MEDIUM ÆVUM MONOGRAPHS
NEW SERIES XV

STUDIES IN
RAGNARS SAGA LOÐBRÓKAR

and its Major Scandinavian Analogues

RORY McTURK

The Society for the Study of
Mediæval Languages and Literature
Oxford
1991

THE SOCIETY FOR THE STUDY OF MEDIEVAL
LANGUAGES AND LITERATURE

http://mediumaevum.modhist.ox.ac.uk

British Library Cataloguing in Publication Data
A catalogue record for this book
is available from the British Library

ISBN-13:
978-0-907570-08-0 (pb)
978-0-907570-97-4 (hb)

First published (as a paperback) 1991
Paperback reprint issued 2015
Hardback reprint issued 2017

Typeset by Oxbow Books
at Oxford University Computing Service

TABLE OF CONTENTS

PREFACE

This monograph was submitted and accepted for the Degree of Ph.D. in the National University of Ireland in 1985. Although I have been working for many years on *Ragnars saga*—which was first suggested to me as a research topic by Professor Turville-Petre as long ago as 1966—it was not until 1981 that I envisaged my work on it taking anything like the form of the present volume. It was originally my intention to supplement the articles I had published in 1975-78 with a study of developments between the saga's ninth-century historical background and its thirteenth-century Icelandic manifestations, but it soon became clear that this was hardly an adequate definition of the subject I had embarked on, and that I needed to revise and extend my views considerably. Hence this monograph, which, though it refers not infrequently to my previous writings on *Ragnars saga*, is intended to stand on its own as a separate work.

Unless otherwise indicated, the expression 'the Analysis', as used in the monograph, refers to the Analysis of *Ragnars saga* and its major Scandinavian analogues in terms of the heroic biographical pattern in ch. II, section (a), see pp. 62–89, below. It may be helpful to note here that the expressions 'the Ragnarr loðbrók tradition' and 'the older Ragnarr loðbrók tradition' are explained on pp. 1–2 and 146–47 respectively; that the main branch of the Ragnarr loðbrók tradition, referred to on p. 187, is the one represented by the vertical line in the centre of the stemma on p. 241; that the saga-tradition of Ragnarr loðbrók (see pp. 132–33 and 165, below), also called the 'saga branch' of the Ragnarr loðbrók tradition (see pp. 183, 194, below), is represented by the same line from the point marked oRs down to the point marked Y; and that the Áslaug-Kráka branch of the tradition (explained on pp. 179–83) is represented in the stemma by the line descending towards the Spangereid-legend from the point on the vertical line at which Áslaug's introduction is noted.

Although the title *Krákumál* is treated as a plural form in Icelandic (see, for instance, Guðnason, 1969, 29), I have treated it as singular in the text of this monograph, mainly because it would seem unnatural and pedantic to do otherwise, but also in order to reinforce my view that the poem is, and always has been, a unified composition (see p. 132, below). On the other hand, I have treated the title *Ragnars kvæði*, which I take to be a plural expression in Faroese, as a plural in English, if only to emphasize that the ballad-sequence in question consists of two distinct parts (albeit unified from the beginning, see p. 166 and cf. p. 58, below). I have omitted the suffixed definite article ('-en') from the Norwegian title 'Lindarormen' and the Danish title 'Ormekampen' when either title is used together with the definite article in English, or adjectivally. The term *vísuorð* has been used to refer to a verse or half line of Old Norse poetry, and also to the type of verse (known as *Vollzeile* in German) that constitutes the third and sixth verse in a normal *ljóðaháttr* strophe (see p. 202, below).

When specific references (i.e. by page or column number) are made to sources in the text, primary and secondary sources are designated by the surnames (or patronymics) of their editors and authors respectively, except in a few cases where abbreviated titles are used. The designation of the source is in each case followed by the date of its publication, which in turn is followed by the relevant page or column number. I have adopted this system partly in order to dispense altogether with footnotes, and partly in order to give an immediate indication of the dates at which the views I discuss were first advanced; where a work referred to has appeared in more than one edition or printing, I have indicated this (as far as my information has permitted) in the Bibliography. I have however adopted a different system in the case of Saxo, where references following Saxo's name in the text are by number to the relevant book, chapter, and paragraph in Olrik & Ræder, 1931 (see further pp. 249, 260, below).

Since I have written at such length on traditions relevant to *Ragnars saga* that originated and developed outside Iceland, it is perhaps necessary for me to emphasize that I have assumed that the three versions of the saga discussed in this monograph (i.e. the older *Ragnars saga* reflected in *Ragnarssona þáttr*, and the X and Y versions reflected in 147 and 1824b respectively) were written in Iceland and by Icelanders.

I am grateful to the late Professor Gabriel Turville-Petre, of Oxford University, for suggesting this subject to me in the first place, and for guiding my work on it in its early stages; to Professor Bo Almqvist, of University College, Dublin, for giving so generously of his time and learned counsel in his capacity as the supervisor of my Ph.D. thesis, on which I began work in 1972; to the late Professor Alan Bliss, also of University College, Dublin, who, as the Head of the Department in which I was registered as a student, always answered promptly and helpfully my questions about the presentation of the thesis, and my requests for additional time in which to work on it; to Professor Bjarni Guðnason, of the University of Iceland, Reykjavík, who placed at my disposal his own expert knowledge of *Ragnars saga* and its Scandinavian analogues; to the late Lektor Helle Jensen, of the Arnamagnæan Institute, Copenhagen, and the Institute's photographer, Mr Arne Mann Nielsen, who supplied the photographs which appear as illustrations on p. 23, below; to Mr John Townsend, Scandinavian Librarian at University College, London (until 1984), who was unfailingly prompt and helpful in answering my requests for books, photocopies, and bibliographical information; to Dr Richard Perkins, also of University College, London, who advised, encouraged, and assisted me in my work in many different ways; to Dr Peter Cox, of the Department of Community Medicine, Leeds University, who advised me on the medical matters discussed on pp. 221–24, below; to my colleague Professor Tom Shippey, of the School of English, Leeds University, who helped me to obtain in 1984 a term's study leave which enabled me to complete my thesis; to Professor Shippey's former secretary, Mrs E. Covemacker, who typed the thesis; to my former pupil at Leeds, Dr Mary Malcolm, who read and checked the typescript; and to Dr Andrew Wawn, who, since he became my colleague at Leeds in 1983, has been a steady source of encouragement and sound advice.

Since being awarded the Degree of Ph.D. I have had special reason to be grateful to Dr Charlotte Brewer, Secretary to the Society for the Study of Mediæval Languages and Literature, my colleague at Leeds from 1985–87, and now of Hertford College, Oxford, who suggested to me that I should submit my work to the Society for consideration for publication in the Medium Ævum Monograph series; to the late Dr Leslie Seiffert, of Hertford College, Oxford, the Society's Editor for Germanic Languages and Literature until his death in December, 1990, for the help and advice he gave me in overseeing the transformation of my thesis into a book; and to the University of Leeds, for a financial grant in aid of the present work's publication.

I am particularly grateful to Mr C. Patrick Wormald, formerly of

Glasgow University and now of Christ Church, Oxford, who read the first chapter of the present work in typescript, and to Dr Peter Orton, formerly my colleague at Leeds and now of Queen Mary and Westfield College, London, who read all three chapters in typescript. Both these scholars have made a number of valuable suggestions, of which I have done my best to take account in this final version of my work. If I have not followed their advice in all particulars, this is no doubt my loss, and does not make me any the less grateful for the time and trouble they have taken. What errors remain are, of course, entirely my own.

Finally, I would thank my wife and children for their support and encouragement during the long time I have been working on *Ragnars saga*, and for their patience with me in my less optimistic moments.

Leeds, May 1989 – March 1990
Rory McTurk

ABBREVIATIONS

(N.B. The abbreviations in the stemma on p. 241, below, are explained on p. 239)

a.	annorum
Abt.	Abteilung
Access.	Accessorium
A.D.	anno Domini
adj.	adjective
AM	Arnamagnæan(sk), (-us, etc.)
AT	Aarne-Thompson (see under AT in the Bibliography)
Barth.	(tomus) Bartholinianus
Bl.	blad (= leaf)
c.	circa
cf.	compare
ch(ap).	chapter
Chr.	Christian
Cl.	Claus
cod.	codex
d.	died
DgF	Danmarks gamle Folkeviser (see under DgF in the Bibliography)
Don. var.	(e) donatione variorum
ed(s).	editor(s), edited (by)
e.g.	exempli gratia
esp.	especially
et al.	and others
etc.	et cetera
f.	feminine
ff.	following
FF	Folklore.Fellows
fig.	figure
Fistr.	fyrsti (= first)
fl.	floruit
fol.	folio

Fs	Fornmanna sögur (see under Fs in the Bibliography)
gen.	genitive
Gl.	gammel (= old)
Hb.	Hauksbók (see under Hb in the Bibliography)
Hist.-filos.	historisk-filosofisk (= historical-philosophical)
Hr.	herre (= sir, mister)
i.e.	id est
inst.	instituted by
introd.	introducer(s), introduced by
Johs.	Johannes
jr.	junior
kgl.	kongelig (= royal)
l(l).	line(s)
m.	masculine
Mbr.	membraneus
ms.	manuscript
n(n).	note(s); neuter
N.B.	nota bene
nom.	nominative
no(s).	number(s)
N.Y.	New York (State)
Ól.	Ólafur, Ólafs
p(p).	page(s)
pl.	plural
pt.	part
q.v.	quod vide
r.	recto
ref.	reference
rpt.	reprint(ed)
saml.	samling (= collection)
sg.	singular
St.	Saint
st.	stanza
str(s).	strophe(s)
Sv.	Svend
trans(s).	translator(s), translated by
v.	verso
viz.	videlicet
vol(s).	volume(s)

&	and
7	ond (= and)
1st	first
4to	quarto
8vo	octavo
147	AM 147 4to
1824b	Ny kgl. saml. 1824b 4to

CHAPTER I

RAGNARR AND LOÐBRÓK

a) New light on the historical Reginheri

In the present section of this chapter, I shall review some recently published work on a ninth-century historical figure, Reginheri, who has long been recognized as one of the models for the hero of Scandinavian tradition known as Ragnarr loðbrók. In section (b) I shall investigate the origins and implications of Ragnarr's second name, Loðbrók; and in section (c) I shall attempt to throw new light on certain historical figures who have been regarded as Reginheri's sons.

In an article published in 1976, I suggested (McTurk, 1976, 93–98, 106–09, 117–23) that the hero known as Ragnarr loðbrók represented a combination of two different historical figures: on the one hand Reginheri (also called Ragneri, Reginerus, Ragenarius), the Viking leader who according to contemporary Frankish sources sacked Paris in 845; and on the other a more shadowy figure, the earliest probable instances of whose name appear in the writings of the eleventh-century historians William of Jumièges (c.1070) and Adam of Bremen (c.1076), the former of whom (see Marx, 1914, 5) refers to a certain 'Lotbroci regis filio, nomine Bier Costae quidem ferreae,' while the latter (see Trillmich, 1961, 208) refers to 'Inguar, filius Lodparchi'. The earliest occurrence of the names Ragnarr and Loðbrók in combination is provided by Ari Þorgilsson (d. 1148), who reports in his Íslendingabók (written between 1120 and 1133, see Benediktsson, 1968, xvii–xviii and 4) that 'Ívarr Ragnarssonr loðbrókar' ('Ívarr son of Ragnarr loðbrók') was responsible for the slaying of the English king, St. Edmund. As in my article, the two names will be used in combination here only when they refer to the two figures as combined into one by Scandinavian tradition; when they refer, in fact, to what I still regard as a legendary rather than a historical figure. The expression 'the Ragnarr loðbrók tradition' will be used to refer to the Scandinavian tradition which in its

surviving forms either exemplifies or presupposes the combined use
of both names for the same person.

In the present section of this chapter, I shall attempt to show
that, thanks to Lukman (1976, 18, 23), more information about the
historical Reginheri is now available than I was aware of when
preparing my 1976 article for publication; and in section (b) I shall
offer some new ideas of my own on the name *Loðbrók*.

In 1976, I concluded (McTurk, 1976, 121–23) that Reginheri,
the leader of the Viking attack on Paris in 845, was associated,
possibly by blood-ties, with the Danish king Horicus I (d. 854), son
of Godofridus I (d. 810); that he had perhaps been active as a
Viking in Ireland in 831; and that he died in 845, shortly after his
attack on Paris. The arguments leading to these conclusions are set
out at length in McTurk (1976, 93–121), and need not be repeated
here. Also in 1976, Lukman (1976, 18, 23) suggested that the
Reginheri of the attack on Paris in 845 was identifiable with a
certain Raginarius mentioned more than once in the *Vita Anskarii*,
that is, the life of Anskar (d. 865), the Frankish missionary to
Scandinavia, written between 865 and 876 by Anskar's pupil and
fellow-monk Rimbert and addressed to the monks of their mother
house at Corbie, near Amiens in Picardy (see Trillmich, 1961, 3–6,
17, 68, 116, 118). As far as I can discover, Lukman is the first to
make this suggestion; it is not made by either Steenstrup (1876,
81–127; 1878, 379–88) or Storm (1878, 34–129) in the course of
their seminal debate on the historical origins of Ragnarr loðbrók, or
by Olrik (1894a, 94–133) or Herrmann (1922, 613–661) in their
commentaries on the relevant part of Saxo's *Gesta Danorum*, i.e.
Book IX, from which Lukman (1976, 18) derives support for the
identification. Rudberg (1965, 125, n. 78), moreover, in a note to
the relevant part of his Swedish translation of the *Vita Anskarii*,
refers to the Raginarius mentioned by Rimbert as 'not otherwise
known'. Lukman, then, if he is right on this point, seems to have
provided evidence for a hitherto unrecognized episode in the life of
Reginheri, about whom so little is known for certain apart from his
attack on Paris in 845.

In ch. 12 of the *Vita Anskarii*, Rimbert (Trillmich, 1961, 44–47)
describes how in 831–32 the Frankish emperor Louis the Pious
established the new archdiocese of Hamburg with Anskar as its
archbishop, and placed the monastery of Turholt (situated some
thirty kilometres south-west of Bruges) within its jurisdiction,
mainly for the purpose of furthering the work of Christian missions

in Scandinavia. Raginarius is first mentioned in ch. 21, where Rimbert (Trillmich, 1961, 68–71) tells how, during the struggle for supremacy in the Frankish empire among the sons of Louis the Pious between the latter's death in 840 and the partitioning of the empire in 843, the monastery of Turholt came to fall within the domain of Louis's son Charles the Bald, who, despite remonstrations from his brothers and many others, deprived it of the function for which his father had intended it, and gave it to one Raginarius, a man who, Rimbert (Trillmich, 1961, 68) makes clear, was well known to his addressees, the monks of Corbie near Amiens ('vobis bene cognito dedit Raginario'). Rimbert (Trillmich, 1961, 76) goes on to complain, in ch. 23, that the missionary activity came to a halt after Charles the Bald deprived the archdiocese of this monastery (in 840); and in ch. 36 (Trillmich, 1961, 116–19) he gives more information about Raginarius, as follows: after being given charge of the monastery by Charles the Bald, Raginarius, much to Anskar's dismay, took into his own service some boys of Scandinavian and Slavonic origin whom Anskar had caused to be trained at Turholt as missionaries. Shortly afterwards, Anskar had a dream in which he found himself upbraiding King Charles and Raginarius with this matter, declaring that he had intended the boys to be the servants of Almighty God, not of Raginarius. It seemed to him then that Raginarius raised his foot and kicked him in the mouth, whereupon Christ seemed to appear at Anskar's side, saying to the king and to Raginarius: 'Why are you treating this man so shamefully? He has a lord of his own, you know, and you will not go unpunished for this.' They were terrified and confused by this intervention, and the archbishop awoke. The divine vengeance which subsequently overtook Raginarius, says Rimbert, bears witness to the truth revealed in this vision, for not long afterwards Raginarius incurred the king's wrath and lost his favour and everything else he had received from him, including the monastery.

Lukman (1976, 18) compares Rimbert's information about Raginarius with Saxo's information about Regnerus Lothbrog, King of Denmark, in Book IX of the *Gesta Danorum*, where Saxo (IX.iv, 15) tells how Regnerus drove out of Denmark into Germany a certain Haraldus, thus defeating the second of three attempts on the throne of Denmark by Haraldus, who commanded some Danish support (see part IX of the Analysis). Regnerus, according to Saxo (IX.iv, 15), tortured to death his prisoners from among the followers of Haraldus and distributed among his own followers the estates of those who had fled with Haraldus, 'for he judged that the fathers would be better punished if they saw the reward of their inheritance go to children they had rejected through their own decision, and the heirs they were fonder of cheated of their patrimony' (Fisher, 1979, 284).

I would advance the following arguments, some of which are implicit in Lukman's own remarks (1976, 18, 23), in support of his identification of the Raginarius of Rimbert's *Vita Anskarii* with Reginheri, the leader of the Vikings who sacked Paris in 845. Firstly, the form of the name *Raginarius* as it occurs in Rimbert's account (Trillmich, 1961, 68, 116), corresponds closely to the forms *Reginheri, Ragneri, Reginerus, Ragenarius*, in which the name of the leader of the 845 attack on Paris appears in the various contemporary and nearly contemporary accounts of the event (see McTurk, 1976, 94–95).

Secondly, Rimbert's clear indication that Raginarius was well-known to the monks of a monastery near Amiens in north-eastern France when the *Vita Anskarii* was written, i.e. between 865 and 876 (Trillmich, 1961, 5), would make particularly good sense if this Raginarius had, in fact, been the leader of the Vikings who sacked Paris in 845, and would also accord well with the evidence assembled by myself and others (see McTurk, 1976, 98–117) to suggest that, in the years leading up to 845, Reginheri was a person of some prominence at the court of the Danish king Horicus I.

Thirdly, Rimbert's account in the *Vita Anskarii* (ch. 36) of how Raginarius took into his own service the boys whom Anskar was training as Christian missionaries bears some resemblance to Saxo's account (IX.iv, 15) of how Regnerus Lothbrog made over to his own followers the estates of those who had fled to Germany with Haraldus. The force of this argument becomes all the clearer when it is borne in mind that there are reasonable grounds (see McTurk, 1976, 95–96) for regarding Reginheri, the leader of the 845 attack on Paris, as one of the historical models for Saxo's Regnerus Lothbrog, and that Saxo's Haraldus (see Herrmann, 1922, 632, 640, 648) is clearly modelled on the ninth-century Danish king Herioldus II, who according to the *Annales regni Francorum* (which for the relevant year may be regarded as a contemporary source, see Rau, 1974, 2–3, 144) was baptized as a Christian in Mainz in 826 with the support of Louis the Pious, and who, according to chs. 7–8 of the *Vita Anskarii* (Trillmich, 1961, 30–38), brought Anskar for the first time to Scandinavia on his return to Denmark from the baptism, and entrusted to him some of his followers for training for the priesthood, thus helping to make possible the creation of a small school for this purpose. It is reasonable to view Herioldus II's conversion, as Storm (1878, 40) and Vogel (1906, 58–60) have done, in the light of his need to win the support of the Franks in the struggle for royal supremacy that he and his relatives were waging with the descendants and relatives of Godofridus I in the first half of the ninth century (see McTurk, 1976, 98–100). Saxo himself (IX.iv, 36–37), following Adam of Bremen (Trillmich, 1961, 186–89; cf. Herrmann, 1922, 648), records the conversion, and adds the information that, although Haraldus was the first to introduce Christianity to Denmark, he later rejected it after Regnerus had re-established the pagan religion there.

Fourthly, Rimbert's account in the *Vita Anskarii* (ch. 36) of Anskar's dream, in which he is kicked by Raginarius in the presence of King Charles the Bald, and in which Raginarius and the king are rebuked for this by Christ, much to their horror and confusion, bears some resemblance to what is told in the earlier and later versions of the *Miracula Sancti Germani* (written respectively in 849–58 and 872–81, see Skyum-Nielsen, 1967, 23, 41) about the death of the Viking conqueror of Paris, who is there called Ragenarius. The relevant chapters are ch. 30 in the earlier version of the *Miracula* (Waitz, 1887, 16), and Book I, ch. 12, in the later (Carnandet, 1866, 789). According to the account they give, which is substantially the same in both versions, Ragenarius came into the presence of King Horicus (I) after returning from Paris to his native land, and boasted to him of conquering the kingdom of Charles (the Bald) and of entering by force the monastery of St. Germanus in the environs of Paris. While he was speaking he suddenly fell in fear and trembling to the ground, crying out that St. Germanus was belabouring him with a stick; this greatly astonished and alarmed the king and his court. After suffering dreadful pain for three days, Ragenarius gave orders for a golden statue to be made and conveyed as a gift to St. Germanus by an ambassador of King Louis (i.e. Louis the German, another son of Louis the Pious) who was then at the court of Horicus. He also promised to become a Christian and remain so, if by the intercession of St. Germanus he might be cured of the sickness that was assailing him. The monk Aimoin, who compiled the later of the two versions of the *Miracula*, adds the details that the statue was

meant to represent St. Germanus himself and that the ambassador
in question was the Saxon count Kobbo (see Skyum-Nielsen, 1967,
39). Both versions agree that Ragenarius's gestures of repentance
were of no avail to him, since he did not belong to Christ's flock
and was not destined to survive; his body swelled up and burst
after being deprived for the most part of the power of its senses,
and so his life ended (for further details of his death as described in
this account, see pp. 221–24, below). It is easy to see how legends
about the same person could have developed in the two rather
different forms found, on the one hand, in Rimbert's *Vita Anskarii*,
and, on the other, in both versions of the *Miracula Sancti Germani*.

Fifthly and finally, Rimbert's indication (in ch. 36 of the *Vita
Anskarii*) that Raginarius incurred the wrath of Charles the Bald
and was overtaken by divine vengeance not long after ('non multo
post', Trillmich, 1961, 116) the affair involving Anskar's pupils at
Turholt—which evidently took place after the death of Louis the
Pious in 840 but before 843 (see Trillmich, 1961, 68–71, 117, n.
170)—is by no means inconsistent with the view that he was the
same person as the Reginheri who, according to the relevant
sources, invaded Charles's kingdom with his attack on Paris in 845,
and who, according to the contemporary *Annales Xantenses* (Rau,
1972, 8–9, 348), died in that year as a victim of divine chastisement
('Domino percutiente', a phrase which, according to de Vries
(1923, 252), may have assisted the development of the legendary
notion, found in both versions of the *Miracula Sancti Germani*, of
Ragenarius being beaten by St. Germanus with a stick).

Thus Lukman (1976, 18, 23) has, in my view, added somewhat
to our knowledge of the historical Reginheri. Not only was this
Reginheri active in Ireland (perhaps) in 831, closely associated with
the Danish king Horicus I, and the leader of the Viking attack on
Paris in 845, in which year he died; he was also, it may now be
concluded, active at Turholt between the years 840 and 843, as a
result of a short-lived association with Charles the Bald.

(b) The origins and implications of the name *Loðbrók*

As indicated above (p. 1), the earliest known instances of the name
Loðbrók seem to be found in the eleventh-century Latin writings of
William of Jumièges and Adam of Bremen, while the earliest
occurrence of the name in combination with *Ragnarr* is found in Ari

Þorgilsson's *Íslendingabók* of the first half of the twelfth century. Only in Scandinavian tradition are the two names found in combination: the name *Ragnall*, occurring in certain Irish writings, may in some cases reflect the name *Ragnarr*, as I have indicated elsewhere (McTurk, 1976, 106–11, 117–23), though strictly speaking the Irish form *Ragnall* corresponds to Old Norse *Ragnaldr* rather than *Ragnarr* (McTurk, 1976, 109, n. 119); while a number of writings of English origin (most of which are in Latin, and some of which are discussed in section (e) of chapter III, below) clearly reflect the name *Loðbrók*. Among non-Scandinavian continental writings, as shown in the first section of this chapter, those dealing with the Viking attack on Paris in 845, and with Charles the Bald's harsh treatment of the Turholt monastery a few years earlier, reflect the name *Ragnarr* in various forms; while William of Jumièges and Adam of Bremen (in contexts not directly related to these events) reflect the name *Loðbrók*. In none of the non-Scandinavian texts in which one or other of these names occurs do the relevant contexts provide clear evidence that the two names designate the same person.

The name *Loðbrók* occurs in Scandinavian writings dating from the twelfth century onwards. The more important instances of it in Scandinavian tradition are noted in part V of the Analysis (see ch. II, section (a), below); much fuller lists are given by Lind (1920–21, 246), and by Knudsen, Kristensen, & Hornby (1954–64, 687–89). The form *loðbrók* clearly suggests the meaning 'hairy breeches', 'shaggy trousers', and this is indeed the meaning agreed on by the two dictionaries just referred to. In *Krákumál*, a poetic monologue dating most probably from the second half of the twelfth century (see pp. 53, 125–33, below), the speaker claims in the first strophe to have acquired the name *Loðbrók* as a result of slaying a serpent in Gautland and so winning Þóra in marriage (see further part V of the Analysis), but the poem gives no explanation of the name. Saxo, on the other hand, writing in the early thirteenth century (see p. 53, below), expressly states (IX.iv, 4–5, 8) that Thora's father Herothus, the king of the Swedes, gave Regnerus the nickname *Lothbrog* because of the shaggy appearance of the breeches he wore when slaying the serpents reared by Thora, whom he won in marriage by the exploit. Neither *Ragnars saga* (as reflected in 1824b; the 147 text does not fully preserve the account of the serpent-fight, see Olsen 1906–08, 116–21, 176–77), dating from the thirteenth century (see further pp. 54–55, 61, 72–73, below), nor *Ragnarssona þáttr*, dating most probably from the turn of the thirteenth to the fourteenth century (see p. 56, below), mentions the acquisition of the nickname, though both make it clear that Ragnarr was wearing hairy breeches when he slew the serpent encircling Þóra's bower; the saga refers to *loðbrøkr* ('hairy trousers', Olsen, 1906–08, 118, l. 3), while the *þáttr* refers to *raggað* (*recte*: *rǫgguð*) *klæði* ('shaggy clothes'), which include *brœkr* ('trousers', Hb, 1892–96, 458, l. 22). It needs to be considered, then, whether *loðbrók*, meaning 'hairy breeches', represents the original form and meaning of the name, and what manner of name this originally was, whether proper noun or nickname.

Schiern (1858, 10–11) suggested that the form *loðbrók* derives by folk-etymology from an unrecorded Old English word **léodbróga*, the existence of which he deduced by analogy with such recorded forms as *léodcyning* ('king of a people') and *herebróga* ('war-terror'), taking it to mean 'terror populi', or 'bearer of terror to a people'. He further suggested that the name was applied to more than just one Viking leader, and that this helps to explain the apparent discrepancy between certain Icelandic genealogies and English annalistic sources as to the likely time of Ragnarr loðbrók's death. In Scandinavia, according to Schiern, the Old English name was misunderstood, and developed the form *loðbrók* under the influence of the well-known story in which Ragnarr had won Þóra as a result of killing a serpent or serpents while wearing a protective costume of hair. Thus he apparently acknowledged the notion of the hairy costume as an ingredient in the story prior to the introduction of the name **Léodbróga* in the form it acquired through misunderstanding; and it would seem to follow from his arguments that its introduction in this form (*Loðbrók*) would have the effect of drawing attention only, or mainly, to the trouser part of the costume. Schiern (1858, 11, n. 3) also mentions, in support of his view, the fact that a form corresponding to *loðbrók* occurs as an English place-name in Domesday Book, without appearing to lend itself to the interpretation 'hairy breeches'. The forms *Lodbroc* and *Ludebroch* are indeed recorded as place-names in Domesday Book, for Warwickshire and Devonshire respectively, as Ekwall (1960) shows. According to him (Ekwall, 1960, 284), the Warwickshire place-name, now *Ladbrooke*, originally meant 'a stream used for the purpose of drawing lots, of divining the future', while the Devonshire place-name, now *Ludbrook* (see Ekwall, 1960, 306), was originally a stream-name meaning 'loud brook'. These interpretations of the name may be compared with Geoffrey of Wells's mid twelfth-century interpretation (in his *de infantia sancti Eadmundi*, ed. Arnold, 1890, 93–103, see 102) of the name of Lodebrok, the father of the northern pirates Hingwar, Ubba and Wern, as 'odiosus rivus', or 'loathed brook'; according to Geoffrey, it was from this 'odious streamlet' that the hateful progeny of Lodebrok flowed. All three of these interpretations do certainly differ from what Schiern regards as the Scandinavian misinterpretation of the name; none of them, however, can be said to support his **léodbróga* theory.

Jessen (1862, 1–37) argued forcefully and persuasively against the historical reliability of most of the Icelandic genealogical material relating to Ragnarr loðbrók, thus removing much of the basis for Schiern's line of reasoning; and he also emphasized (Jessen, 1862, 5) the fact that there is absolutely no recorded instance of the Old English word *léodbróga*, whether used of a Viking or otherwise.

J. Jónsson (1910), on the other hand, supported Schiern's theory as to the original form of the name, and suggested that it was applied in Schiern's proposed meaning (i.e. 'terror populi') to the raven banner which, according to the B, C, D, and E manuscripts of the *Anglo-Saxon chronicle* (see Whitelock, 1979, 195, n. 19), was captured from the army of 'the brother of Inwære and of Healfdene' (see further pp. 43-45, below) in Devon in 878, and which, according to the twelfth-century *Annals of St. Neots* (see Stevenson, 1959, 138), was made by the daughters of Lodebrochus, the three sisters of Hynguar and Hubba, and had the property of forecasting the outcome of a battle whenever it was carried before the army in that a fluttering raven would seem to appear on it if victory was in prospect, while it would droop as an omen of defeat. J. Jónsson (1910, 375-76) argued that the expression 'sons of Loðbrók' was likely to have arisen in England among the Vikings as well as the English as a poetic appellation for the Viking leaders before whom this banner was carried, and that confusion of the forms *léodbróga* and *loðbrók* was perhaps assisted by the use of the noun *brók*, f., for 'banner' by the Vikings.

Storm (1878, 82–86) held the view that *Loðbrók*, which he took to mean 'leather breeches' or 'trousers of pelt' ('Skindbuxe', Storm, 1878, 84, n. 2), was the name of the mother of certain Vikings who came to be regarded as sons of Ragnarr loðbrók. This view, which is by no means as absurd as Steenstrup (1878, 384–88) wished to make it appear, was based on the wording of a runic inscription found in Maeshowe in the Orkneys, and dating from the mid-twelfth century (see A. Liestøl, 1968, 55). The relevant part of the inscription (quoted in normalized spelling, see A. Liestøl, 1968, 60; cf. Storm, 1878, 84) reads as follows: 'Sjá haugr var fyrr hlaðinn heldr Loðbrókar. Synir hennar þeir váru hvatir ...', and may be translated: 'This mound was raised earlier than Loðbrók's; her sons they were bold ...'. (The sons, it should be noted, are not named.) Storm weakened his argument that a woman is here the referent of *Loðbrókar* by concentrating on the feminine gender of the noun *Loðbrók*, thus laying himself open to Steenstrup's well-founded objection that the gender of an Old Norse name or nickname need not correspond to the sex of its bearer. What he should rather have emphasized is the feminine form of the third person singular pronoun, *hennar*, which is used here with reference to Loðbrók, and does indeed suggest that the latter was regarded as a woman by the author of the inscription. A. Liestøl (1968, 60–61) attempted to explain this by suggesting that the use of the feminine form of the pronoun is meant to indicate a lack of respect for Ragnarr loðbrók, who is here being ironically contrasted with his sons. This argument, however, presupposes that the author of the inscription knew a tradition according to which Ragnarr and loðbrók were the same (male) person, and the wording of the inscription, which makes no mention of Ragnarr, gives no grounds for such an assumption.

Schück (1900, 134–40), who clearly regarded *Loðbrók* as a nickname meaning 'hairy breeches' (see Schück, 1900, 138), suggested that a Swedish version of the story of Ragnarr's slaying of Þóra's serpent (which of course takes place in Sweden according to *Ragnars saga* and its major analogues, see part IVA of the Analysis) is pictorially represented on one of the four bronze plates found at Torslunda on the Swedish island of Öland in 1870 and dating from as early as the seventh century. The plate shows a man naked to the waist, wearing what Schück (1900, 139) and more recently Arent (1969, 136) describe as shaggy trousers, holding an axe in his right hand, and with his left grasping what looks like a thick halter hanging from the neck of the monster he is fighting. It should be emphasized that this is no serpentine monster of the kind slain by Ragnarr in the saga and its analogues (see part VI of the Analysis); it is presented as a four-legged creature with a large beak-like mouth and a protruding tongue, sitting up on its hindquarters and itself holding the halter, just above the man's grasping hand, with the claws of its left forefoot. Schück (1900, 139) himself provides an illustration of the plate in question; a clearer one, however, is provided by Arent (1969, facing p. 132). Schück regards as a chain what I have described here as a halter, and sees it as symbolic of treasure, and hence comparable to the gold on which Þóra's serpent lies according to *Ragnars saga* and some of its analogues (see part VI of the Analysis). This is a rather questionable point of similarity between the plate and the various accounts of Ragnarr's serpent-slaying exploit; the trouser-clad warrior is a much more striking one.

Since Schück's time, the Torslunda plates, which were evidently models on which shields and helmets were moulded (see Schück, 1900, 140), have come to be regarded as representing archetypal figures engaged in activities of the kind reflected in the tribal initiation rites of a typical Germanic warrior, rather than as depicting particular heroes (Arent, 1969, 130–45). If this view is correct, it need not of course mean that the subject-matter of the plate just described did not contribute in some way to the figure of Ragnarr loðbrók as he is presented in Scandinavian tradition.

J. de Vries (1928a, 270, n. 33) rejected the **lēodbrōga* theory as propounded by Schiern (1858) and J. Jónsson (1910), without mentioning either of them by name, and implied (de Vries, 1928a, 270) that the name *Loðbrók* never meant anything other than a rough, uncouth Viking clad in shaggy skin garments. In other words, it was an appropriate nickname for a Viking, as de Vries stated more explicitly elsewhere (de Vries, 1928b, 131–33), after suggesting that Adam of Bremen's information (see Trillmich, 1961, 208) that Inguar was the son of one Lodparchus (a corrupt form of Old Norse *loðbrók*, according to de Vries, 1928b, 132) was derived from an English source. J. de Vries's implication that the nickname as he interprets it had connotations of disrespect and fear from the very beginning seems at variance with his implication that the nickname is of Scandinavian (rather than Old English or Frankish) origin. He also pointed out (de Vries, 1928a, 270), as Schück (1900, 138) had done, that the reason why the nickname reflects breeches rather than other garments or the entire costume is not apparent from the surviving traditions about Ragnarr loðbrók. Saxo, the 1824b text of *Ragnars saga* (Olsen, 1906–08, 118–19, cf. 176), and *Ragnarssona þáttr* all mention a cloak as well as breeches (see part V of the Analysis), and the saga in particular indicates that it is the cloak ('loðkápa') that gives Ragnarr the necessary protection. No reason is given (such as an Achilles' heel) as to why his lower parts should especially need protecting, and, as Schück (1900, 138) points out, snakes of the monstrous size described in the saga and its analogues (see part VI of the Analysis) would hardly be adequately guarded against by protective trouserwear alone. An advantage of the **lēodbrōga* theory is the fact that the misunderstanding of this word envisaged by Schiern (1858) and J. Jónsson (1910) does offer an explanation of how and why attention came to be focused on the trouser part of Ragnarr's costume, as indicated above (pp. 8–9). Jessen's (1862, 5) objections to it seem quite valid, however, and de Vries (1928a, 270, n. 33) is surely right in arguing that such a misunderstanding is extremely unlikely. The fact that the Old English word *lēodbiscup* could be borrowed into Icelandic giving the expected forms *ljóðbiskup* and *lýðbiskup* (Bosworth & Toller, 1929, 630; cf. Cleasby, Vigfússon & Craigie, 1957, 394) surely adds to the unlikelihood of Schiern's and J. Jónsson's suggestions.

Mention may be made of Krappe's opinion (1941–42, 327, n. 1), adumbrated by Elton (1894, 366, n. 1), that *loðbrók*, meaning 'Shaggy-breech', was originally an Old Norse epithet for 'hawk' or 'sparrow-hawk'. I can find no real support for this view. *Hábrók* (as opposed to *loðbrók*) occurs, it is true, as a poetic appellation for 'hawk' in the younger of the two groups of *þulur*, or poetic lists, preserved in manuscripts of Snorri's prose *Edda*, that is, in the group dating probably from the thirteenth century (see F. Jónsson, 1912a, 686; 1923, 179, cf. Lie, 1950, 165–66); and *Hábrók* also occurs as the name of the best of hawks in a list of names of the best of various kinds of beings and objects in the eddaic poem *Grímnismál* (strs. 43–44), dating probably from the tenth century (see Sveinsson, 1962, 269–70, 318). In another of the *þulur*, also belonging to the younger (i.e. probably thirteenth-century) group, *hábrók* is listed as a poetic appellation for 'cockerel' (F. Jónsson, 1912a, 687); and it also occurs as a nickname following the proper name *Haukr* (which itself means 'hawk', of course) in ch. 37 of Snorri's *Haralds saga ins hárfagra*, which forms part of *Heimskringla* and thus probably dates from between 1220 and 1235 (see Aðalbjarnarson, 1941, 144–45 and xxv–xxix), and in the *þáttr Hauks hábrókar*, preserved in the late fourteenth-century *Flateyjarbók* and ed. in Fs, 1835, 198–208. In the latter account, Haukr appears to have acquired the nickname as a result of boasting; he was told by King Haraldr hárfagri ('the fine-haired'), whose favourite retainer he was, that he had good reason to boast ('hábrókast') after defeating some champions of Haraldr's enemy King Eirekr of Sweden. Haukr replied that he had had no less reason to boast in England, when (as told at greater length by Snorri, see Aðalbjarnarson, 1941, 145), he placed King Haraldr's infant son Hákon on King Aðalsteinn's knee as a foster-child. King Haraldr smiled at this reply, and from then on Haukr was known as 'hábrók'. Discussing this word as it occurs in *Grímnismál*, A. Kock (1898, 265–66) derives it by folk-etymology from a word meaning 'hawk' borrowed into Old Norse from Old Saxon or Old English (where the relevant forms are *haβok* and *hafoc* respectively).

Whatever the truth about its origins in Norse, the word *hábrók* in the forms and contexts in which it is now known suggests on the one hand the meaning 'with trousers worn high up the leg', and on the other since the adjective *hár*, which forms its first element, can mean 'tall' as well as 'high'—such meanings as 'long-trousered', 'long-legged', and hence also 'tall'. From this last meaning the idea of towering or lording it over others could develop, and so the connection with boasting would arise. Heggstad (1930, 239) takes the word to refer to the feathered thighs of a hawk or cockerel, whereas F. Jónsson (1931b, 314) takes it to mean 'long-trousered' or 'long-legged', but also implies (here and under *haukr*, F. Jónsson, 1931b, 232) that since the word is followed by the partitive genitive plural *hauka* in *Grímnismál* it means there 'one who towers among hawks', and hence 'the best of hawks'. With reference to its use as a nickname, Aðalbjarnarson (1941, 144, n. 1) compares the nicknames *háleggr* ('long leg') and *langbrók* ('long breeches'). A close semantic connection between *hábrók* (meaning 'hawk') and *loðbrók* might seem to be suggested by the examples collected by Solheim (1940, 86–88) from Norwegian folklore of another bird, the eagle, being referred to by sailors as 'skindbukse', meaning 'furry or leather breeches', since it was considered unlucky to use the usual word for eagle (i.e. *ørn*) while at sea. As noted earlier (p. 9), the word *Skindbuxe* is given by Storm (1878, 84, n. 2) as a modern Norwegian translation of *loðbrók*. It must be emphasized, however, that Solheim's examples all seem to be from modern Norwegian folk tradition, and do not include cases of the word *loðbrók* itself being used to refer to an eagle, or to any other bird.

Also relevant here are Mudrak's (1943, 117–19) attempts to explain the nature of Ragnarr's costume by reference to a wide variety of literary and folktale sources. Mudrak draws attention to the fact that, in the 1824b text of *Ragnars saga* (ch. 3, Olsen, 1906–08, 118), Ragnarr prepares his hairy breeches and cloak for the fight with Þóra's serpent by having them boiled in pitch and later rolling in the sand while wearing them, whereas in Saxo's account (IX.iv, 6) Regnerus plunges into cold water wearing his woollen cloak and shaggy thigh-coverings which he then allows to freeze, so as to make them hard to penetrate (this difference between the saga and Saxo's account is discussed at greater length in chapter III, see pp. 161–63, below). Mudrak believes that behind these accounts there lies, among other things, the notion of slaying a monster internally, pointing out that, in the early eleventh-century Iranian *Shah-nama* ('book of kings') by Firdausi (see further de Vries, 1963, 111–12), to which Liebrecht (1861) first drew attention in connection with *Ragnars saga* (cf. Krappe, 1941–42, 332–33), a worm that grows to an enormous size after being generously fed by a maiden who had found it in an apple she was eating, and to whom it brought good fortune in enabling her to spin as much cotton as she wished, is eventually slain by an enemy of the maiden's father pouring liquid metal down its throat. With this account, as with those dealing expressly with Ragnarr loðbrók, Mudrak compares the apocryphal Old Testament story (see p. 207 of the Apocrypha in *The New English Bible with the Apocrypha*, 1970) of Daniel killing a huge snake worshipped by the Babylonians by feeding to it cakes made of pitch, fat, and hair boiled together, and the Russian folktale of Nikita the Tanner (see Afanas'ev, 1946, 310–11).

In this latter story, the Tsar's daughter is abducted by a dragon which, instead of devouring her, marries her. The girl's parents use a dog as messenger to ask her to find out from the dragon whom it regards as stronger than itself. The dragon specifies Nikita the Tanner, who, however, refuses to take the dragon on until he is at last implored to do so by five thousand small children. He then takes thirty hundredweight of flax, smears it with pitch, and wraps himself up in it, 'so that the dragon could not devour him', and, thus equipped, fights the dragon and defeats it. Here the notion of internal slaying is only hinted at; the costume is clearly meant to be unpalatable as well as protective. This story, too, as Mudrak (1943, 118) points out, finds a parallel among Germanic traditions not far removed from those relating to Ragnarr loðbrók in that the German *Lied vom hürnen Seyfrid* (dating, according to King, 1958, 86–90, from *c.*1500, but containing older material), mentions a dragon (King, 1958, 107–12) which plans to seduce, if not to marry, an abducted princess, but which is overcome (King, 1958, 143–45) by the hero Seyfrid, who corresponds to the Sigurðr of *Vǫlsunga saga* and its eddaic sources (cf. pp. 54, 175, 195, below). Mudrak (1943, 119) also compares with the preparations for the serpent-fight as reported in *Ragnars saga* and by Saxo a Tatar legend in which the Mongols conquer a country where the men (though not the women) have canine rather than human form. By jumping into the water despite the winter cold and then rolling in dust the dog-men acquire coats of ice in which they proceed to attack the Mongols.

Lukman's (1976, 19–21) arguments as to the origins of the name *Loðbrók* and its combination with the name *Ragnarr* are considerably weaker than those with which (as shown in the first section of this chapter) he seeks to identify the Raginarius at Turholt between 840 and 843 with the Reginheri at Paris in 845. In general, Lukman (1976) is concerned to suggest influence on the Scandinavian traditions about Ragnarr loðbrók and his sons from material reflected in place-names, personal names, and historical documents relating more or less directly to early mediaeval Flanders, which saw considerable Viking activity in the ninth century, and had close connections with the Danish court at different times during the eleventh and twelfth centuries (see Lukman, 1976, 17). He refers in the present context (Lukman, 1976, 19) to the early twelfth-century and probably Anglo-Latin *Gesta Herwardi* (ed. Hardy & Martin, 1888, 339–404; see lii–liii), whose English hero, Herwardus, marries the fair Turfrida of St. Omer (whose name, beauty and accomplishments are to some extent comparable to those of Þóra as described in *Ragnars saga*, cf. part IVA of the Analysis) at about the time of his involvement in a war against the inhabitants of Scaldemariland (that is, modern Zeeland in the Scheldt estuary), who are described as wearing, by way of armour, felt cloaks steeped in pitch, resin, and spice ('cum feltreis togis pice et resina atque in thure intinctis'), and well-boiled leather jackets ('seu cum tunicis ex coria valde coctis'; see Hardy & Martin, 1888, 361). These garments are certainly comparable to those worn by Ragnarr in the Scandinavian traditions, see part V of the Analysis.

Lukman (1976, 20) next refers to the *Chronicle of the counts of Guines and of Ardres*, composed *c*.1200 by Lambert of Ardres (Lambertus Ardensis) and ed. by Godefroy Menilglaise, 1855, which tells in chs. 19–22 of a certain Regemarus, Count of Boulogne (called Regnier in the French translation of the Chronicle made in *c*.1450, and facing the Latin text in Godefroy Menilglaise, 1855), whose cruelty manifested itself in, among other things, the fact that he put some people to death 'as though preparing a pigling for the food-market' ('more porcelli ad macellum', see Godefroy Menilglaise, 1855, 55). After he had beheaded the foremost nobleman of Ordre, a certain Henfridus (Humfroy), the latter's widow kept her husband's blood-stained shirt and frequently showed it to her children, urging them to vengeance, which they eventually brought about with help from their mother and others by pursuing and killing Regemarus while he was hunting. Lukman (1976, 20) compares what is told in these chapters with *Ragnars saga*'s account (in ch. 15 of the 1824b text, see Olsen 1906–08, 154–59 and cf. 186–89) of how Ragnarr's second wife Áslaug-Kráka-Randalín gave him a protective shirt of hair in return for the gold-embroidered shift that had belonged to his first wife Þóra, and how Ragnarr wore this shirt until forcibly deprived of it in the serpent-pit (see part V of the Analysis), when he said, 'the young pigs would grunt if they knew what the old one was suffering'. It is evidently the name *Regemarus/Regnier*, and the mention of a pig and a shirt in connection with him, that lead Lukman to make this comparison.

Lukman also refers (1976, 20) to chs. 99–103 of Lambert's *Chronicle*, which deal with a certain Herebertus, also called *Herredus*, which latter form corresponds closely to the name of Þóra's father (*Herothus* in Saxo's account, *Herruðr* and *Herrauðr* in the saga and *Ragnarssona þáttr* respectively, see parts IVA and B of the Analysis). According to Lambert, this Herebertus, who lived at Furnes (Veurne), acquired the nickname *Crangroc*, meaning 'with clothes worn inside out' ('ab inversa tunica', see Godefroy Menilglaise, 1855, 223, 225–27), because as a young man he once dressed in such confusion on being called by his father early one summer morning to join a hunt that he put his jacket on inside out. An alternative theory as to the nickname's origin, also given by Lambert (see Godefroy Menilglaise, 1855, 233), is that he wore his jacket that way for niggardly reasons, hoping thereby to save his clothes. According to Lukman (1976, 20), the idea of clothes worn inside out is comparable to that of a skin costume worn with the hairy side outwards; this, the name *Herredus*, and the proximity of Furnes (Veurne) to Turholt, where Raginarius had been active between 840 and 843 (see the first section of this chapter) prompt him to compare this part of Lambert's *Chronicle* with the Scandinavian traditions about the serpent-fight whereby Ragnarr loðbrók wins Þóra, daughter of Herr(a)uðr.

Lukman (1976, 20–21) finally seeks to establish a link between the nicknames *Crangroc* and *Loðbrók* by noting that *Crangroc* shares the -*roc* element with a variant of the name *Lothbrocus* (see Marx, 1914, 6, 8) occurring in certain manuscripts of the *Gesta Normannorum ducum* of William of Jumièges, the work that gives the earliest known reference to Loðbrók, being composed *c*.1070 (cf. p. 1, above). The text of William's *Gesta* as edited by Marx (1914, 5, 8) has the forms *Lotbroci regis*, *Lothbrocus rex*, for the name of the father of Bier Costae ferreae, who as regards his name and nickname surely corresponds to Bjǫrn járnsíða ('Ironside'), son of Ragnarr loðbrók (see part VII of the Analysis). Of the manuscripts from which Marx (1914, 5, 6) gives variants, one group has the form *Lothburcus*, which seems to correspond to the form *Lodparchi* used (presumably in the genitive) by Adam of Bremen (Trillmich, 1961, 208) in designating the father of Inguar (see p. 1, above), as Lukman (1976, 20) notices, and also, it may be added, to the (accusative) form *lodbork* found in the 1824b text of *Krákumál* (str.1; see part V of the Analysis); while another group has the form *Lot(h)rocus*, which Lukman (1976, 21) compares, not only with the nickname *Crangroc*, but also with *Leudericus*, the name of Anskar's episcopal predecessor in the see of Bremen, evidently thinking that the name is likely to have been remembered in connection with that of Raginarius, who, as is shown in the first section of this chapter, usurped Anskar's responsibility for Turholt between 840 and 843. Lukman even seems to suggest a connection between the place-name *Turholt* and the personal name *Þóra*, and explicitly does so between the neighbouring place-name *Wormhout*, meaning 'worm-forest', and the forest in which, according to Saxo (IX.iv, 5), Herothus found the serpents he gave to his daughter Thora, which Regnerus (IX.iv, 7) later slew.

To review the arguments so far assembled: the **lēodbrōga* theory of Schiern (1858), and J. Jónsson (1910), though unacceptable in itself, has the advantage of focusing attention on the question of why the nickname applied to Ragnarr in Scandinavian tradition appears to specify trousers rather than some other garment. Storm's (1878, 82–86) remarks draw attention to reasonably clear evidence from mid twelfth-century Orkney of the appellation *Loðbrók* being applied to a woman, and Schück's (1900) suggest that the notion of a hairy-trousered man fighting a monster is attested in Sweden from as early as the seventh century. Arent's view (1969, 130–45) that the Torslunda plates discussed by Schück show typical scenes from initiation rites, rather than the deeds of particular heroes, differs interestingly from Schück's view without lessening the value of his remarks. J. de Vries's (1928a, 270; 1928b, 130–33) relatively plain, 'no-nonsense' approach to the name *Loðbrók* carries with it a tendency to underestimate the problems the name raises, with the result that his own interpretation of it is not wholly satisfactory; Krappe's (1941–42, 327, n. 1) suggestion that the word means 'hawk' has not found sufficient supporting evidence; and Mudrak's (1943, 117–19) assemblage of material analogous to the Scandinavian accounts of Ragnarr's fight with Þóra's serpent, valuable though it is, does not approach the specific nature of Ragnarr's costume closely enough to explain the name adequately. Although Lukman's (1976, 20–21) views as outlined in the last four paragraphs also have a certain value in drawing attention to analogous material, the specific links he seeks to establish between names occurring in the Scandinavian traditions about Ragnarr loðbrók on the one hand and names of persons and places connected with early Flemish history and legend on the other seem to be based in most cases on only the very vaguest similarity of name and context.

I should like now to draw attention to Sahlgren's (1918, 28–40) view that the name of a Scandinavian harvest-goddess, *Lodhkona* (*Loþkona*), may be deduced from the Swedish place-name *Locknevi*, for which the fourteenth-century form *Lodkonuvi* is attested (Sahlgren, 1918, 33). This last form clearly shows the structure characteristic of a theophoric place-name (Foote & Wilson, 1973, 396), meaning 'the sacred place of Loþkona' (*Loþkonuvé*). As well as noticing this, Sahlgren (1918, 34–35) arrived at the meaning 'harvest-goddess' for *loþkona* by recognizing its first element, *loþ-* (*loð-*), as related to the Old Norse adjective *loðinn*, which means 'hairy, woolly, densely covered with grass', and which shows the past participle form of a (strong) verb not otherwise recorded in Old Norse and related to Gothic *liudan*, 'to grow'. Sahlgren also produced evidence that the second element, *kona*, can have the meaning 'queen' in addition to its more usual one of 'woman' or 'wife'. He concluded that the name was synonymous with another name deducible from Swedish place-names, *Ludhgudha*, the first element of which he also explained by reference to Gothic *liudan*, while the second element is clearly the Old Swedish word for 'goddess'. These names, he suggests, borrowing a term from Polynesian (Sahlgren, 1918, 11), are 'noa' names, that is, names which may be used in place of taboo names without fear of infringing the taboo. In this case he believes that the names *Lodhkona* and *Ludhgudha* were noa names for the fertility goddess whose worship is described by Tacitus in ch. 40 of his *Germania* (ed. Much, 1967, see p. 441), i.e. Nerthus, whose person, to judge from Tacitus's description (quoted below) was clearly taboo, and whose name probably therefore was also. Sahlgren (1918, 22–27) in fact believes that the name *Nerthus*, cognate with Old Irish *nert* and probably meaning 'strength' or 'power', was itself a noa name (of masculine gender) for both this deity and her male counterpart (though the latter is not mentioned by Tacitus), but acquired taboo status with the passing of time, so that other noa names had to be found. These included *Freyja* for the fertility goddess and *Freyr* for her male counterpart; and the name of the Norse fertility god Njǫrðr derives, according to Sahlgren (1918, 27), from the word *Nerthus* itself, surviving in non-taboo contexts (as taboo words often can), but at the same time commanding sufficient recognition of its earlier application to a fertility deity for it to be applied to such a deity once again.

According to Tacitus (ch. 40), the goddess Nerthus was worshipped by a group of seven tribes, living predominantly in northern Germany and on the Danish peninsula (now Jutland; see Much, 1967, 444–49, and his map no. 1). Handford's (1970, 134–35) revised version of Mattingly's translation may now be quoted:

> There is nothing noteworthy about these tribes individually, but they share a common worship of Nerthus, or Mother Earth. They believe that she takes part in human affairs, riding in a chariot among her people. On an island of the sea stands an inviolate grove, in which, veiled with a cloth, is a chariot that none but the priest may touch. The priest can feel the presence of the goddess in this holy of holies, and attends her with deepest reverence as her chariot is drawn along by cows. Then follow days of rejoicing and merrymaking in every place that she condescends to visit and sojourn in. No one goes to war, no one takes up arms; every iron object is locked away. Then, and then only, are peace and quiet known and welcomed, until the goddess, when she has had enough of the society of men, is restored to her sacred precinct by the priest. After that, the chariot, the vestments, and (believe it if you will) the goddess herself, are cleansed in a secluded lake. This service is performed by slaves who are immediately afterwards drowned in the lake. Thus mystery begets terror and a pious reluctance to ask what that sight can be which is seen only by men doomed to die.

From this description it is clear that Nerthus was regarded by her worshippers as a taboo-figure. It is worth noting that, in von Friesen's (1932–34, 30) view, the names *Lodhkona* and *Ludhgudha* as discussed by Sahlgren (1918, 28–40) were virtually 'nomina propria', and that Lid (1942, 118), who largely followed Sahlgren with regard to these two names, also took them to mean 'the hairy woman' and 'the hairy goddess' respectively, and saw them as partly deriving from the primitive custom of decking effigies or real people with plants for the purpose of ritually invoking fertility (cf. de Vries, 1957, 335).

To show the relevance of this information to the form *lodbrók* itself, it is, I suggest, necessary to examine in some detail the verses spoken by the 'trémaðr' or 'wooden man' in the twentieth and final chapter of *Ragnars saga* as preserved in the 1824b text (see pp. 55–56, below). Of the three strophes in question (numbered 38–40 by Olsen, 1906–08, 174–75, and all in the *fornyrðislag* metre, see p. 55, below), only the second and third are relevant here; the first differs from these in also occurring in *Hálfs saga ok Hálfsrekka* (ed. Seelow, 1981, see pp. 170–71), where it seems properly to belong, and de Vries (1928a, 297) indeed suggested that it was borrowed from that saga by *Ragnars saga*, meaning of course what is here called the Y-version of *Ragnars saga* (the only version in which these strophes occur), which I date (see p. 55, below) to the second half of the thirteenth century. Seelow (1981, 165) has however recently shown that the episode in *Hálfs saga ok Hálfsrekka* containing the strophe is unlikely to have formed part of *Hálfs saga* until this saga acquired its final form in the fourteenth century, though the episode may well have had an independent, oral existence during the thirteenth. The simplest solution is that the strophe was taken from *Hálfs saga* and added to the text of *Ragnars saga* by the scribe of 1824b, who was active in *c*.1400 (and who was not identical with the Y-redactor of *Ragnars saga*, see McTurk, 1977a, 582); though it is also possible that the Y-redactor acquired it from a source other than *Hálfs saga* and that it formed part of his redaction. The fact that the first of the two remaining strophes begins with the words 'ok því', meaning 'and therefore', 'and so', might suggest that these strophes originally formed part (perhaps the end) of a longer sequence; Heusler and Ranisch (1903, lxxxii–iii), however, believed that these words represented a somewhat awkward attempt to link the second and third strophes to the first, and de Vries (1928a, 297) believed that the second and third strophes formed a self contained unit. These last two strophes, the ones relevant here, may be of considerable antiquity, perhaps even more than 'ziemlich alt', which is what de Vries (1928a, 297), following Storm (1878, 83) and Koht (1921, 243), considered them; the view quoted, it should be pointed out, is based on the consideration that these verses refer to Loðbrók as opposed to Ragnarr loðbrók, and may thus date from before the two names were combined by Ari, or possibly (see de Vries, 1928a, 258, n. 5) one of his predecessors; they would thus have been composed before *c*.1100, though how long before remains a question.

   Ch. 20 of the 1824b text of *Ragnars saga* consists of the three strophes just discussed preceded by a few lines of prose introducing them and followed by little more than a line of prose rounding them off, and so completing the saga. According to the prose (see

Olsen, 1906–08, 174–75), a man known as Ǫgmundr the Dane, voyaging with five ships, once arrived in Munarvágr off Sámsey (i.e. Samsø, the Danish island north of Fyn and between Jutland and Sjælland). While his 'mathsveinar' (i.e. 'kitchen-knaves', cf. ch. III, pp. 217–18, below) went ashore to prepare food, others of his followers went into a wood to amuse themselves. There they found a certain ancient man of wood ('einn tremann fornann') who was forty ells tall (perhaps; 1824b has only 'XL at hed', but the paper manuscripts add the word *alna* after the numeral, see Olsen, 1962, 22, n. 2 and cf. p. 30, below) and overgrown with moss, though all his features were visible. The newcomers wondered who would have sacrificed to so great an idol as this. The wooden man then spoke the three strophes (of which, as already explained, only the last two are relevant here). The saga then concludes with the prose sentence: 'and this seemed wonderful to them, and they later told other people about it' ('ok þetta þotti monnum undarlight, ok saughdu sidan fra audrum monnum').

Of the two relevant strophes, only the first (numbered 39 by Olsen, 1906–08, 174, cf. 221) presents difficulties of interpretation. One of these difficulties, involving the word **svardmerðlingar** in the second *vísuorð*, has long been recognized; the other, involving what Olsen (1906–08, 174) prints as **lodbrokar** in the fourth *vísuorð*, does not seem to have been noticed before. To deal with **svardmerðlingar** first, there is little doubt that Olsen has printed this correctly; the manuscript (Ny kgl. saml. 1824b 4to, fol. 76v, l. 3 from the bottom) has: **sv^rdm'ðling^r**, and Olsen (1906–08, li; xlvii) makes clear that in this manuscript interlinear **r** is normally to be expanded to *ar*, while *er* is one of the commonest values of the abbreviation mark **'**. The relevant half strophe, as printed by Olsen, reads as follows: **ok þvi settu svardmerðlingar. / svdr hia sallte. / synir lodbrokar**; and the word *svarðmerðlingar*, whatever it means, seems here to be a nominative plural and the subject of the verb *settu*, and to be paralleled by the phrase *synir Loðbrókar*. What *does* it mean? Before an attempt is made to answer this question, it may be pointed out that previous attempts to do so have often been influenced by too great a dependence on the Ragnarr loðbrók tradition as it survives in *Ragnars saga* and elsewhere; for instance, such explanations of *svarðmerðlingar* as meaning 'warriors' or 'piglets' have been found satisfactory, because the Ragnarr loðbrók tradition presents Ragnarr's sons as famous warriors, and because Ragnarr says as he dies in the snake-pit: 'the young pigs would

grunt if they knew what the old one was suffering' (see part X of
the Analysis). This kind of approach is perhaps questionable even
at the best of times, and is surely particularly so in the case of the
two strophes under discussion, which do not appear to have
belonged to the Ragnarr loðbrók tradition from its beginnings,
since they occur only in the 1824b text of the saga, and thus at a
relatively late stage of the tradition's development, i.e. the stage
represented by the Y-version of *Ragnars saga*, before which they
may well have existed independently. Previous commentators have
also been over-bold, sometimes, in emending the text, though this
on the whole has been a less serious failing. Both these pitfalls will,
it is hoped, be avoided here, whatever other limitations my own
suggestions may have; and I shall not hesitate to draw on the
contributions of earlier commentators where they seem to me
valuable.

Olsen (1912, 29–30) followed Torp (in Hægstad & Torp, 1909,
443; cf. Heggstad, Hødnebø, & Simensen, 1975, 422) in reading the
word as *svarðmerðlingar* and taking it as a diminutive form of
*svǫrðmǫrðr, *svarðmǫrðr, a compound noun in which the first
element represents the noun *svǫrðr*, meaning 'the skin with the hair
on' or '(bacon-)rind', while the second element means '(pine-)
marten'. He takes 'rind-marten' as a circumlocutory expression for
'pig', and *svarðmerðlingar*, consequently, as 'piglets', justifying this
translation by referring to the speech in the snake-pit in which
Ragnarr compares himself and his sons to a boar and porkers
respectively (see the preceding paragraph, and part X of the
Analysis). He goes on to suggest that this was a word used by
sailors (in fact as a noa word, though he does not use this term) for
the progeny of a boar-pig, since the normal word for this animal,
gǫltr, was apparently taboo at sea. The advantage of this
interpretation is that no emendation of the text is involved; its
disadvantages, however, are that it is extremely far-fetched, and
that it relies too much on the Ragnarr loðbrók tradition for its
ideas.

Meissner (1921, 350) followed F. Jónsson (1915b, 261) in
reading *sverðmerðlingar*, thus expanding the first interlinear r as *er*
rather than *ar*. He drew attention to the feminine noun *merð*, listed
by Fritzner (1891, 678) with the meaning 'a trap used for catching
fish in rivers or streams', and thus envisaged *sverðmerð, f., meaning
'sword-trap', as a kenning for 'shield', taking *sverðmerðlingar, m.
pl., to mean 'shield-bearers', 'warriors'. The only objections to this

interpretation that I can see are that the interlinear **r** would be
expected to have the value *ar* rather than *er* in the first syllable, as it
does at the end of the word, and that the translation 'warriors'
again seems to show the influence of the Ragnarr loðbrók tradition.
E. A. Kock (1923, 64), who was clearly unaware of Meissner's
reading, poured scorn on various other commentators (not all of
them referred to here), but in fact did rather less well than
Meissner, taking the first syllable of the word, like him, as *sverð*, but
the second as *morð*, n., meaning 'murder', and the word as a whole
as **sverðmorðlingar*, m. pl., 'killers with the sword', 'sword-fighters',
'warriors'. As well as showing the same dependence on the
'warriors' idea, Kock's reading involves still more emendation than
Meissner's.

Gutenbrunner (1937, 140–41) followed Olsen (1912, 29–30) in
reading the word as *svarðmerðlingar* without emendation, and in
deriving it ultimately from the words *svǫrðr* ('skin with hair') and
mǫrðr ('marten'). He also noted, however, that both these words
occur as personal names, and instead of taking **svarðmǫrðr* as a
roundabout expression for 'boar', as Olsen did, suggested that it
was a compound personal name formed from these two names,
which themselves derived ultimately from the habit of wearing
marten-skins and other pelts. **Svarðmǫrðr*, he suggested, was the
name of a Viking leader or sea-king, and the *svarðmerðlingar* were his
sons. Gutenbrunner slightly spoils his argument, which up to this
point has given an impression of commendable independence, by
pointing out that this interpretation fits in well with the phrase
meghir heklinghs (i.e. 'sons of Hœklingr', a sea-king) in the first of
the three strophes spoken by the *trémaðr*, and with the phrase *synir
lodbrokar* ('sons of Loðbrók', to be discussed below) occurring later
in the passage now under discussion. As indicated above (see pp.
17–18), and as Gutenbrunner (1937, 140) himself realized, the first
strophe (no. 38 in Olsen, 1906–08, 174, cf. 221) had originally
nothing to do with the other two and should in no way be allowed
to influence their interpretation; and Gutenbrunner's reliance,
however slight, on the Ragnarr loðbrók tradition shows itself in his
assumption that the Loðbrók of the second strophe was a Viking
leader or a sea-king.

I would follow Olsen (1912, 29–30) and Gutenbrunner (1937,
140) in deriving the first syllable of the word under discussion from
svǫrðr, meaning 'the skin with the hair on'; Meissner (1921, 350) in
deriving the second syllable from *merð*, f., meaning 'trap'; and E. A.

Kock (1923, 64) and Meissner (1921, 350) in taking the suffix -*lingr* to mean 'connected with' or 'having to do with', rather than 'descended from' or as a diminutive. I would give the word *svǫrðr* more of the meaning 'hair of the head' than previous commentators have done, following here the information given in the list of poetic appellations known as 'the little Skálda' (preserved in two manuscripts of Snorri's *Edda* and dating probably from the second half of the thirteenth century, see F. Jónsson, 1931a; lviii–lix, 255–59, see 258) to the effect that the word *svǫrðr* may be used as one of a number of possible words for a person's hair in poetry (all the other words with which *svǫrðr* is here listed in the meaning 'hair' designate different parts of the head in ordinary speech). Thus I would read the word as *svarðmerðlingar* and translate: 'hair-trap wearers', 'wearers of head-dresses'. Further than that I shall not go for the moment, since I wish to avoid preconceived interpretation; I shall not, for instance, assume that the head-dresses in question were helmets, or that the people referred to were therefore warriors.

Turning now to the fourth *vísuorð* of the strophe, which appears in Olsen's edition (1906–08, 174, l. 21) as **synir lodbrokar**, i.e. 'sons of Loðbrók' (see p. 19, above), I would suggest that, while **synir** is undoubtedly the correct reading here, the form **lodbrokar**, as far as its ending is concerned, is open to question. Olsen and other editors (Heusler & Ranisch, 1903, 94, and F. Jónsson, 1915a, 241) have obtained this ending presumably by expanding what they take to be an abbreviated form of terminal -*ar*. It is true that a genitive ending is naturally required here, and that, if *loðbrók* is taken to be the nominative form, *loðbrókar* would be the expected form of the genitive; furthermore, the abbreviated form of -*ar*, whether genitive or otherwise, that would be expected in this manuscript is interlinear **r** (cf. p. 19, above, and Olsen, 1906–08, li; the **w**-like symbol which is used only rarely in this manuscript as an abbreviation for -*ar* may be discounted here, cf. Olsen, 1906–08, xlviii). What the manuscript seems to show, however, if a photograph may be trusted, is: **lodbrok**[v], in which the **k** is immediately followed by interlinear **v** rather than **r** (see fig. 1, which also shows interlinear **r** as an abbreviation of -*ar* in **var**). Now Olsen (1906–08, l, makes it clear that in this manuscript interlinear **v** is generally used as an abbreviation for -*ru* or -*un*, neither of which, of course, provides *loðbrók* with a satisfactory genitive ending. However, he also includes **v** in a list of interlinear letters which, according to him, can sometimes have 'their normal value, without indicating abbreviation' (cf. Olsen, 1906–08, li). He takes the normal value of interlinear v to be u in the case of **nock^{v}t**, where it also follows **k** (see fig. 2 and cf. Olsen 1906–08, ci, ref. to 124, l. 28), and further points out (Olsen, 1906–08, lxii) that in this manuscript **v** and **u** are scarcely distinguishable from each other. These considerations, in my view, provide sufficient justification for taking the correct reading in the present instance as **lodbrok^v**, i.e. *lodbróku*, the genitive singular of a weak feminine noun *lodbróka*.

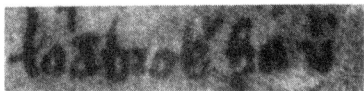　　　　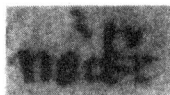

Fig. 1　　　　　　　　　Fig. 2

Figs. 1–2: 1, lodbroku þa *var* (cf. Olsen, 1906–08, 174, ll. 21–22);
2, nockut (cf. Olsen, 1906–08, ci; 124, l. 28).

The two strophes may now be given in normalized spelling with a facing translation:

39.　ok því settu [mik]
　　　svarðmerðlingar
　　　suðr hjá salti,
　　　synir Loðbróku;
　　　þá var ek blótinn
　　　til bana mǫnnum
　　　í Sámseyju
　　　sunnanverðri.

So wearers of head-dresses, sons
of Loðbróka, set me up in the
south by the sea; at that time
I was worshipped with human
sacrifices in the southern part of Samsø.

40.　Þar báðu standa,
　　　meðan strǫnd þolir,
　　　mann hjá þyrni
　　　ok mosa vaxinn;
　　　nú skýtr á mik
　　　skýja gráti,
　　　hlýr hvárki mér
　　　hold né klæði.

There they bade the (wooden) man
(i.e. me) stand near a thorn-bush,
and overgrown with moss, for as
long as the coast endures; now
the tears of the clouds beat upon
me; neither flesh nor cloth
protects me.

As far as I know, the form *lodbróka*, gen. *lodbróku*, is nowhere else recorded. The noun *bróka* is, however, listed in one of the *þulur* belonging to the younger of the two groups of *þulur* preserved in manuscripts of Snorri's *Edda*, that is, in the group dating probably from the thirteenth century (see F. Jónsson, 1912a, 688; 1912b,

677–78; 1923, 179, cf. Lie, 1950, 165–66); it is a brief *þula* of three strophes with the title: 'kvenna heiti ókend', which is probably to be understood as meaning 'poetic appellations for women which may be used without determinants'. A number of the other words listed in this *þula*—notably the word *grund*, f., which appears, like *bróka*, in the second of the three strophes—do occur elsewhere as the basic words in kennings for 'woman', where each of them is naturally combined with a determinant, whether in the form of a prefixed compound element, or a qualifying noun in the genitive. *Grund*, f., for instance, meaning 'earth (goddess)', is used as the basic word in a wide variety of kennings for 'woman' in which the determinants take the form of prefixed compound elements, as well as of nouns in the genitive (see F. Jónsson, 1931b, 206–07). Commenting on this particular *þula*, Meissner (1921, 403) writes: 'In der þula 677, yy (kvenna heiti ókend) werden Namen von Göttinnen und solche Ausdrücke aufgeführt, die in normalen Frauenkenningar als Grundwörter gebraucht werden. Man hat in späterer Zeit sich für berechtigt angesehen, solche Grundwörter als Heiti zu verwenden.' This would imply that the word (or word-element) *bróka* became a poetic word for 'woman' only at a relatively late stage of its history, and that it had earlier functioned either as the name of a goddess, or as a basic word in kennings for 'woman', or as both. Now again as far as I know, the only recorded instance of the weak form *bróka*, apart from the one in the *þula* under discussion, is the genitive singular form occurring as the second element in *Loðbróka* in the *trémaðr* strophe quoted above. Here it is plainly not occurring on its own (i.e. without a qualifier) as the name of a goddess, since it is preceded by the element *Loð-*; nor does it seem to be functioning as the basic word in a kenning for 'woman', since 'sons of a woman' would surely be a very weak and uninformative translation of *synir Loðbróku*, however hard it may be to determine this phrase's true meaning.

Nevertheless, I would suggest that the background of *bróka* as a *heiti* for 'woman' was not so very different from what Meissner (1921, 403) envisages—that this background at any rate included a goddess and an expression comparable to a poetic kenning. I would first recall Sahlgren's (1918, 28–40) view, outlined above, that *Lopkona* developed as a noa name for a fertility goddess so that use of her taboo name could be avoided. Noa names often consisted of circumlocutory expressions (such as *Lopkona*), as Sahlgren (1918, 10) makes clear, and in this respect they may be compared with kennings; it has indeed been suggested, as Lie (1957, 55–59) shows, that the poetic kenning may have had its origin in the constraints imposed by taboo on spoken language in secular as well as religious contexts. Next, bearing in mind Lid's (1942, 118) remarks, referred to above (see p. 17), I would argue that the ritual wearing of shaggy costumes such as *loðbrœkr* ('hairy breeches'; pl. of *loðbrók*, f.) in the cult of the goddess known as *Lopkona* led to the formation of the weak feminine noun *Loðbróka* (on the basis of the strong feminine noun *loðbrók*) as an alternative appellation for this goddess; that *Lopkona* and *Loðbróka* thus became virtually synonymous (the significance of which for the Ragnarr loðbrók tradition will be discussed below, see esp. pp. 30–35); and that an awareness that the element -*bróka* could thus be substituted for the element -*kona* lies in the background of the appearance of the word *bróka* among the poetic expressions for 'woman' listed in the *þula* discussed above. It may even be significant that the name immediately preceding the word *bróka* in this *þula*, and carrying the head-stave of the line in which it occurs, is *lodda*, f., which occurs in poetry in kennings for 'blood' and 'woman' in the primary meanings 'river' and 'island' respectively (see F. Jónsson, 1931b, 381), and which may well be related to the *loð* element occurring in *Loðbróka* and elsewhere (see de Vries, 1977, 362–63).

  If *Loðbróka* is then to be interpreted as the name of a fertility goddess who was also called *Lopkona*, who are 'the sons of Loðbróka'? And why are they described as 'head-dress wearers' in the word *svarðmerðlingar* as interpreted above? If the goddess Lopkona/Loðbróka was originally identical with the goddess Nerthus mentioned by Tacitus, as Sahlgren's remarks help to suggest, it might be thought that the phrase *synir Loðbróku* meant simply 'human beings', the descendants in the most general sense of Mother Earth (cf. the scaldic kenning *jarðar synir*, 'sons of earth', for 'filii terrae', Meissner, 1921, 364, and the fact that, in ch. 2 of his *Germania*, Tacitus describes the god Tuisto, the father of Mannus and through him of the German peoples, as 'born of earth' ('terra editum', see Much, 1967, 44, 51–52)). It is, however, no great compliment to the composer of these two strophes to assume that this was his meaning: the *trémaðr* must surely be saying something less obvious than that he was set up by human beings (cf. the translation 'sons of a woman' considered and rejected in the immediately foregoing discussion). It is clear from the reference to sacrifices in the second half of str. 39 that the *trémaðr* was set up as a cult-object, and the most likely explanation of the phrase *synir Loðbróku* is surely that it refers to the sons of a priestess, who was named after and represented the goddess. *Synir Loðbróku* would thus be a metronymic expression, such as was occasionally used in mediaeval Scandinavia in preference to a patronymic, as Storm (1878, 85) and Hornby (1947, 231–32) have shown.

An example of a priestess's son participating in pagan ritual is provided by the *þáttr Þorvalds ens víðfǫrla* ('the story of Þorvaldr the far-traveller'), dating from the thirteenth century; the relevant episode is also recorded in the thirteenth-century *Kristni saga*, which appears to have borrowed here from *þáttr Þorvalds* (Kahle, 1905, xiv, xvi, xix; de Vries, 1967, 190, 192). According to this last-named source (see Kahle, 1905, 71), the Icelandic convert and missionary Þorvaldr Koðránsson attempted to preach the gospel at Hvammr in Breiðafjarðardalir (in western Iceland), the home of one Þórarinn, who was away at the time. He made little progress, however, as Þórarinn's wife, Friðgerðr, was engaging in pagan worship ('blótaði') while he was preaching, and they could hear each other's words; his own words were moreover mocked by Skeggi, the son of Þórarinn and Friðgerðr. In a verse composed by Þorvaldr about this, the son is described as 'hreyti hlautteins, goða sveini' (F. Jónsson, 1912b, 105), 'the shaker of the sacrificial blood-sprinkling twig, the servant of the divine powers', and is clearly visualized as an acolyte. His mother, the priestess, is not named after a goddess precisely, it is true; but the second element in her name, *gerðr* (described as a 'goddess-name' by Frank, 1970, 25), is the name of the giant Gymir's daughter, Gerðr, who, as Turville-Petre (1969, 253) has shown, 'appears to have some affinities with Nerthus and to be a Terra Mater'.

As for the head-dresses, Olrik (1905) has produced evidence that the religious beliefs and practices of the Lapps are to a large extent borrowed from Old Norse religion; that their three main deities, representing thunder, fertility, and the wind, are modelled on Þórr, Freyr, and Njǫrðr respectively; and that in conducting sacrifices the Lappish celebrant customarily wore a woman's hat of linen, apparently tied round his head, with a wreath of leaves and flowers placed on top of it, and a white apron (*sic*: 'Forklæde', see Olrik, 1905, 53) hanging over his shoulders. If this practice was among those borrowed by the Lapps from a Germanic source, it may be suggested that the *svarðmerðlingar* mentioned by the *trémaðr* wore head-dresses of the kind just described; leaves and flowers would certainly not be out of place in the context of a fertility cult, and a woman's head-dress would presumably be an appropriate accessory to the worship of a goddess; one modern commentator, indeed, cited by Much (1967, 480), maintains that it was only in sacrificing to goddesses (as opposed to gods) that the Lapps wore hats of this type.

I must emphasize that the expressions *svarðmerðlingar* and *synir Loðbróku*, which as far as I know have never before been explained in the ways I have suggested here, are not the only features of these two strophes that may be said to show affinities with the worship of Nerthus as described by Tacitus. My reading of these two expressions may well be disputed; but no one surely will dispute the references to human sacrifices and to the island of Samsø in the second half of str. 39 (see p. 23, above); and these are reminiscent of, respectively, the killing of the slaves described by Tacitus in connection with the worship of Nerthus (a clear instance of human sacrifice, according to Much, 1967, 457, and Turville-Petre, 1969, 248; cf. pp. 20–26, above) and Tacitus's location of the grove where Nerthus is worshipped 'on an island of the sea' (see p. 17, above); the Danish islands are among the possibilities considered by Much (1967, 452–53) as to which island Tacitus may have meant. Tacitus makes no mention of an idol in connection with Nerthus, it is true, and indeed states elsewhere in his *Germania* (ch. 9) that 'The Germans do not think it in keeping with the divine majesty to confine gods within walls or to portray them in the likeness of any human countenance' (Handford, 1970, 109). It has been shown, however, that at least the last part of this statement may be contradicted by archæological and literary evidence, see Much (1967, 182–84) and Turville-Petre (1969; cf. also 1964, 169–73, 236–50, and Olaf Olsen, 1966, 277–82). Tacitus does of course mention a chariot in connection with the worship of Nerthus, and Turville-Petre (1969, 248 -53) has produced evidence to suggest that a wooden idol and a chariot were used in conjunction as part of an ancient Scandinavian ritual procession or drama intended to bring fertility to the crops. He refers to the story of Gunnarr helmingr ('the pied') preserved in *Qgmundar þáttr dytts* ('the story of Qgmundr dint'), which he believes may date from before 1218. Kristjánsson (1956, lv–lxiv), who assigned it to a somewhat later date, nevertheless maintains that the part of it dealing with Gunnarr helmingr preserves a genuine memory of the pre-Christian religious practices of the Swedes.

According to this story (see Kristjánsson, 1956, 111–15), Gunnarr helmingr was a Norwegian Christian who, during the reign of Óláfr Tryggvason (995–1000), was wrongly suspected of a killing and so fled from Norway to Sweden, where he found that great sacrifices were held, and that Freyr was the god most worshipped. The graven image ('líkneski') of Freyr was so charged with magic ('magnat') that the devil spoke to people from inside it ('ór skurðgoðinu'). A young and beautiful woman was appointed to serve Freyr, since it was believed that he was a living being and needed a wife with whom to have sexual intercourse. Gunnarr asked this woman, the wife of Freyr ('konu Freys'), if he might stay in the sacred precincts ('hofstaðnum') of which, together with Freyr, she had charge, saying in his cheerful way that he would rather have her help than Freyr's. She warned him that Freyr was ill-disposed towards him; but because of the popularity he had acquired locally with his cheerfulness and valour she encouraged him to stay for the winter, and to go the rounds with her and Freyr when the time came for the god to bring fertility to the crops ('þá er hann skal gera mǫnnum árbót'); Freyr and his wife would then sit in a chariot ('í vagni') while their attendants walked ahead in procession, and Gunnarr was to lead the horse. In the event, the journey was an arduous one, and Gunnarr in his exhaustion sat in the chariot with Freyr and his wife. She warned him that Freyr would attack him unless he resumed leading the horse, so he did this for a while, but he soon became exhausted a second time, and resolved to take the consequences. Freyr and he then wrestled together and Gunnarr's strength began to fail, but then it occurred to him that if he could defeat this devil and get back to Norway he would revert to the true faith and seek reconciliation with King Óláfr. As soon as Gunnarr had had this thought, Freyr reeled and fell. The devil departed from the image and all that was left was an empty piece of wood, which Gunnarr broke in pieces. The woman and he then agreed that she should say that he was Freyr when they came to human dwellings. He put on the idol's fine clothing ('búnað'), and the weather, which had been stormy before, began to improve. They were received at various banquets, and people were greatly impressed that Freyr had come to visit them in such weather, and by the fact that he now walked among them and ate and drank like other men, though he spoke little. He no longer wanted animals to be sacrificially slain, and would accept no offerings apart from gold and silver, fine clothes and other treasures. As time went on, it emerged that Freyr's wife was with child; and the Swedes became all the more devoted to their god; the weather was mild and everything so auspicious that no one could remember such a season. Eventually Gunnarr was reconciled with King Óláfr, who had become convinced of his innocence; Gunnarr's wife was baptized under the king's auspices, and they kept the true faith ever afterwards.

Although the word *trémaðr* itself is not mentioned in this account, it is clear that Freyr as described here is in several respects comparable to the *trémaðr* of the final chapter of *Ragnars saga* in the 1824b text; both are presented as animated wooden idols; the *trémaðr* of *Ragnars saga* is described in the prose as a god; and it is clear from one of the verses he speaks (str. 39, see p. 23, above) that he was worshipped with sacrifices, like Freyr in *Qgmundar þáttr*, though in the latter case these seem to have involved animals rather than human beings. Turville-Petre (1969, 249–50) moreover suggests that behind the references in *Qgmundar þáttr* to the wife of Freyr lies the idea of a sacral marriage, and hints that this also lies behind Tacitus's account of the relations between Nerthus and her priest. He also draws attention (Turville-Petre, 1969, 251) to the element of Christian propaganda in the story of Gunnarr helmingr, which shows itself in the description of the god as a devil, in the explanation of Gunnarr's victory in wrestling with Freyr, and in his final reconciliation with the king. This does not invalidate the story as a source for Scandinavian paganism, as Turville-Petre (1969, 249–51; 1964, 247) and Krist-jánsson (1956, lvii–lxiii) see it; nor, in their view, do the similarities it shows to (among other things) a story told by the Roman poet Valerius Flaccus in his *Argonautica*, written near the end of the first century A.D., which, according to Krappe (1928–29), may be regarded as a more or less direct source for it. In the Roman account, the women of the island of Lemnos murdered all their men, except that Hypsipyle saved her father. She took him to the temple of Bacchus, disguised him as the god, dressed herself as a Bacchante and led the supposed god to the seashore, saying that she had to wash him. There he boarded a raft, and so escaped from the murderous women. According to Turville-Petre (1969, 252), the differences between this story and that of Gunnarr helmingr are too great for the former to be regarded as a model for the latter, though they both 'may preserve memories of [a] similar ritual procession or drama in which a man impersonates the god and a woman the goddess'; according to Kristjánsson (1956, lxiii), on the other hand, the Roman account helps to suggest that the story underlying that of Gunnarr helmingr originally travelled from southern Europe to Scandinavia, and there combined with local traditions of a fertility deity.

The Roman account is of interest in the present context in that the motif of the women slaying their menfolk is comparable to that of the slaying of the aged, which it will be shown in ch. III, section (d), below, has its own relevance to the Ragnarr loðbrók tradition; and also insofar as the god in the Roman account is Bacchus, the god of wine, since Polomé (1969, 287–90) finds the name *Loþkona* (discussed above, pp. 16–17) etymologically related to *Liber*, the name of the Italic god of growth and vegetation (cf. Sahlgren, 1918, 29), who came to be identified with his closest equivalent in the Greek pantheon, the wine-god Bacchus or Dionysus (Reinhold, 1972, 357). The reference in the story of Gunnarr helmingr to the idol's clothing may be compared with str. 49 of the eddaic poem *Hávamál*, the dating of which is disputed (see McTurk, 1981a, 156, n. 100); here the word *trémaðr* is used (this passage has in turn been compared with the second of the two strophes quoted on p. 23, above, from the *trémaðr* in the 1824b text of *Ragnars saga*, see Clarke, 1923, 107; Gutenbrunner, 1937, 141–42; and Olsen, 1962, 21 25; Olsen indeed argues that a knowledge of the relevant part of *Hávamál* stimulated the linking of these two strophes to the one preserved also in *Hálfs saga*, cf. p. 18, above). The narrator says that he gave his clothes to two wooden men ('tveim trémǫnnum') out in the open country, and that they considered themselves fine men when they had received some clothing, since a naked man is held in contempt. According to de Vries (1956, 386–87), this passage may be used as evidence that in ancient Scandinavia pagan idols were sometimes clothed, at least in part.

It may be suggested, then, that in the first of the two strophes quoted above, the *trémaðr* is saying that he was set up near the sea as an idol in the southern part of Samsø by head-dress wearers, who were sons of Loðbróka, a priestess named after and possibly identified with the fertility goddess Loðbróka/Loþkona, with whom he was closely associated; and that he was worshipped there with human sacrifices. Understanding the first half of the second strophe quoted (see p. 23, above) is made a little difficult, it is true, by the present tense and indicative mood of the verb *þola*; the past subjunctive might rather be expected here, since the verb seems to occur in a subordinate clause linked to an accusative and infinitive construction dependent on a verb of requesting (i.e. *biðja*, *bað*, *beðinn*; see Nygaard, 1905, 324), here in the past tense. However, the meaning seems to be that the sons of Loðbróka set up the *trémaðr* with the intention that he should remain where he was (by a thorn-bush near the sea) at least until he had become covered with moss, and probably also for as long as the coast itself lasted. Then, in the second half-strophe, he complains that he has neither flesh nor clothing to protect him from the rain that beats upon him. What he is probably lamenting here is the passing of the pagan era and the fact that he is no longer regularly decked with clothes as part of a ritual; a less likely possibility, in view of his probable size as recorded in the prose (see p. 19, above) and the interpretation just given of the first half of the second strophe quoted, is that he is expressing regret at no longer being periodically removed from his station in order to travel by chariot with the priestess in a ritual procession. I am not suggesting that everything the *trémaðr* says should necessarily be believed, but would maintain that his verses provide evidence for the existence of a tradition at the turn of the eleventh to the twelfth century (cf. p. 18, above), according to which the sons of Loðbróka, a woman associated in some way with the fertility goddess known by that name, or as *Lǫþkǫna*, were active in the Danish islands.

Returning now to the Maeshowe runic inscription mentioned above (see p. 9), I would note that this is one of a number of runic inscriptions discovered in Maeshowe on Mainland, Orkney, by James Farrer in 1861, and numbered by him I–XXIV (Farrer, 1862, 25–40). Farrer's numbering seems to have been generally followed by subsequent investigators. These have included Dickins, who in 1930 gave helpful transliterations and renderings of the inscriptions, emphasizing (Dickins, 1930, 1) that they are by a number of different hands; and A. Liestøl, who stressed (A. Liestøl, 1968, 55, 60) that they may nevertheless all be 'securely dated to the middle of the twelfth century'. The passage quoted above, referring to the sons of Loðbrók in such a way as to suggest that Loðbrók was a woman, is from nos. XIX and XX, which in fact constitute one inscription, as Farrer (1862, 35–36) himself made clear. Two of the inscriptions, those numbered XIV and XX by Farrer, clearly state that Jerusalem pilgrims ('Jórsalamenn', 'Jórsalafarar') broke into Maeshowe (see Dickins, 1930, 9–11, and cf. A. Liestøl, 1968, 59), and this has given rise to the view, held at least until 1957 (see Gordon, 1957, 259–60), that the pilgrims referred to were those who accompanied Rǫgnvaldr Kali from the Orkneys to the Holy Land in 1151–53, and were also the authors of the inscriptions. If so, then the breakage into Maeshowe and the inscribing of the runes must have taken place either in the winter of 1150–51, when the pilgrims assembled in the Orkneys prior to setting off for the Holy Land, or after their return to the Orkneys late in 1153 (see Guðmundsson, 1965, lxxxviii, cf. 247, n. 1). Dietrichson (1906, 115, referring to S. Bugge), however, showed that by his time of writing doubt had already been cast on whether the pilgrims referred to in the inscriptions were actually their authors; Marwick (1929, xvii) more emphatically stated that 'The reference in two inscriptions to the Jerusalem-pilgrims implies that the writer was not one of themselves'; and A. Liestøl (1968, 60) seems to think that most of the inscriptions were made by followers of Haraldr Maddaðarson when he and a hundred men spent Twelfth Night in Maeshowe in 1152, while Rǫgnvaldr Kali was away on his pilgrimage, as recorded in ch. 93 of *Orkneyinga saga*, dating from *c*.1200 (see de Vries, 1967, 265). This view does not of course exclude the possibility that the pilgrims referred to were Rǫgnvaldr Kali's followers, who, if that was indeed the case, must have broken into Maeshowe in the winter of 1150–51; but it leaves open the possibility that they were a different group of pilgrims altogether, and presupposes no direct involvement of Rǫgnvaldr himself in the inscribing of the runes.

The view that Rǫgnvaldr Kali was not in the immediate background of the inscriptions is if anything an advantage to my argument, as I wish to claim that the Loðbrók mentioned in inscription XIX–XX was indeed a woman, as the feminine form of the pronoun *hennar* (see p. 9, above) surely suggests, and as Farrer (1862, 36, quoting P. A. Munch) and Storm (1878, 82–86) believed; whereas it has been argued by de Vries (1928a, 259) that although only the former of the two names *Ragnarr* and *Loðbrók* is mentioned in what can now be read of *Háttalykill*, the poem attributed to Rǫgnvaldr Kali and Hallr Þórarinsson in ch. 81 of *Orkneyinga saga*, the authors of this poem were nevertheless informed of Ari's equation of Loðbrók with Ragnarr in *Íslendingabók* (referred to above, p. 1). The precise date of the composition of *Háttalykill* is a matter of some doubt; from where it is referred to in *Orkneyinga saga* it might be thought that it was composed in the period 1140–48, before Rǫgnvaldr's pilgrimage to the Holy Land, but de Vries (1967, 28) has argued that *c*.1155, after Rǫgnvaldr's return, is a more likely date of composition. Taking my cue from Dietrichson (1906, 115, who in turn refers to S. Bugge), Marwick (1929, xvii), and A. Liestøl (1968, 60), I would suggest that the Maeshowe inscription no. XIX–XX, with its reference to the Jerusalem

pilgrims as well as to Loðbrók and *her* sons, was made independently of the combination of the names *Ragnarr* and *Loðbrók*
(whether transmitted by Ari or Rǫgnvaldr Kali), and on the basis
of Orkney traditions relating to Scandinavian pilgrimages to the
Holy Land, including information brought to Scandinavia by
returning pilgrims. It will be shown in the next chapter (see pp.
108–10, below) that there is nothing surprising about this information having included, in its turn, references to the sons of Loðbrók.

As already indicated, the Danish island of Samsø (where the
trémaðr says he was set up as an idol) is off the east coast of Jutland,
and it was through Jutland (as will be shown in ch. II, section
(b) (*iii*), below) that one of the main routes lay for Icelandic,
Orcadian and Norwegian pilgrims travelling to and from Rome and
Jerusalem. Since the sons of Loðbróka, to judge from the *trémaðr*'s
verses, were remembered in connection with Samsø, and since
Jerusalem pilgrims are mentioned in the same Maeshowe inscription as that which mentions the sons of Loðbrók, I would venture
to suggest that the Loðbróka of the *trémaðr*'s verse and the Loðbrók
of the runic inscription were the same person, a woman associated
in some way with the worship of the goddess Loþkona/Loðbróka,
who in turn may originally have been identical with the goddess
Nerthus of Tacitus's *Germania*. This may seem a bold suggestion,
not least because the Maeshowe inscription clearly has the genitive
form *Loðbrókar* (see Farrer, 1862, plate X, no. 20; Dickins, 1930, 10;
Elliott, 1963, 23), as opposed to the *Loðbróku* of the verse; but it
can, I believe, be supported by the following arguments.

First I would repeat the suggestion made above (p. 25), with
Lid's observations in mind, that the ritual wearing of shaggy
garments such as *loðbrœkr* led to the formation of *Loðbróka* as an
alternative name for the fertility goddess *Loþkona*, whose name
underlies the Swedish place-name *Locknevi*, as also shown above
(see p. 16). This suggestion implies that the name *Loðbróka* was
formed from the common noun *loðbrók* as used in connection with
the proper noun *Loþkona*; it may thus be said to derive from both
nouns, more directly from the former than from the latter. Like the
name *Loþkona* itself, which as far as I know is clearly attested only
in certain forms of the place-name *Locknevi* (see Sahlgren, 1918,
33–34), the name *Loðbróka* seems to have been extremely rare; the
only surviving instance of it known to me is its mention by the
trémaðr, though an awareness of it very possibly lies behind the
inclusion of *bróka* as a *heiti* for 'woman' in the *þulr*. Its rarity, and

its formal closeness to the common noun *loðbrók*, from which it partly derives, could easily mean that the two forms *Loðbróka* and *loðbrók* would become confused, particularly at a stage when the circumstances of the *Loðbróka* form's origins were no longer fully remembered or understood. I would suggest that this has happened in the case of the Maeshowe inscription numbered XIX–XX, and that the form *Loðbrók*, used there in the genitive (*Loðbrókar*), represents an imperfect recollection of the form *Loðbróka* (gen. *Loðbróku*).

I would further suggest that, except in a few cases represented by the *trémaðr* passage and perhaps the *þula*, the relatively rare form *Loðbróka* came to be remembered as *Loðbrók*, a form more readily to hand because it was a common noun referring to an article of clothing (from which indeed the proper noun *Loðbróka* had itself partly arisen in the first place). That it could also be used as a nickname is of course confirmed by the name-combination *Ragnarr loðbrók*; but since my present intention is partly to explain this combination, I prefer not to use it here as supporting evidence. The probability is that *loðbrók* could be used as a nickname for either a man or a woman; the nickname *hábrók*, applied to a man, has already been noted (see pp. 11–12, above), and the nickname *langbrók*, also noted above, p. 12, is applied in *Laxdæla saga* and *Njáls saga* (both from the thirteenth century), and in the early fourteenth-century *Hauksbók* redaction of the originally twelfth-century *Landnáma* (see Lind, 1920–21, 236; Benediktsson, 1968, 143, n. 5), to a woman, Hallgerðr Hǫskuldsdóttir, who is also called *snúinbrók* ('twisted breeks') in the thirteenth-century *Sturlubók* redaction of *Landnáma* (see Lind, 1920–21, 347; Benediktsson, 1968, 143, n. 5). The probability that *loðbrók* could be applied as a nickname to a person of either sex is strengthened by the evidence that, in mediaeval Scandinavia, women as well as men used trouserwear of the type designated by the word *brók*, f., pl. *brækr* (see Falk, 1919, 121–22), even though the garments in question varied somewhat according to the sex of the wearer. It may well be true that, as Smyth (1977, 81, n. 64) points out, 'Masculine dress in any form for women was frowned upon in the sagas', but it should not be thought that, as Lönnroth (1976, 37) seems to imply, the mere fact of a woman wearing trousers would necessarily have caused raised eyebrows. In ch. 35 of *Laxdæla saga*, Auðr's nickname, *Bróka-Auðr*, arises not so much from the fact that she wears trousers as from the fact that her trousers are of the kind appropriate to a man (see

Sveinsson, 1934, 95); while the force of Skarpheðinn's insult to Flosi in throwing a pair of trousers ('brókum') at him in ch. 123 of *Njáls saga* almost certainly lies in the fact that the trousers in question are a woman's knickers (Sveinsson, 1954, 314, n. 2).

Now Lind (1920–21, iii) implies that Old Norse nicknames were seldom used otherwise than as appendages to personal names; if, therefore, what looks like a nickname is found on its own, i.e. not combined with a personal name, it may be suspected that it represents what was originally regarded as a proper name. This consideration, in my view, strengthens the likelihood that the *Loðbrók* of the Maeshowe inscription, which is not used in combination with any other name, represents the proper name *Loðbróka* in an imperfectly remembered form. There are in fact a number of instances, both in Old Norse and other sources, of the form *Loðbrók* (or its equivalent) being used in this way (see Storm, 1878, 82–83; Lind, 1920–21, 246; Knudsen, Kristensen, & Hornby, 1954–64, 687–89; and pp. 1, 7, 8, above), but Maeshowe is as far as I know the only one that clearly shows its referent to have been female, and some of them (notably the Anglo-Latin ones, of which the accounts of Geoffrey of Wells and Roger of Wendover provide representative examples, see p. 8, above and ch. III, section (e), below) seem just as clearly to present Loðbrók as a man. Since the use of nicknames without attachment to personal names was evidently rare, it may be suggested that not just the Maeshowe instance, but all these instances of *Loðbrók*, represent the proper name, *Loðbróka*, in misremembered form; and the rarity of the latter name encourages the assumption that the Loðbróka in question was identical with the one referred to by the *trémaðr*, as does also the fact that the various references to Loðbrók, including the Maeshowe one, seem, like the *trémaðr*'s reference to *Loðbróka*, to have been occasioned by the sons of the person referred to.

As already indicated (see pp. 32–33, above) the misremembering of Loðbróka's actual name is probably due to the name's formal closeness to the common noun *loðbrók*, and its own comparative rarity; while the fact that her sex came to be remembered inaccurately should be seen against the background of the probability that, as a nickname, *loðbrók* could be applied just as easily to a man as to a woman. None of the non-Scandinavian references to *Loðbrók* (by William of Jumièges, Adam of Bremen, and various English writers, see pp. 1, 7, 8, above, and ch. III, section (e), below) shows any sign of treating Loðbrók as female, and indeed William of Jumièges, who in *c.*1070 provides the earliest known reference to Loðbrók, clearly regards the latter as a king, referring to Bier Costae ferreae as 'Lotbroci regis filio' (see p. 1, above). This suggests that Loðbróka, who, if she was the mother of the Inguar mentioned by Adam of Bremen, must have lived in the ninth century (Trillmich, 1961, 209, n. 178), was already being referred to as *Loðbrók* by the middle of the eleventh; her true name and sex were, however, remembered in the exceptional cases of the *trémaðr's* verse and the Maeshowe inscription respectively. Whoever was the first to combine the names *Ragnarr* and *Loðbrók* (whether Ari Þorgilsson or one of his predecessors, see de Vries, 1928a, 258, n. 5) clearly saw no difficulty in applying the name *Loðbrók* to a man. It is possible indeed that this person obtained the name from a non-Scandinavian source; Ari, at any rate, may have drawn on English and continental Latin writings in the relevant part of his *Íslendingabók* (Benediktsson, 1968, xxii–xxiii). It is not necessary to assume such a source, however, since it is clear from what has been said above that the woman's name *Loðbróka* was already giving way in Scandinavia to the form *Loðbrók*, applicable to either a man or a woman, in the middle of the eleventh century, well before the time of Ari.

Initiation rites have been touched on in the foregoing discussion (see p. 10, above), and so have fertility rites. According to Speirs (1957, 315), 'almost all rites turn out to be creation rites of one kind or another', and de Vries (1963, 217–26) has argued more painstakingly and persuasively that since the tribal initiation rites of many different societies are intended to re-enact creation myths, elements of fertility ritual often play a prominent part in them. According to de Vries (1963, 219–22), conceptions of how the world and humankind were first created were basically much the same in many primitive societies, both within and outside the Indo-European area. Initiation rituals were of great importance in such societies, symbolizing as they did the passage of a young man at the age of puberty through the death of childhood into the new life of adult membership of his tribe. Ideal models for symbols of this kind of rebirth were found in creation myths, which frequently represented organized life as arising out of chaos, often in the form of a fight in which a god slays a monster. In a typical initiation ritual, then, as de Vries (1963, 221–22) imagines it, the young man was confronted with an artificially constructed monster over which he must in some way triumph. The heroic nature of the triumph meant that this and other elements of the ritual became absorbed into stories about particular heroes of history and legend as these developed in different societies. This, in de Vries's view, explains the international distribution of the heroic biographical pattern, which will be discussed more fully in the next chapter; and the sexual implications of the ritual explain why the winning of a maiden so often follows the slaying of a monster in heroic literature, as it does, of course, in the major accounts of Ragnarr loðbrók (see part VII of the Analysis). J. de Vries hardly discusses the question of which came first, the myth or the ritual, and indeed would probably regard it as irrelevant, since he evidently holds the view that 'the myth cannot be separated from the rite', and that 'myth and rite . . . do not stand in a linear or genealogical relation to each other' (de Vries, 1963, 227, 229). The question has since been discussed in a rather more general context, however, by Leach (1983, 17), who holds the view that, in the vast majority of cases, myths derive from rituals, rather than the other way round.

If, however, the essentials of de Vries's views may be accepted, and if Arent's views, outlined earlier, may also, then the Torslunda plate discussed by Schück in 1900 provides seventh-century evidence from the Swedish island of Öland for an initiation ritual in which the rôle of the monster-slayer was played by a shaggy-trousered man. Sahlgren's remarks on the other hand show that the Swedish place-name *Locknevi* has the fourteenth-century form *Lodkonuvi*, which, if Sahlgren is right, reflects the name's pre-christian origins and the cult of a fertility goddess named *Lopkona*, who was originally identical with Tacitus's Nerthus. Lid's observations further suggest that this goddess was celebrated in a ritual in which the wearing of shaggy costumes played a prominent part; and I have drawn on Lid's remarks and the evidence of two of the strophes spoken by the *trémaðr* in the 1824b text of *Ragnars saga* to suggest that this same goddess was celebrated on the Danish island of Samsø under the name *Loðbróka* by a woman of that name (so called after the goddess), and by her sons. The place-name *Locknevi* is recorded from the Kalmar province (Sahlgren, 1918, 33), the part of mainland Sweden closest to Öland, and if this fact is considered together with the close interrelationship of initiation and fertility rituals pointed out by de Vries (1983, 217–41), and with the apparent similarity of the costume depicted on the Torslunda plate to the kind of costume envisaged by Lid as part of the explanation of the name *Lopkona*, it becomes tempting to suggest a connection

between the subject-matter of the plate and the cult of Loþkona/
Loðbróka.

If, as seems probable, the Torslunda plates served as moulds for
ornaments on helmets and shields, it is likely that their subject-
matter would have been more widely known than just in Öland,
their place of discovery; and Arent (1969, 141) emphasizes the
connection between fertility and the initiation rites she believes
these plates depict in pointing out that 'The overcoming of a
chthonic being, monster, dragon, or giant', such as seems to be
represented by the plate showing the shaggy-trousered man, 'may
... have been reenacted yearly in rituals symbolizing the change
from the old cycle to the New Year'. If a definite connection could
be established between this plate and the ritual celebration of
Loþkona, the plate would provide valuable evidence for the
circumstances in which, as suggested earlier (see pp. 25, 32, above),
the form *Loðbróka* developed as an alternative name for her. Once
this development had taken place, it would of course be natural,
because of the close similarity between the forms *Loðbróka* and
loðbrók, for special attention to be paid to the trouser part of the
costume. It is however noteworthy that the major accounts of
Ragnarr loðbrók's fight with the serpent, summarized in the next
chapter (see parts V and VI of the Analysis), do not dwell especially
on his trouserwear; some indeed (such as 'Ormekampen' and
'Lindarormen') do not mention it, while others (such as *Ragnars
saga* and *Ragnarssona þáttr*) seem to attach more importance to his
cloak than to his trousers. This is undoubtedly linked with the fact
that in most of these accounts the serpent is presented as infinitely
larger and more terrifying than the common viper, the only
poisonous snake found in Scandinavia (see Dronke, 1969a, 65), and
which would indeed be well enough guarded against by a sturdy
pair of trousers; but this in turn may be due to a dim recollection
that, in the ritual celebration of Loþkona/Loðbróka, the adversary
of the shaggy-trousered warrior was no mere viper, but a symbolic
monster representing the forces of primeval chaos.

A more tentative suggestion as to the possibility of a link between *Loðbrók(a)* and
creation myths may be made by reference to Polomé's (1969, 287–90) discussion of
Sahlgren's identification of the form *loþkona* as an element in the original form of
the place-name *Locknevi*. Sahlgren (1918, 37–38) suggested that the form *loðvR*
found as the name of a god involved in the creation of mankind in str. 17 of the
eddaic poem *Vǫluspá* (of c.1000, see further below) as edited by Bugge (1867, 14)
from the text in the Codex Regius, dating from the second half of the thirteenth

century (see Helgason, 1953, 26), should be normalized not to *Lóðurr*, as is common editorial practice (see, for instance, Neckel, 1962, 5), but to **Lopverr*, which according to Sahlgren was the original form of the name. Its second element, *verr*, m., means 'man', or 'husband', and the bearer of the name, in Sahlgren's view, was a god of creation and fertility, the male counterpart of *Lopkona*. In response to this suggestion Turville-Petre (1964, 143) pointed out 'the difficulty', as he saw it, that the twelfth-century Icelandic scald Haukr Valdísarson 'rimes *Lóðurr* with *glóða*', in the *Íslendingadrápa* (str. 1, see F. Jónsson, 1912a, 556; 1912b, 539), 'showing that, for him, the root vowels were identical'. Haukr is here using the expression *Lóðurs vinr* ('Lóðurr's friend') as a kenning for Óðinn; and the same kenning (with the order of the words reversed) is used by the tenth-century scald Eyvindr skáldaspillir ('the plagiarist') in str. 10 of his *Háleygjatal* (see F. Jónsson, 1912a, 69; 1912b, 61), as Turville-Petre (1984, 144) also points out; in this latter case, however, the word *Lóðurs* is not required to participate in any form of rhyme, partly because of its position in the line and partly because the metre of the poem is *kviðuháttr* as opposed to *dróttkvætt*. Sahlgren (1918, 37–38) mentions neither of these cases; but presumably he would not be disturbed by the case of *Háleygjatal*, str. 10, since in purely metrical terms the first syllable of *Lóðurs* here (like that of *loðvR* in str. 17 of *Vǫluspá*, see Sahlgren, 1918, 38) *need* not contain a long vowel, provided that the syllable itself is long; and a long first syllable is provided just as easily by the form **Lopvers* (gen.) or (in the case of *Vǫluspá*, str. 17) **Lopverr* (nom.) as by *Lóðurs* or *Lóðurr*. Since the manuscript form of *Lóðurs* in *Háleygjatal* appears to be *loðurs* (see F. Jónsson, 1912a, 69), and since *u* and *v* seem virtually interchangeable in the relevant manuscripts (see F. Jónsson, 1912a, 69, vii; cf. Seip, 1954, 94, 99, 120, 140; and p. 23, above), Sahlgren would presumably normalize here to **Lopvers*, gen. sg. of **Lopverr*. F. Jónsson (1912a, 68) dates *Háleygjatal* to *c.985*, and *Vǫluspá* is generally dated to *c.*1000 (see Nordal, 1978–79; cf. Sveinsson, 1962, 228, 327 29, and de Vries, 1964, 60–62); Polomé (1969, 288, n. 88), however, dates *Vǫluspá* to 950.

If Sahlgren's views on the *loðvR* of *Vǫluspá*, str. 17, are accepted, and if *Háleygjatal*, str. 10, may be regarded as showing another instance of **lopverr*, what is to be done about the form *Lóðurs* occurring in the twelfth-century *Íslendingadrápa*? There can be no doubt that *Lóðurs* (as opposed to **Lopvers*) is the correct reading here, since in this poem the laws of internal rhyme appropriate to the *dróttkvætt* metre (which of course do not apply in *fornyrðislag*, the metre of *Vǫluspá*, any more than in the *kviðuháttr* of *Háleygjatal*) are consistently if not regularly applied. There can also be little doubt that the Lóðurr here referred to is the same deity as the Lóðurr or Lopverr of the other two poems. To explain the form *Lóðurs* in *Íslendingadrápa*, then, while at the same time accepting the forms **Lopverr* and **Lopvers* in *Vǫluspá* and *Háleygjatal* respectively, it would be necessary to argue that **Lopverr* developed into the form *Lóðurr* some time between *c.*1000 (by which time *Vǫluspá* and *Háleygjatal* may be assumed to have been composed) and the twelfth century. Polomé (1969, 287–90) has in fact produced such an argument, though his remarks are made difficult to follow by his failure to emphasize sufficiently strongly that, in the cases of *Vǫluspá* and *Háleygjatal*, it is a long first syllable, and not *necessarily* a long *vowel* in that syllable, that is metrically required of the word *Lóðurr* or **Lopverr*. If this point is kept in mind, it is possible to deduce the following argument from his remarks: between *c.*1000 and the twelfth century, **Lopverr* acquired the form *Lóðurr* in two stages of development. Firstly, **Lopverr* became *Loðurr* by reduction of its unstressed second syllable, so that in metrical terms its first syllable became *Lo-* rather than *Loþ-*, and thus short rather than long. Secondly, the *o* of *Loðurr* became long, if not by compensatory lengthening, which is not necessarily consequent on loss of the vowel of the second syllable in a form such as **Loþverr* > *Loðurr*, then under the influence of the metrical requirement that, if *Loðurr* is to function as a disyllable in poetry, its first syllable must be long; the lengthening was also assisted, according to Polomé, by the influence of such forms as Old Norse *lóð*, f. and n. , meaning 'produce of the land', and Icelandic *lóða*, adj., meaning 'on heat' (both of which, as he points out, have associations of fertility). Thus developed the form *Lóðurr* which the twelfth-century poet of *Íslendingadrápa* was able to rhyme with *glóða*.

If this argument is accepted, it need not be assumed that the manuscripts of *Vǫluspá* and *Háleygjatal* (all of which date from the thirteenth century or later, see Nordal, 1978, 1–2; F. Jónsson, 1912a, 69, vii; cf. Schier, 1970, 14 27) necessarily reproduce the older forms **Loþverr*, **Loþvers*; it could be maintained that these forms were used by the original composers of the poems at the turn of the tenth to the eleventh century, but that the scribes of the thirteenth century or later were using the younger forms *Lóðurr*, *Lóðurs*, which of course had developed by their time. The interpretation of Loþverr/Lóðurr as a fertility god is by no means inconsistent with the qualities which, according to *Vǫluspá*, str. 17, he gave to man; he evidently bestowed both 'lá' and 'lito góða' (see Neckel, 1962, 5). The latter expression clearly means 'healthy colouring', while *lá*, f., though it may mean 'appearance' or conceivably 'blood' (see Polomé, 1969, 283 85), is in Polomé's view (1969, 285 88) most reasonably to be interpreted as 'hair', particularly if attention is paid to Snorri's statement in his prose *Edda* (see F. Jónsson, 1931a, 191) that *lá* is a poetic appellation for 'hair'. This view has found the support of Schach (1983, 92 93), in a recent study of *Vǫluspá*.

While it must be admitted that these considerations provide less certain evidence for the form **Loþverr* than the place-name evidence adduced by Sahlgren does for the form *Loþkona*, it is by no means unreasonable to suggest that a goddess of the latter name (as Sahlgren explains it) was believed to have a male counterpart, since it was common for deities of creation and fertility to be represented as either hermaphrodite or in pairs consisting sometimes of husband and wife, sometimes of brother and sister, and sometimes even of both (see Turville-Petre, 1964, 172). **Loþverr*, with its second element meaning 'man' or 'husband', would be a wholly appropriate name for a male counterpart to Loþkona, the second element of whose name, as noted above, means 'woman' or 'wife'. It may be very tentatively suggested, then, that Loþverr and Loþkona did form a divine pair who were especially associated with creation and fertility. It should be stressed, however, that the arguments given earlier (pp. 16–25, above) in relation to Loþkona/Loðbróka are more solidly based than those just given in relation to **Loþverr*.

(c) Five sons, their father lost, their mother found

I should now like to discuss certain historical figures of the ninth century who, it has been argued, came to be regarded as sons of

Ragnarr loðbrók (cf. de Vries, 1923, 253–74). These are, first, Inwære, who is mentioned in a part of the *Anglo-Saxon chronicle* (the annal for 878; see Earle & Plummer, 1892, 74–75) that may be regarded as a contemporary account (Sweet, 1967, 32), and who seems to have been the prototype of the 'Inguar, filius Lodparchi' mentioned in *c*.1076 by Adam of Bremen (see p. 1, above), and of Ragnarr loðbrók's son Ívarr beinlauss ('the boneless', see part VII of the Analysis); secondly, Hubba, who first appears as an associate of Hinguar (= Inwære) in the late tenth-century *Passio sancti Eadmundi* by Abbo of Fleury (ed. Arnold, 1890, 6–25), and who was probably the model for Ubbo, a son, according to Saxo (IX.iv, 18–19), of Regnerus Lothbrog (see part VII of the Analysis, and pp. 104–07, 154, below); thirdly, Sigifridus, who is mentioned in a contemporary source, the *Annales Fuldenses* for 873 (Rau, 1969, 88–89; cf. Skyum-Nielsen, 1967, 15–16, 65), as a king ruling in Denmark in that year, and who may well be a model for Ragnarr loðbrók's son Sigurðr ormr-í-auga ('snake-in-the-eye'), called Sywardus 'serpentini oculi' by Saxo, IX.iv, 12 (see part VII of the Analysis); and fourthly Berno, who according to the nearly contemporary *Chronicon Fontanellense* for 855 (Pertz, 1829, 304; cf. Skyum-Nielsen, 1967, 16), and the contemporary *Annales Bertiniani* for 858 (Rau, 1972, 96–97, cf. Skyum-Nielsen, 1967, 13), was active between those years as a Viking leader on the Seine; he was in all probability the model for 'Bier Costae...ferreae', mentioned in *c*.1070 by William of Jumièges (see p. 1, above), and for Bjǫrn járnsiða, son of Ragnarr loðbrók (see part VII of the Analysis).

The main theories as to the origins of the nicknames of Ragnarr loðbrók's sons have recently been surveyed by Davidson (1980, 153–56, 158), and will be only briefly considered here. As for Ívarr's nickname *beinlauss*, the most convincing of the theories known to Davidson seems to me to be that of de Vries (1928a, 259–60), who noted that Inguar (= Inwære) was described by Adam of Bremen as 'the most cruel' ('crudelissimus') of a number of Vikings (see Trillmich, 1961, 208), and suggested that Ívarr's nickname might have arisen as a result of the Latin adjective *exosus* ('detesting' or 'detestable') being misread as *exos* ('boneless'); the latter adjective is in fact used of Ívarr by Arngrímur Jónsson, d. 1648, see p. 57, below, and part VII of the Analysis.

Apparently unknown to Davidson, however, are Solheim's (1940, 104–06) examples from modern Norwegian folklore of an adverse wind or storm being referred to by such expressions as *beinlaus*, *Eivind beinlaus*, and *Ivar beinlaus*; the meaning of *beinlaus* here seems to be either 'boneless' or 'without legs', and the expressions appear to derive from an impulse to lessen the fear or apprehension caused by the prospect of an adverse wind by referring to it euphemistically. Rather surprisingly, Solheim makes no reference in this connection to Ívarr beinlauss as a son of Ragnarr loðbrók, or to Ragnarr loðbrók himself or any of his other sons, though in the light of his findings it is of some interest to note that in Saxo (IX.iv, 17, 33; v, 6), Ericus, a son of Regnerus Lothbrog appointed by his father as king of Sweden, is nicknamed 'Ventosi Pillei' or 'wind-hat'. This nickname seems to correspond to *Wäderhatt*, 'weather hat', a nickname applied in Swedish folk tradition to a king named Erik, for which Strömbäck (1835, 138–39) quotes a seventeenth-century Swedish explanation to the effect that this king was believed to have control of the weather, in that the wind would blow from whatever direction in which he turned his hat. As will be shown in more detail in the next chapter (see pp. 89 90, 119, below), a fragmentary strophe (8b) in the mid twelfth-century poem *Háttalykill* appears to refer to somebody called 'Agnarr's brother' as completely boneless; and the foregoing considerations, together with the fact that, apart from in Saxo (IX.iv, 8), the Ragnarr loðbrók tradition presents Eirekr rather than Ívarr as a full brother of Agnarr (see part VII of the Analysis, and cf. ch. II, section (b) (*v*), below), raise the question of whether the reference in *Háttalykill*, str. 8b, is to Eirekr rather than Ívarr. I hope to have the opportunity of discussing this question elsewhere, together with other questions raised by the nickname *beinlauss*, in collaboration with Dr R. M. Perkins, of University College, London, to whom I am indebted for bringing Solheim's references to my attention. Here, however, I would simply point out that all the mediaeval evidence points to Ívarr rather than Eirekr as having been referred to as 'beinlauss'.

It may finally be noted, before the other nicknames are briefly dealt with, that according to Chadwick (1959, 186–87), whose views on this subject also seem to have escaped Davidson's notice, *beinlauss* originally meant 'legless' rather than 'boneless' and was an appropriate name for a dragon (conceived of as a snake-like creature). This view of the nickname may be compared with Smyth's (1977, 94 95), of which Davidson, who refers to Smyth (Davidson, 1980, 153), is presumably aware. The nicknames of Sigurðr and Bjǫrn, sons of Ragnarr loðbrók, are a good deal less problematic than *beinlauss*. Sigurðr's nickname, *ormr-i-auga* ('snake-in-the-eye') probably originally referred to a menacing gaze like that of a snake, such as is mentioned in str. 34 of the eddaic poem *Rígspula* (on the disputed dating of which see McTurk, 1981a, 156, n. 100; on the nickname see Davidson, 1980, 155, though it should be noted that Davidson does not refer, as does Guðnason, 1982, 86, n. 8, to Reichborn-Kjennerud's discussion of it in *Maal og minne*, 1923, 26, in terms of the eye condition known as *nystagmus*). Bjǫrn's nickname *járnsíða* ('ironside') probably referred to a mail-shirt, such as a Viking might be expected to have worn (see Davidson, 1980, 156; Foote & Wilson, 1923, 279).

In addition to the four historical figures already mentioned, it is necessary to consider here a certain Healfdene, who, though he nowhere appears as a son of Ragnarr loðbrók, is mentioned in (among other places) the *Anglo-Saxon chronicle* for 871, 874–76, and 878, and seems to be referred to (in the annal for 878) as a brother of Inwære (Earle & Plummer, 1892, 74 75; McTurk, 1976, 119–20; Wormald, 1982, 142 43). J. de Vries (1923, 266–67) has argued that this Healfdene is identical with one Halbdeni, who, in the *Annales Fuldenses* for 873 (Rau, 1969, 88–89), is clearly referred to as a brother of Sigifridus. If the identification of Healfdene with Halbdeni could be definitely established (and de Vries 1923, 266, regards it as practically certain), it would provide important evidence that Inwære and Sigifridus (and of course Healfdene/ Halbdeni himself) were sons of the same parents. Historians have recently been concerned not so much with this identification (cf. McTurk, 1980, 232–33) as with the possibility that Healfdene was identical with an Albann mentioned in the entry for 877 in the *Annals of Ulster* (see Hennessy, 1887, 390–91; Byrne, 1963, 269; Smyth, 1977, 255–66; Wormald, 1982, 141–44), which for the Viking period may be regarded as for the most part contemporary (Hughes, 1972, 150; see also 101, n. 1). This latter identification is treated with some scepticism, though not altogether rejected, by de Vries (1923, 263–66). A slight advantage of it is that there is a case (though by no means a strong one, see de Vries, 1923, 263–66, and McTurk, 1976, 115–16, 118) for regarding this Albann as the son of one Ragnall, whose name, as already indicated (p. 7, above), corresponds loosely (but only loosely) to *Ragnarr*; another advant- age of it, at least from the point of view of the historians just referred to, is that it provides one argument in support of the view that Healfdene, who according to the *Anglo-Saxon chronicle* gained control of Northumbria in 874–76, was a brother of Imhar (of Dublin), a Viking who, according to the *Annals of Ulster*, was active in Ireland between 857 and 863, and in 871–73; and that the tenth-century Viking kings of Dublin were descendants of Imhar who were motivated in their struggle for the control of York by a wish to reclaim what they saw as their family inheritance. In support of this view it has also been argued that Inwære was identical with Imhar of Dublin. The only serious obstacle to this identification is that, in contrast to the *Annals of Ulster* for 873, which say that Imhar ('rex Nordmannorum totius Hiberniae et Britanniae', see Hennessy, 1887, 386–87) died in that year, the late tenth-century chronicle of Æthelweard, which is based on a lost version of the *Anglo-Saxon chronicle* and has some independent authority (Whitelock, 1979, 118), states that Iuuar (= Inwære), the king of the Vikings responsible for the slaying of King Edmund in 869, himself died in that same year, shortly after King Edmund (see Campbell, 1962, 36).

I would accept now, as I did in 1976 (McTurk, 1976, 108),

Vogel's (1906, 409–10) and de Vries's (1923, 253–55) view that the 'Bier Costae ... ferreae' mentioned by William of Jumièges represents the Berno of the Frankish annals (i.e. the *Chronicon Fontanellense* for 855 and the *Annales Bertiniani* for 858) mentioned above, but would be more inclined now than I was then to accept as historically accurate William's information that this person was the son of someone with a name approximating to *Loðbrók*. Here I am influenced partly by Wormald's recent (1982, 130–31) plea for a less sceptical approach generally to the retrospective mediaeval accounts of the Viking Age, including the non-Scandinavian continental ones; and partly by the reflection that it is methodo-logically more satisfactory to adopt the straightforward view that William of Jumièges based his information here on a reliable tradition than to accept de Vries's (1928b, 132–33) relatively complicated theory that he adapted it from information about Inwære/Inguar in a lost source of English origin from which Adam of Bremen derived his information about Inguar's parentage (cf. McTurk, 1976, 108). This is not to say that William of Jumièges was not, in many respects, 'mehr Dichter als Historiker' (de Vries, 1928b, 133–34), or that the remainder of what he says about Bier Costae ferreae should not be treated with caution (cf. Storm, 1878, 75–79; de Vries, 1923, 254–56; McTurk, 1976, 107–08).

Leaving aside Berno and Hubba for the moment, I should like to return to the Inwære and Healfdene of the *Anglo-Saxon chronicle* for 878, and to the problem of Healfdene's identification with, on the one hand, the Albann mentioned in the *Annals of Ulster* for 877, and, on the other, the Halbdeni, brother of Sigifridus, mentioned in the *Annales Fuldenses* for 873. The *Annals of Ulster* for 877 state that 'Albann, king of the dark heathens', died in a battle between the fair and the dark heathens near Strangford Lough. The *Anglo-Saxon chronicle* for 878 states that 'the brother of Inwære and of Healfdene' ('Inwæres broþor 7 Healfdenes') was killed in Devon with 840 of his men. So far, there is no objection to the equation of Albann with Healfdene. According to Æthelweard's chronicle, however, which, it has been claimed, 'has authentic details of its own, especially in relation to south-western affairs' (Whitelock, 1965, xviii), the Viking leader killed on this occasion was not 'the brother of Inwære and of Healfdene', but 'Healfdene, brother of the tyrant Iguuar' ('Healfdene, Iguuares tyranni frater'); this Healfdene, says Æthelweard, arrived in Devon in 878, and was killed there with 800 of his men (see Campbell, 1962, 43). Æthelweard's statement is less

veiled than that of the *Anglo-Saxon chronicle*, which makes it
tempting to accept his authority; the price of accepting it, however,
is that if, as he states, Healfdene was the Viking leader slain in
Devon in 878, this Healfdene obviously cannot have been identical
with the Albann slain near Strangford Lough in 877. Equally
obviously, Sigifridus's brother Halbdeni (*fl.* 873), who it was noted
earlier has been identified with the Healfdene of the *Anglo-Saxon
chronicle* for 878, cannot also be identified with Albann (d. 877) if
Æthelweard's authority is accepted. On the other hand, if it is
accepted, there is no objection to regarding *either* Albann (d. 877) *or*
Healfdene (d. 878) as identical with Halbdeni, brother of Sigifridus
(*fl.* 873); and it should also be noted that Æthelweard's statement
certainly does not dispel, and if anything strengthens, the
impression given by the *Anglo-Saxon chronicle* for 878 that Inwære
and Healfdene were brothers (cf. McTurk, 1976, 120, 122; 1980,
233). Acceptance of Æthelweard's authority here thus leads to two
rather unsatisfactory alternatives, which may be summarized as
follows: *either* Halbdeni, brother of Sigifridus, was identical with
Albann, but was no relation to the brothers Inwære and Healfdene;
or Halbdeni, brother of Sigifridus, was identical with Healfdene and
hence also a brother of Inwære, but was no relation to Albann.

On this problem, Wormald (1982, 143) has written: 'Aethelweard certainly used a lost text of the *Chronicle* with some superior
information, but he was also translating (with difficulty) and
interpolating his own views. In the case of the 878 entry, the extant
Chronicle's *Inwaeres broður 7 Healfdenes* is certainly a strange phrase;
but, as against Aethelweard's version, it surely deserves all the
credit of a *lectio difficilior*; it is much easier to see how Aethelweard
could have misread or mistranslated what is now in the English
text, than how an English scribe could have made anything so
obscure out of an original corresponding to Aethelweard's text'.
This is surely a cogent argument, which, if accepted, would make it
possible to conclude that Æthelweard's information about Healf
dene's death in Devon in 878 may be dismissed, and that Healfdene,
the brother of Inwære, was identical not only with Albann, but also
with Halbdeni, the brother of Sigifridus. It would also mean that
the phrase 'the brother of Inwære and of Healfdene' would have to
be taken as meaning what it says, rather than as a confused
reference to Healfdene himself; and this in turn would leave open
the possibility that the unnamed brother referred to was Hubba. It
is true that there is no contemporary evidence for this last

identification, but the contemporary reference to the nameless third brother, if accepted as genuine, would provide, as it were, a vacant slot into which the earliest available evidence might be fitted; and there is evidence from the turn of the tenth to the eleventh century, based on apparently reliable oral traditions, that Hubba was closely associated with Inwære as a leader of the Great Army that arrived in England in 865, as Whitelock (1979, 29) and Wormald (1982, 143) have shown; while in the second quarter of the twelfth century (see Keynes & Lapidge, 1983, 199; Bell, 1960, li-lii) the *Annals of St. Neots* identify Hubba as a brother of Hinguar (Stevenson, 1959, 44, 138), and the Anglo-Norman verse chronicler Gaimar, whose sources included a lost version of the *Anglo-Saxon chronicle* (see Whitelock, 1979, 119–20), gives *Ube* as the name of the brother of Ywar and of Haldene who was killed in Devon in 878 (Bell, 1960, 100, cf. 244–45).

I would accept Wormald's argument, quoted above, and conclude that Inwære, Hubba, Healfdene (= Albann = Halbdeni) and Sigifridus were brothers. Remembering that Inguar (= Inwære) is described as 'filius Lodparchi' by Adam of Bremen, and that Bier (= Berno) is called 'Lotbroci regis filio' by William of Jumièges, I would add Berno to this group of brothers and, assuming that they were full brothers, would suggest that their mother was Loðbróka, who, originally as a result of her name becoming confused with the form *loðbrók* (applicable as a nickname to either a man or a woman, as suggested above pp. 32–34), came to be regarded as the father of Inwære, Hubba, Sigifridus, and Berno, if not also of Healfdene (on whom in this context see Mawer, 1909, 85–86; de Vries, 1923, 273; Smith, 1935, 176–78).

This view may be compared with the conclusions of Storm (1878, 85–86) and Vogel (1906, 409–12) in relation to the parentage of these five brothers. I differ from Storm in regarding *Loðbróka* rather than *Loðbrók* as the name of their mother, and from Vogel in regarding the figure remembered as *Loðbrók* as their mother rather than their father, and obviously, therefore, not identifiable with Reginheri, the Viking leader of the attack on Paris in 845, an identification that Vogel (1906, 409) accepts. I also differ from both of them in preferring not to regard Loðbrók(a) as a member of the house of Herioldus I, one of the two warring dynasties in ninth-century Denmark, the other being the house of Godofridus I, to which Reginheri may have belonged (see McTurk, 1976, 111–17). As presented by Vogel (1906, 411–12), the arguments associating the figure remembered as (Ragnarr) loðbrók with the house of Herioldus I depend not only on the view that this figure was historically a man rather than a woman, but also (to a large extent) on non-contemporary sources of dubious reliability, notably the twelfth-century *Annales Lindisfarnenses* and the originally mid eleventh-century *Fragmentary annals of Ireland* now edited by Radner (1978; see p. xxvi), which I have discussed critically elsewhere (McTurk, 1976, 114, 106–11). Storm (1878, 85–86), while maintaining that the Loðbrók figure was historically a woman, also argues that she was a member of the house of Herioldus I and unlikely, therefore, to have been married to Reginheri, since the latter was probably a member of the house of Godofridus I, the rival dynasty (a consequence of this view is, of course, that Reginheri cannot be regarded as the father of the five brothers just discussed). Storm (1878, 43) does however leave open the possibility that she was of independent stock, and I would follow him in this respect.

Before discussing the question, just touched on, of who was the father of Inwære, Hubba, Healfdene, Sigifridus, and Berno, I would note that, as well as rejecting Æthelweard's information that Healfdene died in Devon in 878, Wormald (1982, 143) also dismisses Æthelweard's statement that Iuuar died in 869, shortly after King Edmund, whom Iuuar's followers had slain in that same year. Justifying this dismissal, Wormald (1982, 143) maintains that it is 'a hagiographical commonplace that the perpetrators of such deeds as the slaughter of Edmund met their just deserts'. For Wormald, the advantage of being able to dismiss Æthelweard here is that this would enable the Inwære of the *Anglo-Saxon chronicle* to be identified with the Imhar of the *Annals of Ulster*, who according to those annals died in 873; and this identification, taken together with that of Healfdene with Albann (accepted above), would support the view that the Scandinavian kingdoms of Dublin and York were related by family ties. It is not my primary purpose here to argue in support of this view, but I see no reason why this second stricture of Wormald's in relation to Æthelweard should not also be accepted, particularly if it is borne in mind that Æthelweard was removed in time by about a century from the slaying of King Edmund, and that there is no contemporary evidence that Inwære died in 869.

In a footnote to his remark about the 'hagiographical commonplace', just quoted, Wormald (1982, 151, n. 96) applies the considerations underlying this remark to the death of Reginheri as reported in the *Annales Xantenses* for 845 (Rau, 1972, 348–49), implying that this report should be treated with suspicion, since the death is nowhere else recorded in annalistic (as opposed to hagiographical) sources (see McTurk, 1976, 96–97). It is certainly true that the *Annales Xantenses* for 845 present Reginheri's death as an instance of divine retribution (much more obviously, indeed, than does Æthelweard's report of Iuuar's death, see Campbell, 1962, 36); on the other hand, their account of Reginheri's death differs from Æthelweard's report of Iuuar's in being written by a contemporary (Skyum-Nielsen, 1967, 15), and in my view should be accepted unless really convincing evidence is found to contradict it. The account is not in fact contradicted in the other annalistic sources, even though, as Wormald (1982, 151, n. 96) points out, none of them actually mentions Reginheri's death. The contemporary *Annales Bertiniani* for 845 (Rau, 1972, 66–67) refer to the affliction which, according to the *Annales Xantenses* for that year, caused Reginheri's death, but do not themselves mention Reginheri by name; the equally contemporary *Annales Fuldenses* for 845 (Rau, 1969, 32–33) record the Viking attack on Paris without mentioning the affliction or the name of the Viking leader; while the nearly contemporary *Chronicon Fontanellense* (Pertz, 1829, 302) simply states that the Vikings under the leadership of Ragneri entered Paris on March 28, 845. None of these sources, however, states or implies that Reginheri/Ragneri lived beyond that year, or mentions him in subsequent annals.

As I suggested in 1976 (McTurk, 1976, 103, 116–17), what I have just said about the report of Reginheri's death in the *Annales Xantenses* for 845—that it is the evidence of a contemporary, and should be accepted unless it is contradicted by more convincing evidence—is also applicable to a statement in the *Annales Fuldenses* for 854 (see Rau, 1969, 46–47) to the effect that only one member of the entire royal family, a boy, survived a battle in Denmark in that year between the Danish king Horicus I and his fraternal nephew Gudurm. This statement is relevant to the question of whether or not Reginheri was the father of the five brothers here under discussion, a question to which I now finally turn. Storm (1878, 42) has shown convincingly that the 'royal family' mentioned in this statement must be the house of Godofridus I, and that the boy survivor must be Horicus II; and I have pointed out (McTurk, 1976, 102–03; 1977c, 475) that the two other main sources for this battle—the *Annales Bertiniani* for 854 (Rau, 1972, 88–89), and ch. 31 of the *Vita Anskarii* (Trillmich, 1961, 100–01)—do not contradict the *Annales Fuldenses* on this subject, though they are less specific about it. Now, if the *Annales Fuldenses* for 854 are to be believed, Danish royalty recorded from after that year cannot have belonged to the house of Godofridus I unless clearly descended from Horicus II, the one royal survivor of the battle of 854. The brothers Halbdeni and Sigifridus, who appear in the *Annales Fuldenses* for 873 (as noted above), where they are both described as kings (and Sigifridus as king of the Danes), can hardly have been sons of Horicus II, since this Horicus, who was a boy (i.e. eleven at the oldest, see Herrmann, 1922, 69, and cf. part IVA of the Analysis in ch. II, section (a), below) in 854, is unlikely to have had sons old enough to be kings by 873. Grasping at the brittle straw of evidence (from the twelfth-century *Cogadh Gaedhel re Gallaibh*, 'the war of the Gaedhill with the Gaill', see McTurk, 1976, 115–16; Hughes, 1972, 289) that the Albann slain near Strangford Lough in 877 (according to the *Annals of Ulster*) was a son of one Ragnall, de Vries (who did not take Æthelweard into account, and thus saw no objection to the equation of Albann with Halbdeni) tentatively suggested (de Vries, 1923, 270, 273) that Reginheri was the father of Halbdeni and Sigifridus; at the same time, however, he also argued (de Vries, 1923, 244–49), very much more convincingly (cf. McTurk, 1976, 111–15), that Reginheri was a member of the house of Godofridus I, thus apparently ignoring the evidence of the *Annales Fuldenses* that members of this house appearing after 854 can only be descended from Horicus II (though it is fair to point out that de Vries, 1927a, 122, does show an awareness of the battle of 854 in a quite different context). There is no doubt that the identification of Reginheri as the father of Halbdeni and Sigifridus is attractive; if it could be shown that he was their father, and hence also the father of Inwære, Hubba, and Berno (on the assumption made earlier that all five of them were full brothers), it could be suggested that Reginheri and the mother of these five, Loðbróka, were husband and wife, and this in turn would help to explain how Loðbróka's name, misremembered as *Loðbrók*, came to be combined with that of Reginheri/Ragnarr. To make this identification, however, it is necessary either to discard the evidence of the *Annales Fuldenses* for 854, or to undo de Vries's (1923, 244–49) careful and convincing arguments to the effect that Reginheri was a member of the house of Godofridus I. I am reluctant to adopt either alternative. As for the first, it does not seem to me now, any more than in 1976 (cf. McTurk, 1976, 115–17), that sufficiently strong evidence has been found to contradict the testimony of the *Annales Fuldenses* with regard to the battle of 854; as I showed then, the evidence that Albann (d. 877) was a son of Ragnall is 'by no means water-tight' (McTurk, 1976, 116); and even if it were established that he was, it would still be necessary to dispose of the problem that the name *Ragnall* corresponds to *Ragnaldr* rather than to *Ragnarr*. As for the second alternative, it still seems to me, as it did in 1976 (McTurk, 1976, 115), that de Vries's arguments for Reginheri's membership of the house of Godofridus I hold good, even on the points on which he might conceivably be criticized. Thus the difficulty of identifying Reginheri as the father of Halbdeni and Sigifridus (and their brothers) should not, in my view, be underestimated; but if it can be removed by others better equipped than I am to sift the relevant sources, well and good.

I conclude, then, that the brothers Inwære, Hubba, Healfdene, Sigifridus, and Berno were sons of an unknown father, and of a mother named *Loðbróka*, about whom little is known for certain, but who may well have been named after, and associated with the cult of, a fertility-goddess known by the names *Lopkona*, *Loðbróka*, of which the latter name derived partly from the former, and partly from the common noun *loðbrók*. Through confusion of her name with this common noun, which could be applied as a nickname to either a man or a woman, Loðbróka, the mother of Inwære and his brothers, came to be regarded as their father and identified with Reginheri, the Viking leader of the attack on Paris in 845. This identification is likely to have arisen not so much because of any special connection (such as marriage) between Loðbróka and Reginheri, as because Reginheri, a member of the house of Godofridus I, was a prominent Viking alive in the first half of the ninth century, when the father of Inwære and his brothers must have been alive also. Following Wormald (1982, 141–44) in his rejection of Æthelweard's information on the deaths of Healfdene and Inwære, I would also conclude that Healfdene was identical, not only with the Halbdeni of the *Annales Fuldenses* for 873, but also with the Albann of the *Annals of Ulster* for 877; and that Inwære was identical with Imhar of Dublin. It is thus open to those who are so minded to argue that the Scandinavian kingdoms of York and Dublin were originally linked by the fraternal relationship of Imhar (= Inwære) and Healfdene (= Albann = Halbdeni).

Whereas this chapter has been largely concerned with the historical background to the Ragnarr loðbrók tradition, the remainder of this monograph will be mainly concerned with the development of this and related traditions (notably the originally English one discussed at length in ch. III, section (e), below) in which the historical Loðbróka, a woman, is remembered, under various forms of the name *Loðbrók*, as a man. In discussion of cases where Loðbrók was clearly regarded as male, that figure will be referred to as such in the following pages.

CHAPTER II

THE HEROIC BIOGRAPHICAL PATTERN

(a) Analysis of the pattern as applied to Ragnarr and Áslaug

In the present section of this chapter, I shall attempt to show that the tradition represented by *Ragnars saga* and its major Scandinavian analogues conforms to the pattern of the internationally attested heroic biographical pattern, also referred to as the international heroic biography. As will become apparent, the conformity emerges mainly in the career of Ragnarr, the hero, but also in that of his wife Áslaug.

It has already been noted that, in de Vries's view, the heroic biographical pattern, with its international distribution, was originally closely connected with initiation rituals, and with creation myths in which organized life was represented as arising out of chaos, the latter being often symbolized by monsters (see p. 35, above). Old Norse creation mythology, as de Vries indicates (1963, 222, 224), is essentially of this type. The main sources for Old Norse cosmogony are, of course, the eddaic poems *Vǫluspá* (*c*.1000, see p. 38, above), *Vafþrúðnismál* and *Grímnismál* (both probably from before 1000, see Sveinsson, 1962, 269–70, 318), and Snorri's prose *Edda* (written probably between 1220 and 1241, see Faulkes, 1982, xiii–xv), which includes these three poems among its sources (Faulkes, 1982, xxvi; I leave aside the eddaic poem *Rígsþula*, the date and reliability of which are disputed, and which deals solely with the origins of mankind, see McTurk, 1981a, 156, n. 100, and Martin, 1981, 358–60). While the monster symbolism is certainly not conspicuous in the relevant part of *Vǫluspá* (str. 3), where primeval chaos is represented as a yawning void (cf. Martin, 1981, 360), Snorri's prose *Edda* (*Gylfaginning*, chs. 5–6), elaborating on a passage in *Grímnismál* (strs. 40–41; see F. Jónsson, 1931a, 16) which is closely paralleled in *Vafþrúðnismál* (strs. 20–21), records the doctrine that, in Dronke's words (1969b, 307): 'the physical universe is created out of a death, out of the corpse of the giant

Ymir, killed by the gods'; and in *Vøluspá* (str. 3) itself, according to certain manuscripts (apparently representing a tradition unknown to Snorri, see Nordal, 1978, 11–12), it is said that Ymir inhabited, or lived at the same time as, the primeval void.

The attempts of various scholars to establish a pattern for the international heroic biography have been instructively reviewed by Dundes (1965, 142–44) and Ó Cathasaigh (1977, 1–8). Ó Cathasaigh gives cogent reasons for regarding de Vries's formulation of the pattern as preferable to any other, finding it neither over-rigid nor over-generalized. J. de Vries (1963, 211–17) divides the pattern into ten parts, numbered I to X, and gives examples of each part from many different traditions. Where necessary, he gives variant motifs, designated by the letters A, B, etc., under the heading of a particular part. It is his version of the pattern that is used in the summary Analysis of *Ragnars saga* and its major Scandinavian analogues given below. J. de Vries makes no mention of Ragnarr or Loðbrók in his book on *Heroic song and heroic legend* (i.e de Vries, 1963), though he admits elsewhere (de Vries, 1928a, 269) 'daß sich typische Elemente der Heldensage mit der Figur Ragnars verbunden haben'. The purpose of the Analysis is to show that *Ragnars saga* and its analogues deserve to be considered together with the examples collected by de Vries in support of his book's main thesis, namely that the international heroic biography, with its characteristic patterning, was originally bound up with creation myths and initiation rituals. The suitability of *Ragnars saga* and its analogues for consideration in this light is suggested partly by the link I have tried to establish in the previous chapter between the nickname *loðbrók* on the one hand and, on the other, *Lopkona*, the latter name having associations with fertility rites if not directly with creation myths (see pp. 16–39, above), and by the fact that (to anticipate somewhat) *Ragnars saga* and its main Scandinavian analogues not only in general fit de Vries's pattern with remarkable closeness and thoroughness, but also seem to show a connection with initiation rituals in emphasizing more than once (see part IVA of the Analysis below) that the hero was fifteen—the age of majority in mediaeval Norway—when he slew the monstrous serpent.

In the analysis below, the various items dealt with under each heading or sub-heading are not necessarily in chronological order, but are arranged as far as possible according to their degree of similarity to each other, so that those which are most similar are treated together. All the items analysed are therefore first listed in chronological order, again as far as possible. The order is in fact not wholly consistent, since a number of items which are particularly hard to date, namely the ballads (nos. 7, 8, 10, 13, 15, 16, 17 and 18 of the list below), and the oral traditions related to the ballads and recorded by Torfæus, Ramus, and Müller (nos. 11, 12, and 14 of the list), are placed in the chronological sequence according to the dates of their earliest known recorded versions, while all other items are listed according to their known or presumed dates of origin. The language of a listed item is specified only in cases of languages other than Old Norse. Information is given about the earliest known text of each item listed, and, in cases where an item exists in more than one version, about the earliest known text of each version. For the purposes of the list, the X and Y versions of *Ragnars saga* (nos. 4 and 5 respectively) are treated as separate items; and the X version is given relatively lengthy treatment in the list, since, for reasons to be explained below (see p. 61), it is given relatively brief treatment in the Analysis itself.

List of items analysed

(1) *Krákumál*, a poetic monologue in twenty-nine strophes in a variant of the *dróttkvætt* form (see further pp. 125–33, below) completed most probably by *c*.1200 (de Vries, 1927b, 55–60; cf. Guðnason, 1969, 29, n. 3). The earliest manuscript, Ny kgl. saml. 1824b, 4to (in Det Kongelige Bibliotek, Copenhagen), where the text of the poem immediately follows that of the Y version of *Ragnars saga* (see (5), below), dates from *c*.1400 (Olsen, 1906–08, ii, lxiii); here however the text lacks str. 16 and comes to an end nearly halfway through str. 22 (F. Jónsson, 1912a, 641). The earliest complete text is preserved in Uppsala, Universitets bibliotek ms. R 702 (Salanska saml. 81, 4to), which according to Gödel (1892, 49–52) was owned and perhaps written by the Icelander Magnús Ólafsson í Laufási (*c*.1573–1636).

(2) Book IX of the *Gesta Danorum*, a prose history of the Danish people written in Latin by the Dane, Saxo Grammaticus (d. *c*.1220), and completed by 1216. Book IX was perhaps composed not long before that date if, as has been suggested, it was the last of the sixteen books of the *Gesta Danorum* to be written (Herrmann, 1922,

1–2; cf. Strand, 1980, 272). The earliest complete text of the *Gesta Danorum* is that of Kristiern Pedersøn's edition, printed in Paris in 1514. The work survives in mediaeval manuscripts only fragmentarily, and the fragments in question do not contain any part of Book IX. The oldest of them, the so-called Angers fragment, dating from *c*.1200 and thus from Saxo's lifetime, is apparently part of a draft of Book I written at a relatively early stage of its composition (Olrik & Ræder, 1931, xi–xiv, xxix–xxxiii).

(3) *Vǫlsunga saga*, a prose narrative based largely on heroic poems of the poetic *Edda* and composed either before or at much the same time as the X version of *Ragnars saga*, which in its original form appears to have followed *Vǫlsunga saga* as a sequel, and was most probably written *c*.1250 (see (4), below, and McTurk, 1977a, 571, 583, and n. 128). The earliest surviving manuscript of *Vǫlsunga saga*, from which all others ultimately derive (Finch, 1983), preserves however a version dating most probably from the second half of the thirteenth century (McTurk, 1977a, 583). This manuscript, Ny kgl. saml. 1824b, 4to, itself dates from *c*.1400 (see (1), above). The text of *Vǫlsunga saga* as preserved here immediately precedes that of the Y version of *Ragnars saga* (see (5), below) and is edited together with it by Olsen (1906–08, i–lxxxiii, 1–175). It has forty-four chapters and contains some thirty strophes in eddaic metres (some spoken by the characters, others introduced into the narrative as quotations from older works).

(4) The so-called X version of *Ragnars saga*, a prose narrative written most probably *c*.1250 (McTurk, 1977a, 583 and n. 128), though preserved only in the fragmentary text of cod. AM 147 4to, which dates from the second half of the fifteenth century (Olsen, 1906–08, lxxxiii–iv, and n. 1). In various parts of the prose text it is possible to identify certain verse-passages, in the following order: first, fifteen strophes in irregular *dróttkvætt* measure, spoken by certain of the characters and corresponding in wording, order of occurrence, and apparently also in attribution, to the strophes numbered 1, 6–10, 15–16, 18–20 and 22–25 in Olsen's edition of the 1824b text of the Y version (see (5), below); secondly, a fragmentary text of *Krákumál* (see (1), above) which is here spoken by Ragnarr as he dies in the snake-pit (see parts V, VIII, and X of the Analysis) and thus forms part of the narrative, not (as in 1824b) an appendix to it (see (1) above and (5) below); thirdly, one strophe in irregular *dróttkvætt* measure, also spoken by Ragnarr and

corresponding to str. 26 of Olsen's edition of the 1824b text of Y; and fourthly, one half strophe in the *tøglag* metre, quoted from Sigvatr Þórðarson's *Knútsdrápa* (str. 1 in F. Jónsson, 1912a, 248) in the course of the narrative and corresponding to the eighth of the nine verse-passages in *Ragnarssona þáttr* (see (6), below). The strophes corresponding to those numbered 18, 19, 20, and 22 in Olsen's edition of the 1824b text of Y also correspond respectively to the third, fourth, fifth, and seventh of the nine verse-passages in *Ragnarssona þáttr* (see (6), below).

The surviving text (edited by Olsen, 1906–08, lxxxiii–xcv and 176–94) is largely illegible, having had material quite unrelated to *Ragnars saga* written over it in *c*.1600. It appears to have originally filled twenty-two leaves, the first, sixth, and sixteenth of which are now missing, and to have been preceded, 'if not in this manuscript, then in its original' (cf. Olsen, 1906–08, lxxxvi), by the text of a relatively early version (now lost) of *Vǫlsunga saga* (cf. (3) above). It also appears to have begun at a point corresponding to the beginning of the second chapter of the 1824b text of the Y version, and to have ended at a point corresponding to the end of the seventeenth chapter of that text (see (5), below). It should be noted, however, that its chapter-divisions (where they can be located) do not otherwise always occur at the same points in the narrative as those in the 1824b text of Y (Olsen, 1906–08, xc–xci).

(5) The so-called Y version of *Ragnars saga*, a prose narrative written most probably in the second half of the thirteenth century (McTurk, 1977a, 583). The earliest manuscript (from which all others are here assumed to derive, cf. McTurk, 1977a, 568, and n. 3) is Ny kgl. saml. 1824b 4to (dating from *c*.1400, see (1) above), where the text of Y immediately follows *Vǫlsunga saga* (see (3) above), comprises twenty chapters, and immediately precedes *Krákumál* (see (1) above). The 1824b texts of *Vǫlsunga saga* and of Y (though not of *Krákumál*) are edited by Olsen (1906–08), together with the 147 text of X (see (3) and (4) above). Placed in the mouths of certain of the characters of Y are a total of forty strophes, numbered 1–40 by Olsen; the last three of these are in *fornyrðislag*, the remainder in irregular *dróttkvætt* measure. This larger group, as indicated under (4), above, includes sixteen strophes which can also be identified in the 147 text of X, in the same order and in much the same contexts as in the 1824b text of Y. Furthermore, the strophes numbered 11, 13, and 18–22 in Olsen's edition of the latter text

correspond closely in wording and wholly in attribution and order of occurrence to the first seven of the nine verse-passages in *Ragnarssona páttr* (see (6), below).

(6) The so-called *Ragnarssona páttr* (not an ancient title, see Guðnason, 1969, 29–30), a prose narrative composed most probably in the late thirteenth or early fourteenth century, perhaps by Haukr Erlendsson (d. 1334; see Guðnason, 1969, 30), and preserved in Haukr's own hand in ms. AM 544, 4to, which forms part of the codex known as *Hauksbók*, written by Haukr Erlendsson and others in the early years of the fourteenth century (see Hb, 1892–96, i–lxiii, xci–xciii, and 458–67). In its surviving form, the *páttr* has five chapters and, as already indicated (under (4) and (5) above), contains nine verse-passages, of which the first seven and the ninth are strophes in irregular *dróttkvætt* measure, spoken by certain of the characters, and the eighth, a half-strophe in *tøglag*, is a quotation made in the course of the narrative from Sigvatr Þórðarson's *Knútsdrápa*. The ninth of these verse-passages is preserved only here; the third, fourth, fifth, seventh, and eighth of them correspond to verse-passages in the 147 text of the X version of *Ragnars saga*, as indicated under (4), above; and the first seven of them correspond to strophes in the 1824b text of the Y version in the manner indicated under (5), above. The sources of the *páttr* appear to have included on the one hand the lost *Skjǫldunga saga* (dated by Guðnason, 1982, li–lii, to the period 1180–1200), and on the other a lost version of *Ragnars saga* (here called the older *Ragnars saga*) from which the X version and (less directly) the Y version both descended (McTurk, 1975, 43–64).

(7) 'Regnfred og Kragelil', a Danish ballad in four-line stanzas with a refrain, edited by Grundtvig as no. 22 in DgF I (1853). He prints two texts, A and B, each representing one of the two main versions in its earliest known form. The B text, the older of the two, is based solely on that of no. 158 in Karen Brahe's folio manuscript (Odense, Landsarkivet, Karen Brahe I, 1), the relevant part of which dates from *c*.1570. Here the ballad has twenty-four stanzas. The A text is based solely on that of no. 4b in Peder Syv's collection of ballads, published in 1695, where the ballad has eighteen stanzas (information on the location and dating of texts is here taken from DgF XII, 1976, 303, 376–80; 219).

(8) 'Karl og Kragelil', a Danish ballad in four-line stanzas with a

refrain, edited by Grundtvig as no. 23 in DgF I (1853). He prints three main texts, A, B, and C, each representing one of the three main versions in its earliest known form. B is the oldest of the three, the earliest text on which it is based being that of no. 141 in Karen Brahe's folio manuscript, the relevant part of which dates from c.1570, cf. (7) above. Here the ballad has twenty-two stanzas. The earliest text on which A is based is that of no. 15 in Anna Munk's manuscript (Copenhagen, Det Kongelige Bibliotek, Gl. kgl. saml. 2396, 4to), dating from 1590, where the ballad has twenty-eight stanzas; and the C text is based solely on that of no. 61 in Odense Stiftsbibliotek 32, fol., dating from 1625–40, where the ballad also has twenty-eight stanzas (information on the location and dating of texts is here taken from DgF XII, 302–03, 307–09, 385–86).

(9) The material relating to Ragnarr loðbrók and his sons in *Rerum Danicarum fragmenta*, a prose history of Denmark written in Latin by the Icelander Arngrímur Jónsson (1568–1648) and completed in 1596. The relevant material appears at the beginning of ch. 19 of the first section of the history, and in greater detail in the appendix entitled *Ad catalogum Regum Sveciæ*. The earliest and best manuscript is Don. var. I fol., Barth. XXV (in Det Kongelige Bibliotek, Copenhagen), written at the instructions of the Dane, Thomas Bartholin (1659–90), and completed before 1689; this forms the basis of Benediktsson's edition (see Benediktsson, 1957, 184; 1950, 358–59, 464–66; and 1957, 244, 260–62). Arngrímur's main sources for the relevant passages were the lost *Skjǫldunga saga* (which also formed a source for *Ragnarssona þáttr* and perhaps for the older, lost version of *Ragnars saga* mentioned under (6), above, *q.v.*); and the Y version of *Ragnars saga* (see (5) above, and McTurk, 1975, 43–64). He also refers more than once to Saxo's account (see (2), above), not uncritically.

(10) 'Ormekampen', a Danish ballad in four-line stanzas with a refrain, edited by Grundtvig as no. 24 in DgF I (1853). The earliest known text is that of no. 66 in Sophie Sandberg's manuscript (Copenhagen, Det Kongelige Bibliotek, Thott 1511, 4to), dating from 1622, where the ballad has nineteen stanzas. It is on this text that Grundtvig's is primarily based; information as to its location and dating is here taken from DgF XII (1976), 302, 345–47.

(11) An account in Latin prose, written in 1699 by the Icelander

Þormóður Torfason (Torfæus; 1636–1719) and published in his *Historia rerum Norvegicarum* (1711), of oral traditions relating to Áslaug-Kráka (see esp. parts III and IX of the Analysis below), obtained in 1664 on Spangereid, the isthmus joining Lindesnæs to the southern Norwegian mainland, by Þormóður himself; and later, in 1698, checked and corrected there at Þormóður's request by a local royal official, the Dane Anders Nielsen Toldorph (d. 1711). The earliest known account of the traditions collected by Torfæus on Spangereid is a letter in Danish written by him to Thomas Bartholin (see (9) above) in 1686, before his information had been checked by Toldorph; it is the Latin account that is used in the analysis below and elsewhere in the present discussion. The relevant documents are quoted and discussed by Helgason (1975).

(12) A prose account in Danish by the Norwegian, Jonas Ramus (1649–1718), published in his *Norriges Kongers Historie* (1719), of oral traditions from the Lindesnæs area of southern Norway concerning Áslaug-Kráka (see esp. part III of the Analysis below). The account is based to a large extent on that of Torfæus (see (11) above), but adds certain details, as Helgason (1975, 86) has shown.

(13) *Ragnars kvæði*. A Faroese ballad-sequence in four-line stanzas and in two main parts, the first ending with the death of Ragnar's wife Tóra and the second with Ragnar's acquisition of Ásla Sjúrðardóttir (see esp. part VII of the Analysis below). The sequence is edited as no. 2 in Djurhuus & Matras (1951–63, 215–43), which prints six texts, A–F, each of them based on the earliest (or only) known manuscript recording of one of the six surviving versions; and a seventh text, G, which has relatively little independent value, and must be treated with caution (see further below). Apart from some additional details supplied from Hammershaimb (1851, ii) in the case of G, the following information is taken from Djurhuus & Matras (1951–63, ix–xv, 215–43): [A] is the oldest of the texts, being based on one written down by Jens Christian Svabo in 1781–82 and preserved as no. 9 in vol. II of 'Svabo's quarto', ms. Gl. kgl. saml. 2894 (in Det Kongelige Bibliotek, Copenhagen); this text preserves only the first part of the sequence (here entitled 'Fyrsti Ragnars táttur') and has forty-seven stanzas with a refrain. [B] is based on a text written down by J. H. Schrøter in 1818 and preserved in Copenhagen, Det Kongelige Bibliotek, ms. Ny kgl. saml. 345 8vo; this text preserves the entire sequence (which is here entitled 'Ragnars táttur') and has

102 stanzas with a refrain. [C] is based on a text also written down by J. H. Schrøter (at a date apparently not recorded) and preserved in Hammershaimb's collection (AM, Access. 4); this text preserves the second part of the sequence (which it calls 'annar táttur'), but only the last nine stanzas of the first, having a total of sixty stanzas (no refrain is indicated in what survives of the text). [D] is based on the text written down by Johannes Clemensen in 1823 and preserved as no. 69 in 'Sandoyarbók' (Copenhagen, Dansk Folkemindesamling, 68). This text preserves the entire sequence in 104 stanzas (with no refrain indicated); the first part (entitled 'Ragnars táttur') occupies stanzas 1–56, the second (entitled 'Kráku táttur') stanzas 57–104. [E] is based on a text preserved as no. 70 in 'Fugloyarbók' (AM Access. 4), dating from before 1854; this text preserves only the first part of the sequence (here entitled 'Ragnars táttur') and has sixty stanzas (with no refrain indicated). [F] is based on a text preserved as no. 36 on p. 227 of vol. I (1840) of N. Nolsø's *Liedersammlung* (in Føroya Amts Bókasavn, Tórshavn); this text preserves the entire sequence (with no title indicated) and has eighty-eight stanzas with a refrain. [G] simply reproduces the text printed in Hammershaimb (1851, 59–67), which appears to be based on a later recording than Schrøter's of the version represented by B, but with readings supplied from Schrøter's text of that version, from Svabo's text of the version represented by A, and from elsewhere (see Hammershaimb, 1851, ii, and cf. Djurhuus & Matras, 1951–63, 218). Here the entire text is given (under the title 'Ragnars táttur') in ninety-four stanzas with a refrain.

(14) A prose account in Danish by the Dane, P. E. Müller (1776–1834), published in his *Sagabibliothek* II (1818), 481, of a Faroese ballad ('Qvad') no longer extant (so far as I am aware) and dealing with the upbringing of a girl named Osla by a poor man called Kraaka, and her marriage to a widowed king (see parts III and IX of the Analysis below). Müller does not appear to have had direct access to the ballad itself; according to him, only a prose abstract of it had reached Copenhagen by his time of writing. He links it with *Sjúrðar kvæði* (see under (15), below) and introduces his discussion of it immediately after referring to the 'Fistr. Ragnar Taattur' (*sic*) as one of the Faroese poems collected by Svabo and preserved in Det Kongelige Bibliotek, Copenhagen (cf. (13) above).

(15) 'Brynhildar táttur', the second part of the Faroese ballad-cycle in four-line stanzas known as *Sjúrðar kvæði*, which (except in one

case, see F, below) survives variously in three or four parts. The cycle is edited as no. 1 in Djurhuus & Matras (1951–63, 1–214), which prints nine texts, designated by the letters A, Ba, Bb, C-H. These need not be described in as much detail as those of the *Ragnars kvæði* (see (13), above), since only small parts of the 'Brynhildar táttur' are directly relevant to *Ragnars saga*, that is, those concerning firstly the begetting of Ásla Sjúrðardóttir and secondly the birth of Ásla and her abandonment by Brynhild (see parts I and II of the Analysis below); it should however be noted that the ninth text, H, reprinted from Hammershaimb (1851, 3–58), has relatively little independent value, and must be treated with caution (see Hammershaimb 1851, ii, and cf. (13) above). F is irrelevant here, since it preserves only 'Regin smiður', the first part of the cycle; all the other texts mention the begetting of Ásla, but only four (A, Bb, D, and H) mention her birth and abandonment. A is the oldest of the texts, being based on one written down by J. H. Schrøter in 1818 and preserved in ms. Ny kgl. saml. 345 8vo (see Djurhuus & Matras, 1951–63, 1, and cf. (13) above). The relevant stanza-numbers of each text may be given as follows (II referring to the relevant part of the cycle in cases where the stanza-numbering starts afresh with a new part): AII, 92–93; 161–63; BaII, 89–90; BbII, 113–14; 194–96; C, 163–64; DII, 111; 194–96; EII, 68; G, 174–75; HII, 93; 176–78. Only in the cases of A and H does a ballad-refrain seem to be indicated in the text.

(16) 'Gests ríma' or 'Áslu ríma', a Faroese ballad in two-line stanzas edited as no. 3 in Djurhuus & Matras (1951–63, 244–47), which prints two texts, A and B, each representing the earliest known manuscript recording of one of the two surviving versions; and a third text, C, which has relatively little independent value, and must be treated with caution (see further below). Apart from an additional detail supplied from Hammershaimb (1851, ii) in the case of C, the following information is taken from Djurhuus & Matras (1951–63, ix–xv, 244–47): A is the oldest of the texts, being based on one written down by J. H. Schrøter in 1818 and preserved in ms. Ny kgl. saml. 345 8vo (see (13), above); this text has thirty-seven stanzas with a double refrain. B is based on a text written down 'after July 6, 1831', and preserved as no. 91 in 'Sandoyarbók' (see (13), above); this text has thirty-five stanzas, with no refrain indicated. C simply reproduces the text printed in Hammershaimb (1851, 68–70), which appears to be based on a later

recording than Schrøter's of the version represented by A, but with readings from Schrøter's text and from other sources, including sung versions of the ballad. Here the text has thirty-eight stanzas with a double refrain.

(17) 'Lindarormen', a Norwegian version of 'Ormekampen' (see (10), above) in twenty-six four-line stanzas with a refrain, collected before 1848 by M. B. Landstad, and printed as no. XI in his *Norske Folkeviser* (1853), 139–46, cf. iii.

(18) Seven Norwegian variants of 'Lindarormen', apparently recorded in writing from oral sources (some of them by S. Bugge), and discussed briefly by Bugge in an appendix to DgF III (1862), 798–99. Of the seven variants mentioned, only the fifth and seventh are quoted, neither of them in full.

It will be clear from what has been said under no. (4) of this list about the fragmentary text of the X version of *Ragnars saga* in AM 147 4to that this text does not lend itself readily to summary treatment. It will therefore be referred to in the Analysis only in cases where it can clearly be seen to differ from the text of the Y version preserved in Ny kgl. saml. 1824b 4to (and in the one case, noted under part V of the Analysis, where the name *Loðbrók* can be discerned in it). It should be borne in mind that the X version of *Ragnars saga* as preserved in 147 does not contain material corresponding to the content of chs. 1 and 18–20 of the Y version as preserved in 1824b (see under nos. (4) and (5) of the list above), and may never have done so. Of these four chapters only ch. 1 is relevant to the Analysis. When *Ragnars saga* is referred to in the Analysis, it is the Y version as reflected in 1824b that is meant, unless otherwise stated. Where ch. 1 of this version is referred to in the Analysis (under parts IIIC, IIID, and IX), it must be remembered that this chapter has no counterpart, fragmentary or otherwise, in the 147 text of the X version; and where other chapters are referred to and no reference is made to the X version, it may be assumed that the relevant part of the 147 text of X is either defective or does not differ significantly from the 1824b text of Y.

The word 'hero' will be used in the analysis to refer not only to Ragnarr himself and to the character corresponding to him in each of the relevant analogues, but also to the heroine of *Ragnars saga*, Ragnarr's second wife Áslaug (also called Kráka or Randalín), and to the character corresponding to her in each of the relevant analogues. This use of the term is acceptable according to the important qualification involving an actual as opposed to a formal hero that Olrik makes to the law of concentration on a central character in his various writings on the laws of oral narrative (see e.g. Olrik, 1921, 73; 1965, 139; cf. McTurk, 1981b, 101–15). Olrik in fact specifically mentions Áslaug as an example of 'the actual character who finally has our sympathies', as opposed to 'the character who is the object of formal concentration' (Olrik, 1965, 139–40). The extent to which the lives and actions of the other main characters of *Ragnars saga* (i.e. the sons of Ragnarr loðbrók) also exemplify the heroic biographical pattern will be discussed separately below, under sub-heading (b) of the present chapter.

The Analysis

I. *The begetting of the hero*

A. The mother is a virgin, who . . . has extra-marital relations with the hero's father.

In *Vǫlsunga saga* this is the case with Áslaug's mother Brynhildr, if we may believe what she says in ch. 29 of the saga, where she refers to Sigurðr, 'er ek vann eida a fiallenu, ok er hann minn frumverr' ('to whom I swore oaths on the mountain, and he is my first lover', see Olsen, 1906–08, 68–69), before instructing Heimir to bring up Áslaug, her daughter by Sigurðr (cf. IIID, below). At no stage are Sigurðr and Brynhildr married to each other, although they twice plight their troth (once on Hindarfjall in ch. 22, during their first meeting, and once at Heimir's dwelling in ch. 25); Sigurðr is tricked into marrying Guðrún Gjúkadóttir by Guðrún's mother Grímhildr, who gives him a drink which causes him to forget Brynhildr (ch. 28); and Brynhildr is tricked into marrying Gunnarr Gjúkason when Sigurðr, now married to Guðrún, changes shapes with Gunnarr and in the latter's guise crosses the flame-barrier surrounding Brynhildr's hall, thus making it seem that Gunnarr has qualified for acceptance as her husband (ch. 29).

In 'Brynhildar táttur', the indications are that Brynhild remains a virgin up to the time of her union with Sjúrður, and that this union is not a matrimonial one, and never becomes so. She refuses all suitors in her determination to marry Sjúrður, confident that he will be the only person to cross the flames surrounding her hall. He fulfils her expectations as to the flame-barrier; Ásla Sjúrðardóttir is conceived as a result of their union; and Sjúrður gives Brynhild some rings as a love-bond. Later, however, he is made to forget Brynhild by a drink administered by Guðrun Júkadóttir at the instructions of her mother Grimhild; he then marries Guðrun.

B. The father is a god.

Although this motif does not appear in the Scandinavian traditions relating directly to Ragnarr loðbrók, it may be noted here that, according to *Vǫlsunga saga* (chs. 1–2, 11–13 and 29), Áslaug is descended from the god Óðinn in being the daughter of Sigurðr and thus the great-granddaughter of Vǫlsungr, the great-grandson of Óðinn.

C. The father is an animal, often the disguise of a god.

Although this motif does not occur in the traditions relating directly to Ragnarr loðbrók, reference may be made to the theory that the presentation of Sigurðr and Brynhildr as meeting on Hindarfjall ('Hind's mountain', see IA, above, and IIA, below) may reflect a memory of an ancient Germanic cultic ritual involving the seeking of a hind by a stag (Finch, 1965, xxxiii–iv).

D. The child is conceived in incest.

Although this motif does not occur in the traditions relating directly to Ragnarr loðbrók, it may be noted that it does occur in ch. 7 of *Vǫlsunga saga*, where Signý conceives Sinfjǫtli as a result of sleeping with her brother Sigmundr.

II. *The birth of a hero*

A. It takes place in an unnatural way.

Whether unnatural or not, the circumstances of Áslaug's birth are certainly obscure. Sigurðr and Brynhildr first meet on Hindarfjall in chs. 21–22 of *Vǫlsunga saga*, and the passage quoted from ch. 29 of that saga under IA, above, suggests that it was there they had the union that led to Áslaug's conception. Holtsmark (1966, 16), however, implies that in her view the conception had its origin in the house of Heimir, where Sigurðr and Brynhildr meet in chs. 24–25 of *Vǫlsunga saga*. Brynhildr's instructions about Áslaug's upbringing, referred to under IA, above, are made 'on the same day' ('Þann sama dag', see Olsen, 1906–08, 68) as that on which

Sigurðr has completed a visit to Brynhildr lasting three nights, during which he, disguised as Gunnarr, has shared her bed with a drawn sword between himself and her. It is unlikely, for obvious reasons, that this encounter gave rise to the conception, though Brynhildr later (in ch. 31) implies to Gunnarr that Sigurðr betrayed Gunnarr's trust while sleeping with her on this occasion. The generally ambiguous nature of Brynhildr's relations with Sigurðr led Wechsler (1875, 12) to describe Áslaug as not 'die leibliche Tochter Brynhildens und Sigurds', but rather 'das geistige Kind ihres Bundes', and to see her as an allegorical representation of the spirit of poetry.

In 'Brynhildar táttur', on the other hand, the conception of Ásla Sjúrðardóttir is relatively straightforward. There is no shape-changing arrangement here between Gunnar and Sjúrður, and no physical object separating Sjúrður and Brynhild once they have met as lovers. As for Ásla's birth, this is briefly described in 'Brynhildar táttur' as presented in texts A, Bb, D, and H of the *Sjúrðar kvæði* (see further no. (15) of the list above), where it takes place in dramatic circumstances. After learning of Sjúrður's marriage to Guðrun (cf. IA, above), Brynhild resolves to bring about Sjúrður's death; and Sjúrður, hearing of her distress, visits her and attempts to explain his position. At the sight of Sjúrður, Brynhild gives birth to Ásla, and at once orders her to be exposed in the manner described under IIIA and IX, below.

B. The 'unborn' hero, i.e. the child that is born by means of a caesarean section.

Although this motif does not occur in the traditions relating directly to Ragnarr loðbrók, it may be noted that, in ch. 2 of *Vǫlsunga saga*, Aslaug's great-grandfather, Vǫlsungr (cf. IB, above), is born in this way.

III. *The youth of the hero is threatened*

In Saxo (IX.iii, 1–4), Siwardus Ring succeeds to the throne of Denmark with the support of the Scanians and Sjællanders, but is opposed by his cousin Ringo, who holds Jutland, and who tries in the temporary absence of Siwardus to seize the throne. The Sjælland supporters of Siwardus proclaim his son Regnerus as king, 'though he Ñad scarcely yet been plucked from his cradle' (Fisher, 1979, 279); Siwardus returns, but the Sjællanders continue to fear being outnumbered by Ringo's forces. Regnerus advises pretended reconciliation with the enemy as a temporary measure, and this advice, for which he is much admired, is accepted. As his safety is feared for in Denmark, he is sent to Norway to be brought up.

In Ramus's account, mention is made of an oral tradition at Lindesnæs in southern Norway according to which Asløg as a child floated ashore there in a golden harp, and of a Norwegian ballad about this same harp, still current at Ramus's time of writing, and dealing with a king's daughter who was set afloat on the sea by her stepmother. See further under IIIC, below.

In Müller's account, Osla is washed ashore in a chest and is brought up by a poor man named Kraaka, who treats her badly because she is more beautiful than his own daughter.

In 'Regnfred og Kragelil', Sigurd's daughter (so the A text; the Rose-king's daughter in the B text) is abducted at what is presumably a young age, since she is later referred to as a 'maiden' ('jomfru' A, 'iumfru' B) when found by the hero (Regnfred in the A text, Villemor in the B text).

A. The child is exposed . . by the mother who thus tries to hide her shame.

In the relevant texts of 'Brynhildar táttur' (i.e. *Sjúrðar kvæði* A, Bb, D, and H, cf. IIA above), Brynhild does not wish to see Ásla, her daughter by Sjúrður, after giving birth to her in the circumstances described under IIA, above. At Brynhild's instructions Ásla is set afloat on a river, the current of which carries her off. H. de Boor (1920, 292–93) argues persuasively that the story of Sigurðr being accidentally set afloat as a child in chs. 160–62 of the mid thirteenth-century *Þiðriks saga af Bern* has been influenced by a tradition relating to Áslaug; for a different view of this story, expressed without knowledge of de Boor's but not necessarily inconsistent with it, see McTurk (1977a, 584).

B. The exposed child is fed by animals.

In the B text of 'Regnfred og Kragelil', the abducted daughter of the Rose-king appears to be protected by three bears when found tending cattle in a field by the hero Villemor: 'Hannd leegtte for hynnder meed tthy biørnne / och med thy biørnne three' ('He played with the bears, with the three bears, in her presence'), see DgF I (1853), 333. Grundtvig (DgF I, 1853, 330, 1st n.) compares this situation with that in which, according to Saxo, Lathgertha attempts to protect herself from Regnerus with a bear and a dog; see under IVA and VII below.

C. ... the child is found by shepherds, etc. In some cases it is ... taken to them (fishermen are also included under the heading of 'shepherds, etc.': see de Vries, 1963, 214).

In *Ragnars saga* (ch. 1), Heimir (see IIID, below) fears for the safety of the three-year-old Áslaug after hearing that Sigurðr and Brynhildr are dead. He hides her with some treasure in a skilfully made harp, which he opens only to wash and feed her, and journeys with her until he lodges in Norway at Spangarheiðr (cf. Spangereid, under no. (11) of the list above), the home of the farming couple, Áki and Gríma. These two kill Heimir for his riches, find Áslaug in the harp, and bring her up as their own daughter, calling her Kráka after Gríma's mother and making her work for them. One of her jobs, it later emerges (in chs. 5–6), is to mind their sheep and goats; they thus impose on her the responsibilities of a shepherdess, even if they are not shepherds themselves. There is also a hint that Áki, as well as being a farmer, is a part-time fisherman, since Áslaug-Kráka obtains a trout-net from him in order to meet Ragnarr's requirement that she should visit him 'neither clad nor unclad' (see IVA and cf. VII, below). Lukman (1976, 9, 30) compares Áslaug's fortunes with those of Danaë and her son Perseus in Greek mythology: they were set adrift on the sea by her father Acrisius in a chest, which was washed ashore on the island of Seriphos, where the boy Perseus was taken in hand by Dictys, brother of the king of the island, a name which evidently connoted nets and fishing in ancient Greek.

The 'Gests ríma' or 'Áslu ríma' makes no mention of shepherding or fishing but is otherwise so close to the parts of *Ragnars saga* just outlined that the relevant parts of it may be noted here: Gestur finds a harp by a river and, taking it with him, lodges at the farm of an old couple, Haki and his wife, who treacherously murder him and find inside the harp a maiden who the old woman says will be called Kráka and known as her daughter. In the C text (see no. (16) of the list above) the old woman also prophesies that the maiden will bear a boneless child (cf. VII, below), and the maiden denies that she will do so.

Torfæus relates that, according to local tradition, a girl named Aadlow was found in the vicinity of Spangereid in southern Norway in a golden harp, thus giving rise to the place-name

Gullvigen ('aureus sinus'); that she tended goats and sheep in that area, where the hillock Aadlowhoug and (less certainly) the brook Krakubeck ('Krakæ rivulus') are named after her; and that she later became Queen of Denmark.

In Ramus's account it is told how, according to local tradition at Lindesnæs, Asløg floated ashore there in a golden harp into a cove still known as Guldviig; and then, after reference has been made to the ballad mentioned under the main heading III, above, how this same Asløg, from whom the topographical names *Aatløgs Hougen* and *Kraake-Bækken* seem to derive, tended cattle as a young woman, and was called 'Kraake' (i.e. 'crow') because she wore black clothes.

In 'Regnfred og Kragelil' the hero Regnfred (so the A text; Villemor in the B text, see also under the main heading III, above), searching for the abducted daughter of Sigurd (so A; of the Rose-king, B) hears from a boy (so A; from a dwarf, B) of a certain Herre Habor (so A; of an unpleasant, unnamed mountain-man, B), who has a beautiful maiden with him. He finds her tending Herre Habor's goats (so A; tending robbers' cattle, B), and questions her as to her origins. She replies that her father is an old man 'who chases goats from the moors' ('Hand genner de geder af mose', so A; that he is named Gammelmand, i.e. 'old man', and lives nearby, B). She also gives an assumed name *(Kragelil*, A; *Fragnedlil*, B). Later, however, in response to the production of a weapon by the hero, she reveals that she is the girl he is looking for, and gives her true name *(Svanelil*, A; *Sølverlad*, B).

In the five relevant texts of the *Ragnars kvæði*, i.e. B, C, D, F, G (see no. (13) of the list above), the maiden Kráka, when questioned by Ragnar after being found by his followers (in circumstances explained under VII, below), at the home of Hákar, a giant (so B; of Áki, C; of a person later named as Haki kall, D; of Haki kallur, F; of Haki, G; this figure is later referred to as an old man—'kall', 'kallur'—in all five texts), at first says that this person is her father, that he keeps goats (or, in B, F, G, that her own daily work is to tend goats), and that her name is *Kráka*. Later, however (see under VII, below), she reveals that she is Ásla, the daughter of Sjúrður and Brynhild.

In 'Karl og Kragelil' (the A text of which is here followed, unless otherwise stated), Karl despatches his followers to find him the fairest maiden the sun shines on, and they eventually find a suitably beautiful girl tending some farmers' flocks. Questioned as to her origins, she replies that her father is a shepherd and that her name is *Kragelil*. Later, however, she reveals that *Karl* was the name of her father, who (in the C text also, but not in B) died in a snake-yard (cf. V, VIII and X, below); that her mother's name was *Brynnyll* (i.e. *Brynhildr*; in B and C, however, she gives her mother's name as *Kremolt*, i.e. *Grímhildr*); and that her own name is *Adellrun* (B says nothing further about her parents, and is no longer relevant here). She also says (in A only) that her mother was exiled and (in C also) that the farmers with whom she lives were responsible for her father's death. When Karl offers (or when in C she asks him) to avenge her on the farmers, she requests that he spare the farmer's wife, who was always kind to her (gave her clothes and food, C).

D. In Greek legend various heroes are brought up by a mythical figure; e.g. by Chiron: Achilles, Aeneas, etc.

Mention may here be made of Heimir, to whom Brynhildr in ch. 29 of *Vǫlsunga saga* entrusts the task of bringing up her daughter Áslaug, which he faithfully performs up to the time of his death in ch. 1 of *Ragnars saga* (see IIIC, above). He is perhaps more of a legendary than a strictly mythical figure, though such distinctions need hardly be insisted upon (see Kirk, 1971, 31–34).

IV. *The way in which the hero is brought up*

A. The hero reveals his strength, courage, or other particular features at a very early age.

In *Krákumál*, the narrator speaks first of having acquired the name *Loðbrók* as a result of slaying a serpent in Gautland (i.e. Götaland) and so winning Þóra in marriage (str. 1). He does not say how old he was at the time of the exploit, but goes on to specify that he was very young when he took part in a battle in the Eyrasund (Øresund; str. 2), and that he was twenty years old when he and his companions defeated eight jarls in the mouth of the river Dína (Dvina; str. 3). In the second last strophe of the poem (str. 28) he claims to have engaged in fifty-one battles during his lifetime, and to have begun his martial career at an early age.

In Saxo (IX.iii, 1–4), as indicated under III, above, Regnerus shows remarkable intelligence when scarcely out of his cradle in the advice he gives his father's supporters when they fear the superior strength of the Jutlanders. The age of Regnerus is nowhere specified, but it is evidently soon after he is sent to Norway for his upbringing (see III, above) that his father dies and he succeeds to the throne (IX.iii, 4), and 'about this time' (Fisher, 1979, 280) that his paternal grandfather, the king of the Norwegians, is slain by the Swedish king Frø, with the result that Regnerus returns to Norway and is helped to avenge his grandfather by the woman-warrior Lathgertha. He marries Lathgertha after killing a bear and a dog with which she attempts to protect herself from his advances (cf. IIIB, above, and VII, below). By her he has two daughters (whose names are not given) and a son, Fridlevus. Over three years later he divorces Lathgertha and desires Thora, daughter of Herothus, King of the Swedes (IX.iv, 1–4). The exploit by which he wins her is dealt with under V and VI, below, but it may be noted here that it is from a nurse ('a nutrice') that he receives his protective clothing for combating Thora's serpents; this may represent a tradition according to which he was relatively young at the time. Furthermore, Regnerus is explicitly described as a youth ('iuvenem') in the context of his fight with these serpents (IX.iv, 6–7).

In *Ragnars saga* (ch. 3), Ragnarr, son of the king of Denmark, Sigurðr hringr, slays at the age of fifteen the serpent encircling the bower of Þóra borgarhjǫrtr, daughter of Herruðr, a jarl in Gautland (she is the fairest and most courteous of women, called 'borgarhjǫrtr', 'castle-hart', because she surpasses all other women in beauty as the hart surpasses all other animals, see ch. 2 of the saga). Ragnarr keeps his identity secret; when Þóra, seeing 'a certain large man' ('einn mann mikinn') leave the bower, asks him his name and his business, he replies with a strophe of which the first half may be quoted here (from Olsen, 1906–08, 119):

Hętt heñ ek leyfdv life.	I have risked my allotted life, oh
lit favgr kona vitra.	fair-complexioned woman. At the
va ek at folldar fiske.	age of fifteen I struck at the fish
xv gamall minv.	of the earth (i.e. at the serpent).

In 'Lindarormen', the son of the Danish king is fifteen years old when he responds to an appeal to win the proud Lyselin as his bride by killing a troublesome snake in her possession. He kills the snake, but does not accept Lyselin as his bride, telling her he is already betrothed (in the seventh of Bugge's variants of 'Lindarormen', however, the hero does seem to marry the maiden for whose benefit he has killed the snake, see no. (18) of the list above, and VI and VII, below).

As Olsen (1906–08, 195) has shown, fifteen was the age of majority in mediaeval Norway (from the beginning of the eleventh century onwards). The specification of this age in the verse just quoted from *Ragnars saga* and in 'Lindarormen' is thus obviously significant if, as de Vries claims, the heroic biographical pattern is related to initiation rites (for further examples of the motif 'hero's precocious strength' in Old Norse literature, at fifteen as well as other ages, see Boberg, 1966, 125–26).

In *Ragnars saga* (ch. 5), Áslaug-Kráka seems to show great intelligence ('mikit vit', see Olsen 1906–08, 125) at what is presumably still a young age in the way she responds to the riddling-conditions imposed on her by Ragnarr. She is to visit him 'neither clad nor unclad, neither fed nor unfed, neither alone nor accompanied by man', and fulfils these conditions by wearing nothing but a net (cf. IIIC, above) under her flowing hair, by allowing her lips to smell of a leek she has tasted, and by taking a dog with her.

In the five relevant texts of the *Ragnars kvæði* (B, C, D, F, G) there are only two riddling-conditions, namely 'with a fellow who is not a fellow' and 'both clad and unclad' (in that order, apart from in C), which Kráka fulfils by having a dog as companion and by combing her hair in a special way. In B, C, and G she also bites a leek, which, however, is superfluous, since in no surviving text (so far as I am aware) does this ballad have conditions of the type, 'neither fed nor unfed'. In one text, D, where the two conditions are the same as usual, no mention is made of the hair-combing or of the leek, and a hawk is mentioned in addition to the dog. Kráka-Ásla's intelligence is emphasized at least as much as her beauty in texts B, F, G of the *Ragnars kvæði*, whereas in *Ragnars saga* more is made of her beauty than of her intelligence, and in the 'Gests ríma' the latter quality is not mentioned.

B. On the other hand the child is often very slow in his development: he is dumb or pretends to be mentally deficient.

There is some evidence that Ragnarr as a young man was regarded as a less than perfect ruler, though by his enemies rather than by his subjects. In *Ragnarssona þáttr* (ch. 1), Ragnarr succeeds his father Ring(r) as king of the Swedes and Danes at a time when his realms are being occupied by many invading kings who, since he is a young man, regard him as little suited to decision-making and government. Later, however, he liberates his entire kingdom after winning to wife the exceptionally beautiful Þóra borgarhjǫrtr, the daughter of his liegeman Herrauðr, a jarl in Vestra-Gautland (Västergötland), as a result of slaying a serpent encircling her bower. This exploit (cf. IVA, above, and V, VI, and VII, below) may thus be regarded as a turning-point in his career, much as Beowulf's slaying of Grendel and his mother is regarded by Grønbech (1955, 99). Ragnarr has two sons, Eiríkr and Agnarr, by Þóra, who falls ill and dies when they are only a few years old.

In Arngrímur's account, Ragnerus Lodbroch inherits the extensive domains won by his father, Sigvardus Ringo, from the latter's paternal uncle, Haraldus Hildetǫnn ('war-tooth'), at the battle of Bravǫll. Since his realms are then invaded by neighbouring princes who fear him relatively little because of his young age, Ragnerus seeks to strengthen his position by marrying Thora, the daughter of baron Gautricus of Gautlandia (so Arngrímur's appendix; of Westrogotia in his ch. 19, see no. (9) of the list above), who grants her to him in marriage as a reward for slaying an enormous snake. Thora dies after bearing Ragnerus two sons, Ericus and Agnerus, and Lodbrocus (*sic*) then recovers all his inherited realms.

V. *The hero often acquires invulnerability*

In *Krákumál* (str. 1), the speaker states that he acquired the name *Loðbrók* ('hairy breek') as a result of slaying a serpent in Gautland and so winning Þóra in marriage, but does not explain the name itself (this is the one occurrence of the name in the poem; it appears as *lodbork* in one manuscript, 1824b, see F. Jónsson, 1912a, 641, cf. Lukman, 1976, 20–21, and p. 15, above). He effects the killing with a weapon designated by the expression 'stáli bjartra mála' ('the steel of bright symbols', cf. F. Jónsson 1912b, 649), which, if it is not simply a kenning for 'sword', may indicate a sword or spear on which there are magic symbols, the function of which, however, remains obscure.

In Saxo (IX.iv, 6–8), Regnerus protects himself with a woollen cloak and some hairy thigh-coverings obtained from a nurse (see IVA, above) against the two snakes reared by Thora, daughter of Herothus, whom Regnerus woos in preference to his first wife Lathgertha. He first strengthens the costume by bathing in water while wearing it and then allowing it to freeze. He straps a sword to his side and takes a thonged spear in his right hand. The snakes attempt to batter him with their coiled tails and to cover him with poisonous vomit. He protects himself from their bites with a shield, and from their poison with his costume, and eventually kills them both, apparently simultaneously, by piercing their tails with his spear. Noticing his costume, Herothus gives him the nickname *Lothbrog* (*sic*), the one occurrence of the name in Saxo's account.

In *Ragnars saga* (ch. 3), Ragnarr prepares to attack the snake encircling the bower of Þóra, daughter of Herruðr, by having some hairy breeches and a fur cloak boiled in pitch and later (after travelling to Gautland, cf. IVA, above) rolling in the sand while wearing them. He removes from his spear the nail fastening its head to the shaft, kills the snake as a result of striking at it twice with his spear, and is protected by his costume from its gushing blood, which lands harmlessly between his shoulders. Þóra addresses him as he leaves the bower, and his sole response is the strophe quoted in part under IVA, above. His spearhead remains in the wound he has given the serpent, but he keeps the shaft with him (N.B.: neither of these two points is mentioned in the 147 text of the saga, see Olsen 1906–08, 176). No mention is made of his acquisition of the nickname *Loðbrók* (N.B.: as a name or nickname, the strong feminine noun *loðbrók* occurs only once in the 1824b text of the saga, and then in the genitive; this is in the title of the saga, 'Sagha Raghnars lodbrokar', see Olsen, 1906–08, 111, cf. lxiii and lxxix. The weak feminine form *loðbróka* also occurs only once in the text, and then apparently as a proper noun in the genitive, in str. 39, l. 4, 'syn*ir* lodbrokv', see ch. I, pp. 22–23, above and cf. Olsen, 1906–08, 174. As far as can be gathered from the fragmentary state of the 147 text of the saga, the weak feminine noun *loðbróka* occurs nowhere in that text, and the strong feminine noun *loðbrók* occurs there only once, and then in the genitive also: 'lodbrokar syn*ir*', see Olsen 1906–08, 194).

In *Ragnarssona þáttr* (ch. 1), Ragnarr prepares to attack the snake encircling the bower of Þóra, daughter of Herrauðr, by dressing in shaggy clothes consisting of trousers, a sleeved cloak and a hood, with tar and sand pressed into them, and equipping himself with a spear and a sword. The snake rises up and breathes poison at him, but he protects himself with a shield, spears the snake in the heart, and beheads it with his sword. No mention is made of his acquiring the nickname *loðbrók* (this name occurs only four times in *Ragnarssona þáttr*, always as a strong feminine noun in the genitive case: 'synir Loðbrokar' occurs once, Hb, 1892–96, 459, l. 33, and

'Loðbrokar syn*ir*' three times, Hb, 1892–96, 462, l. 11; 464, l. 12; 465, l. 13).

In the six relevant texts of the *Ragnars kvæði* (A, B, D, E, F, G), Ragnar (son of Sjúrður Ring, A, B, D, F, G) prepares to attack a snake of alarmingly large size in the possession of Tóra Borgarhjørt (jomfru Borgarhjørt, E), the daughter of a king in Suðurlønd (so A, D; in Upplønd, B, G; in Uppland, F; of no named country, E), by treating his clothes with tar and sand (and stone, A, B, D, E). In the D text this is the beginning of his being called *Ragnar loðbrók*; in A and G, however, the nickname stems from the moment when he puts on a scarlet costume after killing the snake and discarding the tarred garments (in none of the other texts is the nickname mentioned). He kills the snake after a brief exchange with it in which he rouses it from sleep; he then takes away with him the shaft of his weapon (which in all the relevant texts except E is later declared by the king's daughter to have been a spear; in E no weapon is specified). In removing the shaft he leaves behind what is variously called 'the point' ('oddurin', A, G), 'the sword' ('svørðið', B, F), and 'the contrivance' ('vælin', D), though in E, where the shaft is mentioned as usual, all that appears to have been left behind in this context is blood ('blóðið tað stóð har aftur', 'the blood remained behind').

In 'Ormekampen', Peder Riboldsøn (Rimboltsøn) prepares to kill an unmanageably large and fierce worm in the possession of Herre Helsing's daughter by putting on the skin of a bull, smeared with tar, over his red jacket, coat of mail, and silk shirt, and by having eight trenches dug to contain the worm's blood, standing in a ninth trench himself. He thus succeeds in destroying the worm.

In 'Lindarormen', the fifteen-year-old Danish prince (see under IVA, above) is advised by his little brown foal, who has the gift of human speech, that in order to defeat the troublesome snake belonging to the maiden Lyselin he will need to have hands like stone and a heart like steel, and must roll in tar and sand, as this will serve him better than corslet or sword. When he arrives in Iceland, where Lyselin lives, he meets 'the scarlet-clad maid-servant of the snake' ('den orme-terna / var sveipt i skarlaki röð'), whom he asks if the snake is at home, whereupon it crawls out of a window. He fights the snake for two days, cuts it into a hundred small pieces with a sword, sticks its head on a spear, and rides to Lyselin's residence.

In the first five of Bugge's seven variants of 'Lindarormen', the hero's name is Daniel Kongens Søn ('Daniel, the king's son); in the fifth it is his mother who advises him to treat his costume with tar and sand, and in this variant also the hero's meeting with the maiden on his way to attack the snake receives relatively lengthy treatment; she offers him ale, which he refuses; she then goes to an upper room to inform the snake of his arrival. In Bugge's sixth variant it is an old woman who advises the hero to roll in tar and sand.

In *Ragnars saga* (ch. 15), when Ragnarr rashly decides to invade England with only two merchant-ships, his second wife Áslaug (here called Randalín) gives him a protective shirt of hair in repayment for a richly-embroidered shift which had belonged to his first wife, Þóra, and which Ragnarr had offered to Áslaug (then called Kráka) on first meeting her in chs. 5–6 (her acceptance of the shift is not in fact recorded in the saga; when Ragnarr offers it to her in ch. 6 she replies in str. 5 that only wretched garments are fit for her, and that her name *Kráka* (= 'crow') has to do with the coal-black clothes she has worn as a goatherd, cf. Ramus's account under IIIC, above). When defeated (later in ch. 15) by King Ella of England and thrown into a snake-pit at the king's instructions, Ragnarr remains unharmed until the shirt is forcibly removed.

In *Ragnarssona þáttr* (chs. 2–3) Ragnarr also decides to invade England with only two merchant-ships, despite the forebodings of his second wife Áslaug. He proceeds with the invasion and is defeated by King Ella of Northumbria. He is captured and placed in a snake-pit, but is at first protected physically by a silk tunic given him by Áslaug as a parting-gift; only when this is removed at Ella's instructions does he succumb finally to the snakes.

Although the motif of death caused by snakes is found in *Krákumál* (strs. 24–29), in the accounts of Saxo (IX.iv, 38–39) and Arngrímur (the latter of whom refers to the former in this context), and in the A and C texts of 'Karl og Kragelil' (though here in a rather different context, see IIIC, above), none of these traditions mentions a protective garment in this connection.

VI. *One of the most common heroic deeds is the fight with a dragon or another monster*

In *Krákumál* (str. 1), the speaker (who is otherwise unnamed) states that he acquired the name *Loðbrók* as a result of slaying a serpent in Gautland and so winning Þóra in marriage. The serpent is designated by the kennings *lyngǫlun* ('heather-fish') and *storðar lykkju* ('loop of the earth'), see F. Jónsson 1912b, 649. The latter kenning may refer solely, as Meissner (1921, 114) seems to suggest, to the idea of a snake as a coiled inhabitant of the earth's surface, though it is surely possible that it also refers to the idea of the world-serpent encircling the earth as a whole so that its head and tail meet, as in Snorri's prose *Edda* (F. Jónsson, 1931a, 60); cf. the serpent encircling the bower in *Ragnars saga* and *Ragnarssona þáttr* as summarized below under the present heading.

In Saxo (IX.iv, 4–8), Regnerus slays in the manner described under V, above, the snakes belonging to Thora, daughter of Herothus. They had been found in a forest by some companions of her father when he was hunting, and he gave them to her to rear. Unaware of the possible consequences, she fed them daily on an ox-carcase, and they grew to the extent of becoming a public menace with their venomous breath. By the time Regnerus fights them they have grown to an enormous size; one is said to be 'inusitatæ magnitudinis' and the other 'granditate par priorisque'.

In *Ragnars saga* (chs. 2–3), Ragnarr slays in the manner described under V, above, the snake that Þóra's father Herruðr, who loved her dearly, had given her as one of his daily presents to her; the snake is said to have been small and very beautiful ('litin lynghorm ... akafligha fagran', Olsen 1906–08, 116–17) when he gave it to her. She was pleased with the snake and put it in a box on top of some gold, and the gold increased in bulk as the snake grew in size. The snake outgrew and encircled its box, and later outgrew even Þóra's bower, while the gold underneath it continued to increase. Its head and tail met as it encircled the bower, and it became such a troublesome charge that the only person who dared approach it was the keeper who fed it the ox it required for each meal. When Ragnarr kills it, its death-throes are so noisy that the entire bower shakes and he is protected by his costume (cf. V, above) from its gushing blood. Those (*þeir*, m.pl.) who had been inside the bower are awakened by the noise and leave it; then Þóra sees and questions Ragnarr with the result described under IVA, above.

In *Ragnarssona þáttr* (ch. 1), Ragnarr slays in the manner described under V, above, the snake that Þóra's father, Herrauðr, had given her as a morning-gift ('morgin giof', Hb, 1892–96, 458, l. 11) when it was a mere 'yrmlingr', i.e. a little or young snake. She at first reared it in a box, but it grew so large that at last it encircled her bower, biting its own tail, and became so fierce that only those who gave it food or were personal servants of Þóra dared to approach it; it needed an ox to eat each day, and its increased size and ferocity caused great alarm.

In Arngrímur's account, as indicated under IVB, above, Ragnerus seeks to strengthen his position as a young king by marrying Thora, daughter of Gautricus, who grants her to him as a reward for slaying an enormous snake. In describing the snake Arngrímur uses the expression 'inusitatæ magnitudinis', which he has presumably borrowed from Saxo (IX.iv, 7), see no. (9) of the list above, and Saxo's account of the serpent-fight as described above under the present heading; cf. also the final paragraph of V, above.

In the relevant texts of the *Ragnars kvæði* (A, B, D, E, F, G), Ragnar kills in the manner described under V, above, a glittering snake ('fræna[r]ormur') belonging to Tóra (or jomfru, E) Borgarhjørt (see also under V, above), which has been found by some maidens in a wood (so B, F, G; in a garden, D). In E, it is jomfru Borgarhjørt herself who finds the snake in some grass, though maidens are mentioned here also; in A, the actual finding of the snake is not mentioned. The snake was placed in a box together with a gold ring (so B, D, F, G; in A only the ring is said to have been placed in the box; in E neither box nor ring is mentioned), and grew to an enormous size (encircling the maiden's bower, A; outgrowing it, B, F, G; outgrowing and encircling it, D; encircling the maiden within the bower, E); in B, E, F, and G it stretches its tail over its head, and in B, F, and G it forms towering coils (in E it forms eighteen coils, though not until Ragnar is about to attack it). The king (see also under V, above) offers his daughter in marriage to the man who will kill the snake (see also under VII, below; this offer is not made in E, however). A count (or a certain Sjúrður frægi, 'the renowned', E) sails to attack it, but turns homeward in terror while still at sea on hearing its bellowing. Ragnar then sails to attack it, before (or in B, F, G after) preparing to do so in the manner described under V, above; while still at sea he, too, hears the snake bellowing. Ragnar then attacks and kills the snake in the manner described under V, above.

In 'Ormekampen', Peder Riboldsøn (Rimboltsøn) destroys in the manner described under V, above, the worm belonging to Hr. Helsing's daughter. This highly-coloured ('spraglitt') worm had been given her as a present by a little shepherd-boy who found it in some grass. She looked after it for three years, in the course of which it became unmanageably large and fierce, and her father offered her hand in marriage to the man who could kill it. A certain Sivord Ingvorsøn lost his life in attempting to do so, and Hr. Helsing then offered all his property as well as his daughter's hand to its prospective slayer. Peder Riboldsøn then undertakes the task and succeeds.

In 'Lindarormen', the Danish prince (see under IVA, above) slays in the manner described under V, above, the snake belonging to Lyselin. It had been brought to her by a little shepherd-boy who found it in some grass. She put it in a chest, and in two days it grew so large that the chest broke, after which it played on the floor and reposed in her bosom. On his way to Iceland (see under V, above) to kill the snake, the prince hears its utterances ('deð orme-mál') from his ship, but proceeds undaunted.

In the seventh of Bugge's 'Lindarorm' variants, a maiden living in Iceland begs for release from a snake which has greatly increased in length in the course of eight years. Eivind the king's son beheads it with his sword; he then takes hold of its head while the maiden grasps its tail, and their disposal of its body obscurely involves the breaking of some masonry.

VII. *The hero wins a maiden, usually after overcoming great dangers*

In *Krákumál* (str. 1) the speaker states that he acquired the name *Loðbrók* as a result of slaying a serpent in Gautland and so winning Þóra in marriage.

In Saxo (IX.iv, 2–3), Regnerus wins Lathgertha after killing a bear and a dog which she has placed at the door of her dwelling to protect her (cf. IIIB and IVA, above). The children of this marriage are noted under IVA, above. Regnerus divorces Lathgertha on falling in love with Thora (IX.iv, 4), whom he wins (IX.iv, 8) as a result of slaying some snakes in the manner described under V and VI, above; Thora's father had offered her in marriage to the man who could remove these pests, and a number of young men tried unsuccessfully to do so before Regnerus (IX.iv, 5). By Thora Regnerus has the sons Rathbarthus, Dunwatus, Sywardus (later nicknamed 'serpentini oculi', '[of the] snake-like eye', IX.iv, 12), Biornus (later nicknamed 'ferrei lateris', 'ironside', IX.iv, 17), Agnerus, and Ivarus. Thora falls ill and dies (IX.iv, 13), and mention is subsequently made of a third wife of Regnerus, Suanlogha, by whom he has the sons Regnaldus, Withsercus, and

Ericus (IX.iv, 17; Ericus, it later emerges, is nicknamed 'Ventosi Pillei', 'wind-hat', IX.iv, 33). Suanlogha incites Regnerus to vengeance after the death of their son Withsercus (IX.iv, 31), and dies herself as a result of illness (IX.iv, 34). While married to Suanlogha, Regnerus also seduces the lowly-born daughter of Hesbernus (IX.iv, 18–19), gaining access to her carefully guarded quarters by disguising himself as a woman. By her he has the son Ubbo (on the nicknames of the sons, see ch. I, pp. 40–41, above).

In *Ragnars saga* (chs. 3–4), Ragnarr wins Þóra after being identified as the slayer of the snake described under VI, above. Þóra's father had promised his daughter in marriage to the man who could kill the snake, with the gold on which the snake lay as her dowry. Though the news of this offer spread widely, no one prior to Ragnarr felt equal to the task. After killing the snake in the manner described under V (cf. also IVA and VI), above, Ragnarr attends an assembly at which Þóra's father invites the slayer to identify himself by producing a spear-shaft to fit the spear-head found in the snake's body. When Ragnarr's spear-shaft is found to fit the head perfectly, he is identified as the slayer. By Þóra, Ragnarr has two sons, Eirekr and Agnarr; she dies as a result of illness. He later (in chs. 5–6) goes to visit his many friends and relatives in Norway, where he meets Kráka (not knowing her to be really Áslaug, the daughter of Sigurðr and Brynhildr, see IIA and IIIC, above), and the hand he extends to her in greeting is bitten by a dog, which his men kill at once. She had brought the dog with her in response to Ragnarr's request that she should visit him 'neither alone nor accompanied by man', which together with other requests (cf. IVA, above) he had made on hearing from some servants of his, who had gone to Spangarheiðr to bake bread, that they had burnt the bread as a result of looking at a woman no less beautiful than Þóra. He threatened to punish them severely if they were lying, and the purpose of his curious requests seems to have been to find out if Kráka was as marvellous as they said, though it was her beauty, and not her intelligence, that they had stressed. As part of the process of wooing her, Ragnarr offers her the shift referred to in the discussion of *Ragnars saga* (ch. 15) under V, above. She eventually makes it clear to him that she will grant him her favours only if he takes her home with him and marries her, and Ragnarr agrees to this. By her he has (in ch. 7) the sons Ívarr (described as 'beinlaus', 'boneless'), Bjǫrn (later referred to, in chs. 15 and 18, as 'Biornn iarnnsida', 'Ironside'), Hvítserkr (later referred

to, in ch. 16, as 'Hvitserkr hvati', 'the bold'), Rǫgnvaldr, and later
(in ch. 9), Sigurðr ormr-í–auga ('snake-in-the-eye'; on the nicknames, see ch. I, pp. 40–41, above). The circumstances in which
Ragnarr becomes aware of Kráka's true identity are described
under IX, below.

  In *Ragnarssona þáttr* (ch. 1), Ragnarr wins Þóra as a result of
slaying the snake described under VI, above. Her father had sworn
to marry her only to the man who would kill the snake or would
dare to go and speak to her in defiance of it, and Ragnarr succeeded
in killing it in the manner described under V, above. He has two
sons, Eiríkr and Agnarr, by Þóra, who dies after an illness when
they are only a few years old (cf. IVB, above). He then marries
Áslaug, 'er svm*ir* kalla Randalin dottor Sigvrðar Fafnis bana *ok*
Brynilldar Bvdla dottor' ('whom some call Randalín, the daughter
of Sigurðr, Fáfnir's slayer, and of Brynhildr Buðladóttir', see Hb,
1892–96, 459, ll. 3–4), and by her has four sons: Ívarr beinlausi ('the
boneless'), Bjǫrn járnsíða ('ironside'), Hvítserkr, and Sigurðr
ormr-í–auga ('snake-in-the-eye'; on the nicknames see ch. I, pp.
40–41, above). Note that no mention is made of Rǫgnvaldr.

  In Arngrímur's account, Ragnerus is granted Thora's hand in
marriage by her father, Gautricus, as a reward for slaying an
enormous snake, Arngrímur's description of which is noted under
VI, above. Thora dies after bearing Ragnerus two sons, Ericus and
Agnerus (cf. IVB, above), and later, after recovering his inherited
realms (cf. also IVB, above), Ragnerus marries Aslauga, daughter
of Sigvardus Foffnisbane ('Fáfnir's slayer'). By this marriage he has
five sons: Ivarus (later said to be nicknamed 'Beinlaus', i.e. 'exos',
'boneless'), Witsercus, Biorno (later said to be nicknamed 'Jarnsijda', i.e. 'ferreus latus', 'ironside'), Raugnvaldus, and Sigvardus
(later said to be nicknamed 'Snogoey', i.e. 'serpentinus oculus',
'snake-like eye'; on the nicknames see ch. I, pp. 40–41, above).

  In the relevant texts of the *Ragnars kvæði* (A, B, D, E, F, G),
Ragnar kills a snake in the circumstances described under V and
VI, above, leaving behind an object variously described in the
different texts, as also shown under V, above. A slave (who finds
the object in question in all the relevant texts apart from A and E;
in E only blood is left behind, cf. V, above) applies to the king,
claiming to have killed the snake and so won his daughter in
marriage (only the first of these two claims is made in E, however,
which does not mention the king's offer of his daughter in marriage
as a reward for killing the snake, cf. VI, above). The king's

daughter (called Tóra in all relevant texts except E, cf. V, above) nevertheless insists that it was a prince and no slave who did the killing, specifying (in all texts except E) that he did it with a spear (cf. V, above). Ragnar reappears (attending Tóra's wedding, A; attending an assembly held by the king, B, F, G; arriving by ship, A, D, E, G) and marries the king's daughter in place of the slave. She then dies after prophesying that her clothes will suit his next wife perfectly (and that the lady in question will be Ásla Sjúrðardóttir, A, D; of noble birth, Á, B, D, F, G). At this stage the A and E texts cease to be relevant, and C becomes so (see no. (13) of the list above); thus the relevant ones from now on are B, C, D, F, and G. Confident that he will never love another woman (so B, C, F, and G), Ragnar now sails southwards (eastwards, C, D), calling at a place where his men attempt to bake bread at the home of an old man—variously designated in the different texts (as shown under IIIC, above)—and his supposed daughter, on whose exceptional qualities (of combined wisdom and cheerfulness, B, C, F, G; and beauty, C) the men report to Ragnar, implying that her presence has distracted them from their baking, and comparing her with Tóra (in D the comparison is made somewhat later, and in C they bring him a lock of the girl's hair. In C also Ragnar threatens them with the gallows in case they are mocking him). He requests that she should visit him under the conditions described under IVA, above, and she fulfils them in the manner there described; in doing so she gets her dog to accompany her. She goes on board Ragnar's ship, and apart from in D (where it is presented as a noteworthy feature of her appearance: 'mikið man um tað varða', 'this is a matter of great importance'), no one notices the snake (or shell, C) which, as the daughter of Sjúrður, she has in (or in D over) her eye. Questioned by Ragnar as to her parentage, she replies in the manner described under IIIC, above, finally revealing that she is the daughter of Sjúrður and Brynhild after Ragnar has made her try on some clothes (which in B, D, F, G suit her literally down to the ground) and questioned her a second time (so B, F, G; a second and third time, C; simply doubted her, D). After the second question-and-answer sequence Ragnar takes her off with him, giving the old man gold and other gifts in exchange for her (according to C only, Ragnar travels to England before discovering her true identity and marrying her, see further under IX, below, and they later have children, including a number of sons).

Although the 'Gests ríma' or 'Áslu ríma' makes no mention of

Ragnar actually winning or marrying Ásla-Kráka, its events are in some ways so close to those of *Ragnars saga* and the *Ragnars kvæði* as outlined here that the relevant part of it may be summarized (cf. IIIC, above, where it is noted that the C text refers briefly to a boneless child). Ragnar's men come to Haki's farm to bake bread; they take a hair from the maiden's head back to Ragnar, explaining to him that they have burnt the bread because they were looking at a maiden fairer than Tóra. He takes this news as mockery and threatens them with the gallows. The ballad ends with the maiden, Ásla, calling her little dog to her when the men have returned to the farm to summon her to Ragnar.

In the B text of 'Regnfred og Kragelil', Villemor, the Molmer king's son, finds the Rose-king's daughter in the circumstances described under IIIC and IIIB above; that is, under the protection of an unpleasant old mountain-man and some bears. He takes her off with him, paying gold and silver to the old man in compensation, and gives her a crown and the title of queen. In the A text, where the names of the characters are different (cf. IIIC, above), the unpleasantness of the maiden's guardian is not specified, and no mention is made of bears. The A text also differs from B in that the relationship between its hero and heroine (Regnfred and Kragelil-Svanelil, cf. IIIC, above) is ambiguous: it seems at first that they are brother and sister (unless Regnfred, who is described as 'the king's son', is meant to be the son of some other king than Sigurd, the heroine's father), while the last two stanzas, which describe them sleeping in each other's arms, suggest that they are lovers (no mention is made in A, either, of the heroine being given a crown or the title of queen).

In 'Karl og Kragelil', the hero, Karl, wins a maiden in the circumstances described under IIIC, above. She reveals her true parentage after being dressed in scarlet and silk (so A; in silk, B, C) and taken into Karl's presence; finally he marries her. In the B and C texts (though not in A) Karl's followers return and report to him on the maiden they have found, before finally carrying out his instructions to bring her to him.

In 'Ormekampen', Peder Riboldsøn (Rimboltsøn) wins Hr. Helsing's daughter after killing a worm in the circumstances described under VI and V, above. The danger of the exploit is emphasized by the fact that Sivord Ingvorsøn loses his life in attempting it, thus causing great distress to the various scarlet-clad women who attend his funeral at the Grimersløv (Grindesløv, Brynesløv) monastery.

In 'Lindarormen', the Danish prince (see under IVA, above) is invited by Lyselin to eat and sleep with her after he has slain her snake in the circumstances described under VI and V, above. However, his foal (cf. V, above) advises him against accepting 'the lady of Sønderliðborg', so he bids Lyselin a thousand good nights after telling her that he has already betrothed himself to the Roman emperor's daughter, to whom he must return.

Bugge's fifth 'Lindarorm' variant (in which the prince is advised by his mother, noted under V, above) ends with his claiming, after killing the snake, to be engaged to a girl living far in the east, who awaits his return; though his seventh variant (summarized in part under VI, above) ends with the maiden sleeping in prince Eivind's arms.

VIII. *The hero makes an expedition to the underworld*

In Saxo (IX.iv, 22–25), Regnerus leads an expedition to Biarmia, the inhabitants of which have caused by magic the death of many of his followers through exposure to abnormal weather and disease. Regnerus, the conqueror of the Holy Roman Empire, almost suffers the humiliation of defeat in Biarmia once its king has joined forces against him with Matullus, prince of Finnmarchia, though he eventually defeats both parties by means of an ambush. In *Ọrvar-Odds saga* (dating probably from between 1265 and 1275, see de Vries, 1967, 487), which Koht (1931, 147) calls 'The typical Viking saga', and which is comparable in many ways to *Ragnars saga*, the hero experiences difficulties of much the same kind as Regnerus in Bjarmaland and Finnmǫrk, including exceptionally severe winds caused by Lappish magic (Boer, 1892, 20, ll. 6–16). Koht (1931, 147) has compared the supernatural adventures of Ọrvar-Oddr in these north-eastern regions with those of Odysseus in the cave of the Cyclops, which Graves (1958, 728) takes together with certain other adventures of Ulysses, including his visit to the underworld, as 'metaphors for the death which he evaded'. 'The cavern of the Cyclops', in Graves's view, 'is plainly a place of death'.

The world of the dead was often depicted as a realm of serpents in Scandinavian tradition, a notion which, according to Dronke (1969a, 66), need not be of exclusively Christian origin. It is obviously significant in the present context, then, that in *Krákumál*, Saxo's account, *Ragnars saga*, *Ragnarssona þáttr*, and Arngrímur's account, the hero's death is caused by snakes. In Saxo's account (IX.iv, 38) it is said to have taken place in a prison ('carcerem'); in *Ragnars saga* (ch. 15) and *Ragnarssona þáttr* (ch. 3) in a snake-yard ('ormgarð'). As noted under IIIC and V, above, the motif of death in a snake-yard ('vorme-gaard', 'orme-gaard') also occurs in the A and C texts of 'Karl og Kragelil', in the rather different context of the heroine revealing that her father died such a death. The motif, noted under V, above, of the protective garment given to Ragnarr by his wife, which occurs only in *Ragnars saga* and in *Ragnarssona þáttr*, may be compared with that of the thread given by Ariadne to Theseus so that, after slaying the Minotaur, he can find his way safely out of the Cretan labyrinth, which de Vries (1963, 223) regards as symbolic of the realm of the dead. J. de Vries also suggests (1963, 224) that a memory of the labyrinth motif may lie behind the account in *Vǫlsunga saga* (ch. 18) of how Sigurðr, in preparing to kill the dragon Fáfnir, is advised by Óðinn to dig some ditches and pierce Fáfnir to the heart while sitting in one of them, letting the other ditches receive the dragon's blood. Sigurðr follows this advice and kills Fáfnir. It has been noted under V, above, that in 'Ormekampen' much the same method is used, with no less success, by Peder Riboldsøn in slaying the worm belonging to Hr. Helsing's daughter.

IX. *When the hero is banished in his youth he returns later and is victorious over his enemies. In some cases he has to leave the realm again which he has won with such difficulty*

In Saxo (IX.iv, 4), Regnerus defeats, among others, some Jutlanders, a people who, under the leadership of Ringo, cf. III, above, had endangered his safety as a child (IX.iii, 1–4) by opposing his father's accession to the throne, so that he was sent in his own interests (rather than banished) to Norway. In alliance with the Scanians (IX.iv, 4), the Jutlanders support Haraldus against Regnerus as a rival claimant to the throne of Denmark (IX.iv, 9–11). Regnerus defeats Haraldus with the help of his divorced wife Lathgertha, who still loves him; later (IX.iv, 15) he drives him out of Denmark into Germany. Later still (IX.iv, 26–28), he suppresses a rebellious attempt on the throne by his son Ubbo, killing Ubbo's grandfather Hesbernus, who had encouraged the rebellion. He checks (IX.iv, 36–37) another attempt on the throne by Haraldus, who is then converted to Christianity at Mainz by Louis the Pious and introduces the new religion into Denmark, though he reverts to paganism after Regnerus, a lifelong heathen, has once again defeated him.

In *Ragnarssona þáttr* (ch. 1), Ragnarr, though he does not suffer banishment, is apparently in a vulnerable position when he succeeds to his father's throne; kings who regard him as too young to be an effective ruler make incursions on his realms. Later, however, he frees his entire kingdom from invaders after winning to wife Þóra, daughter of Herrauðr, as a result of slaying the serpent encircling her bower (cf. IVB, above).

In Arngrímur's account, similarly, the realms of Ragnerus Lodbroch are at first invaded by kings who fear him relatively little because of his youth. After strengthening his position by marrying Thora, however, whom he wins as a reward for slaying a snake, he recovers all his inherited realms (cf. IVB, above).

In *Vǫlsunga saga* (ch. 29), Áslaug, though not banished, is entrusted as a baby by her mother Brynhildr to Heimir (see IIID, above). In *Ragnars saga* (ch. 1), Heimir hears of the deaths of Sigurðr and Brynhildr when Áslaug is three years old, and, fearing for her safety, journeys with her until he is murdered in Norway by Áki and Gríma (cf. IIIC, above). Gríma decides to call her Kráka and to pass her off as her own daughter and Áki's in bringing her up; with this in mind she further decides to shave the girl's head and rub it with tar, so that she will look appropriately ugly, and to give her the worst chores. After meeting Ragnarr in the circumstances described under VII and IVA, above, Áslaug leaves Áki and Gríma (ch. 6) in order to marry him, but first wishes them a life of ever-increasing misery, telling them she knows they murdered Heimir (it is possible that her mention of Heimir does not form part of the 147 text of *Ragnars saga*, see McTurk, 1975, 58, n. 59). She then marries Ragnarr, who believes her to be a mere farmer's daughter, and who later (ch. 9), therefore, secretly seeks the hand of Ingibjǫrg, the daughter of King Eysteinn of Sweden. Áslaug learns of this from some birds, however, and reveals to Ragnarr that she is really Áslaug, the daughter of Sigurðr and Brynhildr, and that her true name is *Áslaug*. She prophesies that their fifth son will be born with a snake-like mark around his eye, and when Sigurðr ormr-í–auga ('snake-in-the-eye') is born, Ragnarr believes her true identity. He abandons his idea of a Swedish marriage, and Áslaug's true parentage is universally acknowledged. Lukman (1976, 15–16) compares Áslaug's fortunes with those of the Danish princess Ingeborg (d. 1236), the wife of King Philip Augustus of France.

In Arngrímur's account, Ragnerus plans to divorce Aslauga (cf. VII, above), believing her to be of humble birth and upbringing; he changes his mind, however, when Aslauga assures him that the child she is bearing him will have a snake-like mark in one of its eyes, proving that its grandfather was Sigvardus the serpent-slayer. This child, Sigvardus, their fifth son (cf. also VII, above) thus comes to be nicknamed 'Snogoey', or 'snake-like eye'.

In the relevant texts of 'Brynhildar táttur' (i.e. *Sjúrðar kvæði* A, Bb, D, H, cf. IIA and IIIA, above), Ásla, the daughter of Sjúrður and Brynhild, is set afloat on a river at the instructions of her mother, who does not wish to see her after giving birth to her in the circumstances described under IIA, above. In the relevant texts of the *Ragnars kvæði* (B, C, D, F, G) she is taken off (and in D later married) by King Ragnar (as he is called in all the relevant texts) after meeting him in the circumstances described under VII, IIIC, and IVA, above. As well as in the ways already noted under VII, above, C differs from the other relevant texts in briefly mentioning Ragnar's engagement (in England) to Ingibjørg, which takes place after he has departed with Kráka from where they first meet, but before he has discovered her true identity by questioning her a third time (after which, of course, he abandons Ingibjørg for her; cf. the paragraph above under the present heading on *Vǫlsunga saga* and *Ragnars saga*).

In the 'Gests ríma' or 'Áslu ríma', Gestur finds a harp by a river and lodges with Haki and his wife, who murder him. In the harp they find a maiden whom the wife decides to call Kráka and pass off as her own daughter (cf. IIIC, above, and the remarks on *Vǫlsunga saga* and *Ragnars saga* above, under the present heading), and who is later summoned to meet King Ragnar in the circumstances described under VII, above.

Torfæus tells how, according to local tradition, a girl called Aadlow was found near Spangereid in a golden harp, tended goats and sheep there, not far from the brook known at Torfæus's time of writing as Krakubeck, and became Queen of Denmark (cf. IIIC, above).

Müller relates that the king of the country where Osla was brought up by a poor man (see under the main heading of III, above) had become a widow and would marry no-one but the person whom his dead wife's clothes would fit (cf. the *Ragnars kvæði* and *Ragnars saga* as outlined under VII, above). They are found to fit Osla, who thus becomes queen; and when she is criticized for her humble origins she produces a letter which her mother had placed in the chest in which she was washed ashore (see also under III, above). Her mother, who is still alive, is then contacted, and recognizes her.

The process by which the abducted maiden is found (and in the B text given the title of queen) by the hero in 'Regnfred og Kragelil' is made sufficiently clear under IIIC, IIIB, and VII, above.

The process whereby, in the A and C texts of 'Karl og Kragelil', the maiden Adellrun marries Karl after being tragically separated from her parents as a child and then living with the farmers who were responsible for her father's death, has been outlined under IIIC and VII, above. It may be added here that the old retainer who, in the A text, brings her to Karl on his horse, reassures her while doing so that he is taking her to a noble knight.

X. *The death of the hero.*

'Heroes often die young ... In many cases their death is miraculous' (de Vries, 1963, 216).

The motif of the garment which protects the hero from death until its removal—occurring among the relevant traditions only in *Ragnars saga* and *Ragnarssona þáttr* has been noted under V, above; while the manner of the hero's death in the relevant traditions— *Krákumál*, Saxo's account, *Ragnars saga*, *Ragnarssona þáttr* and Arngrímur's account—has been noted under V and VIII, above.

In *Krákumál*, the speaker says that he had not expected Ella would be the cause of his death (str. 24), though he rejoices at the prospect of attending Óðinn's banquet for slain warriors (str. 25); he forecasts that his sons will take vengeance on Ella in their anger at the death he is suffering from snakes, one of which has just entered his heart (str. 27); and claims to have engaged in fifty-one battles during his lifetime (str. 28).

Saxo (IX.iv, 38–39) reports that, when the snakes had gnawed at Regnerus's liver and approached his heart, he recited in order all the deeds of his life and said: 'If the young pigs only knew the distress of their boar, they would certainly break into the sty and release him from his suffering without delay' (Fisher, 1979, 291).

Suspecting that this may mean that Regnerus's sons are still alive, Hella (cf. Ella, see p. 74, above) orders the snakes to be removed, but too late.

N.B.: in Saxo's account, Regnerus's death appears to take place in Ireland; just before he describes it, Saxo says that Hella had 'betaken himself to the Irish' ('collatus ad Hibernos', IX.iv, 38). *Krákumál* does not specify the whereabouts of the speaker's death; *Ragnars saga* places Ragnarr's death in England, *Ragnarssona þáttr* more specifically in Northumbria; and Arngrímur, aware of both Saxo's account and that of *Ragnars saga* (see no. (9) of the list above), also places it in England. According to Saxo, Regnerus had earlier fought against a usurper king, Hella, son of Hamo ('Hamonis filium'), at York (IX.iv, 34; just possibly Norwich, see Herrmann, 1922, 648, n. 2), and earlier still had raised hostilities against Britain ('Britanniam'), and slain its king, Hama (*sic*), 'father of a most noble youth, Hella' ('Hamam, Hellæ nobilissimi iuvenis patrem', IX.iv, 14). Quite apart from the unlikelihood of there being snakes in Ireland, Saxo's reference to the Irish is hardly consistent with the other accounts of Ragnarr loðbrók's death or with his own earlier information about Hella, and is probably an error; Herrmann (1922, 649, n. 1) certainly thought so, and de Vries (1928b, 140; cf. 1923, 251) suggested that Saxo's *Hibernos* (= Irishmen) represented a misreading of *Humbros* (= Northumbrians). This is not to say that the location of the death in England is necessarily any more accurate historically; there is of course little or no historical accuracy in any of the accounts of Ragnarr loðbrók's death in a snake-pit (cf. McTurk, 1976, 97, 108-09) and similarly little point in discussing the historical superiority of one to another. Smyth's recent suggestion (1977, 83-100) that Saxo's account, with its reference to the Irish, is historically more reliable than the others certainly cannot command acceptance (see Ó Corráin, 1979, 290-96). See further p. 108, below.

In *Ragnars saga* (ch. 15), after Ragnarr's protective shirt has been removed (see under V, above), he says, 'Gnydia mundu nu grisir, ef þeir visse, hvat enn gamle þyldi' ('the young pigs would grunt if they knew what the old one was suffering', Olsen, 1906–08, 158), and recites two strophes before dying, in the first of which (str. 26) he claims to have engaged in fifty-one battles, and says he did not expect snakes would be the cause of his death, while in the second (str. 27) he repeats his hint as to the probable reaction of his sons, using the image of young pigs and a boar (in the 147 text of the saga, Ragnarr recites the greater part of *Krákumál* before also reciting the first, at least, of the two strophes corresponding to strs. 26 and 27 of the 1824b text, see Olsen, 1906–08, 187–89, and cf. McTurk, 1975, 62, n. 70). Ella, suspecting and anxious to confirm that it is indeed Ragnarr who has been his victim, sends messengers to Ívarr and his brothers to test their reaction to the news.

In *Ragnarssona þáttr* (ch. 3), Ragnarr dies a heroic death in the snake-pit after his protective tunic has been removed (see under V, above). No dying statements of his, either in prose or verse, are quoted or mentioned.

In Arngrímur's account, Ragnerus boasts in the course of a rash invasion of England (undertaken with only two ships) of having been victorious in fifty-one battles. He who first made his name—after coming to the throne in c.810—by subduing a monstrous snake is himself destroyed by snakes after ruling for some thirty-seven years (this figure, and the date of Ragnerus's accession, are found only in Arngrímur's ch. 19 and not in his appendix, see no. (9) of the list above and cf. IVB, above). Arngrímur refers to Saxo for an account of Ragnerus's death and of his sons' revenge.

Mention may briefly be made, finally, of the heroine's father's death in a snake-yard in the A and C texts of 'Karl og Kragelil', cf. IIIC above.

The only one of these accounts which comes at all close to giving the hero's age at the time of his death is Arngrímur's, which says that Ragnerus Lodbroch succeeded to the throne in c.810, initially had difficulties as a king because of his young age (cf. IVB and IX, above), and died after ruling 'hardly longer' ('vix ... diutius') than thirty-seven years. Arngrímur's view as to the length of Ragnerus's reign (which evidently derives from the late fourteenth-century *Flateyjarannáll*, Benediktsson, 1957, 82, 244) would make the date of his death c.847, which accords interestingly with the information in the *Annales Xantenses* (Rau, 1972, 348–49; cf. ch. I, above, pp. 6, 46 47) that the historical Reginheri died in 845. It would hardly make him a young man at the time of his death, however, quite apart from the fact that the various relevant accounts all seem to presuppose that his sons were old enough to avenge him at that time. On the other hand it may be noted that Saxo (IX.iv, 38–39) hints at the untimeliness of Regnerus's death in seeing it as a punishment for his disparagement of Christianity and as a lesson in the turns and changes of fortune; and that, in *Ragnars saga* (ch. 15), *Ragnarssona þáttr* (chs. 2–3) and Arngrímur's account, Ragnarr's decision to invade England with only two ships (cf. V, above) is more what would be expected of a rash, youthful hero than of an experienced warrior.

As to whether the hero's death is presented as 'miraculous' in the Scandinavian traditions relating to Ragnarr loðbrók, it may be recalled here that, in the earlier and later versions of the Frankish Latin *Miracula Sancti Germani* (cf. Waitz, 1887, 16; Carnandet, 1866,

789), the death of the Viking leader Ragenarius is seen as a miraculous instance of divine vengeance, brought about by St. Germanus, whose monastery Ragenarius had desecrated while leading a Viking attack on Paris in 845 (cf. ch. I, section (a), above). According to both versions of this account Ragenarius returned from Paris to Denmark, where he eventually died after collapsing in dreadful agony and crying out that St. Germanus was belabouring him with a stick—a notion which, according to de Vries (1923, 252), has its origin in the phrase 'Domino percutiente', used with reference to the death of Reginheri in the *Annales Xantenses* for 845. While acknowledging the considerable differences in the manner of the Viking leader's death between the Frankish accounts on the one hand and the Scandinavian ones on the other, de Vries (1923, 252) nevertheless comments: 'beide Male ist die Todesart eine recht wunderbare'. He suggests that the knowledge of Ragnarr loðbrók's death in a snake-yard arose under the influence of the story lying behind Gunnarr's death in a snake-pit as reported in the Atli-lays of the poetic *Edda* (i.e. *Atlakviða* and *Atlamál in grœnlenzko*, dating probably from the ninth and twelfth centuries respectively, see Dronke, 1969a, 44, 111) and in *Þiðriks saga* (dating from the mid-thirteenth century, see McTurk, 1977a, 583), and that memories in Denmark of the miraculous associations of the death of Ragenarius made stories about it particularly susceptible to this influence.

* * *

What preliminary conclusions can be drawn from this Analysis? According to de Vries (1927c, 81–85), the serpent-slaying exploit whereby Ragnarr wins Þóra, and his death in the snake-pit, are motifs which belong to relatively early stages of the development of legends about Ragnarr loðbrók and his sons, though not the earliest of all. At the very earliest stages, which appear to have taken place among Scandinavian inhabitants of the Danelaw, the notion rather than the manner of Loðbrók's slaying was of primary importance, since it provided a reason for representing the Viking invasion of Northumbria in 866 as an act of vengeance by his sons. Once this notion was established, more interest was taken in the manner of the father's death and in his earlier career. In a series of partly fragmentary strophes, *Háttalykill*, a poem attributed to the Icelander

Hallr Þórarinsson and the Orcadian jarl Rǫgnvaldr, and dating from the mid-twelfth century (de Vries, 1967, 28), mentions the following legendary figures (see F. Jónsson, 1912b, 489–92): Ragnarr (str. 6a); Ella (apparently describing him as Ragnarr's slayer: 'Ella ... Ragnars bani', str. 7a); someone not named in what can now be read of the text but described as 'the boneless one' ('enn beinlausi', str. 8a); 'Agnarr's brother' ('Agnars bróður', str. 8b); Bjǫrn (str. 9a); Sigurðr (str. 10a); and Hvítserkr (str. 11a) (cf. part VII of the Analysis). This series follows on from another, also partly fragmentary, in which Gunnarr and Fáfnir's bed ('Fáfnis láð', i.e. 'gold', str. 4a), Atli and the sons of Gjúki ('sonum Gjúka', str. 4b), and also Helgi (str. 5a) are mentioned. The poem thus shows that by the time of its composition legends relating to Ragnarr, Ella, Ívarr, etc. had come into contact with ones relating to the Vǫlsungar and Gjúkungar, and were thus open to influence from that quarter as regards both serpent-slaying and death caused by serpents—since Sigurðr the Vǫlsungr slays the serpent Fáfnir and Gunnarr Gjúkason dies in a snake-yard (see *Vǫlsunga saga*, chs. 13–20, 35–40, and the eddaic sources noted by Olsen, 1906–08, 31–47, 90–105). It must be stressed, however, that, as far as can be gathered from its fragmentary state, *Háttalykill* makes no mention of Ragnarr's nickname *loðbrók* or of his slaying a serpent, or of his winning Þóra, or of his dying in a snake-pit. All of these four items nevertheless figure in *Krákumál* (strs. 1, 24–29), which is cast in the form of a monologue apparently spoken by Ragnarr, though the name *Ragnarr* itself (as opposed to the name *Loðbrók*) occurs nowhere in the poem's text. This means, then, that by the time of *Krákumál*'s composition (probably the second half of the twelfth century, see p. 53, above and cf. de Vries, 1967, 39), the following parts of the heroic biographical pattern had become established as components of the tradition relating to Ragnarr loðbrók: V ('invulnerability'), VI ('the fight with a dragon or other monster'), VII ('the hero wins a maiden'), and X ('the death of the hero'). This would be enough to make the pattern recognizable to subsequent bearers of the tradition, and hence to make it likely that the tradition would attract further elements of the pattern in the course of its transmission.

In *Krákumál* (str. 26), the speaker briefly mentions Áslaug (who is not mentioned in *Háttalykill*) in hinting that her sons would be likely to avenge his death in the snake-pit. If de Vries (1928a, 286–89) is right in claiming that Áslaug already existed as a legendary daughter of Sigurðr and Brynhildr before becoming the legendary second wife of Ragnarr loðbrók, then *Krákumál* shows here what is probably an early stage of the absorption into the legends about Ragnarr loðbrók of legends about a daughter of Sigurðr and Brynhildr named Áslaug. In what follows the expressions 'the Áslaug-figure' and 'the Ragnarr-figure' will be used to refer not only to the characters bearing these names in *Ragnars saga*, but also to the characters corresponding to them respectively in the relevant analogues. From the foregoing Analysis it is clear that the Áslaug-figure provides the tradition of Ragnarr loðbrók with parts I and II of the heroic biographical pattern (the 'begetting' and 'birth' of the hero respectively), and that neither of these parts is supplied by the Ragnarr-figure. It is also clear that the Áslaug-figure contributes strikingly to the tradition under the heading of part III ('the youth of the hero is threatened'), and hardly less strikingly, although less strictly in accordance with the pattern, under the heading of part IX ('the hero returns and is victorious'). For the Áslaug-figure's career to fit part IX neatly, it is necessary to revise de Vries's formulation of this part of the pattern by giving it some such summary designation as 'the hero comes into his own'. Now the Ragnarr-figure also exemplifies parts III and IX of the pattern, but for the most part only in Saxo's account, which shows little if any awareness of the Áslaug-figure (though the latter may conceivably be represented by Suanlogha, the briefly-mentioned third wife of Regnerus, see part VII of the Analysis and pp. 124–25, below). In Saxo, Regnerus exemplifies part III of the pattern no less adequately than the Áslaug-figure elsewhere, and part IX more in accordance with de Vries's formulation of it than the Áslaug-figure. This implies that Saxo's account represents a relatively early stage of the tradition prior to the introduction of the Áslaug-figure, at which the Ragnarr-figure exemplified parts III and IX of the pattern; and that these were taken over by the Áslaug-figure (more appropriately in the case of part III than in that of part IX) as the tradition developed. One result of this process is the fact, pointed out by Olrik (see p. 62, above), that Áslaug is the 'actual' hero of *Ragnars saga*, while Ragnarr is merely the 'formal' hero.

Part IVB of the pattern ('the child is slow in his development') is applied to the Ragnarr-figure in *Ragnarssona þáttr* and Arngrímur's account, which reflect relatively early stages of Áslaug's incorporation in the story of Ragnarr loðbrók, but is nowhere applied to the

Áslaug-figure. This part of the pattern obviously presents the Ragnarr-figure in a somewhat unfavourable light, and contrasts with the manner in which part IV is applied to him in Saxo's account, which, as has just been shown, may reflect a stage of the tradition prior to the introduction of the Áslaug-figure. Here Regnerus, with his remarkable intelligence as a youth, exemplifies part IVA ('the hero reveals his particular features at a very early age') rather than part IVB. The application of part IVB to the Ragnarr-figure possibly reflects an early stage of the process whereby the Ragnarr-figure became less important than the Áslaug-figure after the latter's introduction; for the Ragnarr-figure to be able to take second place it was perhaps necessary to present him initially in a not wholly favourable light. However this may be, it should be emphasized that part IVA, which is applied to both figures, is in general exemplified rather more impressively by the Ragnarr-figure than by the Áslaug-figure, who, indeed, exemplifies it exclusively in her rôle as Kráka. This implies that it was used in connection with the Áslaug-figure only at a relatively late stage of the tradition, since it seems likely that the Kráka story was not developed fully until after the Áslaug-figure's introduction (de Vries, 1928a, 273–74). The relevant part of the Kráka story is of course Áslaug-Kráka's display of intelligence in her response to the riddling-conditions imposed on her by Ragnarr; this shows the influence of the popular tale known as 'the clever peasant girl', AT no. 875, as de Vries (1928a, 274 77; 1928d, 214–30) clearly demonstrates, and forms part of an episode which, according to him, was introduced after the association of the Áslaug-figure with the Ragnarr-figure and was meant to prepare the way for the explanation given in *Ragnars saga* of the bonelessness of Ívarr, Ragnarr's eldest son by Áslaug; according to the saga as preserved in 147 and 1824b (see Olsen 1906–08, 128–29, 179), Ívarr was born boneless as a result of a curse placed on Kráka by the farming-couple who had brought her up (see further pp. 93–94, 227, below). It should be emphasized here that, in spite of the poem's title, the Kráka story plays no part whatever in *Krákumál*; the application of this title to the poem now known by it appears to have been either secondary or else originally quite unrelated to the word *Kráka* as a personal name or nickname (see further pp. 125–32, below). It may finally be noted, for the sake of completeness, that part VIII of the pattern ('the hero makes an expedition to the underworld') is hinted at with reference to the

Ragnarr-figure in a number of texts, but is nowhere applied to the Áslaug-figure, as the foregoing Analysis shows.

It is obviously impossible to give anything like a precise chronology of the gradual attachment of the heroic biographical pattern to the various legends about Ragnarr loðbrók, but it will be clear from what has just been said that the earlier stages of this process are reflected in what the relevant texts have to show of parts V, VI, VII, and X of the pattern, and that parts I and II, which are exemplified by the Áslaug-figure but not by the Ragnarr-figure, are unlikely to have featured in legends about Ragnarr loðbrók until the Áslaug-figure had entered this group of legends. Parts III and IX appear to have been applied first to the Ragnarr-figure, and later transferred to the Áslaug-figure; part IVA appears to have been applied more to the Ragnarr-figure than to the Áslaug-figure, and to the latter only at a relatively late stage of the tradition; and part IVB, which is not applied to the Áslaug-figure, appears to have been applied to the Ragnarr-figure at a relatively early stage of the Áslaug-figure's incorporation in the tradition. All that can be said about part VIII, finally, is that it is applied to the Ragnarr-figure, but not to the Áslaug-figure.

(b) The pattern as applied to Ragnarr's sons

(i) The procreation of Ívarr

I shall now consider certain motifs which raise the question of how far the lives and actions of the other main characters of *Ragnars saga* (i.e. Ragnarr's sons) exemplify the heroic biographical pattern; and I shall indicate the stage or stages at which each relevant motif, as applied to one or other of Ragnarr's sons, is likely to have entered the Ragnarr loðbrók tradition. I shall discuss Ívarr's procreation, and the heroic precocity of Sigurðr ormr-í-auga, in relation to parts I, II, and IV of the pattern; the death of Rǫgnvaldr in relation to part X; Ívarr's cow-slayings in relation to part VI; and the deaths of Eirekr, Agnarr, and Hvítserkr in relation to part X, and to a lesser extent part VIII. It will be convenient to conduct the discussion in the order indicated here, rather than in the order in which the parts of the pattern were discussed in the preceding section.

Two of Ragnarr's sons by Áslaug, Ívarr and Sigurðr, are presented as exceptional figures from birth, the former in being boneless and the latter in having a snake-like mark around his eye, but their actual births are in no way presented as unnatural or mysterious, in the manner of Áslaug's birth in *Vǫlsunga saga* (see part IIA of the Analysis), and do not correspond to either of the variant motifs given by de Vries (1963, 212) under the heading of part II ('the birth of the hero'; cf. part II of the Analysis). Furthermore, the circumstances of Ívarr's procreation, though dwelt on at some length in the 147 and 1824b texts of *Ragnars saga* (see Olsen, 1906–08, 128–29, 179–80), do not correspond precisely to any of the four motifs listed by de Vries (1963, 211–12) under the heading of part I ('the begetting of the hero'; cf. part I of the Analysis). In ch. 6 of the 1824b text Ragnarr marries Kráka (whom he does not yet know to be Áslaug, the daughter of Sigurðr and Brynhildr), and seeks to consummate the marriage at once. Kráka excuses herself, saying that there will be serious consequences if she does not have her way; and Ragnarr, who evidently interprets this as meaning that she believes herself to be placed under a curse by the farming couple who have brought her up, declares that this couple do not have the gift of prophecy. Kráka then recites a verse (str. 6), which is not perfectly understood (see Olsen, 1906–08, 198–99; cf. E. A. Kock, 1927, 85), but which implies that unless she and Ragnarr wait for three nights, their child will be born without bones, and which also mentions some divine beings ('heilug goð'), to whom they may sacrifice ('blótim') only at the end of the three-night period. Ragnarr then consummates the marriage, disregarding her recitation, and in the next chapter Ívarr is indeed born without bones, having only a kind of gristle where his bones ought to be. This account, as de Vries (1928a, 276–77) points out, is clearly intended as an explanation of the nickname *beinlauss*, the earliest known instance of which occurs in a poorly preserved part of *Háttalykill* (from the mid-twelfth century, see pp. 31, 89–90, above), apparently with reference to Ívarr, though it should be noted that what appears to be an explanation of the nickname also occurs in the *Chronicon Roskildense*, dating from *c.*1140 (Gertz, 1917–18, 4, 16), somewhat earlier than *Háttalykill* (see further pp. 105–06, below and cf. the discussion in ch. I, pp. 40–41, above).

J. de Vries (1928a, 277) also points out a close parallel to the *Ragnars saga* account in Saxo, IX.xi, 2–4, where Thira, daughter of the English king Hedelradus (Æthelred), requires of her husband, King Gormo III of Denmark, abstention from intercourse for three days after their marriage, ostensibly because of feminine modesty, but in fact because she is privately resolved not to make love until she has been reassured in a dream that the marriage will be fruitful. Her husband co-operates with her by placing a naked sword between them in bed. Then, however, he himself has a dream in which he sees two birds issuing from her womb, and on hearing of this she allows him to consummate the marriage, later bearing him two sons, Haraldus and Kanutus. J. de Vries (1928a, 277) shows that this account derives ultimately from an episode in Book III, ch. 12, of the so-called *Chronicle of Fredegarius*, which was compiled by three anonymous writers at different stages of the seventh century; here Childericus I, King of the Franks, abstains from intercourse on his wedding night and as a result sees his family's future in a vision (Krusch, 1888, 1–9, 97). J. de Vries (1928a, 277, 279, 285) implies that the account in *Ragnars saga* derives partly from 'Fredegarius' (by way of Danish historical legend) and partly from the tradition reflected in *Vǫlsunga saga*, ch. 29 (see part IIA of the Analysis), according to which Sigurðr and Brynhildr share the same bed for three nights with a drawn sword between them. The use of the sword in this connection is also recorded in the eddaic poem *Sigurðarkviða in skamma* (str. 4), dating most probably from the turn of the eleventh to the twelfth century (Sveinsson, 1962, 229, 522–23), and the reason for it, according to Sigurðr in *Vǫlsunga saga* (see Olsen, 1906–08, 68, ll. 19–22) is that he is doomed to die unless he marries his wife in this way. It should be remembered, however, that Sigurðr is here visiting Brynhildr disguised as Gunnarr and on Gunnarr's behalf; his reasons for holding back from her may be different from those he states, or Gunnarr's rather than his own. J. de Vries (1956, 187) points out that the idea of the three nights of continence just after marriage (known as the 'nights of Tobias' in the Middle Ages because the idea occurs in the Vulgate version of the apocryphal book of Tobias, see Gordon, 1957, 198) has its origin in the fear in which, among many primitive peoples, carnal relations between the sexes are held, a fear which sometimes finds expression in the use of someone other than the husband for the purpose of taking the bride's virginity. The winning of Brynhildr by Sigurðr, her 'first lover', on behalf of Gunnarr, who marries her (see parts IA and IIA of the Analysis) may indeed reflect this ancient practice. According to de Vries (1956, 187), the divine beings referred to by Kráka in str. 6 of the 1824b text of *Ragnars saga* (and in the corresponding strophe of 147, see Olsen, 1906–08, 179) cannot be certainly identified, but are probably fertility gods.

It has already been assumed that Áslaug was regarded as the daughter of Sigurðr and Brynhildr before being brought into connection with Ragnarr loðbrók as the latter's wife, and that the account in *Ragnars saga* of the circumstances leading up to Kráka's delivery of Ívarr the boneless represents a later stage in the development of traditions about Ragnarr loðbrók than Áslaug's association with him (see pp. 90–93, above). Arguments in favour of these assumptions will be offered in the next chapter (see ch. III, sections (a)–(d), below); if for the moment they may be accepted, and if it is also borne in mind that Áslaug and her parents are apparently unknown to Saxo (see further pp. 123–25, below), then it may be concluded that the account in *Ragnars saga* of the procreation of Ívarr by Ragnarr and Áslaug-Kráka shares with Saxo's account of Gormo III and Thira a source in Danish historical legend deriving from 'Fredegarius', but has independently borrowed from the story of Sigurðr and Brynhildr the idea that a curse may be fulfilled unless certain restraints are observed in the early days (or nights) of marriage.

(ii) The precocity of Sigurðr ormr-i-auga

The career of Sigurðr ormr-i-auga certainly conforms to part IVA of the pattern, 'the hero reveals his particular features at a very early age'. Like Egill Skalla-Grímsson in *Egils saga* (Nordal, 1933, 80–82), Sigurðr in the 1824b text of *Ragnars saga* is presented as being able to compose scaldic poetry at the age of three (Olsen, 1906–08, 142–44), and the strophe he recites (str. 19 in the 1824b text; it is also preserved in *Ragnarssona þáttr*, see Hb, 1892–96, 461, and fragmentarily in the 147 text of the saga, see Olsen 1906–08, 183) finally persuades his brothers Bjǫrn járnsíða, Hvítserkr, and Ívarr to join their mother Áslaug in taking vengeance on King Eysteinn of Sweden for the deaths of their stepbrothers Eirekr and Agnarr, Ragnarr's sons by Þóra. Sigurðr contributes five well-equipped ships to the expedition against King Eysteinn, and is helped in doing so by a 'foster-father' ('fostra'; see Olsen 1906–08, 146, l. 12), a detail which, as Lukman (1976, 10) has ingeniously hinted, may be related to the information given by William of Jumièges that, when the Danish king Lothbrocus expelled his son Bier Costae ferreae and many other young men from his kingdom because of impending overpopulation, he sent Hastingus with him as a 'pedagogus', i.e. a kind of foster-father. In the 1824b text of *Ragnars saga* (see Olsen, 1906–08, 150, ll. 4–6), the expedition against Eysteinn is a turning-point in Sigurðr's career; from then on he accompanies his brothers on all their Viking raids.

Sigurðr ormr-í-auga has been regarded as an important figure in the development of legends about Ragnarr loðbrók, since his name (if not also his nickname, which may have developed later, see de Vries, 1928a, 289–90), is likely to have given rise to the idea of Áslaug's marriage to Ragnarr loðbrók, so that a genealogical link could be established between the latter's descendants and Áslaug's father, Sigurðr the Vǫlsungr, who was, of course, like Ragnarr loðbrók, the slayer of a monstrous serpent. According to de Vries (1928a, 289–90; cf. also 1927c, 86), this link was made in the later stages of a gradual development of contact between the two groups of legends dealing respectively with the Vǫlsungar and with Ragnarr loðbrók, the earlier stages being represented by the story of Ragnarr's death in King Ella's snake-pit, which shows the influence of the story of Gunnarr's death in King Atli's snake-pit. This gradual development, in de Vries's view, was made inevitable by the recurrent motifs characteristic of heroic legend. I would certainly not contest this argument, or deny the importance of the name *Sigurðr* in connection with it, but would add that if the motifs of heroic legend were originally connected with fertility rites, as de Vries also claims (1963, 217–41), and if the origins of the name *Loðbrók* suggested in the previous chapter are acceptable, then the latter name, with its associations of fertility, is likely to have played a part from the very beginning in assisting the growth of contact between the two groups of legends in question, particularly since it has been shown, by de Vries (1956, 455) and others (see Finch, 1965, xxxv-vi), that the stories of Sigurðr and his forbears Sigmundr and Vǫlsungr have their origins in, among other things, cultic rituals associated with creation and fertility.

Though it has little specific content, the heroic precocity of Sigurðr ormr-í-auga, as it appears in *Ragnars saga*, is in a sense more striking than that of either the Ragnarr-figure or the Áslaug-figure in the saga and elsewhere, since (in the 1824b text at least) he reveals his special qualities at the exceptionally early age of three. It is true that, in Saxo's account (IX.iii, 2–4), Regnerus shows exceptional eloquence and intelligence when scarcely out of his cradle, but the precise age at which he does so is not stated (cf. part IVA of the Analysis). With regard to the sons of Regnerus in Saxo, it is the youthful heroism of Iwarus (at the age of seven) that is emphasized (IX.iv, 10), rather than that of Sywardus serpentini oculi. In *Ragnarssona þáttr*, which seems to reflect a stage of the tradition later than that represented by Saxo but earlier than those represented by the 147 and 1824b texts of *Ragnars saga*, Sigurðr ormr-í-auga recites (in ch. 2) the verse which in the saga he recites at the age of three, though in the *þáttr* his age is not specified. I would suggest that the emphasis in *Ragnars saga* on his early emergence as a heroic figure represents a relatively late addition to the story of Ragnarr loðbrók, made at a stage by which Áslaug was established as its actual hero, and Ragnarr as its formal hero (cf. pp. 62 and 90–91, above), when it was felt, perhaps, that neither of these figures exemplified the heroic qualities appropriate to part IVA of the pattern at a sufficiently early age.

(iii) The death of Rǫgnvaldr

It is noteworthy that Rǫgnvaldr dies as a young man; in this respect he meets the requirements of part X of the pattern better than the Ragnarr-figure does (cf. part X of the Analysis). In ch. 8 of *Ragnars saga* his brothers leave him with part of the army to guard their ships while they attack the town of Hvítabœr, because they consider him too young to fight. The boneless Ívarr, who is carried on a shield in the battle, kills with bow and arrow the two sacred cows that have hitherto protected the town from attack. Rǫgnvaldr, who is anxious to be involved, joins the battle with his part of the army only to fall to the enemy, though his brothers are finally victorious. Bjǫrn járnsíða then recites a verse (str. 7 in 1824b) announcing a victory won with swords in Gnípafjǫrðr off Hvítabœr. This story is recorded in full only in the 1824b text of *Ragnars saga*, though it may be assumed that it was also in the 147 text in the latter's original form, since traces of it can be glimpsed in that text, see Olsen 1906–08, 180. The death of Raugnvaldus as a young man is also noted by Arngrímur, who, however, probably derived his information on this point from the Y version of *Ragnars saga*, if not from the 1824b text itself (Benediktsson, 1957, 260–62). In view of this probability, and since the story is not mentioned at all in *Ragnarssona þáttr* (cf. part VII of the Analysis), it would seem likely that it was a relatively late addition to the tradition of Ragnarr loðbrók and his sons. J. de Vries (1928a, 265–66, 293–94), however, while admitting that it shows late features, believes that it formed part of the older *Ragnars saga* drawn on by the compiler of *Ragnarssona þáttr*, but was disregarded by this compiler as irrelevant to his purposes; he further points out that in str. 15 of *Krákumál* mention is made of the death of one Rǫgnvaldr (at no specified age) in the Hebrides. Saxo (IX.iv, 4) notes a victory of Regnerus over the Scanians at Whiteby (a name which corresponds to *Hvítabœr*), and also makes brief mention, in a different context (IX.iv, 17), of a son of Regnerus by Suanlogha named Regnaldus (cf. Rǫgnvaldr), who, like his brothers Withsercus and Ericus, was too young to join his father in an expedition against Sorlus, the successor of Herothus as King of Sweden. Lukman (1976, 12), moreover, has pointed out a possible connection between the story of Rǫgnvaldr's early death and the death of one Orin/Orrum recorded by Gaimar in his *L'estoire des Engleis* of the mid-twelfth century (see Bell, 1960, 87–90, 241; cf. Hardy & Martin 1889, 88–91). This Orin, a nephew of King Elle of Northumbria (cf. part X of the Analysis), was imprisoned by the latter in a tower for his own safety when the Danes marched on York, as a blind man had prophesied he would be the first to fall at their hands. He escaped, however, and was slain as had been prophesied; and Elle himself was defeated and slain.

J. de Vries (1928a, 265) sees a connection between the Rǫgnvaldr of *Ragnars saga* and Rægnald, the Viking king of York from 919 until his death in 921 (Stenton, 1971, 333, 338), who may have been descended from Imhar of Dublin (McTurk, 1977b, 473), a possible historical prototype of Ívarr the boneless (McTurk, 1976, 117–20; cf. ch. I, section (c), above). He accepts that Hvítabœr in the saga, like Whiteby in Saxo, refers to the inland town of Vitaby in south-eastern Skåne, some four kilometres due west of Kivik, but believes that the name originally referred to the Northumbrian harbour town of Whitby, which was much more important than the Scanian town in Viking times and which, with its location on the coast of modern Yorkshire, fits well with his suggestion of a link between Rǫgnvaldr on the one hand and Rægnald of York on the other. In *Krákumál*, the strophes immediately preceding and following the one (str. 15) recording Rǫgnvaldr's death in the Hebrides mention respectively Northumbria ('Norðimbraland') and Waterford ('Veðrarfjǫrðr'), places where Rægnald of York is known to have been active (Stenton, 1971, 333).

Before these arguments can be discussed further, the events of chs. 9–12 of the 1824b text of *Ragnars saga* must be summarized; it may be assumed that, unless otherwise stated, the corresponding events of the 147 text are not significantly different. Ch. 9 begins with a description of King Eysteinn of Sweden, of his daughter Ingibjǫrg, and of the cow Síbilja, whose fearful bellowing protects his country from invaders by driving them insane in battle and causing them to fight among themselves. Believing Kráka to be a mere farmer's daughter, Ragnarr secretly plans to divorce her and marry Ingibjǫrg, but Kráka finds out about this from some birds (an obvious borrowing from the tradition according to which Sigurðr the Vǫlsungr learns of Reginn's proposed treachery from some titmice, see the prose subsequent to str. 31 of the eddaic poem *Fáfnismál* [which dates partly from the tenth century and partly from considerably later, see Sveinsson, 1962, 458–62]; see also *Fáfnismál*, strs. 32–39, and *Vǫlsunga saga*, chs. 19–20). She tells Ragnarr that she is really Áslaug, the daughter of Sigurðr and Brynhildr, and, when Ragnarr does not believe her, prophesies that the son she is soon to bear him will have a snake-like mark around his eye; she implies to Ragnarr that he may indeed leave her for Ingibjǫrg if this does not turn out to be true. When Sigurðr ormr-í-auga ('snake-in-the-eye') is born, Ragnarr recites a verse (str. 8) noting the mark in his eye, and also (in the view of at least two commentators, e.g. Olsen, 1906–08, 200–01, and S. Bugge, quoted by Olsen, 1906–08, 201) comparing him with Sigurðr the serpent-slayer. When the child appears to reject a gold ring which Ragnarr offers him, Ragnarr recites two more verses (strs. 9 and 10), commending him in the first of these for his sturdiness in rejecting the ring, and emphasizing in the second the uniqueness of the mark in his eye. Ragnarr abandons his idea of a Swedish marriage, and Áslaug's true parentage becomes universally known. In ch. 10, Eysteinn takes offence at Ragnarr's failure to claim his daughter's hand, and for no clear reason Ragnarr's two sons by Þóra, Eirekr and Agnarr, decide to invade Sweden. In the course of their preparations Agnarr's ship slips from its launching-rollers and kills a man; and although this occurrence, known as 'roller-reddening' ('hlunrod', i.e. *hlunnroð*) augurs ill, they proceed with the invasion nonetheless. Eysteinn defeats them with the help of Síbilja in a battle in which Agnarr falls and Eirekr is captured. Eysteinn offers Eirekr his daughter in marriage, but Eirekr recites a verse (str. 11) in which he refuses compensation for his brother, as well as Eysteinn's stated offer, and asks to be transfixed by spears. Then in the prose text he asks to die by impalement on

upstanding spears, and Eysteinn reluctantly agrees. Before he dies
he recites three more verses. In the first of these (str. 12) he stresses
the glorious manner of his death; then in the prose he sends a ring
('hring') to Áslaug and in the second verse (str. 13) bequeaths his
valuables ('bauga' = 'valuables' or 'rings') to her, declaring that
she, his stepmother, will tell her sons of his death. In the third verse
(str. 14), finally, he comments on a raven hovering overhead. His
messengers are received in Denmark by Áslaug, since Ragnarr is
away; she tells them in str. 15 that she has heard of the 'hlunnроð'
incident and asks for further news. One of them tells her, in str. 16,
that Þóra's sons are dead, and in the prose goes on to tell her of the
verse recited by Eirekr when he bequeathed the ring ('hringin') to
her. Áslaug is now as anxious for them to be avenged as if they
were her own sons. Of the latter, only the three-year-old Sigurðr
ormr-í-auga is at home with her when the others (Bjǫrn járnsíða,
Hvítserkr, and Ívarr) return and report Rǫgnvaldr's death. In str. 17
(which is apparently not in the 147 text, see Olsen, 1906–08,
182–83), Áslaug comments on their long absence from home and
stresses that Rǫgnvaldr at the time of his death (which clearly took
place before the birth of Sigurðr) was the youngest of her sons; she
then encourages them to avenge Eirekr and Agnarr, pointing out,
in str. 18, that they themselves would not have remained long
unavenged if they had died before those two. She meets with
resistance from Ívarr in particular, however, because of the
apparently invincible cow Síbilja. Sigurðr ormr-í-auga then recites
str. 19, advocating a revenge mission to Sweden, and this verse, as
noted earlier (see p. 96, above), finally persuades his brothers to
change their minds. The three of them recite a verse each (Bjǫrn:
str. 20; Hvítserkr: str. 21; Ívarr: str. 22), expressing in different
ways their determination to avenge their stepbrothers. In ch. 11
preparations are made for the Swedish expedition, Sigurðr ormr-
í-auga's contribution to which has already been described (see
part (ii) of the present section). The brothers sail to Sweden and
Áslaug leads part of the army there by land, adopting the name
Randalín. In ch. 12 they join battle with King Eysteinn, who here
describes Síbilja as a deity ('god vart', Olsen, 1906–08, 147, l. 28).
Ívarr instructs his followers to attempt to drown the cow's noise; to
throw him at her after carrying him as close to her as possible; and
to make him a bow and arrows. He fires an arrow into each of the
cow's eyes, whereupon her noise grows worse than ever; but he is
then thrown onto her back, where he becomes as heavy as a rock

after being as light as a child to throw, and every bone in her body is broken. Eysteinn is slain, and the brothers are victorious.

J. de Vries (1928a, 264–66) notes the close similarity of the story of Ívarr's slaying of Síbilja to the story of his slaying the cows at Hvítabœr in ch. 8, and argues that the Síbilja story, with its Swedish location, arose as a consequence of the name Hvítabœr becoming associated with Vitaby in Skåne rather than with Whitby in Northumbria. He believes that the references to Síbilja in the surviving texts of *Ragnars saga*, including the entire episode of her slaying by Ívarr, represent additions to a story of hostilities between, on the one hand, Ragnarr's sons Eirekr and Agnarr and, on the other, King Eysteinn of Sweden; and that these additions were prompted by the incorporation of Rǫgnvaldr and the story of the cows at Hvítabœr in the tradition of Ragnarr loðbrók and his sons. Now the story of Eysteinn's hostilities with Eirekr and Agnarr appears in *Ragnarssona þáttr*, which reflects earlier stages of the tradition than those represented by the X and Y versions of *Ragnars saga* (see pp. 56, 98, above) and makes no reference to Síbilja or (as was noted earlier, pp. 79 and 98–99) to Rǫgnvaldr and the events at Hvítabœr; it also gives much more logical reasons for the hostilities than the saga appears to do in its surviving forms (see p. 118, below, and cf. p. 100, above). It is true that Arngrímur's account, which partly also reflects a relatively early stage of the tradition (see p. 57, above), refers to a diabolical cow belonging to King Eysteinus and slain by Ivarus, but Arngrímur has almost certainly borrowed here from the Y version of *Ragnars saga* reflected in 1824b (Benediktsson, 1957, 261–62). J. de Vries (1928a, 293–94) claims that the death of Rǫgnvaldr and the slaying by Ívarr of the cows at Hvítabœr, and the references to Síbilja, were all in the older *Ragnars saga* used by the compiler of *Ragnarssona þáttr*, who, however, omitted to mention them in the *þáttr* because their supernatural character, and Rǫgnvaldr's relative unimportance, made them irrelevant to his purposes, which were strictly historical and genealogical. It is indeed likely that *Ragnarssona þáttr* does not reflect the older *Ragnars saga* fully or precisely, and that this version of the saga contained material not reproduced in the *þáttr*; on the other hand it is dangerous to make more assumptions about this material than are warranted by the evidence. There is little or no evidence for assuming that the cows at Hvítabœr, or the cow Síbilja, were included in the tradition at an earlier stage than that represented by the 147 text of *Ragnars saga* (i.e. the X stage). It

is true that *beli*, Eysteinn's nickname in *Ragnarssona þáttr*, may be
related to the verb *belja*, meaning 'to bellow', but there is no reason
to suppose, with Lidén (1928, 361–64), that the nickname's
background included associations with a bellowing cow (see further
section (b) (*iv*) of the present chapter). Furthermore, while the
passages in *Krákumál*, Saxo, and Gaimar noted earlier (see p. 99)
perhaps provide just enough evidence, if considered together with
the surviving texts of *Ragnars saga*, for tentatively assuming that a
story of Rǫgnvaldr's heroism existed in association with the name
Loðbrók in Viking Northumbria (see further pp. 110–13, below), it is
by no means certain that this story of Rǫgnvaldr (or any other) was
available to the redactor of the older *Ragnars saga*.

According to de Vries (1927a, 145–46; 1927c, 81–84) the main
route whereby the Ragnarr loðbrók tradition as it developed in
Scandinavia was supplied with material of English provenance lay
first from Northumbria to the Orkneys (as witness *Háttalykill* and
the Maeshowe inscription on the literary and popular levels
respectively, cf. ch. I, pp. 30–35, above), and then from the Orkneys
to southern Norway, the latter stage perhaps involving the
influence of the Orcadian jarl Rǫgnvaldr Kali (d. 1158), who had
close southern Norwegian ties. In this part of Norway the tradition
also acquired material from other sources and developed orally into
forms close to those in which it survives in its two fullest
manifestations, the Icelandic *Ragnars saga* on the one hand, and
Saxo's Latin account of Regnerus Lothbrog on the other. Saxo,
however, insofar as his account is a relatively disjointed series of
episodes, represents the Norwegian oral tradition more faithfully,
in de Vries's view (1927a, 146–49; 1927c, 88–89), than does *Ragnars
saga*, which in its surviving forms shows an organizing tendency
more characteristic of a written tradition, particularly in its
development of Áslaug as a unifying figure. As will be shown
below, there are reasons for thinking that *Krákumál* was composed
in the second half of the twelfth century, and this poem shows clear
signs of Orcadian connections, even though, as will also be shown,
it may have been composed in the Hebrides (see section (b) (*v*) of
the present chapter). Now *Krákumál*, it should be emphasized, does
not present Rǫgnvaldr as a son of Loðbrók (the speaker of the
poem, see part V of the Analysis) or as dying anywhere near
Whitby; the relevant strophe (15) presents him as one of the
speaker's followers, and as falling in battle against a certain
Herþjófr in the Hebrides. J. de Vries's view (1927a, 126–27; 1928c,

127–28) that Hvítabœr (= Whitby) was mentioned in a lost version of *Krákumál* known to Saxo involves the dangerous assumption, against which I shall argue below (in section (b) (*v*) of this chapter), that the poem existed in a number of versions differing widely from each other and from the version which survives. If, as Guðnason (1963, 270) suggests, the older *Ragnars saga* represented in *Ragnarssona þáttr* was composed before 1230, and if the route by which it derived its information from Northumbria was the one envisaged by de Vries, it is by no means certain that its redactor, if he knew of Rǫgnvaldr at all, would have regarded him as a son of Ragnarr loðbrók, and most unlikely that he would have regarded Hvítabœr as the scene of his death. It seems safest to assume that neither Rǫgnvaldr nor Hvítabœr was mentioned in the older *Ragnars saga*, and that this is the reason why neither of them is mentioned in *Ragnarssona þáttr*. The story of Rǫgnvaldr's death at Hvítabœr, it may be suggested, had not yet become established as part of the tradition, and did not emerge as such until the composition of the X version of *Ragnars saga*.

If this suggestion is accepted, and if, as de Vries believes (1928a, 265–66), the story did originate in Northumbria, it is of course still possible that it reached the X redactor of *Ragnars saga* by the route through the Orkneys and Norway just described. There was however another route whereby information of English provenance relating to Ragnarr loðbrók is likely to have reached Scandinavia: from the Danelaw direct to Denmark. Though de Vries (1927a, 117–18) mentions this route, he does so in connection with Ubbo rather than with Regnaldus (= Rǫgnvaldr; see 1927a, 132–33), and in general attaches relatively little importance to it, pointing out (1927a, 118) that, while the Danish colonizers of England evidently maintained contact with their original homeland (de Vries, 1928b, 163), this contact is unlikely to have remained close or frequent after the death of Cnut the Great in 1035. Linked with his sceptical view of this route as a channel of relevant information is the fact that he finds little evidence that Saxo, in his account of Regnerus Lothbrog, was indebted to local Danish tradition; according to de Vries (1927a, 117–18), Danish contacts with England did not provide a sufficient basis for the development of a specifically Danish tradition of Ragnarr loðbrók. In de Vries's view (1927a, 119–20, 145–49), Saxo, albeit a Dane writing about Danish heroes in his account of Regnerus Lothbrog and his sons, derived the bulk of his information from Norwegian oral tradition, conveyed to him partly by Icelanders. However this may be, de Vries also acknowledges (1927a, 132–33; 1928b, 163) that an awareness of English traditions continued in Denmark well after the time of Cnut the Great, showing itself in, among other things, the work of the Danish chroniclers, which begins in the twelfth century (Mitchell, 1957, 28). Gertz (1917–18, 14) more specifically suggests that personal consultation with one or another of the many English clerics in Denmark by the anonymous author of the *Chronicon Roskildense*, written in *c*.1140, may account for the material with which this chronicle supplements Adam of Bremen's information in dealing with the Viking raids in England. It is true that the *Chronicon Roskildense* does not mention Rǫgnvaldr, whose name is mentioned in a relevant context in Danish historiographical tradition only by Saxo, in the form *Regnaldus*. It does however mention 'rex crudelissimus Normannorum Ywar, filius Lothpardi' (Gertz, 1917–18, 16), here drawing on the passage in which Adam of Bremen names 'Inguar, filius Lodparchi', as the cruellest of a number of Scandinavian kings engaged in piratical raids on France (Trillmich, 1961, 208; cf. ch. I, p. 1, above).

The *Chronicon Roskildense* does not list these kings, as Adam does, but gives the information, not found in Adam's account, that Ywar 'was said to lack bones' ('quem ferunt ossibus caruisse') and that his brothers, who 'ruled the northern peoples' ('aquilonis gentibus prefuerunt') were Ingvar, Vbbi, Byorn and Vlf. After mentioning that Ywar called together the kings of the Danes to destroy the realm of the Franks, the *Chronicon Roskildense* goes on to describe his cruel conquests in Northumbria and East Anglia. The names it gives for Ywar's brothers are also found, in somewhat different form and order, in a passage in the *Annales Lundenses* (Jørgensen, 1920, 53, cf. note s), dating from *c*.1265 (Kristensen, 1969, 156), where they are added to Adam's list of kings and together with them called 'principes' (as opposed to Adam's 'reges') and 'filii Lothbrochi'. This passage, however, shows, according to Kristensen (1969, 121–22, n. 4), the influence of the *Chronicon Roskildense* as well as of Adam; if so, it cannot have the independent value that Olrik (1921, 51) seemed to assign to it. The *Chronicon Roskildense* thus provides the earliest Danish mention of Loðbrók (in the form *Lothpardus*) and of the Vikings it presents as his sons. Though it shows no awareness that Ywar and Ingvar were historically the same person, presenting them instead as brothers, it is the first Scandinavian source to treat Ingvar and Vbbi as brothers, and sons of someone with a name corresponding to *Loðbrók*, a combination which first finds clear expression in the *Annals of St. Neots* (Stevenson, 1959, 138; cf. Whitelock, 1969, 224, 228), written probably at Bury St. Edmunds in the second quarter of the twelfth century (Keynes & Lapidge, 1983, 199). As a son of Ragnarr loðbrók, Ubbi is virtually unknown to West Scandinavian tradition, though it may be pointed out that *Ragnarssona þáttr* (ch. 3), after quoting Sigvatr Þórðarson's *Knútsdrápa* as a source for its information that Ívarr and his brothers had a blood-eagle cut on Ella's back in York (see further ch. III, section (e) below), relates that two illegitimate sons of Ragnarr named Yngvarr and Hústó tortured St. Edmund at Ívarr's command and took over Edmund's kingdom (see Hb, 1892–96, 464). Like the *Chronicon Roskildense*, the *þáttr* shows no awareness that the names *Ívarr* and *Ingvarr* originally designated the same person (they may indeed have been variant forms of the same name, see Janzén, 1947, 81); and it has been suggested (by Finnur Jónsson in Hb, 1892–96, xcii) that *Hústó* is a corrupt form of *Hubbo*, showing the indirect influence of a foreign, and most probably Latin, source. An Ubbi fríski ('the Frisian'), corresponding to the Ubbo Fresicus of Saxo, VII.x, 9 and VIII.ii, 4 and iv, 7, is described by the mid to late thirteenth-century *Sǫgubrot af fornkonungum* (Guðnason, 1982, xl–xli, 65), as well as by Saxo, as fighting for Haraldr hilditǫnn against Hringr at the battle of Brávellir. This figure seems to reflect the historical Hubba (cf. ch. I, section (c) above), remembered as 'Ubba dux Fresciorum' in the *Historia de sancto Cuthberto* (Arnold 1882, 202), written at Chester-le-Street in the mid-tenth century (Craster, 1954, 178), and it is of some interest in the present context to note that the Ubbi of the *Sǫgubrot* slays at Brávellir a certain Rǫgnvaldr hái ('the tall'), also known as Ráðbarðr hnefi (= 'fist' or 'board-game piece'; perhaps a corruption of *nefi* = *nepos*, Lind, 1920–21, 150); that this figure appears briefly in Saxo's Book VIII (iii, 12) as 'Regnaldus ... Rathbarthi nepos', a supporter of Ringo (= Hringr) at Brávellir; and that *Rathbarthus* and *Regnaldus* appear as names of sons of Regnerus Lothbrog, by Thora and Suanlogha respectively, in Saxo's Book IX (iv, 8 and iv, 17; cf. part VII of the Analysis). Now de Vries argues (1927a, 130–34) that Saxo in preparing Book IX derived the notion of Ubbo's martial prowess, and the name *Rathbarthus*, from a lost Icelandic poem based on southern Norwegian legends about the battle of Brávellir. On the origins of Regnaldus in Book IX de Vries is less specific, confining himself

(1927a, 147) to the remark that Saxo knew only the name of this figure, and no story about him. He does however suggest (1927a, 132–33) that Saxo must have known of Ubbo's (i.e. Hubba's) historical association with Inwære/Inguar (cf. McTurk, 1976, 108) in order to have connected him with (Ragnarr) loðbrók in the first place, and that he acquired this knowledge either personally from an English informant or, more probably, from a Danish annalistic source containing material of learned English origin (de Vries could have mentioned here, though he does not do so, the *Chronicon Roskildense*, which, according to Gertz, 1917–18, 8, was occasionally used by Saxo as a source).

There is thus evidence that information about Vikings who came to be regarded as sons of Ragnarr loðbrók passed from England to Denmark through reasonably direct channels after as well as before the death of Cnut the Great, and up to the time of Saxo.

Certain other material relating to Ragnarr loðbrók in the Latin historical writings of mediaeval Denmark may briefly be noted here. Saxo's contemporary Sven Aggesøn, whose *Brevis historia regvm Dacie* was completed soon after 1185 (Gertz, 1917–18, 59), records in the fourth chapter of this work that 'Siuardus, filius Regneri Lothbrog' conquered Denmark, killed its king, and married the king's daughter (Gertz, 1917–18, 106–07). In his twelfth chapter he notes that one of the twelve sons of Haraldus Kesia (Haraldr kesja, 'halberd', d. 1135) was named Biorn Ferrei Lateris ('ironside'; Gertz, 1917–18, 130–31), and the thirteenth-century *Knýtlinga saga* (written after 1235), ch. 82, confirms that Haraldr kesja had a son named Bjǫrn járnsíða (Guðnason, 1982, clxxix, 240). The form in which Sven gives the nickname is the same as that in which Saxo accounts for the *agnomen* of Biornus, son of Regnerus Lothbrog: 'a ferrei lateris firmitate' (IX.iv, 17; cf. Arngrímur's 'Berno Jarnsijda: ferreum latus', Benediktsson, 1950, 465). According to Gertz (1917–18, 59–61), most of Sven Aggesøn's information came to him from Danish oral tradition; he knew the *Chronicon Roskildense*, but made no use of Adam of Bremen or other foreign sources, and was aware only at second hand that Saxo's work was in progress. The *Series ac breuior historia regum Danie*, which is to some extent independent of Saxo though written after 1219 (Storm, 1878, 53–54; Gertz, 1917–18, 149–50), is a list of Danish kings partly supplemented with historical information. According to Storm (1878, 53–56), the *Series* reflects a process whereby information of foreign origin became combined with native Danish traditions in the twelfth century; from Godofridus I (d. 810, here called 'Gøtric hin Giafmildi', 'the generous') down to and including 'Sueno Magnus' (= Sven Estrithsøn, d. 1070) it draws extensively on Adam of Bremen. In Gertz's edition (1917–18, 161–66), where the kings listed are conveniently numbered, 'Gøtric hin Giafmildi' (i.e. Godofridus I) appears as no. 46, and 'Lothbroki, filius Siward Ring' as no. 50. 'Harald Clac, qui et Herioldus dictus est', appears as no. 51, and is followed by 'Eric, filius eius, christianus' (no. 52), under whose name is included part of Adam's passage about Inguar and other Vikings, referred to above, p. 105.

Inguar's name is given here as 'Inguar, filius Lothbroki'; no new names are added to Adam's list; and the extract is immediately followed by another passage from Adam (cf. Trillmich, 1961, 212–13), given in slightly adapted form, and mentioning two Viking leaders connected with Northumbria: Haldan (= Healfdene, the Viking conqueror of Northumbria in 847–76, see ch. I, pp. 41–42, above), and Gundredus (= Guthfrith, d. 895, the first known Viking ruler of Northumbria after Healfdene, cf. Stenton, 1971, 252–53, 262, 433). No. 53 in the *Series* is 'Eric Vngi, filius Eric, christianus', and no. 54 is 'Syward, filius Regneri Lothbroki'. While there is thus some evidence that Saxo was not the first Danish historian to use the names *Ragnarr* and *Loðbrók* in combination, he seems to be the earliest Danish authority for their combined application to a king of Denmark. As pointed out in the first chapter (see pp. 1, 6–7, above), it is of course the Icelander Ari Þorgilsson (d. 1148) who provides the earliest known instance of the two names in combination, in his *Íslendingabók*, written between 1120 and 1133 (Benediktsson, 1968, xvii–xviii, 4; cf. McTurk, 1976, 95); and in view of the relatively late date of the Danish writings in which it occurs, it would be rash to assume that the combination was known in Denmark prior to the time of Ari, or independently of his influence.

Material relating to Ragnarr loðbrók is also found in the *Annales Ryenses* of the second half of the thirteenth century (Jørgensen, 1920, 67; cf. Kristensen, 1969, 30); in the so-called *Compendium Saxonis*, an anonymous 'shorter Saxo' completed between 1342 and 1346 (Gertz, 1917–18, 338–52, 203); and in Cornelius Hamsfort's *Series regum Daniae*, compiled in 1585 (Langebek, 1772, 234). These writings are too late and secondary to be relevant in the present context, though they have recently been referred to by Smyth (1977, 83–100) in support of his view that Saxo, in writing about the death of Regnerus Lothbrog, 'used a Latin manuscript source which was ultimately of Irish origin' (Smyth, 1977, 96). The first two of them agree with Saxo in placing the death of Regnerus in Ireland, while the third states that he was killed in prison (cf. Saxo, IX.iv, 38 and parts VIII and X of the Analysis) after being captured 'ab *Hella* Hybernorum regulo' (Langebek, 1772, 36). Ó Corráin (1979, 290–96) has effectively demonstrated the weakness of Smyth's arguments, though he may have been somewhat hard on the *Compendium Saxonis*, which, being based on Saxo's original manuscript, has some authority for. determining his meaning in cases of difficulty (Olrik & Ræder, 1931, xxxiii). My own view is that the idea of Regnerus's death in Ireland originated with Saxo, who was led to place it there by a confused recollection of Regnerus's earlier expedition against Hella (who is not mentioned in the relevant part of the *Annales Ryenses* but who seems to appear as an English king in Saxo and the *Compendium*, if not quite so unambiguously as Ella in *Ragnars saga* and the *þáttr*, see Gertz, 1917–18, 342, 346, 347–48; part X of the Analysis; and Herrmann, 1922, 648, nn. 1, 2; 649, n. 1). According to Saxo's own account of this expedition (IX.iv, 34–35), Regnerus defeated Hella at York (or perhaps Norwich, see Herrmann 1922, 648, n. 2), and after a year in England proceeded to Ireland, slew its king, Melbrictus, and besieged Dublin.

It is possible that de Vries has underestimated the importance of the relatively direct route from England to Denmark as a channel of information relating to Ragnarr loðbrók and his sons. He does not in any case seem to consider the possibility that relevant information conveyed by this route was also conveyed from Denmark to southern Norway, and there made its contribution to the oral tradition which in his view supplied *Ragnars saga* with the bulk of its material (see p. 103, above). He does suggest (de Vries, 1928a, 266–69; 1927c, 84), however, that the subject-matter of chs. 13 and 14 of the 1824b text of the saga, which deal respectively with the conquest of Vífilsborg by Ragnarr's sons and with their dissuasion in Lúna by an old man from proceeding as far as Rome (and in which there is hardly a grain of historical truth, as Storm, 1878, 126–29, and de Vries, 1928a, 266–69; 1928b, 122–25, agree), derives from stories heard and repeated by Scandinavian pilgrims travelling southwards through Europe on their way to the Holy Land, and northwards by the same route on their return. The Icelander Abbot Nicholas of Þverá (d. 1159) makes it clear in his pilgrim itinerary (preserved in AM 194 8vo of the late fourteenth century) that stories of Germanic and Scandinavian heroes (including the sons of Loðbrók) had become attached to Vífilsborg, Lúna, and other places on this overland route by the time he made his own pilgrimage in *c*.1150. Between Poddubrunnar (Paderborn) and Meginzoborg (Mainz), according to Nicholas (Kålund, 1908, 13–16), is Gnitaheiðr, 'where Sigurðr fought against Fáfnir' ('er Sigurdr va ath Fabni'); this place, mentioned as the scene of the encounter in several eddaic sources (see Neckel, 1962, 165, 176, 180) and in *Volsunga saga* (ch. 13), has not been certainly identified (see Magoun, 1944, 323–24; Rossenbeck, 1974, 243–48). Nicholas also mentions Vivilsborg (i.e. Wiflisburg or Avenches, a town in Switzerland), saying that 'it was large before the sons of Loðbrók destroyed it, but now it is small' ('hon var mikil, adr Lodbrok[ar]-synir brutu hana, enn nu er hon litil'). He mentions Lúna (modern Luni) in northern Italy, drawing attention to the nearby stretches of sand in which, 'some people claim, is the serpent-pit into which Gunnarr was put' ('I Lunu-sòndum kalla sumir menn ormgard, er Gunnar var i settr'), and says that in Luka (the Tuscan town of Lucca), which according to him is a day's journey from Lúna, there is a crucifix ('roda', i.e. *róða*) 'which has spoken twice; on one occasion it gave its shoe to a poor man, and on another it bore witness on behalf of a slandered person' ('hon hefir II sinnum mellt, annat sinn gaf hon sko sinn aumum manni, en annath sinn bar hon vitni rẻgdum manni'). Lukman (1976, 14) has noted a likely connection between the idea of a crucifix giving its shoe to a poor man and the story in ch. 14 of the 1824b text of *Ragnars saga* of the old man (who also describes himself as a beggar, 'stafkarl' see Olsen, 1906–08, 153, l. 7) telling Ragnarr's sons that he has all but worn out two pairs of iron shoes in travelling to Lúna from Rome.

From Nicholas's account it appears that Icelandic pilgrims on the outward journey sailed first from Iceland to Norway, and from there to Denmark; no place of arrival or departure in Norway is specified, but it is clear that the pilgrims assembled in Denmark at Álaborg (Ålborg), the starting-point of the long journey by land to southern Italy, where they took ship for Jerusalem (Kålund, 1908, 13–20). As well as being the first clearly designated point on the pilgrim-route as Nicholas describes it (Kalund, 1908, 13), Álaborg is also the last place he mentions at the end of his account, where he gives a brief description of the return journey (Kålund, 1908, 23). It is reasonable to assume that, for Icelandic pilgrims following Nicholas's route—one of the so-called 'eastern routes' (Springer, 1950, 102–06)—the homeward journey, like the outward one, was by way of Norway. According to chs. 89–90 of the *Orkneyinga saga* of the early thirteenth century (Guðmundsson, 1965, viii, 236–38), Rǫgnvaldr Kali himself visited Norway after travelling overland from southern Italy to Denmark on his return to the Orkneys from the Holy Land, where he had travelled (chs. 86–88) mainly by sea. It was an Icelander, Þórhallr Ásgrímsson, who shipped Rǫgnvaldr and his followers back to the Orkneys on his way home, and who doubtless brought with him to Iceland much information about Rǫgnvaldr's pilgrimage, which took place in 1151–53 (Guðmundsson, 1965, lxxviii, lxxxviii).

It will be clear from the foregoing remarks that, while there is little evidence for a Danish tradition of Ragnarr loðbrók existing wholly independently of West Norse tradition, there is some evidence that relevant information travelled direct from England to Denmark independently of the route to Norway through the Orkneys, and that this information could then have been brought from Denmark to Norway by West Scandinavian pilgrims returning homewards. It may be assumed that de Vries is right in seeing a connection between Rægnald of York and Rǫgnvaldr, son of Ragnarr loðbrók (cf. p. 99, above). It may also be suggested that Rægnald was already thought of in connection with the name *Loðbrók* in tenth-century Northumbria. The earliest surviving English reference to Loðbrók (as far as I know) is that found in the twelfth-century *Annals of St. Neots*, and referred to earlier (p. 106, above); this source, it is true, does not connect the name specifically with Northumbria, and later English authorities link it not with Northumbria but with East Anglia (Whitelock, 1969, 227–30). J. de Vries (1928b, 132–33) has however suggested that the lost *Gesta Francorum*, referred to by Adam of Bremen (Trillmich, 1961, 208) as the source for his information about Inguar, son of Lodparchus (i.e. Loðbrók), may derive this information from the lost *Gesta Anglorum*, also referred to by Adam (Trillmich, 1961, 212, 258), which, it has recently been suggested (Trillmich, 1961, 148), were of Northumbrian origin. Furthermore, Rægnald's conquest of York in 919 must have meant that he was thought of in connection with Iguuar, the Viking conqueror of York in 866 (according to Æthelweard, see Campbell, 1962, 35) and a historical prototype of Ívarr, son of Ragnarr loðbrók (McTurk, 1976, 119; cf. ch. I, section (c) above). Rægnald's partly Irish background (cf. p. 99, above) must also have meant that he was thought of in connection with Imhar of Dublin, whose grandson he may indeed have been (McTurk, 1977b, 473), and who was probably identical with Iguuar (= Iuuar; see ch. I, pp. 40–46, and cf. McTurk, 1976, 117–23).

It may be suggested that *Krákumál* on the one hand, and, on the other, Saxo, the 147 and 1824b texts of *Ragnars saga* (as opposed to *Krákumál*, cf. pp. 53, 54 56, above, and 132–33, below), and Arngrímur (who is here following the Y version of the saga reflected in 1824b, cf. p. 98, above), represent two separate branches of an originally Northumbrian tradition of Rægnald, which connected him with the name *Loðbrók* from the start. *Krákumál* represents what may be called a western branch, which spread in the direction of the Hebrides and the Orkneys, while the other authorities represent an eastern branch which, after developing in Northumbria independently of the western branch, spread to Scandinavia by way of Denmark.

The western branch of the tradition, represented by *Krákumál*, obviously connects Rægnald in some way with Loðbrók, but not explicitly as that person's son, and also seems to connect him with Northumbria and Ireland, to judge from the respective references to those places in the strophes of *Krákumál* immediately preceding and following the one (str. 15) dealing with Rǫgnvaldr's death, which the poem clearly places in the Hebrides. The eastern branch, on the other hand, seems at first to have emphasized the untimeliness rather than the specific location of Rægnald's death, an emphasis which is perhaps to be explained by the brevity of his reign. Since a Danish attack on York forms the background to Gaimar's story of King Ella's nephew Orin/Orrum (see pp. 99, 103, above), who, like Rǫgnvaldr in the saga, was killed as a result of joining a battle from which he had been excluded for his own safety, it is possible that some such story was already attached to Rægnald in Northumbria. This eastern branch then travelled to Denmark, as is shown by Saxo's brief reference to Regnaldus (see p. 99, above) being too young to join his father in fighting against King Sorlus of Sweden; Saxo thus also represents a stage by which Rægnald had come to be regarded as a son of Ragnarr loðbrók, though he gives no account of the death of Regnaldus. This branch of the tradition was then conveyed from Denmark to Norway by the route described above (pp. 108–10), and there became fully integrated with traditions of Ragnarr loðbrók; this seems to have been a relatively late development, however, since *Krákumál* (drawing on material from Norway as well as from the British Isles, see de Vries 1928a, 291–92; 1927c, 84–85) shows no traces of the eastern branch's influence, and there is no evidence that Rǫgnvaldr was even mentioned in the older *Ragnars saga* reflected in *Ragnarssona þáttr* (cf. Guðnason, 1982, 76, n. 11). In the early stages of its development in Scandinavia, when memories of Rægnald's Northumbrian connections were still fresh, the eastern branch of the tradition, it may be assumed, located his death at Whitby, a harbour-town well known to Danes and Norwegians; later, however, when these connections were forgotten, it came to be thought that the Scanian town of Vitaby was the place in question, and this is presumably the Whiteby of Saxo's account and the Hvítabœr of the 1824b text of *Ragnars saga*—though in Saxo's account, it must be remembered, the town is mentioned in connection with Regnerus rather than with Regnaldus, and not in any context of a heroic death. It may finally be noted that the phrase 'fyr Hvítabœ útan' occurring in str. 7 of the 1824b text of *Ragnars saga*, and meaning 'outside' or 'off' Hvítabœr, may just possibly preserve a memory that the town in question was a coastal one.

   It was noted earlier (p. 102) that de Vries assigns the story of Rǫgnvaldr's death at Hvítabœr, together with the two stories of Ívarr's cow-slayings, to relatively early stages in the development of the Ragnarr loðbrók tradition. The reasons for this are apparently related to his view that, in its earliest stages, the tradition was more preoccupied with the sons of Loðbrók than with their father, whose prominence developed only secondarily (de Vries, 1915, 194; 1928a, 264). This is indeed likely to have been the case; on the other hand, it has emerged from the foregoing discussion that, although Rægnald of York, from an early, Northumbrian stage of the development of traditions about him, appears to have been associated in some way with the name *Loðbrók*, he does not appear to have been counted among the sons of Loðbrók at that early stage. The general point must also be made that a preoccupation with the sons as opposed to the father in the relevant texts should not always be taken as indicating an early stage in the development of the Ragnarr loðbrók tradition. It is admittedly likely that, in the very earliest stages, the Viking activities of the sons were of primary importance, and that an interest in the father's career did not develop until after the notion of his death had been introduced as an acceptable explanation of these activities. Once the father's career was reasonably well established, however, as for example in *Krákumál*, which appears to have drawn largely on southern Norwegian tradition for its account of Loðbrók's heroic career (de Vries 1928a, 291–92), a stage was evidently reached at which, in de Vries's own words (1927c, 85), 'man bestrebt war für die Loðbróksöhne mehr Heldentaten zu erfinden.' There seems to be no reason why the introduction of the cow-slaying episodes, and the final absorption by the tradition of a story locating at Hvítabœr the death of Rǫgnvaldr, son of Ragnarr loðbrók, should not be regarded as examples of this later tendency.

I would therefore agree with de Vries that Rǫgnvaldr's connection with the Ragnarr loðbrók tradition is of early, Northumbrian origin; but would conclude that the stories of Rǫgnvaldr's death at Hvítabœr and of the cow-slayings by Ívarr arose at later stages of the tradition's development than de Vries (1928a, 293–94) maintained (see p. 102, above); these stories, in my view, did not form part of the older *Ragnars saga* represented by *Ragnarssona þáttr*, but made their first appearance in the X version of the saga. The untimeliness of Rǫgnvaldr's death, emphasized by what has here been called the eastern branch of the Rægnald tradition, no doubt proved useful to the Ragnarr loðbrók tradition in stressing more than was possible in the case of Ragnarr's death the idea of a hero dying young (in accordance with part X of the biographical pattern, see that part of the Analysis), while the purpose of introducing the cow-slaying episodes may have been to provide one of Ragnarr's sons with an achievement comparable to that with which Ragnarr so well exemplifies part VI of the pattern: his slaying of Þóra's serpent.

(iv) Ívarr's cow-slayings

If the cow-slayings in *Ragnars saga* seem poor or ludicrous imitations of Ragnarr's slaying of the serpent, this is surely because a cow, with its docile, milk-producing qualities, is much less readily imaginable as hostile to man than a snake. There is evidence, in fact, that the cow was regarded as symbolic of fertility in ancient Scandinavia. Little can be made of the cows which draw the chariot of the fertility-goddess Nerthus in ch. 40 of Tacitus's *Germania* (as shown in the last chapter, see p. 17, above), since these are probably to be regarded first and foremost as draught-animals rather than as representative of the deity's special attributes (de Vries, 1956, 368). More relevant here, though to be treated with caution because of their much later recording, are two accounts by Snorri Sturluson (1179–1241). One of these, in *Óláfs saga Tryggvasonar*, chs. 63–64 (Aðalbjarnarson, 1941, 311–14), tells of King Ǫgvaldr, after whom Ǫgvaldsnes on the south-west Norwegian island of Kǫrmt (Karmøy) was named, and who used to make sacrifices to a cow which he kept with him wherever he went, finding it healthy to drink her milk. The other account, in *Gylfaginning*, chs. 5–6 (F. Jónsson, 1931a, 12–16), tells how the primeval cow Auðumla was formed, like the giant Ymir, from melting hoar-frost, and how she nourished Ymir with her milk, deriving her own nourishment from licking salty ice-blocks. This latter process brought about the creation of Búri, the father of Borr, who in turn became the father (with Bestla, daughter of the giant Bǫlþorn) of Óðinn, Vili, and Vé. These three killed Ymir, and it was from Ymir's corpse, as is told in other sources as well as by Snorri (see pp. 51–52, above), that the earth was created. According to Turville-Petre (1964, 277), 'it cannot be doubted that Snorri's tale of Auðumbla [*sic*] is, in essentials, age-old'. He mentions parallels from ancient Iran, India, and Egypt, as also does de Vries (1957, 365–66), who specifically refers in this connection to the cow in Hindu mythology known as Surabhi. This cow, 'the fountain of milk and curds', was produced, according to Book I, ch. 9, of the *Vishñu Puráña* (Wilson, 1972, 64–66) at the churning of the ocean, an event which formed part of the secondary stage (known as Pratisarga) of the creation. The gods applied to Vishnu for help against their enemies, the demons known as the Asuras or Daityas, and he advised the gods to make peace with the demons and enlist their help in preparing the ambrosia known as Amrita, which would confer immortality; he would see to it that the demons had no share in the drink once it was made. Gods and demons were to throw herbs into the sea, which evidently consisted of milk, and then churn the sea, using the mountain Mandara as a churning-stick, and the serpent Vásuki as a rope to activate the stick. In carrying out this advice the gods held the tail of the serpent; the demons, however, held its head and neck, and were distressed by the flames issuing from its hood. Vishṇu himself helped the gods by acting as a pivot to the mountain-stick in the form of a tortoise. From the ocean thus churned emerged, among other beings, the cow Surabhi. The demons seized the ambrosia, but Vishṇu recovered it and gave it to the gods, who after drinking it and thus acquiring new energy soon defeated their enemies. The idea of a serpent encircling a mountain, and the references to its head and tail, are of course reminiscent of the world-serpent in Old Norse mythology, and Þóra's serpent in *Ragnars saga* (cf. part VI of the Analysis).

Hindu mythology knows moreover of a cow which, as well as providing sustenance, also shows a warlike capacity comparable to that of Síbilja in *Ragnars saga*. The *Ramayana*, Book I, cantos 52–56 (Griffith, 1870, 224–42), tells of a 'cow of plenty' belonging to the sage Vasishṭha; this cow provided the sumptuous food for the banquet with which Vasishṭha entertained King Viśvámitra at his hermitage. Viśvámitra coveted the cow on this occasion and offered for it vast numbers of elephants, horse-drawn chariots, and heifers, all of which, however, Vasishṭha refused. When Viśvámitra then tried to take the cow by force, the cow looked for aid to Vasishṭha, lowing in her distress, and then created at his command, lowing again as she did so, several hordes of warriors who proceeded to attack Viśvámitra and his followers, but were defeated and slain. The cow then lowed once more and produced still more warriors from various parts of her body, and this time Viśvámitra was defeated.

It is not clear whether this latter cow is to be identified with Surabhi, or regarded as closely related to her (see Dowson, 1968, 147, 218, 309, 366). One of the Sanskrit names by which she appears to have been known, however, is *Savala*, meaning 'piebald, variegated', a name which, according to Hüsing (1906, 143–44, cf. Mudrak, 1943, 127), is likely to have become known to the

Germanic peoples by way of the Middle Iranian language known as Saka, in which the form of the name would have corresponded closely to *Síbilja*. If this argument can be accepted, then it may be suggested that the story of Síbilja in *Ragnars saga*, and the name *Síbilja* itself, have their ultimate origins in Hindu mythology. Lidén's view (1928, 361–64) of the name's origin should not be disregarded, however; after rejecting the theory that it derives from the Latin name *Sibylla* he argues that the forms of the name in 1824b (*Sibilia*) and 147 (*Sibyli[a]*) suggest that the second element reflects the verb *bylja*, meaning 'to boom, roar, echo', while the first is an adverbial prefix meaning 'constantly' or 'powerfully'. Because of the manuscript forms he chooses *bylja* in preference to the verb *belja*, meaning 'to bellow', as the basis of the name's second element, even though, as he admits, the two verbs are closely related, semantically and phonologically. He identifies Eysteinn's nickname, *beli*, with the giant's name *Beli*, oblique forms of which, occurring in the poetic and prose Eddas, show it to be related to the verb *belja*; no oblique forms of the nickname appear in *Ragnarssona þáttr* or the *Ragnars saga* manuscripts, however. On this basis he posits, as the original form of the Eysteinn beli episode in *Ragnarssona þáttr*, a story about a bellowing giant accompanied by a booming cow.

It is not certain that Eysteinn's nickname *beli* is in fact identifiable with the giant's name *Beli*, and so related to the verb *belja*, meaning 'to bellow'; the nickname may rather be related to the noun *belgr*, meaning 'animal-skin' or 'skin-bag' (Lidén, 1928, 364, n. 2). The fact remains, however, that, in its nominative form (the only form in which it occurs in the relevant texts), the nickname is identical with the nominative form of the giant's name, and may well have conveyed the idea of bellowing, whether accurately or not. It would not be surprising, therefore, if the nickname attracted stories about cows or oxen, since it is apparently in connection with these animals that the verb *belja* is most often used (Fritzner, 1973, I, 124). It is of some interest to note that it is only in *Ragnarssona þáttr*, where no cows are mentioned, that the nickname *beli* is at all prominent; it occurs twice there (Hb, 1892–96, 459, l. 20, 461, l. 4), only once in what can be read of the 147 text of *Ragnars saga* (Olsen, 1906–08, 183, Bl. 9r, l. 26), and not at all in the 1824b text; this may suggest that the nickname was felt to be superfluous once the bellowing function suggested by it had been taken over by a cow. Now it is clear that the Síbilja story, and the verse dealing with the fight at Hvítabœr (corresponding to str. 7 in the 1824b text), were both in the 147 text of *Ragnars saga* in its original form; and it may be assumed that the cow-episode in the Hvítabœr story also originally formed part of the 147 text, as indicated earlier (see p. 98, above). As they appear in 1824b, the cows at Hvítabœr and the cow Síbilja provide an example of the law of oral narrative known as progression (Olrik, 1921, 69; cf. McTurk, 1981b, 106), whereby a hero's adventures become progressively more difficult: the Hvítabœr cows appear only briefly, and Ívarr despatches them with little difficulty, whereas Síbilja's activities are reported at some length in three separate instances (in chs. 9, 10, and 12 respectively), before the complex process whereby Ívarr kills her (in ch. 12) is finally described.

It may be concluded that the X version of *Ragnars saga* represented by 147 derived the episode of the cows at Hvítabœr and the Síbilja story from the same source, a tale orally current in Scandinavia dealing with supernatural and fearsome cows, one of which was called Síbilja, and which were defeated by a hero in a series of increasingly difficult encounters. The name *Síbilja* was originally the Sanskrit name meaning 'piebald', but because of the form in which it had reached Scandinavia (by the route suggested by Hüsing, as above, p. 115), it was interpreted there as meaning 'constantly booming or bellowing', as Lidén's arguments (see p. 116, above) help to show, and was so understood by the X redactor of *Ragnars saga*. He must have been tempted to include the story by, among other things, the apparent appropriateness of linking a cow of this name with a king nicknamed 'beli'. If the quality of his work may be judged on the basis of the 1824b text of the saga, he appears to have adapted the story to its new environment with considerable skill, using it to form a link between the story of Rǫgnvaldr's death at Hvítabœr and that of Eysteinn's hostilities with Eirekr and Agnarr, and thus assisting the process whereby the former story came to be integrated with the Ragnarr loðbrók tradition. This process seems to have been carried further by the Y redactor, with his inclusion in the saga of str. 17 of the 1824b text, a strophe which appears neither in *Ragnarssona þáttr* nor apparently in the 147 text of the saga (cf. p. 101, above). This strophe, which Áslaug recites just before encouraging her sons to avenge Eirekr and Agnarr, refers in its second half to Rǫgnvaldr's valour and relative youthfulness at the time of his death.

(v) The deaths of Eirekr and Agnarr

Before the death of Eirekr can be discussed, it is necessary to examine the origins of the story of his and Agnarr's hostilities with Eysteinn. As indicated above (p. 102), *Ragnarssona þáttr* (ch. 2) preserves an older version of this story than does either of the surviving texts of *Ragnars saga*, and gives a more logical explanation of the hostilities than the saga does. In the saga, the hostilities arise with the invasion of Sweden by Eirekr and Agnarr at the beginning of ch. 10 of the 1824b text. Why they undertake the invasion is not clear, however; it might indeed be thought more appropriate for Eysteinn to be invading their own homeland at this stage of the narrative, since Ragnarr, their father, has just offended Eysteinn (see p. 100, above). In the *þáttr*, on the other hand, the hostilities arise logically enough. Fearing that his sons may extend their domains into Sweden, which forms part of his own kingdom, Ragnarr makes Eysteinn beli a surrogate king of Uppsvíariki (the territory of the northern Swedes), instructing him to defend that region if necessary. When Ragnarr is away in the east, his two sons by Þóra, Eiríkr and Agnarr, try to persuade Eysteinn to become subject to them rather than to Ragnarr, and Eiríkr asks to marry Eysteinn's daughter, who is here called Borghildr. After consultation with his countrymen Eysteinn decides on a hostile response to Eiríkr and Agnarr, and defeats them in a battle in which Agnarr falls and Eiríkr is captured. Eysteinn then offers Eiríkr compensation for Agnarr, and Borghildr's hand in marriage, but Eiríkr prefers death to reconciliation after suffering such a defeat and chooses to die by impalement on spears over the bodies of the slain. Before dying he recites two verses, corresponding respectively to strs. 11 and 13 in the 1824b text of *Ragnars saga*. Áslaug receives in Selund (i.e. Sjælland) the news of his and Agnarr's deaths, and announces it to her sons by Ragnarr, namely Bjǫrn, Hvítserkr, Sigurðr, and Ívarr, the first two of whom are playing a board-game at the time (as they apparently also are in the 147 as opposed to the 1824b text of the saga, see Olsen, 1906–08, xcii, 183; see further ch. III, section (g), below). After a discussion consisting of five verses, corresponding in wording, order, and attribution to strs. 18–22 of the 1824b text (see pp. 55–56, 101, above), the brothers leave by sea for Sweden while Áslaug proceeds there by land, taking with her fifteen hundred knights and adopting the name *Randalín*. The five then join forces in Sweden and defeat Eysteinn in a great battle.

It is noticeable that, in the *þáttr* as well as in the saga, considerably more is made of Eiríkr's (Eirekr's) death than of Agnarr's. Agnarr, on the other hand, is mentioned in both *Háttalykill* and *Krákumál*, whereas Eirekr is mentioned in neither. As already noted (see pp. 40–41, 90, above), there is a reference to 'Agnarr's brother' in a fragmentary strophe (8b) of *Háttalykill*; it is almost certainly Ívarr the boneless, however, who is meant here. The correct reading of the *vísuorð* immediately following this reference is apparently *án gǫrvallra beina* (E. A. Kock, 1940, 22), meaning 'without any bones at all', and the expression *enn beinlausi*, 'the boneless one', is used in the immediately preceding strophe, 8a, which is true that Ívarr is not presented as a full brother of Agnarr in *Ragnars saga*, *Ragnarssona þáttr* or Arngrímur's account (cf. part VII of the Analysis); but Ivarus and Agnerus appear as *fratres* in Saxo (IX.iv, 8), where they are listed among the sons of Regnerus by Thora; and the word *bróðir* (used by *Háttalykill*, str. 8b, in the oblique form *bróður*) need not in any case mean 'brother on both sides' (see Cleasby & Vigfusson, 1957, 82). In *Krákumál*, in which Eirekr nowhere appears (see further pp. 123, 125–33, below), Agnarr is mentioned in str. 17, where the speaker reports that his son Agnarr was slain by a certain Egill. It would thus seem that Agnarr was originally more prominent than Eirekr in the tradition of Ragnarr loðbrók, and later became less so. According to de Vries (1928a, 281–84), Agnarr was borrowed from this tradition into that of Hrólfr kraki ('pole'), and gave his name to the Agnerus (son of Ingellus) who, in Book II (vi, 9–10) of Saxo's *Gesta Danorum*, seeks to marry Ruta, sister of Rolvo (= Hrólfr), but is slain at his own wedding-feast by Biarco, and dies smiling. This last feature, which is reminiscent of the closing words of *Krákumál*: 'læjandi skalk deyja' ('I shall die laughing'), was also borrowed, in de Vries's view, from the Ragnarr loðbrók tradition, where Agnarr could no longer remain prominent after becoming part and parcel of the tradition of Hrólfr kraki.

As for the position of Eirekr in the Ragnarr loðbrók tradition, de Vries (1928a, 278–81) argues with great ingenuity for a connection here between this tradition on the one hand and, on the other, the story of Ericus Disertus ('the eloquent'), which forms a major source for Book V of Saxo's *Gesta Danorum*. This Ericus has in common with the Eirekr of the Ragnarr loðbrók tradition a father named Regnerus (= Ragnarr) and a stepmother named Craca

(= Kráka). The starting-point of de Vries's argument is the fact that, in *Ragnars saga* (in 147 as well as 1824b), Kráka-Áslaug differs from the 'cruel stepmother' figure of folklore in her evident sorrow at the loss of her stepsons and her anxiety to see them avenged. She seems indeed more concerned for revenge on their behalf than on that of her own son, Rǫgnvaldr (see Olsen, 1906–08, 141–47; cf. 182–84). Now the Craca of Saxo's Book V shows a comparable concern for the welfare of her stepson Ericus, for the following reasons (V.ii, 6–9): she had prepared for him and for her son Rollerus a stew, made partly from the saliva of snakes, which she served in two sections, one darker than the other, intending that her own son, Rollerus, should eat the darker section. It was in fact her stepson Ericus who did so, however, and as a result he acquired increased understanding and eloquence, including an ability to understand the language of animals. When Craca realized what had happened, she at once became concerned that Ericus, now possessed of the gifts she had intended for her son, should help and protect the latter, and assured him that by calling her name in time of trouble he could obtain supernatural aid for them both. She is as good as her word later in Book V (iii, 34), when Ericus invokes her aid while engaged in the deception whereby he wins from King Gotarus of Norway the latter's daughter, Alvilda, as a bride for King Frotho III of Denmark.

J. de Vries (1928a, 279–80) lists further similarities between the story of Ragnarr loðbrók and that of Ericus Disertus as evidence for the interaction of the two stories during their parallel growth: firstly, in *Ragnarssona þáttr*, the 1824b text of *Ragnars saga*, and certain of the ballads (see part V of the Analysis and cf. ch. III, section (b), below), the Ragnarr-figure treats his protective costume with tar and sand when preparing to fight the serpent, and in Saxo's Book V (iii, 12) Ericus smears the soles of his leather sandals with resin and sand to give them a firmer grip in a battle to be fought on ice; secondly, in *Ragnars saga* (1824b, ch. 10, and the corresponding part of 147, see Olsen, 1906–08, 137, 141 and 182), Eirekr and Agnarr are undeterred by the 'roller-reddening' ('hlunnroð') incident (see p. 100, above) from invading Sweden, even though it is a bad omen, and in Saxo's Book V (iii, 1) Ericus stumbles on leaving his ship and interprets this (it would appear rightly) as a good omen; thirdly, in the saga (1824b, ch. 13, and the corresponding part of 147, see Olsen, 1906–08, 151–52 and 185–86), the sons of Ragnarr loðbrók prepare to take Vífilsborg by carrying up to it bundles of branches from a nearby forest and setting fire to them before attacking the castle with catapults, and in Saxo's Book V (iv, 1) Ericus defeats the Slavs by first trapping them with the use of some ships camouflaged by leafy branches and then catapulting them with stones; fourthly, in the *þáttr* and the saga (in 1824b and probably also 147, see Olsen, 1906–08, 146–47, 184), the expedition to Sweden to avenge Eirekr and Agnarr is divided into two groups, one of which proceeds there by land and the other by sea, and in Saxo's Book V (iv, 3) Ericus advises Frotho to divide an expedition against the Slavs in the same way; fifthly, in the *þáttr* and (it may be assumed, cf. ch. III, pp. 178–82, below) both texts of the saga, Áslaug in the role of Randalín gives support and protection to her sons in leading part of the Swedish expedition to avenge her stepsons, and in Saxo's Book V (ii, 9; iii, 30–31, 34), as shown above, Craca promises and gives supernatural aid to her stepson Ericus in time of need; sixthly and finally, the eloquence which, in Saxo's Book IX (iii, 2–4), Regnerus shows as a boy, and the ingenuity with which, in *Ragnars saga* (1824b, ch. 5; cf. also 147, Olsen 1906–08, 178, bottom footnote) and the relevant texts of the *Ragnars kvæði* (see part IVA of the Analysis), Kráka responds to the riddling-conditions imposed on her by Ragnarr, are comparable to the eloquence and wit shown by Ericus in Saxo's Book V (ii, 2 to the end) at all stages of his career.

Whether or not it is possible to agree with de Vries that these points provide cumulative evidence of contact between the two stories, there can be little doubt that the agreement between them as to the names of Eirekr/Ericus and his father and stepmother does provide evidence of such contact. On the difficult question as to which of the two stories is primarily the lender or the borrower, de Vries does not commit himself fully, though he argues that, as far as the stepmother's fondness for her stepson is concerned, the story of Ericus Disertus is likely to be the lender, since this feature is more logically motivated in that story than in the story of Ragnarr loðbrók. While this last consideration may be valid, the argument itself is weakened by the fact that in *Ragnars saga* it is not, as de Vries (1928a, 278) seems to suggest, in her rôle as 'Kráka, später als Aslaug anerkannt' that Áslaug laments and seeks to avenge the deaths of her stepsons; it is in fact after her true name and parentage have been acknowledged that she does so, as has already been shown (see pp. 99–102, above). Furthermore, de Vries fails to reckon adequately with the fact, also indicated earlier (see p.

118, above), that Áslaug's rôle as an avenging stepmother is well established in *Ragnarssona páttr*, which reflects an older *Ragnars saga* than either of those represented in 147 and 1824b, and makes no mention of Kráka. It may also be noted here that the Craca of Saxo's Book V and the Áslaug of *Ragnars saga* differ from each other as stepmothers in that the former is active on behalf of her stepson exclusively during his lifetime, while the latter is active on behalf of her stepsons exclusively after their deaths.

A more persuasive argument of de Vries's (1928a, 278–79), in my view, is that the name *Kráka* has a more appropriate application in the story of Ericus Disertus than in that of Ragnarr loðbrók, and is thus likely to have passed from the former story to the latter, rather than the other way round. In the older of the two groups of *þulur* preserved in manuscripts of Snorri's *Edda*, that is, in the group dating probably from before 1200 (see F. Jónsson, 1923, 179; Lie, 1950, 165–66), the name *Kráka* occurs in a list of 'trǫllkvenna heiti', i.e. poetic appellations for giantesses or witches (Jónsson, 1912b, 659–60; the same list, incidentally, includes the name *Gríma*, which is also the name of Áslaug's none too benevolent foster-mother in the 1824b text of *Ragnars saga*, see parts IIIC and IX of the Analysis and cf. p. 61, above). Furthermore, Norwegian folk-tradition (see K. Liestøl, 1917, 107) has examples of the name *Kráka* being used for the evil stepmother on the one hand, and for the ugly sister on the other, in tales of the Cinderella type; the ugly sister figure is also called Krákudóttir ('Kráka's daughter') in Faroese folk-tales. In the story of Ericus Disertus, as de Vries (1928a, 278–79) points out, Craca's preparation of the magic stew seems a wholly appropriate activity for a 'trǫllkona', and although she is presented in that story as a benevolent stepmother, it should be remembered that her benevolence only becomes concentrated on her stepson when it emerges that he, rather than her own son, has eaten the darker and clearly more beneficial section of the stew.

Although de Vries, as already indicated, is relatively non-committal on the nature of the relationship between the tradition of Ericus Disertus and that of Ragnarr loðbrók, what seems to emerge from his remarks is the conclusion that Eirekr and Kráka were borrowed *together* from the former tradition into the latter (see de Vries, 1928a, 278–92; cf. 1927c, 87). As far as I can see, this view involves at least three difficulties, which de Vries has not dealt with wholly satisfactorily. These are as follows: first, the fact that Eirekr plays a significant rôle in *Ragnarssona páttr*, which, however, makes no mention of Kráka, even though it presents Áslaug-Randalín, the daughter of Sigurðr and Brynhildr and Ragnarr's second wife, as the avenging stepmother of Eiríkr and Agnarr, Ragnarr's sons by Þóra; secondly, the fact that a son of Regnerus Lothbrog named Ericus appears in Saxo's Book IX, where, however, no mention is made of Kráka or indeed of Áslaug; and thirdly, the fact that no mention is made of Eirekr in *Krákumál*, the title of which seems to betray an awareness of Áslaug's rôle as Kráka, since although the name *Kráka* occurs nowhere in the poem's text, Áslaug is mentioned in it (str. 26) briefly.

Further discussion of these difficulties will show only the third to be unreal, and the first and second to have enough validity to outweigh the unreality of the third. As for the first of them—the absence of Kráka from *Ragnarssona þáttr*, where Eiríkr nevertheless appears—de Vries argues (1915, 164–65; cf. 1928a, 293–94, 273) that the Kráka-story did form part of the older *Ragnars saga* drawn on by the *þáttr*, without, however, having yet acquired the fullness of detail that it shows in the 147 and 1824b texts. It was omitted from the *þáttr*, he claims, because its folktale elements made it inappropriate to that work's primarily historical and genealogical purposes, but was developed into the form it has in the surviving texts of the saga in order to help explain Ívarr's nickname 'the boneless'. It will be recalled that de Vries advances very much the same argument in relation to Rǫgnvaldr, the cows at Hvítabœr, and Síbilja, three items which appear to have occurred in both the X and Y versions of *Ragnars saga*, but none of which occurs in *Ragnarssona þáttr*, and that this argument was rejected earlier (see p. 102, above) with the preliminary comment that it is dangerous to make more assumptions than the evidence allows about the content of the older *Ragnars saga* drawn on by the *þáttr*. This comment may be repeated here. It may also be noted as a matter of interest that Arngrímur, though he records Ragnerus's plan to leave Aslauga for the supposedly more nobly-born daughter of Eysteinus (cf. part IX of the Analysis), and Aslauga's later encouragement to her sons to avenge Ericus and Agnerus, makes no mention of the names *Kráka* or *Randalín*.

As for the second difficulty, the absence of Kráka from Saxo's Book IX where, however, Regnerus Lothbrog has a son named Ericus, further details of this Ericus may now be given: he is one of the three sons of Regnerus by Suanlogha (IX.iv, 17), and is nicknamed 'Ventosi Pillei' ('wind-hat', IX.iv, 33, cf. ch. I, p. 41, above). He is appointed King of Sweden by Regnerus and assists the latter in his defeat and slaying of King Murial of the Orkneys (IX.iv, 33). Later, after the death of Regnerus, it emerges that Ericus has been slain in Sweden by a certain Ostenus, whose name seems to correspond to *Eysteinn*; and Agnerus, one of Regnerus's six sons by Thora, is himself slain in attempting to avenge Ericus (IX.v, 6). Although de Vries does not discuss Saxo's account of this Ericus directly in relation to the question of how Kráka came to form part of the Ragnarr loðbrók tradition, he does argue (1927a, 146–47) that, in comparison with the compilers of *Ragnarssona þáttr* and *Ragnars saga*, Saxo shows only a very superficial knowledge of the story of Eirekr, son of Ragnarr loðbrók; and de Vries would no doubt have used this argument if confronted with the difficulty now under discussion. He might even have argued that Saxo, if he had known a story in which Eirekr, the son of Ragnarr loðbrók, was also the stepson of Kráka, would not have dwelt to the extent that he does in Book V on Craca, stepmother of Ericus Disertus (see pp. 119–22, above). This last assumption is perhaps a rash one, however, since de Vries (1927a, 140–43, 147) and others (Olrik, 1894a, 111; Kuntze, 1917, 463–64; cf. Herrmann, 1922, 624–25) have in fact argued that, although Saxo shows no obvious knowledge of a tradition linking Regnerus Lothbrog with a daughter of Sigurðr and Brynhildr, or with anyone named Áslaug, Kráka, or Randalín, he nevertheless shows a dim, ill-informed awareness of such a tradition in his presentation of Lathgertha and Suanlogha as wives of this Regnerus. Lathgertha, like Áslaug-Kráka-Randalín, has long hair and warlike characteristics (Saxo, IX.iv, 2; cf. Olsen, 1906–08, 122–24, 141–47), and in leaving her for another (Saxo, IX.iv, 4; cf. part IVA of the Analysis) Regnerus treats her in much the same way as Ragnarr plans to treat Kráka, before discovering that she is really Áslaug, the daughter of Sigurðr and Brynhildr (see part IX of the Analysis). Suanlogha (= Svanlaug) shares the second element of her name with Áslaug, and the first with Svanhildr, who, according to *Vǫlsunga saga* (chs. 41–44) and its relevant sources (see Olsen, 1906–08, 105–10), was the daughter of Sigurðr by Guðrún, was trampled to death under horses' hooves on the orders of her husband Jǫrmunrekr, and was avenged by her half-brothers Hamðir and Sǫrli, sons of Guðrún by Jónakr. A version of this story appears in Book VIII (x, 7–14) of the *Gesta Danorum*, where Saxo tells how Iarmericus (= Jǫrmunrekr) had his wife Suanilda (= Svanhildr) trampled to death by horses, and how she was avenged by her brothers. It is true that Saxo shows no real awareness of Suanilda's parentage, but he does mention that, when preparing to avenge her, her brothers consulted a sorceress named Guthruna; and in Book XIII (vi, 7) he briefly refers to Grimilda (= Kriemhilt), the figure corresponding to Guðrún in German traditions of the Nibelungs (cf. Finch, 1965, xvi, n. 1). These arguments are interesting and by no means entirely unconvincing; it is particularly interesting, for instance, to note that Arngrímur, in the context of Aslauga's attempts to dissuade Ragnerus from invading England, seems to equate Aslauga with the Suanluga (*sic*) of Saxo's account ('Asl[a]uga quam Saxo Suanlugam', Benediktsson, 1950, 466). The fact remains, however, that no actual mention of Áslaug, Kráka, or Randalín is made at any stage of Saxo's narrative about Regnerus Lothbrog.

The third difficulty, the absence of Eirekr from *Krákumál*, the title of which suggests an awareness of Kráka, and in which Áslaug appears, requires relatively lengthy treatment. The title *Krákumál*, which appears to mean either 'the words of Kráka' or perhaps 'the story of Kráka' is applied to this poem in its earliest known manuscript, Ny kgl. saml. 1824b 4to (Kålund, 1900, 236), where, as shown above (p. 53), the poem immediately follows *Ragnars saga*. The title seems on the face of it hardly appropriate, since the name *Kráka*, as already indicated (p. 92, above), occurs nowhere in the poem's text, and although the poem does refer briefly to Áslaug it shows no awareness of her appearance in the role of Kráka as this is recorded in *Ragnars saga* and elsewhere (see parts IIIC, IVA, V, VII, and IX of the Analysis, and ch. III, section (d), below). Indeed, the poem in its surviving form has little to do even with Áslaug; it is spoken in the first person by Loðbrók as he awaits his death in King Ella's snake-pit, but makes no mention of the protective garment given to Ragnarr by Áslaug in *Ragnars saga* and *Ragnarssona þáttr* (cf. part V of the Analysis); the name *Loðbrók* is accounted for in the opening strophe, but the name *Ragnarr* occurs nowhere in the text (cf. p. 90, above). The first twenty-one strophes deal with battles in which the speaker has been to a greater or lesser extent involved, while the last eight express his heroic resolve in the face of death; his hope that Áslaug's sons will avenge him; and his expectation of a favourable reception in Óðinn's hall. Nevertheless, the prominence of Kráka in the Ragnarr loðbrók tradition generally (cf. the parts of the Analysis just referred to) surely means that the use of the title *Krákumál* in 1824b for the poem in question cannot easily be dismissed as a mistake (as can, I believe, the title *Bjarkamál*, which is applied to it in Uppsala Universitets bibliotek, ms. R 702, see Gödel, 1892, 50, and cf. p. 53, above); it may be considered a possibility that the poem was known as *Krákumál* prior to its recording in 1824b, and perhaps even at an early stage of its existence. Now, if the poem was known as *Krákumál* from its early stages, and if what I take to be de Vries's suggestion is to be upheld, i.e. that Kráka and Eirekr were borrowed together into the Ragnarr loðbrók tradition from the story of Ericus Disertus, it does indeed seem to be a difficulty that Eirekr is nowhere mentioned in *Krákumál*. In *Ragnarssona þáttr* and *Ragnars saga*, as we have seen (pp. 118 and 99–102, above), the brothers Eirekr and Agnarr both fall to King Eysteinn, who is eventually defeated by the combined forces of their stepmother Áslaug-Randalín and her sons; Arngrímur, moreover, gives essentially the same information without, however, mentioning the name *Randalín* (cf. p. 123, above) or the fact that Áslaug accompanies her sons on the revenge mission. Now str. 7 of *Krákumál* mentions a battle at Ullarakr ('the field of wool'), where King Eysteinn fell, and the name *Ullarakr* seems to correspond to *Laneus* ('woolly'), the name, according to Saxo (IX.iv, 10), of the plain on which Regnerus is for the first time victorious over Haraldus (cf. part IX of the Analysis). Neither Ericus nor Ostenus, however (neither, that is, of the two characters who, in Saxo's Book IX, appear to correspond to Eirekr and Eysteinn respectively), is involved at this stage of Saxo's narrative. Str. 17 of *Krákumál*, further, reports a battle in which the narrator's son Agnarr was slain by one Egill; the location of the battle is not given. These two references represent *Krákumál*'s closest approximation to the story of Eysteinn's defeat of Eirekr and Agnarr, preserved in the *þáttr*, in the saga, and by Arngrímur.

Although de Vries does not address himself directly to this difficulty, he develops what might be interpreted as a counter-argument to it with his theory as to the origins and structure of *Krákumál* (de Vries 1927b, 1928c); a theory which, however, presents its own problems, as I shall attempt to show. He notes that in its surviving form the poem has twenty-nine strophes, all of which, except for the last, begin with the refrain 'hjoggum vér með hjǫrvi' ('we hewed with the sword'), and all of which, except for the last and one other, have ten *vísuorð* each, including the refrain. The two exceptions here, strs. 23 and 29, have eight *vísuorð* each, in the manner of a normal *dróttkvætt* strophe. Following Olrik (1894a, 97), de Vries (1927b, 53) notes a close similarity in content and wording between, on the one hand, str. 26 of *Ragnars saga* in the 1824b text, and, on the other, strs. 28 and 24 of *Krákumál*. Str. 26 of *Ragnars saga*, the first of the two strophes recited by Ragnarr in the snake-pit according to the 1824b text (which differs here from the 147 text, see part X of the Analysis), has eight *vísuorð*, like virtually all other strophes in the 1824b text of *Ragnars saga* (though see the discussion of str. 21 in ch. III, pp. 198–202, below), and does not, of course, have a refrain.

From a discussion of these various points de Vries concludes that the composition of *Krákumál* took place in three main stages: first, a stage at which the strophes consisted of eight *vísuorð* each, without a refrain; secondly, a stage at which the refrain was inserted in place of the first *vísuorð* of each of these eight-*vísuorð* strophes, thus necessitating in at least one case (so de Vries claims) the transference of part of the content of one strophe (28) to another (str. 24; close examination of str. 28 reveals that no such transference would in fact be necessary here, even if the refrain had been inserted as de Vries suggests); and thirdly, a stage at which two *vísuorð* were added at the end of each strophe, thus forming the ten-*vísuorð* strophe beginning with a refrain that is now characteristic of virtually the entire poem. In this view the final strophe, which has only eight *vísuorð* and no refrain, is a relic of the first stage; and str. 23, which begins with the refrain, but also has only eight *vísuorð*, is a relic of the second stage. Such a view obviously implies, as de Vries (1927b, 54–60) himself emphasizes, that the poem went through a number of different versions in the course of its composition, and that it cannot be regarded as a unity in its present form. He regards the last eight strophes, the death-song proper, as indicative of the original form of the poem, and the first twenty-one, the battle-catalogue, as representing a secondary development. Many of the references to persons and places in the battle-catalogue, including the mention of Rǫgnvaldr (str. 15), noted earlier (see section (b) (*iii*) of the present chapter) appear to reflect historical events of the tenth to the twelfth centuries. Furthermore, both parts of *Krákumál* show marked stylistic similarities to the poetry of Einarr Skúlason, an Icelandic scald active mainly between 1150 and 1165; and marked similarities of subject-matter as well as style to the poetry of Rǫgnvaldr Kali, who appears to have been the co-author, with Hallr Þórarinsson, of

Háttalykill, dating from the mid-twelfth century (cf. pp. 31 and 89–90, above). The last eight strophes of *Krákumál* seem to reflect the revival of interest in the Viking way of life that developed in the second half of the twelfth century, and the remainder of the poem shows, among other things, a balancing against each other of warlike and amorous preoccupations (in strs. 13, 14, 18, and 20) in a manner reminiscent of the poetry composed by Rǫgnvaldr Kali in the course of his pilgrimage to the Holy Land in 1151–53 (cf. p. 110, above). From these considerations de Vries concludes that the poem was composed around the middle of the twelfth century, the second part somewhat earlier than the first, and that the process of its composition may well have taken place in the Orkneys, in the environment of Rǫgnvaldr Kali, who, if he was indeed a joint author of *Háttalykill*, was one of the very first to give literary expression to legends about Ragnarr and heroes described elsewhere as his sons. The Maeshowe inscriptions, moreover, as de Vries (1927b, 55) notes, provide evidence of interest in the sons of Loðbrók in mid twelfth-century Orkney (cf. ch. I, section (b), above).

As for the title *Krákumál*, de Vries (1928c) argues, on highly dubious grounds, that the first part of the poem, the battle-catalogue, does not always seem appropriately attributed to Ragnarr, and was originally meant to be spoken by Áslaug. This part of the surviving poem thus represents, in de Vries's view, the original *Krákumál* or 'words of Kráka', so called because of Áslaug's nickname *Kráka*. The last eight strophes of the poem, on the other hand, represent a death-song originally attributed to Ragnarr, and the poem acquired its present form as a result of the original *Krákumál* becoming combined with the original death-song, or 'Ragnarsmál' (see de Vries, 1928c, 126), and becoming attributed to Ragnarr in the process, but at the same time retaining the title *Krákumál*, which came to be applied to the entire poem in its new form. In support of his view that the first part of the poem was originally meant to be spoken by Áslaug-Kráka, de Vries argues mainly that the battle-catalogue proper shows a preoccupation with the loss in battle of certain of the speaker's sons, and is in this respect comparable to the verses in which Áslaug laments the loss of her sons Rǫgnvaldr and Hvítserkr in the 1824b text of *Ragnars saga*, and Sigurðr ormr-í-auga in *Ragnarssona þáttr*. The relevant verses in the 1824b text of *Ragnars saga* are str. 17, in the second half of which Áslaug emphasizes Rǫgnvaldr's relative youthfulness at the time of his death, and strs. 30 and 31, in which she tells how Hvítserkr was burnt to death on a pile of human heads in Eastern Europe, points out that he chose the manner of his death himself, and emphasizes his heroism, raising rhetorically the question of how a warrior could find a nobler bed ('beð') than that on which he died (Olsen, 1906–08, 169, 215–16). None of these occurs in the 147 text of the saga. The relevant verse in *Ragnarssona þáttr* is the ninth and final one quoted there, which is nowhere else recorded: here Áslaug, after hearing the news of Sigurðr ormr-í-auga's death in a battle against the emperor Ǫrnulfr, tells in a *dróttkvætt*-strophe how some ravens are watching in vain for Sigurðr now that he has met his untimely death.

Returning now to *Krákumál*, we find that, of the twenty-one strophes which according to de Vries represent the original *Krákumál* (i.e. the poem spoken by Áslaug as opposed to Ragnarr), only one, str. 17, can definitely be said to deal with a son of the speaker. It is true that str. 15 reports the death in the Hebrides of Rǫgnvaldr, who, as shown above (in section (b) (*iii*) of this chapter), seems to correspond somewhat loosely to Rǫgnvaldr, the son of Ragnarr and Áslaug mentioned in *Ragnars saga*, as well as to the Regnaldus and Raugnvaldus of Saxo and Arngrímur respectively. It has also been indicated above, however, that the *Krákumál* strophe does not specify that the Rǫgnvaldr it mentions is the speaker's son, whereas the second half of str. 17 of *Ragnars saga* does so (see pp. 103, 101, above).

Str. 17 of *Krákumál*, then, is the only strophe in the poem that reports the death of someone explicitly stated to be the speaker's son; it uses the expression 'syni mínum' ('my son') in recording the death of Agnarr at the hands of Egill. Agnarr, however, is a son of Ragnarr by Þóra in all the relevant analogues, including Saxo (see part VII of the Analysis), which surely means that if the strophe is to be attributed to anyone other than Ragnarr it should be attributed not to Áslaug, but to Þóra. This adds, if anything, to the difficulty now under discussion, i.e. that Eirekr is nowhere mentioned in the surviving *Krákumál*, even though, in de Vries's implied view, he was borrowed into the Ragnarr loðbrók tradition from the story of Ericus Disertus together with his stepmother Kráka (see pp. 122–23, 125–26, above). Not only is Eirekr not referred to in the extant poem, but Agnarr, who in the relevant analogues is a stepson, like Eirekr, of Áslaug-Kráka, is referred to in the poem as a son, rather than a stepson, of the speaker.

As will be evident, de Vries regards the verses in *Ragnars saga* and the *þáttr* dealing with the deaths of Rǫgnvaldr, Hvítserkr, and Sigurðr ormr-í-auga as representing the original *Krákumál*. He would explain the absence from the surviving *Krákumál* of references to the deaths of Hvítserkr and Sigurðr by the view that such references would be inappropriate once the original *Krákumál* had become combined with Ragnarr's death-song and attributed to Ragnarr, since these two die *after* Ragnarr in all the relevant analogues in the case of Sigurðr (de Vries, 1928c, 126), and in all of them except Saxo's Book IX (iv, 30) in the case of Hvítserkr. Although he does not explain the failure of the surviving *Krákumál* to mention Eirekr, he could perhaps have argued that in Saxo's account (IX.v, 6) the death of Ericus also occurs after that of Regnerus, even though in all the other relevant analogues (i.e. *Ragnarssona þáttr*, the 147 and 1824b texts of *Ragnars saga*, and Arngrímur's account), Eirekr's death precedes Ragnarr's. He would still have to explain, however, why in str. 17 of the surviving poem Agnarr is referred to as the speaker's son, if, as he wishes to claim, the speaker of the original *Krákumál* was Áslaug, the stepmother of Eirekr and Agnarr in all the analogues where she and they appear (i.e. *Ragnarssona þáttr*, both texts of *Ragnars saga*, and Arngrímur's account, cf. pp. 128–29, above, and part VII of the Analysis). Has Agnarr's relationship to the original speaker been altered to suit the new speaker, Ragnarr loðbrók? From asking this sort of question it is only a short step to adjusting the surviving text to make it fit a hypothetical, lost one, and such a dangerous course should be pursued no further. This means, then, that the only strophe in *Krákumál* that provides anything like positive evidence in support of de Vries's theory of the poem's origins is str. 15, which deals with Rǫgnvaldr; but its similarities to the second half of str. 17 of *Ragnars saga* simply are not close enough for so complex and far-reaching a theory to be confidently based on them; in particular, it must be repeated that the *Krákumál* strophe does not refer to Rǫgnvaldr as the speaker's son, as the one in the saga does.

To be fair to de Vries, he seems to recognize that, apart from its title, the surviving *Krákumál* shows few, if any, clear signs of what he regards as the original *Krákumál*. Of the latter, he says (1928c, 126): 'Selbst ging es verloren, aber einige Trümmer wurden in der Saga gerettet'. There is certainly an element of ingenuity in his theory, and in putting it forward he draws attention to a number of interesting facts about the style and structure of the surviving poem. From what has been said above, however, it will be clear that the theory rests on too weak a basis, and necessitates too many assumptions, to command acceptance.

A more acceptable theory, in my view, is that of Olsen (1935), whose discussion differs from de Vries's and from what I have said so far in taking account of the fact that, as well as being a personal name, the word *kráka* means 'crow'. Olsen recognizes the possibility that *Krákumál* was composed in the Orkneys, but suggests the Hebrides as an even more likely place of composition, in view of the phrase 'í Suðreyjum sjálfum' used in str. 15 of the poem. This phrase, meaning 'in the Hebrides themselves', implies that the poet either lived in the Hebrides or had close ties with them. I see no reason to disagree with this view, or to accept F. Jónsson's more complicated view, evident from his translation of the strophe (F. Jónsson, 1912b, 652), that the pronoun *sjálfum* here belongs to the phrase 'várum mǫnnum' ('our men') of the following *vísuorð*. One of the implications of Olsen's view is that *Krákumál* was composed in an environment of close linguistic and cultural contact between Scandinavians and Celts. He points out that the word *Krákumál*, if translated literally into Old Irish, would give the compound word *badbscél*, which occurs in the eighth or early ninth-century Irish saga, *Fled Bricrend* (ed. Henderson, 1899, see pp. lxii, 90; on the date of the saga, see further Dillon, 1948, 18; Murphy, 1971, 41). The second element, *scél*, m., meaning 'story' or 'piece of news', corresponds closely enough to *mál*, n. pl., meaning 'sentences' or 'things said', and the first element, *badb*, f., means 'crow' or 'war-goddess', and in early Irish literature is often applied to a war-goddess who appears in battle-scenes in the form of a crow. The word *Krákumál* would thus be a Norse calque of Hebridean origin on Old Irish *badbscél*, the meaning of which was apparently 'tale of slaughter' (Carney and O Daly, 1975, 5). Such a term seems readily applicable to the poem now known as *Krákumál*, which deals with battles and slayings of one kind or another from beginning to end. It may just be significant here that in the twenty-ninth and final strophe of the surviving poem, the speaker says that the female spirits ('dísir') sent by Óðinn from the latter's palace are inviting him there, since there is at least one instance in Old Norse literature (in ch. 1 of *Vǫlsunga saga*, see Olsen, 1906–08, 4, l. 10) of a female messenger of Óðinn taking the form of a crow. In general, however, it is the raven rather than the crow that appears in Old Norse literature as a (male) messenger of Óðinn and a bird of battle; *Krákumál* itself, indeed, illustrates the latter rôle of the raven in no fewer than six instances (in strs. 2, 8, 9, 16 [twice], and 24). The only instance I have found of a crow appearing as a bird of battle in Old Norse literature is in the clearly derogatory context of a verse in which the twelfth-century scald Þórarinn stuttfeldr ('short-cloak') accuses a certain Árni fjǫruskeifr ('shore-gawk') of hardly having provided even a crow with food on the battle-field (F. Jónsson, 1912b, 464). On the other hand, there is a crow that advises Konr, the youngest son of Jarl, to engage in warfare rather than bird-taming in the penultimate strophe of *Rígsþula* (Neckel, 1962, 287), a poem which it has also been suggested shows Celtic influence (Young, 1933; on the dating of the poem, see p. 51, above). If Olsen's theory is correct, then, it seems likely that the original implications of the title *Krákumál* were understood only in the Norse-Celtic environment of the poem's composition, and that after the poem had become known elsewhere in Scandinavian territory, outside the sphere of Celtic influence, the title remained attached to it without being fully understood.

According to Olsen (1935), then, the title *Krákumál* originally had nothing to do with the Norse personal name *Kráka,* and signified a tale of slaughter. Olsen's theory has the great advantage over de Vries's of allowing for a relatively simple view of the poem's origins. If it can be accepted that Olsen is right, then it is reasonable to regard *Krákumál* as a unified composition from its beginnings, and it is not necessary to assume, with de Vries, that the poem as it survives is the result of a complicated process whereby two poems were gradually combined into one. An apparent further advantage of accepting Olsen's theory is that it makes it possible to regard *Krákumál* as never having referred to either Eirekr or Kráka (as opposed to Áslaug), and thus to dismiss it as an obstacle to de Vries's view that these two figures were borrowed together from the story of Ericus Disertus into the Ragnarr loðbrók tradition; the poem could reflect a stage before the borrowing took place. This advantage is apparent rather than real, however, since the obstacles to de Vries's view offered by *Ragnarssona þáttr* and Saxo's account, and discussed above (pp. 123–25) still remain in force.

In contrast to de Vries (1928a, 294), who seems to be puzzled by the fact that *Krákumál* does not appear in *Ragnarssona þáttr*, I would maintain that *Krákumál* did not form part of the saga-tradition of

Ragnarr loðbrók until the X stage of that tradition's development. As with Rǫgnvaldr and the stories of the cows (see section (b) (*iii*) of the present chapter), I would suggest that the reason why *Krákumál* is not found in *Ragnarssona þáttr* is quite simply that it did not form part of the older *Ragnars saga*, which the *þáttr* had as a source. As noted above (pp. 54, 87), the X redactor appears to have included *Krákumál* in his text of the saga, and I have suggested elsewhere (McTurk, 1975, 52, 62, n. 70) that this redactor was not fully aware of the narrative inconsistencies that were bound to result from his doing so. One of these must have been *Krákumál*'s location in the Hebrides of Rǫgnvaldr's death, an event which the saga (at the X as well as the Y stage, as I have argued above, see pp. 98–99, 113–14), locates at Hvítabœr. This consideration, together with the increased knowledge of Rǫgnvaldr's death implied by str. 17 of the 1824b text of the saga (which is not found in 147), must have been one of the factors that prompted the Y redactor to remove *Krákumál* from the text of the saga, and relegate it to the position of an appendix (see McTurk, 1975, 62–63, cf. pp. 53–55, above).

The foregoing discussion, which began (on p. 118) as an investigation of the origins of the story of Eysteinn's hostilities with Eirekr and Agnarr in *Ragnars saga*, has taken in the question of Kráka's introduction into the Ragnarr loðbrók tradition as well. Certain conclusions may be drawn from the information so far assembled, after this has been summarized. Agnarr is mentioned in *Háttalykill*, *Krákumál*, Saxo's Book IX, *Ragnarssona þáttr*, *Ragnars saga* (in 147 and 1824b), and Arngrímur's account. In all but the first two of these he appears unambiguously as a son of Ragnarr loðbrók by Þóra, but in *Háttalykill* Ragnarr (as opposed to Loðbrók) is mentioned, though Agnarr's relationship to him is not made clear, while in *Krákumál* Agnarr appears as the son of the narrator, who claims to have acquired the name *Loðbrók*, though the poem makes no mention of Ragnarr. Agnarr's death is not referred to in *Háttalykill*, which mentions him only in indicating that he was the brother (*sic*) of Ívarr the boneless; in *Krákumál* he is slain by one Egill, but in all the other authorities he dies in battle against Eysteinn (Ostenus in Saxo). Eirekr is not mentioned in either *Háttalykill* or *Krákumál*, but is otherwise mentioned by the same authorities as Agnarr. In *Ragnarssona þáttr*, *Ragnars saga*, and Arngrímur's account he is a son of Ragnarr loðbrók by Þóra, like Agnarr, whereas in Saxo's account he is a son of Regnerus Lothbrog by Suanlogha. In Saxo's account, however, both he and Agnerus fall to Ostenus, much as in the other relevant works they both fall to Eysteinn. Eysteinn himself (called Ostenus by Saxo) appears in all the works in which Agnarr is mentioned apart from *Háttalykill*. In *Krákumál* he appears to be an opponent of the narrator Loðbrók, who claims to have been involved in a battle at Ullarakr where King Eysteinn fell, but in all the other relevant accounts he is the opponent of Eirekr and Agnarr. Of the works in which Agnarr is mentioned, Kráka appears for certain only in the two texts of *Ragnars saga*. She is nowhere mentioned in *Háttalykill*, Saxo's Book IX, or *Ragnarssona þáttr*; nor does she appear anywhere in the text of *Krákumál*, though her name is at least apparently mentioned in the title of that poem; and Arngrímur, though evidently aware of Ragnarr's plan to leave Áslaug for the supposedly more nobly-born daughter of Eysteinn, makes no mention of Kráka by name. The fact that Kráka appears in a number of other accounts (mostly ballads, to be dealt with in ch. III, below) relating more or less directly to Ragnarr loðbrók has been disregarded here, since these accounts, which show practically no awareness of the sons of Ragnarr loðbrók, form virtually no part of the immediately preceding discussion. It should finally be noted that, in Saxo's Book V, the hero Ericus Disertus has a stepmother named Craca and a father named Regnerus.

I assume that, although *Krákumál* does not mention the name *Ragnarr*, its presentation of *Loðbrók* as a name acquired by the speaker as a result of slaying a serpent (see part V of the Analysis) presupposes an awareness of the latter name's attachment to *Ragnarr* as a nickname. Thus, as far as Eysteinn is concerned, I would suggest that *Krákumál*, which records Eysteinn's death in one of the battles at which Loðbrók was present, represents a relatively early stage in the development of the Ragnarr loðbrók tradition, at which Eysteinn was regarded as an enemy primarily of (Ragnarr) loðbrók, as distinct from any of the latter's sons, whereas the other works in which he is mentioned represent a later stage at which he was presented as the enemy primarily of Eirekr and Agnarr, sons of Ragnarr loðbrók, perhaps in response to the need remarked on by de Vries, and noted earlier (pp. 112–14, above), for providing more heroic deeds for the sons once the heroic career of their father was reasonably well established. Among the 'other works' just mentioned is of course Saxo's Book IX (v, 6), which presents Ostenus as an enemy of Ericus and Agnerus, while at the same time seeming to preserve, in the different context of Regnerus Lothbrog's victory over Haraldus at Laneus (Saxo, IX.iv, 10), a memory of the battle at Ullarakr where, according to *Krákumál* (str. 7), Eysteinn was slain. The foregoing argument does not, of course, exclude the possibility that at a still later stage it became necessary to emphasize hostile relations between Eysteinn on the one hand, and Ragnarr loðbrók as well as his sons on the other; the 1824b text of *Ragnars saga*, when compared with *Ragnarssona þáttr*, suggests that such a development in fact took place, as I have argued elsewhere (McTurk, 1975, 60–61).

As for Eirekr and Agnarr, the fact that Eirekr, unlike Agnarr, is not mentioned in either *Háttalykill* or *Krákumál* need not mean what de Vries perhaps wishes to imply, i.e. that Eirekr did not enter the Ragnarr loðbrók tradition until Kráka also did; Ericus does after all figure in Saxo's Book IX, where Kráka is not mentioned. It does suggest, however, as de Vries (1928a, 282) clearly recognizes, that Agnarr was originally more important in the tradition than Eirekr. This state of affairs is perhaps also reflected in Saxo's Book IX, which mentions both Ericus and Agnerus, but which contrasts with the other works that do so in placing the death of Agnerus after that of Ericus rather than before it (and also, incidentally, in placing both their deaths after, rather than before, their father's death). Even so, Saxo gives no special prominence to the death of either Ericus or Agnerus; it is not until the stage of the tradition reflected in *Ragnarssona þáttr* (where Kráka is not mentioned) that the death of Eirekr can be clearly seen to receive fuller treatment than Agnarr's. By this stage also, Eirekr and Agnarr are clearly presented as stepsons of Áslaug-Randalín (on these points Arngrímur's account seems to follow the Y version of *Ragnars saga* rather than *Skjǫldunga saga*, cf. p. 57, above, and has no independent value). As suggested earlier (see p. 119, above), Agnarr's absorption into the tradition of Hrólfr kraki is the most likely reason for his decline in prominence in the Ragnarr loðbrók tradition.

With regard to Kráka, it may be suggested that the prominence acquired by Eirekr in the Ragnarr loðbrók tradition in the manner just described, the coincidence of his name with that of Ericus Disertus, and the fact that he is presented as a stepson of Áslaug, were sufficient to attract the name of Craca, stepmother of Ericus Disertus, from the story of the latter into the Ragnarr loðbrók tradition. The name *Craca* or *Kráka*, however, with its folktale associations of the cruel stepmother and ugly sister, was hardly appropriate for Áslaug in her heroic rôle as an avenging stepmother, the warlike aspect of which seemed to derive partly from memories of Áslaug's valkyrie connections, which came to be acknowledged by the application to her in the older *Ragnars saga* of the additional name *Randalín*, as the *þáttr* indicates; this will be discussed more fully in ch. III, sections (c) and (d). The name *Kráka* therefore came to be used of Áslaug mainly in the early stages of her career, before she revealed her true parentage. Here, as de Vries (1928a, 278–79) implies, it acquired its own appropriateness in assisting the development of the story of Áslaug's upbringing by foster-parents—in supplying, for instance, the name *Kráka* for Gríma's mother (and perhaps also, I would add, the motif of Gríma's attempt to disguise Áslaug's beauty by shaving her head and rubbing it with tar, found in ch. 1 of the 1824b text of *Ragnars saga* though not in 147, see pp. 84, 61, 67, 74, above). My own argument in relation to Kráka thus differs from de Vries's in disallowing the possibility, which de Vries (1915, 164–65; 1928a, 294) seems to entertain, that Kráka was known to the Ragnarr loðbrók tradition at the stage represented by *Ragnarssona þáttr*, i.e. in the older *Ragnars saga*. It is possible that the poem's title, *Krákumál*, particularly if felt to be obscure for the reasons suggested above (pp. 131–32), provided an additional incentive for borrowing the name *Kráka* into the Ragnarr loðbrók tradition from the story of Ericus Disertus. Since the father of this Ericus is named Regnerus (= Ragnarr), it might be thought that the name *Ragnarr* itself provided a stimulus for the borrowing, as may perhaps be the case. Here, however, it should be noted that Regnerus the father of Ericus Disertus is merely a colourless figure in comparison with his son Ericus and the latter's stepmother on the one hand, and with Ragnarr loðbrók on the other. He is described by Saxo as a fighter (*pugilis*, V.ii, 3) and a man of considerable wealth (V.ii, 5), and seems to have no function in Saxo's Book V beyond providing a name for the father of Ericus and first husband of Craca (V.iii, 25). In the circumstances it seems most reasonable to regard his presence in the story of Ericus Disertus as the result of reactive influence from the Ragnarr loðbrók tradition. Such a view would be quite consistent with de Vries's idea, outlined above (pp. 119–22), that the stories of Ericus Disertus and Ragnarr loðbrók influenced each other during their parallel growth.

Returning now to the manner of Eirekr's death and its relevance to the heroic biographical pattern, I see no reason to agree with de

Vries (1928c, 124) that the idea of death by impalement on spears arose as a misunderstanding of the strophe occurring as no. 11 in the 1824b text of *Ragnars saga*, a strophe which is also preserved, in an apparently less corrupt form, in *Ragnarssona þáttr*, where the prose text also interprets the manner of the death as by impalement on spears. The relevant part of the strophe may be quoted with my own facing translation from the *Ragnarssona þáttr* text as edited in Hb, 1892–96, 460:

<table>
<tr><td>

monk øfstr of val deyja,
ok geirtré í gǫgnum
gǫrr, látið mik standa.

</td><td>

I shall die higher up than anyone
else over the heap of slain, (and
be) ready (*gǫrr*) to do so. Let
spearshafts transfix me!

</td></tr>
</table>

It does not seem necessary or even permissible to follow de Vries in taking this to mean: 'I shall be transfixed by spears while standing upright on the battlefield'; *øfstr* surely means 'uppermost', or just possibly 'last', rather than 'upright', and *valr* surely refers to the slain rather than to the battlefield itself (F. Jónsson, 1931b, 98, 591). In support of his argument that a misunderstanding has taken place, de Vries (1928c, 124) refers to the strophe occurring next (i.e. as no. 12) in the 1824b text of *Ragnars saga*, where Eirekr declares that no prince, as far as he knows, will ever die on a more glorious bed ('beð') than he (see Olsen, 1906–08, 140, 203–04). J. de Vries (1928c, 124) seems to think that the idea of a bed of spears has arisen from the word *beð* being wrongly taken to refer to the word *geirtré*, 'spearshafts', rather than to the word *val*, 'the slain', in the passage quoted above. Now it is indeed likely that the Y redactor understood the reference to a bed in this manner (provided that 1824b can be taken as an accurate representation of his text), since the word *val* does not occur in the 1824b text of the strophe quoted; the relevant *vísuorð* here reads (Olsen, 1906–08, 139): 'm[un e]k eptir avldrecka', 'I shall be drinking ale afterwards' (presumably in Valhǫll). However, the strophe referring to the bed (str. 12 in the 1824b text of *Ragnars saga*) simply does not occur in *Ragnarssona þáttr*, which, it must be repeated, interprets the manner of the death in its prose text as by impalement on spears. In order to get round this difficulty de Vries (1928c, 124) argues that the older *Ragnars saga* drawn on by the *þáttr* contained the strophe quoted above in the relatively corrupt form later reproduced in the 1824b text, that is, without the word *val*. The redactor of *Ragnarssona þáttr* later corrected the strophe, in de Vries's view, to give the version which the *þáttr* now preserves, but omitted to remove the account of the impalement from the prose text. Though de Vries fails to do so, he would have to argue further, in order to carry his point, that the strophe containing the reference to a bed also formed part of the older *Ragnars saga* drawn on by the *þáttr*, but was omitted by the latter's redactor. In failing to proceed so far, de Vries seems to be concealing one of the complications of an argument which is already tortuous enough in the form in which he presents it. Surely the passage in question, as quoted and translated above, is not seriously at variance with the idea of a man meeting his death by impalement on spears. Even if *ofstr* is taken to mean 'last', as is possible (F. Jónsson, 1931b, 98), and the meaning of the first *vísuorð* quoted is 'I shall be the last to die on the heap of slain', the speaker could still mean that he envisages being the last person to be thrown onto a heap of slain and dying there as a result of prior impalement. While I do not think it is necessary to follow E. A. Kock (1927, 86) in emending the nominative singular masculine *gǫrr* in the relevant passage to the accusative plural neuter *gǫr*, so as to give the meaning that the spears, rather than the speaker, are 'ready', or 'prepared', it is of some interest that Kock should wish to make this emendation, since it shows that for him, at any rate, there is no discrepancy between the content of the strophe and the prose information surrounding it.

If the prose text of *Ragnars saga* does show a misunderstanding of any of the strophes spoken by Eirekr prior to his death, this is more likely to be apparent in the prose account of Eirekr sending Áslaug a ring, which occurs just before str. 13 in the 1824b text. The prose account mentions only one ring, whereas the strophe refers to 'rings' or 'valuables' ('bauga'; cf. p. 101, above). The strophe in question also occurs in *Ragnarssona þáttr*, but without any elaboration there in the prose. It is doubtful, however, whether the saga-text does show a discrepancy here between the strophe and the prose. If Eirekr intends to leave all his valuables to Áslaug, as the strophe indicates, it is hardly inconsistent for him to take from his arm and send to her, as he does in the prose, what is presumably the only costly object he has on him at the time of his death. Whatever the explanation of the single ring, I agree with de Vries (1928a, 278, n. 53) that Olrik (1894a, 132) and Herrmann (1922, 623–24) are probably going too far in seeing it as indicative of a secret passion on Eirekr's part for his stepmother.

It may be significant that Edzardi (1880, li–liv), who gave
thorough treatment to the discrepancies between verse and prose in
the 1824b text of *Ragnars saga*, did not include either of the cases
just discussed in his list of such discrepancies.

As for the relevance of Eirekr's death to the heroic biographical
pattern, Mudrak (1943, 128) draws attention to a passage in
Herodotus (Godley, 1957, 294–96) which shows a connection
between the motif of impalement on spears and the idea of a visit to
the underworld; he also suggests a connection between this passage
and the story of Eirekr's death, which he sees as illustrating 'eine
besondere Art der Jenseitsreise'. The passage in question deals with
the Thracian tribe known as the Getae, who, according to
Herodotus, believe that, instead of dying, they go to join a divine
being named Salmoxis, also known as Gebeleizis. Every five years
they choose a messenger by lot to visit Salmoxis with requests for
their needs to be supplied, and they dispatch the messenger by
throwing him onto a number of javelins held pointing upwards. If
he is killed, this means that Salmoxis is in a favourable mood; if he
survives, he is reproached for his unsuitability for the task, and
another messenger is substituted. That the abode of Salmoxis is the
underworld is suggested by an alternative account of him, also
given by Herodotus (Godley, 1957, 297), according to which
Salmoxis was an ordinary human being who built a hall in which he
generously entertained guests, teaching them that neither he nor
they would ever die, but would go to a place of perpetual happiness.
He convinced them of the truth of this doctrine by disappearing for
three years into an underground chamber he had built and finally
reappearing after he had been missed and mourned as though he
were dead.

It is difficult to argue convincingly for a connection between
Herodotus's account and that of Eirekr's death. The motif of
impalement does, it is true, occur in both accounts, but there are
hardly enough further similarities between them to suggest that this
is anything more than a coincidence. Mudrak (1923, 128) emphasizes the fact that Eirekr himself chooses to die by impalement,
comparing this with the fact that, in Herodotus's account, death by
this means is presented as enviable, inasmuch as the one who dies
by it is favoured by Salmoxis. This latter idea is in turn comparable
to the ancient Scandinavian notion of fallen warriors becoming the
chosen heroes of Óðinn, whom they join as drinking companions in
Valhǫll (see *Snorra Edda*, *Gylfaginning*, ch. 25, F. Jónsson, 1931a,

43). However, the main emphasis in the accounts of Eirekr's death is on his heroic reasons for choosing it rather than on the afterlife in store for him. He chooses to die in such a spectacular and horrific way because he would rather be seen to die bravely than live with the knowledge of his defeat; his brief reference to drinking ale after death is secondary both in origin and importance (cf. pp. 137–38, above). Nevertheless, if the consequences of Mudrak's view could be accepted, i.e. that the older *Ragnars saga* drawn on by the *þáttr* was influenced (presumably indirectly) by the information preserved in Herodotus, and that the *þáttr* thus reflects an association of the motif of impalement on spears with the idea of a visit to the underworld, then it might be argued that this motif came to be used in connection with Eirekr because it was felt that Ragnarr himself did not exemplify part VIII of the biographical pattern ('The hero makes an expedition to the underworld'), sufficiently strikingly. The Analysis above (see section (a) of the present chapter) in fact suggests that, of the ten numbered parts of the pattern, part VIII is the one least adequately represented by the hero-figure (in the sense of the term 'hero' explained above, pp. 61–62) in the Ragnarr loðbrók tradition; and a connection of some kind between this tradition and Herodotus seems to be indicated by William of Jumièges, who, as well as referring to Lothbrocus, the father of Bier Costae ferreae ('ironside') in the manner already discussed (see pp. 1, 42–43, 96–97, above), mentions in much the same context (see Marx, 1914, 7–8) a certain Zalmoxes, King of the Goths, whose name and tribe can hardly fail to recall the Salmoxis of Herodotus and his association with the Getae, a tribe whose name was apparently sometimes applied to the Goths by mediaeval Latin writers (see Marx, 1914, 6, nn. 1 and 2).

Whatever the relevance of Eirekr's death to part VIII of the heroic biographical pattern, it is clear that it has certain of the characteristics of part X, 'the death of the hero', and may reasonably be regarded as a partial imitation of the manner of Ragnarr's death as reported in the saga and its relevant Scandinavian analogues (see under part X of the Analysis above). It resembles Ragnarr's death in being relatively exceptional (if not exactly 'miraculous', cf. pp. 86, 88–89, above), and although Eirekr's youthfulness at the time of his death is nowhere emphasized, as Rǫgnvaldr's is in the 1824b text of *Ragnars saga* (and in Arngrímur's account), it is clear that in *Ragnarssona þáttr*, both texts of *Ragnars saga*, and Arngrímur's account, Eirekr dies at a younger age than

Ragnarr does, since Ragnarr, his father, is still alive at the time of his death. In this respect, at least, Eirekr fulfils the requirements of part X of the pattern better than Ragnarr does. In Saxo's account, as already noted, the death of Ericus (= Eirekr) occurs after that of his father, though it is perhaps just worth noting that Saxo at one point mentions the youthfulness of Ericus, albeit at an earlier stage of his career; according to Saxo (IX.iv, 17), the three sons of Regnerus by Suanlogha, Regnaldus (= Rǫgnvaldr), Withsercus (= Hvítserkr), and Ericus (= Eiríkr, Eirekr), were too young to join Regnerus on his campaign against Sorlus, the regent who succeeded King Herothus of Sweden on his death.

(vi) The death of Hvítserkr

The death of Hvítserkr as reported in the 1824b text of *Ragnars saga* (ch. 18; hence not in the 147 text, see p. 61, above) and by Saxo (IX.iv, 29–30) is also reminiscent of part X of the heroic biographical pattern, yet appears to be modelled on the story of Eirekr's death, as de Vries (1927a, 136–37; cf. 1928c, 125) suggests, rather than on that of Ragnarr's. Here it must be remembered that Saxo does not report the death of Ericus in any detail, which means that, if de Vries's suggestion is to be accepted, it must be concluded that a story of Eirekr's defeat and death, comparable to the accounts of these events in *Ragnarssona þáttr* and the saga, existed by Saxo's time, but was either unknown to him or suppressed by him. That he was at least partly aware of such a story is shown by his brief reference (Saxo, IX.v, 6) to the death of Ericus (Eirekr) at the hands of Ostenus. Hvítserkr is mentioned in a fragmentary part of *Háttalykill* (str. 11a), in Saxo's Book IX, in *Ragnarssona þáttr*, in the 147 and 1824b texts of *Ragnars saga*, and by Arngrímur. Accounts of his death are found only in Saxo and in the 1824b as opposed to the 147 text of the saga; his death does not appear to have been reported in the X version of the latter. In Saxo's account Withsercus, who had been appointed King of the Scythians by his father Regnerus (IX.iv, 21), is treacherously attacked by Daxon, King of the Hellespont, and is eventually captured from the top of a pile of corpses while fighting off his assailants. Daxon is moved by his physical beauty to offer him his daughter in marriage, but Withsercus prefers to be bound and burnt to death with his captive friends, and Daxon grants his request. Regnerus avenges his death on Daxon by banishing the latter to Utgarthia; later he restores

Daxon to his kingdom, but insists on an annual tribute from him (IX.iv, 201–32). In the 1824b text of *Ragnars saga* (ch. 18), it is told how, after avenging their father's death, Hvítserkr, Bjǫrn, and Sigurðr return from England to Denmark while Ívarr stays behind to rule England. Their mother, Randalín, lives to hear, as an old woman, the news of Hvítserkr's heroic death in Eastern Europe; once defeated and captured, he chooses to burn to death on a pile of human heads. It is in this connection that she recites strs. 30 and 31, the essential content of which has been given above, see p. 129. J. de Vries is surely right to suggest (de Vries, 1927a, 136–37) that the story of Hvítserkr's death, as reflected in these two accounts, has been influenced by that of Eirekr's death as reflected in *Ragnarssona páttr* and the saga. In Saxo's account, and in the 1824b text of the saga, Withsercus/Hvítserkr chooses the manner of his own death, as Eiríkr/Eirekr does in the *páttr* and the saga; and in Saxo's account Withsercus, like Eiríkr/Eirekr in the *páttr* and the saga, chooses to die rather than accept his enemy's offer of his daughter's hand in marriage. The idea in Saxo's account of Withsercus being captured from the top of a pile of corpses, paralleled in the 1824b text of the saga by Hvítserkr dying on a pile of human heads, was no doubt suggested by the verse passage discussed earlier (see p. 137, above; preserved in the *páttr* and as str. 11 in the 1824b text of the saga) in which Eiríkr speaks of dying high up over the slain.

J. de Vries is probably also right to suggest (de Vries, 1928c, 125) that the image of a bed, used in the second of Áslaug-Randalín's two strophes about Hvítserkr's death with reference to the pile of heads on which he dies (str. 31 in the 1824b text of the saga, see Olsen, 1906–08, 169, 215–16) was influenced by the same image as used with reference to the spears (as I believe, see p. 138, above) in one of the strophes (no. 12 in the 1824b text) spoken by Eirekr just before his death.

Here however it should be remembered that, as noted above (p. 137), while the strophe in which Eirekr speaks of dying high up over the slain (str. 11 in 1824b) is preserved in *Ragnarssona páttr*, the one in which he uses the image of the bed (str. 12) is not. This means that the former strophe may be assumed to have formed part of the older *Ragnars saga* and also of the older Ragnarr loðbrók tradition that influenced Saxo's account, while no such assumptions can be made about the latter strophe. It is uncertain whether this strophe (str. 12 in 1824b) was introduced at the X or the Y stage of *Ragnars saga*'s development; the state of AM 147 4to makes it impossible to say for certain whether it formed part of the X version of the saga (see Olsen, 1906–08, 182). It may be assumed that it was introduced either by the X or by the Y redactor, and that the latter composed Áslaug-Randalín's two strophes on Hvítserkr's death, inspired partly by the image of the bed in Eirekr's strophe, and partly by a familiarity, gained independently of the saga-tradition of Ragnarr loðbrók, with Hvítserkr's death as reported in the older Ragnarr loðbrók tradition underlying Saxo's account.

The story of Eirekr's death thus influenced that of Hvítserkr's in two stages: firstly in the older Ragnarr loðbrók tradition, in providing the motif of death accepted in preference to the enemy's offer of a daughter in marriage, and the motif of the victim in question being physically uppermost among the slain; and secondly, at the stage represented by the Y version of *Ragnars saga*, after Eirekr's verse containing the image of the bed had been introduced, in stimulating the composition of two strophes on Hvítserkr's death, the second of which also contains the image of the bed. This view is surely preferable to regarding the three strophes as having already existed in the older Ragnarr loðbrók tradition drawn on by Saxo; if that view were adopted, it would be necessary to explain why Eirekr's strophe (no. 12 in 1824b) is not found in *Ragnarssona þáttr*, and why the two strophes on Hvítserkr's death (nos. 30 and 31 in 1824b) were not in either *Ragnarssona þáttr* or the 147 text of the saga; and, since Áslaug (whether called Áslaug, Randalín or Kráka) had not yet been introduced at the stage of the Ragnarr loðbrók tradition represented by Saxo's account, it would also be necessary to suggest that the two strophes about Hvítserkr were originally spoken by someone other than Áslaug-Randalín, whether by Suanlogha (the mother of Withsercus according to Saxo) or (since in Saxo's account Withsercus, like Eirekr elsewhere, cf. pp. 140–41, dies before Regnerus) by Ragnarr himself. It is moreover consistent with the view I have proposed that the second strophe on Hvítserkr's death mentions the piling up of human heads, a more fantastic notion than the pile of corpses mentioned by Saxo (IX.iv, 29). This could well imply that the strophe was of later origin than the relevant part of Saxo's account.

(vii) Conclusions

From the foregoing discussion it will be clear that the parts of the heroic biographical pattern mainly relevant to Ragnarr's sons are IVA, VI, VIII, and X. Part I is hardly relevant here, though the story of Ívarr's procreation, as shown above (in section (*i*)), comes near to exemplifying it. This story seems to have been introduced after, rather than before, Áslaug's incorporation in the Ragnarr loðbrók tradition; not only does it partly show the influence of traditions relating to Áslaug's parents Sigurðr and Brynhildr, as already indicated; it also forms an integral part of the Kráka episode of *Ragnars saga*, an episode which did not develop until after Áslaug's introduction, as will be shown more fully in the next ·chapter. Since Ívarr's bonelessness seems to pose no real threat to him in the Ragnarr loðbrók tradition, either in his youth or later, I have not considered it as an example of part III; and although Bjǫrn's nickname *járnsíða* ('ironside') suggests invulnerability, this idea is not developed in relation to Bjǫrn in the Ragnarr loðbrók tradition, where the nickname seems to function simply as a label. I have not, therefore, considered it as an example of part V, though it may be noted that William of Jumièges explains Bier's nickname *Costae ferreae* (cf. pp. 1, 40–41, above) with a brief account of how Bier was protected from weapons by powerful drugs prepared by his mother (see Marx, 1914, 9, and cf. Davidson, 1980, 156).

It is no easier than in the first section of this chapter to provide a clear chronology for the attachment of the relevant parts of the heroic biographical pattern to the characters under discussion. Part IVA, as it shows itself in the heroic precocity of Sigurðr ormr-í-auga, seems to have been introduced after Áslaug's incorporation in the Ragnarr loðbrók tradition (see section (*ii*), above), and this also seems to have been the case with part VI as it reveals itself in the stories of Ívarr's cow-slayings at Hvítabœr and in Eysteinn's realm; these stories, indeed, do not appear to have formed part of the tradition until they were included in *Ragnars saga* by the X redactor (see sections (*iii*) and (*iv*), above). Part VIII is perhaps exemplified by the story of Eirekr's death by impalement on spears, a story which, though the manner of his death is not recorded by Saxo, probably existed by Saxo's time, since the story of Withsercus's death, recorded by Saxo, seems to show its influence. Since Saxo's account represents a stage of the tradition prior to Áslaug's introduction, it may be concluded that part VIII of the pattern, as applied to Eirekr, preceded Áslaug in becoming attached to the tradition, though the story in which it is so applied apparently influenced that of Hvítserkr's (Withsercus's) death after as well as before her introduction (cf. pp. 139–43, above). Eirekr's death also exemplifies part X of the pattern and seems if anything to have come to do so more as the tradition developed; it is at any rate presented as occurring after the death of Regnerus in Saxo's account, which represents a relatively early stage of the development, and elsewhere as occurring before it, so that the untimeliness of his death is so much the more emphasized (see pp. 140–41, above). Part X is, however, exemplified most impressively by Rǫgnvaldr, who, though he appears to have been loosely connected with the tradition from an early stage, does not come to exemplify the pattern until the stage represented by the X version of *Ragnars saga* (see section (*iii*), above), i.e. well after the introduction of Áslaug (he dies, it is true, in *Krákumál*, where Áslaug is briefly mentioned, cf. p. 90, above, but there he is presented neither as a son of Ragnarr loðbrók, nor as dying at a young age, or in any 'miraculous' way).

It has emerged from the discussion that where the careers of Ragnarr's sons fit the heroic biographical pattern, this seems to be due to the influence of the pattern as exemplified by either the Ragnarr or the Áslaug figure, or both. Ívarr's exemplification of part VI seems to represent an imitation of Ragnarr's slaying of Þóra's serpent (see section (*iv*), above), and Sigurðr ormr-í-auga's exemplification of part IVA seems to have developed in reparation for the fact that neither Ragnarr (at least at the later stages of the tradition's development, cf. pp. 91–92, above) nor Áslaug represents this part of the pattern at a very early age (see section (*ii*), above). The Ragnarr-figure's total failure to exemplify parts I and II of the pattern is of course made up for by the Áslaug-figure's fulfilment of them, as shown in section (a) of this chapter, see pp. 91, 93, above; reparation for his partial failure to exemplify parts VIII and X, on the other hand, seems to have been attempted prior to Áslaug's introduction with the story of Eirekr's death by impalement on spears (cf. pp. 139–44, above), and, in the case of part X, to have been continued after her introduction with this same story (see pp. 142–43, above), and, most significantly, with the story of Rǫgnvaldr's death as a young man at Hvítabœr (see section (*iii*), above).

In the foregoing discussion it was also suggested that, as well as showing the influence of traditions about the sexual relations of Sigurðr and Brynhildr, the story of Ívarr's procreation derives in part from the account of Childericus I's bridal night in the so-called *Chronicle of Fredegarius* (see section (*i*), above); and that Rǫgnvaldr, originally the tenth-century Northumbrian king Rægnald, came to the notice of the *Krákumál* poet by a more or less direct route from England to the Hebrides, and to that of the X redactor of *Ragnars saga* partly by way of *Krákumál*, cf. pp. 132–33, above, but also, and independently, by a route from England to Iceland by way of Denmark and Norway (see pp. 103–14, above). The importance of this latter route for the development of the Ragnarr loðbrók tradition will be made clear in a different context in section (e) of the next chapter. It was further suggested that, at least as far as Síbilja is concerned, the stories of Ívarr's cow-slayings have their ultimate origins in Hindu mythology (see section (*iv*), above); that Agnarr, originally more prominent than Eirekr in the Ragnarr loðbrók tradition, became less so after being adopted by the tradition of Hrólfr kraki (p. 119, above); that Eirekr, after developing his own prominence in the Ragnarr loðbrók tradition, was instrumental in attracting into it the name and certain other features of Craca, the stepmother of Ericus Disertus in the traditions preserved in Book V of Saxo's *Gesta Danorum* (pp. 119–22, 135–36, above); that *Krákumál* differs little in its surviving form from that in which it was composed (pp. 125–32, above), and that its title, originally a calque on Old Irish *baðbscél*, meaning 'tale of slaughter', was also instrumental in drawing the Craca figure (i.e. Kráka) into the Ragnarr loðbrók tradition (pp. 131–32, 136, above); that the story of Eirekr's death by impalement on spears is in some way connected to Herodotus's account of Salmoxis, where the motif of impalement also occurs (pp. 139 40, above); and that the story of Hvítserkr's death was influenced by that of Eirekr's in two stages—first in the older Ragnarr loðbrók tradition, before Áslaug's introduction, and later at the stage represented by the Y version of *Ragnars saga* (section (*vi*), above).

J. de Vries (cf. p. 103, above) is clearly right in maintaining that the introduction of Áslaug gave increased form and coherence to the Ragnarr loðbrók tradition. As will be evident, the expression 'the older Ragnarr loðbrók tradition' has been used here to refer to the tradition in its relatively formless, disjointed state, before the introduction of Áslaug. This older stage of the tradition is reflected in different ways in *Krákumál* and Book IX of Saxo's *Gesta*

Danorum; it is true that Áslaug is mentioned in *Krákumál*, but the mention is only a brief one, and it is legitimate to regard her presence in the poem as due to secondary influence from the Ragnarr loðbrók tradition. The content of the older tradition may be summed up as follows: Ragnarr kills Þóra's serpent (thus acquiring the nickname *loðbrók*), has sons by her and various other wives (not including Áslaug), engages in various battles, dies in King Ella's snake-pit, and is avenged by his sons (*Krákumál* concentrates more than Saxo on Ragnarr's battles, and Saxo dwells more than *Krákumál* on his wives and sons). Such, very briefly, was the state of the tradition prior to the introduction of Áslaug, the main subject of the next chapter.

CHAPTER III

RAGNARR AND ÁSLAUG IN BALLAD AND LEGEND

(a) Previous attempts at synthesis; scope of the present investigation

In this chapter, after reviewing earlier work on the subject in the present section, I shall attempt in section (c) to trace the development of the Áslaug-figure prior to its incorporation in the Ragnarr loðbrók tradition, while in sections (b), (d), and (e) I shall argue that the Faroese *Ragnars kvæði* derive primarily from two Norwegian oral sources, both independent of *Ragnars saga*. These are, on the one hand, a ballad about a serpent-fight, drawing its material from the pre-Áslaug stages of the Ragnarr loðbrók tradition, and on the other a local legend (called the Spangereid-legend), behind which there lay from the beginning an awareness of Áslaug's parentage, of her marriage to Ragnarr, and of her rôle as Kráka, and which was also influenced by oral sources deriving by way of Denmark from England and the continent. In section (f) I shall argue for the influence of *Tristrams saga* on the Y version of *Ragnars saga*, and in section (g) I shall summarize the chapter's argument in a stemma, and attempt to tie up certain loose ends of the discussion.

It is now appropriate to discuss in detail the introduction of Áslaug into the Ragnarr loðbrók tradition, and her appearance in the rôles of Kráka and Randalín, which it may be assumed were in no sense clearly defined, and were certainly not identified by those names, prior to the introduction of Áslaug herself (cf. pp. 123–25, above). 'Bei der Betrachtung der Aslaugfigur ist die spätere Balladentradition von besonderer Bedeutung', as de Vries (1928a, 286) emphasizes, and it is necessary to discuss here the relationship of the ballad-analogues of *Ragnars saga* to each other, to the saga itself, and to the other major analogues.

The conclusions on this subject reached by de Vries in 1915, and summarized in the stemmata reproduced on p. 240, below, were as follows: the Ragnarr loðbrók tradition originally knew nothing of either Áslaug or Kráka, while the Spangereid-legend of Aadlow recorded by Torfæus (and summarized under headings IIIC and IX of the Analysis) originally had nothing to do with Ragnarr loðbrók. The Ragnarr loðbrók tradition and the Spangereid-legend combined, however, and together formed the basis of the now lost original version of *Ragnars saga*, in which a story of Áslaug-Kráka deriving from the Spangereid-legend was included, and from which descended, independently of each other, *Ragnarssona þáttr*, the Faroese *Ragnars kvæði*, a Norwegian ballad concentrating on the serpent-fight and no longer extant in its original form, and another lost version of *Ragnars saga*, called the 'older' version as distinct from the younger, surviving versions (cf. McTurk, 1975, 60), yet also distinct from its parent version, the 'original' one (see de Vries, 1915, 135, 167). This use of the term 'older' in relation to *Ragnars saga* thus differs from the way the term is applied to the saga elsewhere in this monograph, and is distinguished by quotation marks. The Norwegian ballad has, as its two main reflexes, the Norwegian 'Lindarorm' (see p. 61, above) on the one hand and the Danish 'Ormekamp' (see p. 57, above) on the other; in the former it has been considerably altered and augmented by independent influence from the Danish ballad known as 'Gralver Kongesön' ('Prince Gralver'), edited by Grundtvig as no. 29 in DgF (1853, 374–84), which contributes the foal with human speech, the title 'the lady of Sønderliðborg', the Roman emperor's daughter, and the setting in Iceland (for these details, see under headings V and VII of the Analysis). As well as providing source-material for the original version of *Ragnars saga*, the Spangereid-legend also gave rise, independently of the Ragnarr loðbrók tradition, to the Norwegian ballad referred to by Ramus (see under headings III and IIIC of the Analysis); from this ballad, which is no longer extant, are derived independently of each other the two Danish ballads 'Regnfred og Kragelil' and 'Karl og Kragelil' (see pp. 56–57, above). 'Regnfred og Kragelil' appears to have influenced the Faroese *Ragnars kvæði* in supplying them with the motif of gold being paid to the old man in exchange for his adopted daughter (see part VII of the Analysis, and de Vries, 1915, 172–73), while the surviving *Ragnars saga*, which descends from the 'older' *Ragnars saga* as de Vries defines it, appears to have influenced 'Karl og Kragelil' in supplying it with the name *Brynnyll* (= *Brynhildr*) for the heroine's mother (see part IIIC of the Analysis and de Vries, 1915, 175–76). The motif in 'Karl og Kragelil' of the heroine's father's death in a snake-yard (see part IIIC of the Analysis) is also due to secondary influence, though in this case (see de Vries, 1915, 178) from poetic traditions about Gunnarr Gjúkason and Ragnarr loðbrók (presumably the eddaic Atli-lays, see p. 89, above, and *Krákumál* respectively). The Faroese 'Gests ríma' in its surviving form derives from an older 'Gests ríma', now lost, which in turn derives from the surviving *Ragnars saga* (de Vries, 1915, 182–88). Finally, as I have indicated elsewhere (McTurk, 1975, 56–57), de Vries (1915, 188–206) argues that *Vǫlsunga saga* and *Ragnars saga* were originally mutually independent.

Such in sum are de Vries's arguments in the fourth chapter of his book on the Faroese ballads, the chapter dealing with the *Ragnars kvæði*. As will be evident, he believes, among other things, that the *Ragnars kvæði* preserve traces of an earlier, more original version of *Ragnars saga* than either of the surviving versions (though in his book he uses only 1824b of the two surviving texts, and does not discuss similarities and differences between it and 147). In his chapter on 'Brynhildar táttur' (ch. 2), by contrast, he concludes that roughly the first five sixths of this ballad derive from the surviving *Vǫlsunga saga* (i.e. the version reflected in 1824b, see p. 54, above), while the remainder derives from *Þiðriks saga*. These first five sixths include the stanzas dealing with the begetting of Ásla Sjúrðardóttir and her birth and abandonment to the river, summarized under headings IIA, IIIA, and IX of the Analysis; these stanzas, according to de Vries in 1915 (see de Vries, 1915, 70, 77, 98–99) were interpolated. Later, however, in response to the writings of Neckel (1920) and de Boor (1923), de Vries (1928a, 286–89) came to regard not only these stanzas, but also the prose summary recorded by Müller of a lost Faroese poem, and reproduced under headings III and IX of the Analysis, as preserving an older account of Áslaug's early history than is provided by either *Vǫlsunga saga* or *Ragnars saga*. He was somewhat more reluctant to abandon a view which is manifest from his stemma (see p. 240, fig. 3, below) and from the summary just given, i.e. that the Spangereid-legend of Aadlow recorded by Torfæus originally had nothing to do with Ragnarr loðbrók. It is indeed striking that Torfæus makes no mention of Ragnarr loðbrók in the immediate context of the local traditions he is reporting, even though his report does follow on from a discussion of Ragnarr's marriage to Kráka in *Ragnars saga* (see Helgason, 1975, 82); and that Ramus's account, which is largely based on Torfæus's and also deals with these traditions in the general context of Ragnarr loðbrók (Helgason, 1975, 85–86), makes no mention of the latter when discussing them specifically. J. de Vries's unwillingness to abandon his view is apparent in his remark on the lost Faroese poem lying behind the prose account given by Müller, the content of which has much in common with the Spangereid-legend recorded by Torfæus and Ramus: 'daß sich diese Erzählung gar nicht mit der Krakasage der Ragnarssaga verträgt' (de Vries, 1928a, 288). If it is borne in mind that, in the account in question, Osla is brought up by a man named Kraaka who is not her father, this remark is surely at variance with de Vries's own view, expressed in the same article (1928a, 278–80) and discussed in the last chapter (see pp. 119–22, 135–36, above), that the name *Kráka* entered the Ragnarr loðbrók tradition from the story of Ericus Disertus, where it is the name of the hero's stepmother, was applied to Áslaug in the early stages of her career, and, since an explanation for this was needed, was also applied, by 'eine Verdoppelung des Stiefmutter-motivs' (de Vries, 1928a, 279), to the mother of Áslaug's foster-mother, Gríma, who is presented as naming the girl Kráka after her own mother. If this was indeed the process whereby Kráka became part of the Ragnarr loðbrók tradition, a process which, as will be evident, presupposes that Áslaug was already part of it, then it follows that any account mentioning both Áslaug and Kráka together, even if it does not mention Ragnarr loðbrók, must also presuppose a stage of development at which Áslaug had come to be associated with Ragnarr, provided, of course, that pure coincidence can be safely discounted. If this is accepted, and if it is also acknowledged, as it surely must be, that the name *Osla* is strikingly similar to the name *Áslaug*, then it seems likely that an association of Áslaug and Kráka with Ragnarr loðbrók lies somewhere in the background of the lost Faroese poem referred to by Müller.

The same logic may be applied to the topographical names *Aadlowhougen* and *Krakubecken*, which according to Torfæus (cf. part IIIC of the Analysis) occur in close proximity to each other in the Spangereid area, and for which Ramus uses the forms *Aatløgs Hougen* and *Kraake-Bækken*. K. Liestøl (1917, 105–06) and Helgason (1975, 79–80) have removed doubts raised by Storm (1878, 116–18) and de Vries (1915, 157) as to whether the forms *Aadlow* and *Aatløg* used by Torfæus and Ramus respectively in fact correspond to *Áslaug* (rather than to *Oddlaug*). In 1915, de Vries (1915, 155, 160, 163–65) argued that the names *Aadlowhougen* and *Krakubæk* (*sic*), together with the name *Gullvigen/Guldviig* also used by Torfæus and Ramus and meaning 'the golden cove' (see part IIIC of the Analysis), pointed to the localization in the Spangereid area of a popular tale about a girl named Áslaug-Kráka and a golden harp, a tale which, in his view, had at first no connection with the Ragnarr loðbrók tradition, but later combined with it and thus provided source-material for the original version of *Ragnars saga*. In the light of de Vries's more recent explanation (1928a, 278–80) of Kráka's presence in the Ragnarr loðbrók tradition, however, it must be concluded, as with the lost Faroese poem just discussed, that, provided pure coincidence can be safely ruled out, a connection with Ragnarr loðbrók must underlie the geographical closeness to each other of the two names in question, even though there are no local traces of Ragnarr loðbrók, and no references to him in the relevant parts of Torfæus's and Ramus's accounts. The information recorded by Torfæus that Aadlow became Queen of Denmark (see parts IIIC and IX of the Analysis) in any case suggests that his informants were aware of a tradition of her marriage to Ragnarr loðbrók, as K. Liestøl (1917, 105) points out. K. Liestøl (1917, 106–07) also argues that *Kraaka*, a reasonably common river name, originally existed as the name of a brook at Spangereid (in the form *Kraakebekken*, cf. *Krakubecken*) quite independently of any story about Ragnarr loðbrók or his wife Áslaug or a woman named Kráka, but that after stories on these subjects had developed and combined, they became localized at Spangereid by attraction of the woman's name to the brook's name. From this it would seem to follow that the name *Aadlowhougen* developed only after the localization had taken place. H. de Boor (1923, 112–13), on the other hand, seems to think that the three names *Aadlowhougen*, *Krakubecken* and *Gullvigen* all arose in the Spangereid area as a result of influence from stories about Áslaug and Kráka, which were already part of the Ragnarr loðbrók tradition.

It seems likely, then, that the Spangereid-legend of Aadlow had Ragnarr loðbrók as part of its background from the very beginning. Can it also be said that Áslaug was regarded from the very beginning as the daughter of Sigurðr and Brynhildr? J. de Vries (1915, 163–64) thought not in 1915, a fact which does not emerge from the summary of his conclusions given above (pp. 150–51), or from his stemma (see p. 240, fig. 3, below); he later (de Vries, 1928a, 286–90, cf. 274, n. 45 and 278, n. 55) came to change this opinion, however, apparently as a result of reading reviews of his work by K. Liestøl (1917) and de Boor (1923). In 1915 he argued (de Vries, 1915, 154–64) that the idea that Áslaug was the daughter of Sigurðr and Brynhildr did not emerge until after the Spangereid-legend had become combined with the Ragnarr loðbrók tradition and the story of Ragnarr imposing riddling-conditions on Áslaug-Kráka (see part IVA of the Analysis) had also developed. In this view, Áslaug-Kráka was to outward appearances little more than a peasant-girl when she became associated with Ragnarr loðbrók (though her double name and the motif of her arrival in a harp as a child indicated that she was no ordinary human being, see de Vries, 1915, 159); only later was it thought necessary to provide her with illustrious parents. Before this view is criticized, it may be noted that it serves as a reminder that, in Book IX of Saxo's *Gesta Danorum*, which seems to reflect a stage of the Ragnarr loðbrók tradition prior to the introduction of Áslaug and Kráka, neither of whom it mentions (see pp. 123–25, above), and which makes no mention either of Sigurðr the Vǫlsungr or of Brynhildr, Regnerus has sexual relations with a girl of humble origin ('famulam', Saxo, IX.iv, 18), the unnamed daughter of Hesbernus and mother of his son Ubbo. The usefulness of this reminder will be made clear below (pp. 226–27).

Apart from this, however, de Vries's earlier view just outlined has little to recommend it. In the first place, it can hardly have been to his own advantage to suggest that Áslaug came to be regarded as the daughter of Sigurðr and Brynhildr only after her association with Ragnarr loðbrók, since this would make it necessary to posit a troublesome extra stage—not in fact included in de Vries's stemma, see p. 240, fig. 3, below—between, on the one hand, the combination of the Spangereid-legend with the Ragnarr loðbrók tradition, and, on the other, what de Vries calls the 'original' version of *Ragnars saga*. This original version must have presented Áslaug as the daughter of Sigurðr and Brynhildr, since she appears as such in all the relevant works supposed to descend from it—*Ragnarssona þáttr*, the *Ragnars kvæði*, and *Ragnars saga* in its surviving forms ('Lindarormen' and 'Ormekampen', which according to de Vries also descend from it, see p. 150, above and p. 240, below, are irrelevant here, since they deal with a stage of Ragnarr's career prior to his meeting with Áslaug-Kráka, who is thus neither mentioned nor represented in them.)

In the second place, K. Liestøl (1917, 105) and de Boor (1923, 113) have emphasized that there is no reason to attribute to secondary influence from the Ragnarr loðbrók tradition the name *Brynnyll* for the heroine's mother in the A-text of 'Karl og Kragelil' (see part IIIC of the Analysis), as de Vries did in 1915, see pp. 150–51, above; on the other hand their failure to mention in this connection the names *Regnfred* and *Sigurd* that occur in the A-text of 'Regnfred og Kragelil' (see also part IIIC of the Analysis) presumably means that they accept de Vries's well-documented view (de Vries, 1915, 167–68) that these names are here due to such influence.

Thirdly, de Boor (1923, 113) has argued convincingly that, on the one hand, the story of Heimir and Áslaug in the 1824b text of *Ragnars saga*, and that of Gestur and Ásla in the 'Gests ríma' (see part IIIC of the Analysis) and, on the other, the stories of Ásla being set afloat in 'Brynhildar táttur', and of Osla coming to land in Müller's account of the lost Faroese poem (see under the main heading III, and part IIIA, of the Analysis), go back to sources which in combination helped to form the Spangereid-legend recorded by Torfæus and Ramus, and which also descended from an old tradition according to which Áslaug was the daughter of Sigurðr and Brynhildr.

Fourthly and finally, de Boor (1923, 113–14) finds independent evidence that Áslaug belonged originally to the Sigurðr-legend in the group of Faroese ballads about the 'dvørgamoy' or 'dwarf-maiden', which according to him represent variants of the legend of Sigurðr and Sigrdríf(a), the valkyrie figure whose rôle is fulfilled by Brynhildr in the Hindarfjall episode of *Vǫlsunga saga* (chs. 20–22). These ballads deal with the relations, amorous and otherwise, of Sjúrður, son of Sigmundur, with a dwarf-maiden variously referred to by the names *Ása*, *Ásla* and *Aldiruna*; and the last of these names is applied in certain texts of the Faroese ballad 'Regin smiður' (which forms part of the *Sjúrðar kvæði* described above on pp. 59–60) to a woman visited by Sjúrður in circumstances comparable to those of Sigurðr's relations with the valkyrie figure named Sigrdrífa in the eddaic poems *Fáfnismál* (on the dating of which see p. 100, above) and *Sigrdrífumál* (probably completed by *c.*1000, see Sveinsson, 1962, 467); unnamed but distinguished from Brynhildr in the eddaic poem *Grípisspá* (dating from the twelfth century or even later, see Sveinsson, 1962, 528); and corresponding to

Brynhildr as she appears in ch. 21 of *Vǫlsunga saga* (see Olsen, 1906–08, 47–54). He visits this Aldiruna after slaying the serpent at Glitraheiði and then leaves, causing her to mourn (see Djurhuus & Matras, 1951–63, 91, 195, n. 7). The names *Ásla* and *Aldiruna* are thus applied in Faroese tradition to a figure corresponding to Sigrdrífa-Brynhildr, the valkyrie visited by Sigurðr in Old Norse-Icelandic tradition. Now in the Danish ballad 'Karl og Kragelil', *Adellrun* is the real name of the girl who at first gives her name as *Kragelil*; whose mother's name is given as *Brynnyll* in the A-text of the ballad; and who corresponds to Aadlow in Torfæus's account. All this suggests that Áslaug belonged originally to legends connected with Sigurðr rather than with Ragnarr loðbrók, and that she was regarded as the daughter of Sigurðr and Brynhildr, if not from the very beginning of her existence, then at least from a stage prior to her incorporation in the Ragnarr Loðbrók tradition. It is noteworthy that, by 1928 (see de Vries, 1928a, 286–89), de Vries appears to have largely adopted de Boor's conclusions.

Among the reviewers of de Vries's work of 1915, K. Liestøl (1917, 85–86, 102–10, cf. also 1915, 213–15, and 1970, 44–51, 101–02), von Sydow (1919), and Neckel (1920) were especially critical of his general tendency to find the Faroese ballads more closely related to their Icelandic saga-analogues than to their continental Scandinavian ballad-analogues. It was Liestøl who made this criticism in most detail, and although de Vries (1931, 129–30) has replied to his remarks as far as the bulk of the *Sjúrðar kvæði* is concerned, he has not, as far as I know, replied to them in relation to the *Ragnars kvæði* or the other Faroese ballad-material relevant in particular to Ragnarr loðbrók. For the purposes of his discussion, K. Liestøl divides the *Ragnars kvæði* into two main parts, as was done in the last chapter (see p. 58, above), noting that the first part, dealing with Ragnar's fight with the serpent, his winning of Tóra and her death, has its ballad-analogues in the Norwegian 'Lindarorm' and the Danish 'Ormekamp', while the second part, dealing with Ragnar's acquisition of Ásla Sjúrðardóttir, who at first presents herself as the low-born Kráka, is paralleled in Ramus's account of the otherwise unrecorded Norwegian ballad about an abandoned princess (see part III of the Analysis), and in the Danish ballads 'Regnfred og Kragelil' and 'Karl og Kragelil', both of which K. Liestøl (1915, 215), like de Vries (cf. p. 150, above), sees as deriving from the ballad referred to by Ramus.

With regard to the first part of the *Ragnars kvæði*, K. Liestøl

(1917, 102–10) criticizes de Vries's view, evident from the summary given above (pp. 150–51) and from his stemma (p. 240, fig. 4, below) that, if secondary borrowing is left out of account, there is no direct relationship between the *Ragnars kvæði* on the one hand and the ballad-tradition represented by 'Lindarormen' and 'Ormekampen' on the other, the similarities between the Faroese and mainland Scandinavian ballads being here due to the fact that they have a common source in the 'original' version of *Ragnars saga*, to which the Faroese ballads are more closely related than the others. Arguing against this view, K. Liestøl shows that the *Ragnars kvæði* have in common with 'Lindarormen' and 'Ormekampen' a number of elements which are not found in the Icelandic saga tradition represented by *Ragnars saga*, *Ragnarssona þáttr* and *Bósa saga* (K. Liestøl, 1970, 45, 102; *Bósa saga* need not, however, be taken any further into account in the present context, since I accept Jiriczek's view, 1893, ivl-iiil, that, in relation to *Ragnars saga* and *Ragnarssona þáttr*, it has no independent value; cf. p. 237, below.) The elements in question are as follows: firstly, the information found in the *Ragnars kvæði* and in 'Ormekampen' that, before the hero destroys the snake or worm, another warrior attempts to do so, but fails (see part VI of the Analysis); secondly, a concentration in the accounts of the hero's preparations for the serpent-fight in the *Ragnars kvæði* and in 'Lindarormen' on his use of tar and sand (both of which are, however, used by him in *Ragnarssona þáttr*, as are pitch and sand in *Ragnars saga*, see part V of the Analysis; K. Liestøl seems to ignore these two Icelandic examples of the motif in question); thirdly, the information in the *Ragnars kvæði* and in 'Lindarormen' that the noise made by the snake can be heard out at sea by those approaching it by ship (see part VI of the Analysis); fourthly, the information in the *Ragnars kvæði* and in one of the versions of 'Lindarormen' noted by Bugge (see part V of the Analysis) that the snake is warned of the hero's hostile presence in the *Ragnars kvæði* by Ragnar himself, who rouses the snake from sleep, and in the relevant version of 'Lindarormen' by the maiden; and fifthly (see K. Liestøl, 1970, 46, only), the references in the *Ragnars kvæði* and 'Ormekampen' to a red garment worn by the hero (see part V of the Analysis).

According to K. Liestøl, who evidently accepts de Vries's view that both 'Lindarormen' and 'Ormekampen' derive from a Norwegian ballad, i.e. the 'Lindarorm' ballad in its original form (see K. Liestøl, 1915, 213–15), these five points represent additions

made by the composer of this ballad to its main source, a relatively
early version of the relevant part of *Ragnars saga*, though in what
form this was available to the ballad-poet Liestøl does not specify.
He concludes (K. Liestøl, 1970, 47; 1917, 110) that the first part of
the *Ragnars kvæði* derives primarily from the original 'Lindarorm'
ballad, but that the *Ragnars kvæði* nevertheless show more in
common with the Icelandic saga-tradition than with the relevant
ballad-analogues because they have as a secondary source a written
version of *Ragnars saga* close or identical to that which survives in
1824b. Where the Norwegian ballad differed in content from the
written saga, the *Ragnars kvæði* have adapted it to the latter, but they
have retained the additional elements just listed since these do not
disturb the plot of the saga as preserved in 1824b.

As for the second part of the *Ragnars kvæði*, K. Liestøl (1917,
104–10; 1970, 47–51) considers this together with the 'Gests ríma'
and with the parts of 'Brynhildar táttur' dealing with Ásla
Sjúrðardóttir (see under parts I, II, III, VII, and IX of the Analysis),
and finds that these Faroese ballads show similarities with Ramus's
account and with the two 'Kragelil' ballads that are not shared by
the Icelandic saga-tradition, here represented by *Ragnars saga* and
(to the extent only that it mentions Ragnarr's marriage to Áslaug
and the latter's parentage) by *Ragnarssona þáttr* (see part VII of the
Analysis). The similarities are as follows: firstly, the Áslaug-figure
is set afloat by her mother in 'Brynhildar táttur' and by her
stepmother in Ramus's account, and is washed ashore in the latter
and apparently also in the 'Gests ríma' (see part IIIC of the
Analysis; the stepmother-figure may reflect the duplication of the
stepmother-motif following the introduction of Kráka into the
Ragnarr loðbrók tradition from the story of Ericus Disertus, and
referred to earlier, see p. 152, above; for another possible explanation, however, see pp. 194–196, below). Secondly, when the
hero meets the maiden in the Faroese and mainland Scandinavian
ballads he is not motivated by a wish to visit friends and relations in
going to the place where he finds her, as Ragnarr is said to be in
Ragnars saga (see part VII of the Analysis). In the *Ragnars kvæði*,
Ragnar's purpose in making the journey is not specified; in
'Regnfred og Kragelil' and 'Karl og Kragelil' the hero is actually
looking for the maiden. (According to K. Liestøl, 1917, 108, and
1970, 50, who must surely be wrong on this point, this is also the
case with Ragnar in the *Ragnars kvæði*; see part VII of the Analysis.)
Thirdly, in the *Ragnars kvæði* and in 'Regnfred og Kragelil' the

hero, prior to taking the maiden off with him, gives gold and other gifts to the old man at whose home she had been living (see parts IIIC and VII of the Analysis).

From these considerations K. Liestøl (1917, 110) concludes that the second part of the *Ragnars kvæði* also derives primarily from a Norwegian ballad (in this case the one referred to by Ramus), and secondarily from the surviving *Ragnars saga*, while the ballad itself derives from the Spangereid-legend, which independently influenced *Ragnars saga* (K. Liestøl, 1915, 215). I would add here that this influence is apparent in the surviving texts of *Ragnars saga* (i.e. 147 and 1824b as edited by Olsen, 1906–08), which contain references to Spangarheiðr and to Kráka, but does not appear in *Ragnarssona þáttr*, and thus cannot be assumed to have affected the older *Ragnars saga* which the *þáttr* represents. It will be shown below (in sections (c) and (d)) that the older *Ragnars saga* is, in fact, unlikely to have borrowed from the Spangereid-legend the information (conveyed by *Ragnarssona þáttr*, see part VII of the Analysis) that Ragnarr's second wife was Áslaug, also known as Randalín, the daughter of Sigurðr and Brynhildr (or indeed to have borrowed at all from that source). K. Liestøl (1917, 110) further concludes that the *Ragnars kvæði* have combined into one the two Norwegian ballads which provide their basic material (i.e. the original version of 'Lindarormen' and the ballad referred to by Ramus), and have adapted the accounts of both to fit *Ragnars saga* as preserved in 1824b.

These observations of K. Liestøl's are not always entirely accurate, as I have indicated in connection with the second item in each of his two lists. In seeking to assert the uniqueness of the ballad-tradition in relation to the saga-tradition, Liestøl has ignored the fact that one of the features he lists as unique to the ballad-tradition—the hero's use of tar and sand in preparing to fight the serpent—is in fact paralleled in the saga-tradition, and must therefore have been in the original source of both, provided, of course, that secondary influence by one tradition on the other can here be safely discounted. In seeking also to relate the Faroese ballads more closely to the mainland Scandinavian ballads than to the Icelandic saga-tradition, Liestøl exaggerates the similarities between the Faroese *Ragnars kvæði* and the Danish 'Kragelil' ballads by giving the false impression that not only the latter ballads, but also the *Ragnars kvæði*, present the hero as actually looking for the maiden when he sets out on the journey that leads to his meeting her. Apart from these inaccuracies, however, Liestøl has performed a useful service in drawing attention to the various similarities and differences he lists; and his arguments as to the relationship of the *Ragnars kvæði* to *Ragnars saga* are, I believe, essentially valid, though in need of modification in different ways, as I shall indicate below.

In summary it may be recalled that de Vries in his work of 1915, which prompted K. Liestøl's discussion of 1917 and other reviews, found no direct relationship between the Faroese *Ragnars kvæði* and their mainland Scandinavian ballad-analogues. He derived the Norwegian 'Lindarorm' and the Danish 'Ormekamp' independently of each other from the original Norwegian version of the 'Lindarorm' ballad, which he placed in a collateral relationship with the *Ragnars kvæði*, *Ragnarssona þáttr*, and an 'older' lost version of *Ragnars saga*, and traced together with these to an 'original' version of *Ragnars saga*, also lost. As for the two Danish 'Kragelil' ballads, he saw these as descending collaterally from the Norwegian ballad referred to by Ramus, which he placed at a still further remove from the *Ragnars kvæði*, deriving it independently of the 'original' *Ragnars saga* from one of the latter's sources, the Spangereid-legend, which according to him supplied the 'original' *Ragnars saga* with the story of Áslaug-Kráka, but did not in itself connect her in any way with Sigurðr and Brynhildr, or with Ragnarr loðbrók. He later (de Vries, 1928a) came to modify this last opinion, at least as far as Sigurðr and Brynhildr were concerned, in the light of K. Liestøl's (1917), Neckel's (1920), and de Boor's (1923) reviews. K. Liestøl (1915, 213–15) agreed with de Vries in deriving 'Lindarormen' and 'Ormekampen' from the original Norwegian version of the former ballad, and the two 'Kragelil' ballads from the Ramus ballad. In contrast to de Vries, however, K. Liestøl (1917) found the Faroese *Ragnars kvæði* no less closely related to their Scandinavian ballad-analogues than to their Icelandic saga-analogues. According to Liestøl, they made use of the surviving *Ragnars saga* in acquiring their final form, but derive primarily from two Norwegian ballads, namely 'Lindarormen' in its original form and the Ramus ballad. As for the sources of these two ballads, K. Liestøl (1915, 213–14) apparently followed de Vries in deriving the original 'Lindarorm' ballad from an early, lost version of *Ragnars saga*, though he was no clearer than de Vries as to whether this was available to the ballad-composer in oral or written form, and gave even less idea than de Vries did of its length or scope. He followed de Vries in deriving the Ramus ballad from an oral source, the Spangereid-legend, and in believing that this gave rise independently to the Kráka-Áslaug episode of *Ragnars saga*; unlike de Vries in 1915, however, he believed that the Spangereid-legend had behind it from the very beginning a tradition according to which Áslaug was the daughter of Sigurðr and Brynhildr (cf. also Neckel, 1920, and de Boor, 1923) and wife of Ragnarr loðbrók.

Before an attempt is made to synthesize the various suggested relationships reviewed here, it may be noted that de Boor (1923, 112–13), who had rather less respect than either de Vries or K. Liestøl for the antiquity or independent value of the Spangereid-legend as recorded by Torfæus and Ramus, differed from de Vries in regarding the motif of Aadlow-Asløg's arrival in a golden harp as a particularly late, secondary feature of the legend, and Neckel (1920, 18) more specifically suggested that its presence in the Norwegian traditions available to Torfæus and Ramus was due to secondary influence from *Ragnars saga* as preserved in 1824b, where Heimir conceals Áslaug in a harp (see part IIIC of the Analysis).

While it is not certain how far the prose accounts of Torfæus, Ramus, and Müller represent actual ballad-traditions, it is natural to consider them together with the ballad-analogues of *Ragnars saga*, partly because of their closeness in subject-matter to the surviving ballad-analogues, and partly because Ramus and Müller seem to refer explicitly to ballad-sources (Ramus with the words 'endnu siunges en Viise i Norrige', 'a song is still sung in Norway', see Helgason, 1975, 86; and Müller, 1818, 481, in mentioning 'Et andet færøisk Quad', 'another Faroese song'). For the purposes of the present discussion they may be counted among the saga's ballad-analogues, though their secondary character, and the fact that Torfæus makes no reference to a ballad-source, must not be forgotten.

It is clear that the ballad and saga traditions of Ragnarr loðbrók are more closely related to each other than either of these traditions is to Book IX of Saxo's *Gesta Danorum*, which, consequently, has played virtually no part in the immediately foregoing discussion. The reason for this is that the ballad-tradition is mainly concerned with events corresponding to two episodes of *Ragnars saga*, only one of which is at all closely paralleled in Saxo's account. These are, firstly, Ragnarr's winning of Þóra as a result of slaying the serpent, and her subsequent death; and secondly, his marriage to the ostensibly low-born Kráka, who eventually reveals herself as Áslaug, the daughter of Sigurðr and Brynhildr. As indicated earlier (see pp. 123–25, above) the second of these two episodes has virtually no parallel in Saxo's account; Saxo shows at best only a faint awareness of its events, and makes no mention of Kráka, Áslaug, Sigurðr, or Brynhildr.

The main events of the first episode, on the other hand, are, it is true, paralleled in Saxo's narrative: here (Saxo IX.iv, 4 8) Regnerus slays two serpents and as a result wins to wife Thora, who later (Saxo IX.iv, 13) dies (cf. parts V, VI, and VII of the Analysis). As in *Krákumál*, str. 1, and certain texts of the *Ragnars kvæði* (see part V of the Analysis), Regnerus in Saxo's account (IX.iv, 8) acquires the nickname *Lothbrog* (i.e. *loðbrók*) as a result of his serpent-slaying exploit; but whereas *Krákumál* does not elaborate on the hairy costume to which the nickname seems to refer, Saxo, the relevant ballads, and the saga-tradition give detailed accounts of the hero's preparation of his costume for the serpent-fight (see part V of the Analysis). Saxo (IX.iv, 6) relates that Regnerus strengthened the costume by first bathing in it and then allowing it to freeze on his body; whereas the ballad and saga traditions, as will be shown in more detail below (see section (b)), agree with each other in reporting that the hero treated the costume with tar and sand. While the latter type of treatment seems from a modern point of view far more logical and sensible than the one recorded by Saxo, it must be emphasized that Saxo's description of Regnerus's use of ice for added protection is neither as unparalleled nor as absurd as de Vries (1928a, 271) seemed to think; folklore parallels from Transylvania and Hungary were pointed out long ago by Wlislocki (1887; cf. Krappe, 1941–42, 334–35), and the Tatar legend referred to by Mudrak (1943, 119) has been noted earlier (see p. 13, above). Davidson (1980, 152), moreover, has recently drawn attention to evidence that grizzly bears sometimes wet their fur deliberately and then roll in the snow, thus acquiring coats of ice which protect them against arrows and even bullets. It thus seems likely that Saxo's account arose out of an interpretation of the name *Loðbrók* that developed independently of the one involving tar and sand, rather than, as de Vries (1928a, 271) seems to suggest, out of a misunderstanding of the tar and sand motif.

Saxo's account, then, seems in general to be at a rather further remove from the ballad and saga traditions than these are from each other. It is true that a special link between Saxo and the ballad tradition is indicated by the fact that in Saxo's account, and in two of the Norwegian variants of 'Lindarormen' noted by Bugge, the hero is helped by a woman in his measures for self-protection: in Saxo's account (IX.iv, 6) Regnerus obtains his costume from a nurse, and in the ballad-variants the hero is advised in the one case by his mother, in the other by an old woman, to make use of tar and sand (see parts IV A and V of the Analysis). In Landstad's text of 'Lindarormen', by contrast (see also under part V of the Analysis), it is a foal who gives him this advice; but the talking foal, as already indicated (see p. 150, above), is one of the features borrowed by 'Lindarormen' from the Danish 'Prince Gralver' ballad; the woman in the rôle of helper or adviser seems to represent an earlier stage of the ballad's development. This was pointed out by de Vries (1915, 137–38, 146–47), who also acknowledged the presence of the adviser-motif in Saxo's account; somewhat questionably, perhaps, he did not go so far as to regard it as one of the oldest features of the story. Whether or not he was right in this respect, however, he was undoubtedly right in his claim (de Vries, 1915, 136–37) that Landstad (1853, 141, n. 3), in commenting on certain other features of 'Lindarormen' in relation to Saxo's Book IX, had tended to exaggerate the similarities between Saxo's and the ballad's accounts.

Neither *Krákumál* nor Arngrímur's account is, any more than Saxo's account, directly relevant to the present discussion. It is true that in the first strophe of *Krákumál* the narrator speaks of having acquired the name *Loðbrók* as a result of slaying a serpent and so winning Þóra in marriage, but the poem's treatment of this episode is too brief to permit detailed comparison with the ballad and saga traditions. Its mention of Áslaug (in str. 26) is also too brief to be of any value in the present context; and its title, as argued earlier (see pp. 125–33, above), need not and very possibly does not imply any awareness of the Kráka story, of which not the slightest trace appears in the poem itself. Arngrímur's account has as its main sources the lost *Skjǫldunga saga*, the Y version of *Ragnars saga*, and Saxo's account, as noted above (see p. 57); it thus has independent value only insofar as it conveys the content of *Skjǫldunga saga*. *Ragnarssona þáttr*, which Arngrímur evidently did not use (Olrik, 1894b, 147–48, 148 n. 1; Benediktsson 1957, 261), also includes *Skjǫldunga saga* among its sources, which further include the lost older *Ragnars saga* (cf. p. 56, above).

Comparison of Arngrímur's account with *Ragnarssona þáttr* on the one hand and the 1824b text of *Ragnars saga* on the other shows that *Skjǫldunga saga* differed from the Y version of *Ragnars saga* in, among other things, stressing the political importance for Ragnarr of his marriage to Þóra (cf. part IVB of the Analysis), but it is impossible to say how far, if at all, the actual serpent-fight formed part of *Skjǫldunga saga*'s account. In ch. 19 of the first section of his *Rerum Danicarum fragmenta* Arngrímur does not mention it in connection with Ragnerus's marriage to Thora, which may suggest that it was not mentioned in *Skjǫldunga saga* either; in his appendix he does mention it, and in describing the serpent clearly borrows a phrase from Saxo (see part VI of the Analysis), though unlike Saxo he mentions only one serpent rather than two. What little he says about the serpent-fight, however, could easily have been condensed from the Y version of *Ragnars saga*; his account does not tell us anything about the fight itself that is not conveyed by the Y version of the saga or by Saxo. *Ragnarssona þáttr*'s treatment of the serpent-fight, which is a good deal fuller than Arngrímur's, does, it is true, differ in certain ways from Saxo's account on the one hand and that of the Y version of *Ragnars saga* on the other (see part V of the Analysis and cf. pp. 161–63, above, and section (b), below); but the differences need not be due to the influence of *Skjǫldunga saga*; they could equally well be attributed to the influence of the older *Ragnars saga*, to which the *þáttr*, after describing Ragnarr's victory over the serpent, refers in the following terms (Hb, 1892–96, 458, ll. 29–31): 'ok for þat sva sem seg*ir* i sogv Ragnars k*onungs* at h*ann* feck sið*an* Þorv borgarhiort *ok* sið*an* lagþiz h*ann* i hernað *ok* frelsti allt sitt riki' ('and it turned out as told in the saga of King Ragnarr, that he won Þóra borgarhjǫrtr and then embarked on warfare and liberated his entire kingdom'). This passage may suggest that the older *Ragnars saga* resembled *Skjǫldunga saga* and differed from the Y version of *Ragnars saga* in emphasizing the political implications of Ragnarr's marriage to Þóra, though the information contained in the quotation from the words '*ok* sið*an*' ('and then') onwards may, of course, derive solely from *Skjǫldunga saga*. AM 147 4to, which contains the X version of *Ragnars saga* and stands in a closer relationship to *Skjǫldunga saga* than does Ny kgl. saml. 1824b 4to (which contains the Y version; see McTurk, 1975, 64) is of no help here; not only is it insufficiently legible in the relevant part of the text (see Olsen 1906–08, 176–77), but the extent of its inheritance from *Skjǫldunga saga* as opposed to the older *Ragnars saga* is in general no easier to determine than in the case of *Ragnarssona þáttr*.

Whatever the truth about Arngrímur's sources for the Þóra episode, his own treatment of it is too brief to be of immediate value in the present discussion. The same is true of his treatment of the Kráka-Áslaug episode. He must of course have been aware of the Kráka story from the Y version of *Ragnars saga*, whether or not the story occurred in *Skjǫldunga saga*; as noted earlier (see pp. 123, 134, above), however, he makes very little of it, and does not even mention Kráka by name. Kráka certainly figures in the X version of *Ragnars saga* (see Olsen, 1906–08, 177–81), if not quite so fully as in the Y version, but *Ragnarssona þáttr* shows no awareness at all of the Kráka story, though it does record Ragnarr's marriage to Áslaug-Randalín, the daughter of Sigurðr and Brynhildr (see part VII of the Analysis). It seems likely that, as Guðnason (1969, 32) has argued, the Kráka story did not enter what may be called the saga-tradition of Ragnarr loðbrók (cf. pp. 132–33, 135–36, above) until the X stage, and did not appear in the older *Ragnars saga* or in *Skjǫldunga saga*. Guðnason (1969, 32; 1982, xlv) indeed argues convincingly, mainly on the basis of Arngrímur's account, that little more was told of Áslaug in *Skjǫldunga saga* than that she became Ragnarr's wife after Þóra's death and was the daughter of Sigurðr Fáfnisbani, to whom Arngrímur refers as follows (Benediktsson, 1950, 464): 'celeberrimus Europæ pugil Sigvardus Regibus Sveciæ oriundus; illi cognomen Foffnisbane, qvasi serpenticidam dixeris'.

Krákumál and the accounts of Saxo and Arngrímur will therefore continue to occupy something of a background position in the present discussion, though they will, of course, be referred to below as and when they become relevant. In particular, it must be remembered that they differ from the ballad-tradition and resemble *Ragnarssona þáttr* and the X and Y versions of *Ragnars saga* in dealing to a greater or lesser extent with the activities of the hero's sons, and in following his own career up to the time of his death, which they agree with the *þáttr* and the saga in placing in a snake-pit. The ballad-tradition is not, it is true, entirely free of references to Ragnarr's sons and to the manner of his death; the sons are briefly referred to in the 'Gests ríma' and the C text of the *Ragnars kvæði* (see part VII of the Analysis), and a snake-pit is mentioned in the A and C texts of 'Karl og Kragelil' (see part IIIC of the Analysis) as the scene of the heroine's father's death; these references will be explained below (see pp. 180–81, 186–88; cf. also pp. 168–69).

(b) The serpent-fight in the ballad-tradition

Neither the Norwegian 'Lindarorm' nor the Danish 'Ormekamp' gives any very convincing impression of having ever formed part of a narrative sequence comparable to what is found in the Icelandic saga-tradition as represented by *Ragnarssona þáttr* and by the X and Y versions of *Ragnars saga*, or in the Faroese *Ragnars kvæði*. 'Ormekampen' seems to come to a natural end after the hero has destroyed the worm and won the maiden (see part VII of the Analysis), and gives no hint that the story is likely to continue with anything comparable to Ragnarr's marriage, after Þóra's death, to Áslaug the daughter of Sigurðr and Brynhildr: this development, found in all surviving texts of the second part of the *Ragnars kvæði*, i.e. texts B-D and F-G, as well as in the *þáttr* and the saga, seems to be assumed even in the two cases where only the first part of the *Ragnars kvæði* is preserved, i.e. in texts A and E. (Here, Ragnar's first wife Tóra Borgarhjørt so A; jomfru Borgarhjørt E— prophesies that after her death he will marry the woman for whom his present wife's clothes are found to be a perfect fit, and in A explicitly states that this will be Ásla Sjúrðardóttir; it is a reasonable assumption that the Faroese *Ragnars kvæði* formed a two-part ballad-sequence from the earliest stages of their existence.) It is true that 'Ormekampen' shows the influence of the Sigurðr legend in presenting the hero as digging trenches to catch the worm's blood; but this feature, which may or may not have been in the original version of the ballad, need not imply any awareness of the notion that Sigurðr's daughter became the wife of Ragnarr loðbrók—a notion which, according to de Vries (1928a, 289–90; cf. pp. 90–91, above), arose relatively late in the development of contacts between the traditions of these two heroes. It is also true that 'Lindarormen' hints at a continuation of its story insofar as the hero does not marry proud Lyselin, the maiden he wins as a result of killing the snake, but leaves her for the Roman emperor's daughter, to whom he says he is betrothed (see part VII of the Analysis); but this seems to be due to the influence of the Danish 'Prince Gralver' ballad, and to have nothing to do with the Sigurðr legend. Neither 'Lindarormen' nor 'Ormekampen', moreover, makes any mention of sons born to the hero or of the hero's death, whether in a snake-pit or other circumstances, and in this respect they differ from the *þáttr* and the saga but resemble the *Ragnars kvæði*; while they differ from the *Ragnars kvæði* and the saga but resemble the *þáttr* in having nothing comparable to the Kráka episode.

On the other hand, it does seem likely that the name or nickname *loðbrók*, though not mentioned in either 'Lindarormen' or 'Ormekampen', forms part of the background of both. Storm (1878, 96–98) has convincingly suggested that the nickname gave rise to a variety of legendary accounts more or less consistent with the idea of preparing a hairy costume for use as protection in fighting a serpent, and there can be no doubt that the motif of the hero treating his garments with tar and sand in 'Lindarormen', and the mention of tar in connection with his costume in 'Orme-kampen' (see part V of the Analysis), fit this idea very neatly. Furthermore, although the names of the characters in the two ballads in no way correspond to those of the characters in the serpent-slaying episodes of the *þáttr*, the saga, and the *Ragnars kvæði*, a link with Ragnarr loðbrók (as opposed to just Loðbrók) seems to be suggested by the fact that the hero of 'Lindarormen' is described as the son of the Danish king (see parts IVA and V of the Analysis): the form 'Daniel, kongens søn', 'Daniel, the king's son', found in most of the variants of this ballad recorded by Bugge, is almost certainly a corruption of 'Danerkongens søn', 'the Danish king's son' (see DgF III, 1862, 798, n.). This implies that the tradition underlying the ballad (though not necessarily the ballad itself) was informed of a connection between the names *Ragnarr* and *Loðbrók*, since there is evidence that Reginheri/Ragnarr was associated historically with one of the Danish royal families of the ninth century (McTurk, 1976, 100, 111–23; cf. pp. 47–49, above), and may have been a son of one Sigifridus (d. 812), while Saxo (IX.iii, 1–4) and the 1824b text of *Ragnars saga* (ch. 3) describe Regnerus/Ragnarr as the son of Siwardus Ring/Sigurðr hringr, King of Denmark (see parts III and IVA of the Analysis; cf. also Arngrímur's account under heading IVB of the Analysis, and the *Ragnars kvæði* under part V). (I differ here from de Vries, 1915, 142–43, who does not allow to the expression 'Danerkongens søn' the significance I have attached to it, though I would not of course claim that it need imply a direct relationship between 'Lindar-ormen' and any of the surviving texts in which Ragnarr is presented as a Danish king's son, and would agree with de Vries, 1915, 137, that no such relationship between 'Lindarormen' and the Y version of *Ragnars saga* is implied by the fact that the hero is said in both to have been fifteen at the time of the serpent-slaying, see part IVA of the Analysis.)

It may be accepted here, as it is by K. Liestøl (1915, 213–14), that de Vries (1915, 148) is right in deriving both 'Lindarormen' and 'Ormekampen' from a Norwegian source, the 'Lindarorm' ballad in its original form. This original 'Lindarorm' ballad was evidently not so very different from the one that survives, but lacked the elements imported from the 'Prince Gralver' ballad, and listed earlier (see p. 150, above); the hero was advised about his protective covering by his mother rather than by a foal (see part V of the Analysis), and the ballad ended with his marrying the maiden he won as a result of slaying the serpent (cf. part VII of the Analysis). It may also be assumed that the tar and sand motif formed part of the original 'Lindarorm' ballad; as de Vries (1915, 142) indicates, the fact that tar only is mentioned in connection with the hero's garments in 'Ormekampen' is probably due to the fact that in this ballad, which seems to represent a younger stage of the ballad-tradition than 'Lindarormen', the tar and sand motif has had to make room for an increasing preoccupation with the hero's scarlet costume, one of the items listed by K. Liestøl (see pp. 156–57, above) as characteristic of the ballad-tradition as opposed to the saga-tradition. The tar and sand motif also occurs in the *Ragnars kvæði*, as Liestøl recognizes, and in *Ragnarssona þáttr* and the 1824b text of *Ragnars saga*, as Liestøl fails to notice (see p. 157, above); but these three works, as already indicated (see p. 166, above), all contain material additional to what is found in 'Lindarormen' and 'Ormekampen', including the information, on which they all agree, that Ragnarr married Áslaug, the daughter of Sigurðr and Brynhildr, after Þóra's death (see part VII of the Analysis). Nothing comparable to this development is found in either of the two ballads under discussion, and there is no reason to suppose that it formed any part of their common source, or was known to the tradition out of which that source arose.

I would suggest on the basis of these arguments that the original 'Lindarorm' ballad derived from a Norwegian oral tradition dealing solely or mainly with the slaying of a serpent and winning of a maiden by a hero named Ragnarr loðbrók, and not involving any sequel to speak of. I say 'to speak of', since it is hard to believe that the tradition here envisaged was never at any stage aware of the hero's sons or of his death in the snake-pit, partly because sons of Lodparchus, Lotbrocus are referred to in sources dating from as early as *c*.1070 (see ch. I, sections (a) and (c), above), and partly because the slaying of a serpent plays such a prominent part in the ballad; and the more prominent this feature was in the Ragnarr loðbrók tradition, the more likely the latter is to have attracted to itself the story of Gunnarr's death in the snake-pit, a development which seems to have taken place at a relatively early stage of contact between legends of Ragnarr loðbrók on the one hand and legends of the Vǫlsungar and Gjúkungar on the other (see pp. 89–90, above). This contact must in any case have arisen partly as a result of the similarity of Ragnarr's serpent-slaying exploit to that of Sigurðr the Vǫlsungr, who may also have come to be regarded, apparently independently of the Ragnarr loðbrók tradition, as having met his death in a snake-yard, see Grundtvig in ▶gF I (1853, 334). If it may indeed be admitted that the serpent-slaying exploit in 'Lindarormen' and 'Ormekampen' presupposes a tradi- tion which included the story of the hero's death in a snake-pit, it may also be suggested that this story in turn presupposes the involvement of his avenging sons. The tradition behind the two ballads cannot be seen as identical to the tradition known to Saxo, since Saxo's account, as we have seen, differs from the ballad and saga traditions in its treatment of the serpent-fight and the preparations for it; it may, however, be regarded as comparable to the tradition behind Saxo's account insofar as the latter records Regnerus's death in prison from the bites of snakes (see part VIII of the Analysis), and allows him a fair number of sons by various wives who, though they include Thora, do not include Áslaug (see parts IVA and VII of the Analysis). What I am suggesting is that the extant 'Lindarorm' and 'Ormekamp' ballads reflect a stage of the Ragnarr loðbrók tradition prior to the introduction of Áslaug, the daughter of Sigurðr and Brynhildr, as Ragnarr's wife.

In making this suggestion I am, of course, also suggesting that either the original 'Lindarorm' ballad or the tradition underlying it, or both, must at some stage or stages have been selective with the material forming the basis of the tradition; that is, that, in addition to the story of the serpent-fight, the tradition included material relating to Ragnarr's sons and to his death which came to be omitted either before or during the process of the ballad's composition. As I have assumed this much about the underlying tradition, it may be asked why I have not also assumed that it included a story of Ragnarr's marriage to Áslaug-Kráka, the daughter of Sigurðr and Brynhildr, and that this too, came to be omitted either before or during the ballad's development. Here various considerations need to be kept in mind. On the one hand it is generally rash to assume more about the background of extant texts than the evidence permits; on the other hand, there is also a danger of assuming too little about the background of surviving ballads, since ballad-traditions are often selective in relation to their source material (Nolsøe, 1976, 18). It should be remembered that Saxo's account in particular provides evidence that a considerable body of tradition accumulated around Ragnarr loðbrók before Áslaug-Kráka came to be associated with him; she does not seem to have been introduced into the tradition, in fact, until after it had become established that he was a serpent-slayer, had sons by various wives, and was himself killed by serpents (see pp. 146–47, above). Since I can find no hint in either 'Lindarormen' or 'Ormekampen' of anything resembling the story of Ragnarr's relations with Áslaug-Kráka, I have chosen to assume that this story formed no part of their background. Since on the other hand sons of Loðbrók are so much earlier attested than Aslaug-Kráka, and since a serpent plays such a prominent part in each ballad, I have assumed that Ragnarr's sons and his death in the snake-pit figured at some stage, somewhere, in the background of these ballads. I may have gone too far in assuming this, since neither the hero's sons nor his death are mentioned in either ballad; but would defend myself on the grounds that, at least as far as the hero's death is concerned, it is important to guard against the mistake de Vries (1915, 159–63) seemed to make in relation to the oral tradition attached to Spangereid and recorded by Torfæus when he refused to take the hint that a reference to Áslaug's marriage to Ragnarr loðbrók might lie behind the tradition reported by Torfæus that Aadlow became Queen of Denmark (see parts IIIC and IX of the Analysis). If the prominence given to the serpent in 'Lindarormen' and 'Ormekampen' does provide a hint that a story of the hero's destruction by snakes formed part of the ballad-tradition's background, it would surely be wrong to ignore it. Not that de Vries is guilty of this mistake in relation to 'Lindarormen' or 'Orme-kampen', of course; on the contrary, he seems to assume too much rather than too little about their background in deriving their common source from a lost 'original' version of *Ragnars saga* which, as he envisages it, must have included the story of Ragnarr's marriage to Áslaug-Kráka, the daughter of Sigurðr and Brynhildr (see p. 154, above).

What I am suggesting, then, is a compromise, which allows a measure of selectiveness to the ballad-composer or some predecessor of his in admitting that more than actually appears in the ballad's extant texts may originally have formed part of the tradition from which it descends, but not so much selectiveness as would have to be allowed if it were admitted that the tradition also included a story of Ragnarr's marriage to the daughter of Sigurðr and Brynhildr. I am also suggesting that this was an oral tradition, comparable though not identical (for the reasons already given, see p. 169, above) to that which seems to have informed Saxo's account, and comparable also, though again not identical, to that which appears to underlie *Krákumál*, a poem which, despite its title, seems to have no knowledge of the Kráka story, and shows scarcely more awareness of Áslaug (though it does once refer to her, in str. 26) than Saxo does with his references to Lathgertha and Suanlogha (see pp. 123–25 and 161–62, above). An advantage of this suggestion is that it allows for a measure of fluidity in the tradition from which the ballad originally emerged; it involves the assumption that elements additional to those of the surviving ballads formed part of this tradition, but does not insist that these additional elements were dominant or even present in the form in which the tradition became available to the ballad-composer. If, on the other hand, one assumes that the ballad derives more or less directly from a tradition of Ragnarr loðbrók close or identical to one of those surviving in the *þáttr*, the saga, or the *Ragnars kvæði*, one is immediately committed to the view that the ballad-tradition was selective with its source-material to a more or less ruthless extent.

It is in any case unlikely that the original 'Lindarorm' ballad derived from the Y version of *Ragnars saga* as reflected in 1824b. As already indicated (see p. 168, above), the evidence suggests that the tar and sand motif formed part of the original 'Lindarorm' ballad; only tar is mentioned in 'Ormekampen', but in 'Lindarormen' the hero is advised to roll in sand as well as tar; and this is comparable to what is told in the *þáttr*, where Ragnarr uses garments into which tar and sand have been pressed, and in the *Ragnars kvæði*, where Ragnarr treats his costume with tar and sand (see part V of the Analysis). In 'Lindarormen', the *þáttr*, and the *Ragnars kvæði* the impression is given that the tar and sand are applied more or less simultaneously; in 1824b, on the other hand, Ragnarr rolls in the sand so long after having his garments boiled in pitch that the latter's adhesive quality (as opposed to its protective quality) cannot logically be effective. This illogicality is noticed by de Vries (1928a, 271) and Mundt (1971, 130), and attributed by the latter to a scribal misplacing of the clause describing the rolling in the sand. The ballad-tradition thus differs here from the 1824b text of *Ragnars saga* and is relatively close to *Ragnarssona þáttr*, which according to Storm (1878, 97) gives the most authentic of the various accounts of Ragnarr's serpent-slaying exploit (among which he includes 'Ormekampen', though he does not mention in this context the Norwegian or Faroese ballads, or the relatively brief accounts of *Krákumál* and Arngrímur). This suggests that, if the original 'Lindarorm' ballad derived from a written version of *Ragnars saga*, this version must have been closer to the older *Ragnars saga* reflected in *Ragnarssona þáttr* than to the Y version reflected in 1824b (unless of course it is assumed that the ballad-tradition corrected this version's illogical use of the motif in question).

Now this older *Ragnars saga*, as I see it, did not include the Kráka story but did include, as the *þáttr* shows, Ragnarr's marriage to the daughter of Sigurðr and Brynhildr, various activities of his sons, and his death in the snake-pit; if it were seen as the source of the original 'Lindarorm' ballad, it would have to be assumed that these items of information were deliberately discarded by the ballad-tradition in the course of its development; and the same assumption would have to be made if it were suggested that *Ragnarssona þáttr* itself, as preserved in *Hauksbók*, were the ballad's source. Still more drastic pruning by the ballad-tradition would have to be assumed if credence were given to de Vries's view (1915, 148) that the common ballad-source of 'Lindarormen' and 'Ormekampen' derived from what he called the 'original' version of *Ragnars saga*, since this version, which he also believed was the one drawn on by *Ragnarssona þáttr*, included in his view the Kráka episode, even though the *þáttr* makes no mention of it. This at least was his opinion in 1915; by 1928, it is true, he had somewhat modified his view of the extent to which the Kráka episode formed part of what by then he called 'die ältere Ragnarssaga, welche Hauk vorlag' (de Vries, 1928a, 294; cf. p. 56, above). A similarly high degree of selectiveness would have to be attributed to the ballad-tradition if it were suggested that the X version of *Ragnars saga* preserved fragmentarily in 147 were the source of the original 'Lindarorm' ballad. This version of the saga certainly included the Kráka episode, if not in so developed a form as in the Y version preserved in 1824b (cf. McTurk, 1975, 58, n. 59), and also dealt at length with Ragnarr's sons and his death in the snake-pit; it cannot unfortunately be said how it handled the tar and sand motif, since the relevant part of the 147 text is defective (Olsen, 1906–08, lxxxvi, 176).

One other possibility may finally be considered, that is, that the original 'Lindarorm' ballad derived from the *Ragnars kvæði*, which in turn derived from a written version of *Ragnars saga*. If the *Ragnars kvæði* were thus seen in relation to the original 'Lindarorm' ballad as Grundtvig (in DgF I, 1853, 331) saw them in relation to 'Regnfred og Kragelil' (i.e. as representing a transitional Faroese stage in a development from Icelandic saga to mainland Scandinavian ballad), it would have to be assumed that the *Ragnars kvæði* developed out of the saga-tradition after the latter's adoption of the story of Áslaug-Kráka (since this appears in the *Ragnars kvæði*) and before the tar and sand motif came to be used illogically (since it is used logically in the *Ragnars kvæði* and in 'Lindarormen'). The X version of *Ragnars saga* might seem to represent such a stage in the saga-tradition's development, if only it could be discovered how it treated the tar and sand motif; but this unfortunately cannot be discovered, for the reasons already explained. This view would of course imply that the responsibility for discarding source-material was shared by the Faroese and mainland Scandinavian ballad-traditions; the tradition represented by the *Ragnars kvæði*, though it retained the Kráka-Áslaug story, would have discarded the material relating to Ragnarr's sons and to his death, and the tradition underlying the 'Lindarorm' ballad would have discarded the Kráka-Áslaug story.

None of the possibilities considered here can be excluded altogether, but the one involving the oral tradition described above (see pp. 168–69) seems to me the safest and the most reasonable; I would suggest that this oral tradition was the source of the original 'Lindarorm' ballad, and also contributed source-material to the older *Ragnars saga* drawn on by *Ragnarssona þáttr*. If this suggestion is accepted, it is not necessary to consider any further the possibility, which K. Liestøl seems to leave open (cf. pp. 157–58 and 160, above), that the original 'Lindarorm' ballad derives from a written version of *Ragnars saga* no longer extant.

(c) From Áslaug to Áslaug-Randalín

In order to trace the development of the Áslaug-figure prior to its incorporation in the Ragnarr loðbrók tradition, it is necessary to return to de Boor's remarks of 1923 on the Faroese 'Dvørgamoy' ballads, referred to above (see p. 155), and to draw attention to an article by de Boor published in 1920, devoted exclusively to the 'Dvørgamoy' ballads, and referred to by de Boor himself (1923, 113, n. 1). Djurhuus & Matras (1951–63, 263–310) follow Hammershaimb (1851, iii, 80–113, 184–200) in numbering these ballads I–V. This numbering, which de Boor (1920, 209) also follows, is adopted here, and in cases where it is necessary to designate variant texts by letter, Djurhuus & Matras (1951–63) have been followed. They, it should be noted, differ somewhat from de Boor (1920) in their designation by letter of variant texts. From de Boor's (1920, 254 56, 260–64) observations, then, it emerges that the dwarf-maiden with whom Sjúrður has dealings in the 'Dvørgamoy' ballads is called Ása in 'Dvørgamoy' IIIA and B, Ásla in 'Dvørgamoy' IV, and Áldurimma in 'Dvørgamoy' IIIC. As de Vries (1928a, 287) indicates, the element *Ás-* in the names *Ása* and *Ásla*, the latter of which is clearly a variant of *Áslaug* (de Boor, 1920, 256), suggests divine associations; and indeed the dwarf-maiden in 'Dvørgamoy' IIIC and IV implies that she is a daughter of the god Óðinn in saying that her father ruled in Óðinn's kingdom (cf. de Boor, 1920, 269–70). The name *Áldurimma* appears to be a variant of *Aldiruna*, the name of a woman visited by Sjúrður according to certain texts of the Faroese 'Regin smiður', the first ballad in the cycle known as *Sjúrðar kvæði*, after he has slain the serpent at Glitraheiði (as shown above, p. 156), and before his meeting with Brynhild (which takes place in 'Brynhildar táttur', the second ballad in the cycle, see part IA of the Analysis). The *-runa* element in *Aldiruna* appears to be a weak form of the name-element *-rún*, and to mean 'confidante', 'a purveyor of secret information', as de Boor (1920, 261–62) suggests.

All this is consistent with de Boor's view (1920, 254–99) that the 'Dvørgamoy' ballads derive from the legend of Sigurðr's encounter on a fiery mountain with the valkyrie referred to obliquely in *Grípisspá* (strs. 15–17), named as Sigrdríf(a) in *Fáfnismál* (str. 44) and *Sigrdrífumál* (prose between strs. 4 and 5) (on the dating of these three eddaic poems see p. 155, above), and identified with Brynhildr in *Vǫlsunga saga* (chs. 21–22), Snorri's prose *Edda* (*Skáldskaparmál*, ch. 49) and the fourteenth-century *Nornagests þáttr* (ch. 6; for the date see de Vries, 1967, 478): Sigurðr, according to the legend, woos the valkyrie after rousing her from sleep, learns runic and other wisdom from her, and subsequently leaves her. As noted earlier, de Boor (1923, 113–14; cf. 1920, 288–94) believes that the 'Dvørgamoy' ballads show that Áslaug belonged originally to the Sigurðr legend rather than to the Ragnarr loðbrók tradition, and de Vries (1928a, 286–89) came to accept this view. J. de Vries indeed develops this view in an interesting way, as will be shown below.

It may first be noted that the 'Dvørgamoy' ballads contain much that is reminiscent of Sigurðr's relations with Sigrdrífa-Brynhildr on the one hand, and Ragnarr loðbrók's with Áslaug-Kráka-Randalín on the other. In the first place, the dwarf-maiden in 'Dvørgamoy' I gives Sjúrður advice on how to handle her father, who is here presented as a dwarf with hostile intentions towards him; this may be compared with the more general but no less useful advice given by Sigrdrífa-Brynhildr to Sigurðr in *Sigrdrífumál* and *Vǫlsunga saga*, chs. 21–22. Secondly, the question-and-answer sequences in 'Dvørgamoy' IIIB, C, and IV, whereby Sjúrður finds out, among other things, the dwarf maiden's name and parentage, are comparable to the questioning process whereby, in the *Ragnars kvæði*, 'Regnfred og Kragelil', and 'Karl og Kragelil', the Ragnarr-figure eventually discovers the Áslaug-figure's true name and origins (see parts IIIC, VII, and IX of the Analysis). Thirdly, the close association with Óðinn implied by the dwarf-maiden's hint, already referred to, that she is a daughter of Óðinn (in 'Dvørgamoy' IIIC and IV) tends to reinforce de Boor's notion (1920, 259–60, 275) that she was originally a valkyrie figure, as seems to have been the case with Sigrdrífa (whose name may indeed mean 'valkyrie', see Kuhn, 1968, 184, but contrast F. Jónsson, 1931b, 494), since the valkyries are frequently described in Old Norse-Icelandic tradition as the handmaids of Óðinn (Munch, 1967, 67), if not explicitly as his daughters. Fourthly, in 'Dvørgamoy' IIIB and C the dwarf-maiden offers Sjúrður a protective hat (called a *huldanhatt*) which will make him unrecognizable. This feature, which de Boor (1920, 277–79) derives from Icelandic and Faroese folk traditions of the *huldufólk*, or elves, is surely most readily comparable to the 'Tarnkappe', or cloak of invisibility, worn by Siegfried in the *Nibelungenlied* (when winning Brünhild on Gunther's behalf, see de Boor, 1956, 71–85), or to the 'Nebelkap', or 'mist-cloak', with which Seyfrid is protected from a giant in the *Lied vom hürnen Seyfrid* (King, 1958, 128–29); the influence of German traditions is evident elsewhere in the 'Dvørgamoy' ballads, as de Boor (1920, 226–49) has shown. It may also be compared, however, if less strikingly,

with the protective garment given to Ragnarr by Áslaug-Randalín
in *Ragnars saga* and *Ragnarssona þáttr* (see part V of the Analysis)
and used by him in the snake-pit; and it may be remembered in this
connection that in Saxo's account and certain variants of the
'Lindarorm' ballad the Ragnarr-figure is helped by a woman in
preparing his protective covering for the serpent-fight (see pp.
162–63, above). Fifthly, Sjúrður's begetting of a daughter with the
dwarf-maiden in 'Dvørgamoy' IIIA and B is comparable to
Sigurðr's begetting of Áslaug with Brynhildr in *Vǫlsunga saga* and
'Brynhildar táttur' (see parts I and II of the Analysis), though it
should be noted that, in the 'Dvørgamoy' ballad, neither mother
nor child survives the birth. Sixthly and finally, in 'Dvørgamoy' IV
the dwarf-maiden tells Sjúrður that her father ('who ruled in
Óðinn's kingdom') searched on her behalf in a rune-stream
(*rúnarstreymi*) for a wondrous ring, and that her mother Gunhild
had dreamt that there was gold at the bottom of this stream.
Whatever the meaning of this somewhat obscure information, the
first element in the word *rúnarstreymur* (to give it its nominative
rather than dative form), like the last element in the name *Aldiruna*,
discussed above, is reminiscent of the runic wisdom which, in
Sigrdrífumál and *Vǫlsunga saga*, is presented as such a speciality of
Sigrdrífa-Brynhildr.

Following on from de Boor's conclusions, de Vries (1928a,
286–89) uses the evidence of the 'Dvørgamoy' ballads to suggest
that, in the earliest versions of the story, the maiden awakened by
Sigurðr on the mountain was called variously Ása, Ásla(ug),
Aldirúna, and Sigrdríf(a). Of these four names the first two and the
last were especially indicative of her valkyrie nature, while the third
suggested her wisdom. *Sigrdríf(a)* eventually became the dominant
name, thanks to the prominence it acquired through being
mentioned in the compilation of which the greater part survives in
the Codex Regius of the poetic *Edda*, and Sigrdríf(a) later came to
be identified with Brynhildr. J. de Vries does not discuss this last
stage in the development, even though his argument implies it and
indeed requires that it be acknowledged; support for it can,
however, be found in the more recent writings of Helgason (1953,
59) and Finch (1965, xxiii–xxiv). The idea that Sigurðr and the
maiden had a daughter may well have existed in the earliest stages,
even though no mention of it is made in the poetic *Edda*. This is
suggested by the fact that it occurs in 'Dvørgamoy' IIIA and B,
apparently quite independently of influence from traditions about

the Vǫlsungar and Ragnarr loðbrók (cf. de Boor, 1920, 288–94); in the 'Dvørgamoy' ballad, however, the daughter is not named, and dies at birth. With characteristic ingenuity de Vries (1928a, 287–88) argues that once the names *Sigrdríf(a)* and *Brynhildr* had superseded the names *Ása, Ásla(ug)* and *Aldirúna* for the daughter's mother, these last three names were free to be applied to the daughter herself when attention came to be focused on her. *Áslaug* of course became the dominant name for the daughter, but the application to her of the name *Aldirúna* seems to be attested by the Danish ballad 'Karl og Kragelil', where the maiden gives her true name as *Adellrun* in all three texts of the ballad, and her mother's as *Brynnyll* in the A-text (see part IIIC of the Analysis). To anticipate somewhat, the name *Aldirúna*, with its connotations of wisdom, seems to have contributed to the adoption by the Ragnarr loðbrók tradition of the motif of Kráka-Áslaug's cleverness in fulfilling the three conditions imposed on her by Ragnarr; though it must be emphasized that the Kráka-figure, according to the present argument, was not intro-duced until after the incorporation of Áslaug in the Ragnarr loðbrók tradition, a stage which the argument has not yet quite reached.

As the daughter of Sigurðr and Sigrdrífa-Brynhildr, the Áslaug-figure was in its earliest stages, according to de Vries (1928a, 288), 'ganz ohne Inhalt', though he goes on to argue, rather surprisingly in view of this decisive phrase, that these earliest stages are represented by the story recorded by Müller of Osla being washed ashore in a chest, brought up by a poor man called Kraaka, and marrying the king whose dead wife's clothes are found to fit her perfectly (see parts III and IX of the Analysis). I have already argued (p. 152, above) that the occurrence of the name *Kraaka* in addition to the name *Osla* in Müller's account implies a stage of development after Áslaug's introduction into the Ragnarr loðbrók tradition, even though the account itself makes no mention of Ragnarr loðbrók; and I would now suggest that its mention of Osla's marriage to a king, even though the king is not named, presupposes an awareness of Áslaug's marriage to Ragnarr loðbrók (as K. Liestøl would surely agree, see pp. 152–53, above). I would also suggest, in contrast to de Vries, that the motif of the dead wife's perfectly fitting clothes reflects the attempt also reflected in the *Ragnars kvæði* and *Ragnars saga* (though in the latter only dimly, see part VII of the Analysis) to link Ragnarr's marriage to Áslaug with his earlier marriage to Þóra by making Þóra prophesy before her death that her clothes would be a perfect fit for her husband's next wife, whom he would thus be able to identify. I would in fact argue that the 'Inhalt' of Müller's account derives mainly from the Ragnarr loðbrók tradition and from the Kráka story, and that the Áslaug-figure was originally a good deal more 'ohne Inhalt' than de Vries himself believed. I see no reason to regard even the motif of the girl being washed ashore in a chest, which finds parallels in the accounts of Torfæus and Ramus (see part IIIC of the Analysis), and presupposes her being set afloat in the manner described in certain texts of the 'Brynhildar táttur' (see parts IIA and IIIA of the Analysis), as having become attached to Áslaug prior to her incorporation in the Ragnarr loðbrók tradition; there is certainly no trace of it in *Ragnarssona þáttr*, which, in reflecting the older *Ragnars saga*, also reflects a relatively early stage of this incorporation. When Áslaug as such was introduced into the tradition, I suggest, the application to her of the name *Aldirúna/Adellrun* was forgotten (though it later influenced the tradition independently, appearing in the 'Karl og Kragelil' ballad and contributing to the development of the Kráka-figure, as indicated above, p. 177) and little more was known about her than is recorded in the stanzas of 'Brynhildar táttur' referring to her conception (see part IIA of the Analysis): her name, *Áslaug*, the fact that she was the daughter of Sigurðr and Brynhildr, and her valkyrie background (of which both her name and her parentage would serve as reminders).

The relatively little information about Áslaug was no doubt to the advantage of the Ragnarr loðbrók tradition, which was able to adapt her freely to its needs. It made her the second wife of Ragnarr, the mother of his sons Ívarr, Bjǫrn, Hvítserkr, and Sigurðr (Rǫgnvaldr, as argued in ch. II, section (b) (*iii*), did not become prominent in the tradition until later), and the stepmother of Eirekr and Agnarr, his sons by his first wife Þóra (cf. part VII of the Analysis). In case she should thus seem to become too humanized and domesticated, the tradition acknowledged her valkyrie background by giving her the additional name *Randalín*, which, as Sveinsson (1936, 195) has shown, may well derive from the form *Randa-Hlín* ('shield-goddess', 'shield-woman'), a likely kenning for a valkyrie, and by making her adopt this name in the appropriate context of her warlike revenge of her stepsons (cf. pp. 101, 118, above). She was also made to give Ragnarr a silk tunic as a parting-gift from her before he set sail for England; this gave him protection in King Ella's snake-pit until it was removed. This idea, which was doubtless suggested by the story of Ragnarr's use of a protective costume in fighting Þóra's serpent, seems to represent an attempt to unify the narrative by indicating similarities between the two snake-episodes (as does also the fact that, in the 1824b text of *Ragnars saga*, ch. 15, Ragnarr is said to have had with him in England the spear he used on Þóra's serpent, see Olsen, 1906–08, 157); on the other hand, the story of Þóra's clothes being given to Áslaug, which provides a link between these two episodes in allowing repayment for the shift to be the reason for Áslaug giving Ragnarr the tunic (cf. parts V and VII of the Analysis), seems to represent a later or (more probably) independent development, as I shall argue below (see p. 181). If the story of Áslaug acquiring Þóra's clothes is left aside, then the account just given may be said to summarize her position in the older *Ragnars saga* reflected in *Ragnarssona þáttr*. If the name *Randalín (Filippusdóttir)*, bestowed by the Oddaverjar on a member of their family born in *c*.1230, derives from *Ragnars saga*, as Sveinsson (1936, 194–95) and Guðnason (1969, 37) suggest, then it must derive from the older *Ragnars saga* (cf. Guðnason, 1982, 78, n. 4), since there is reason to believe that neither the X nor the Y version of *Ragnars saga* was written before *c*.1240 (see McTurk, 1977a, 583 and n. 128). If their suggestion can be accepted, then it may be concluded that the older *Ragnars saga* was in existence prior to 1230.

(d) Áslaug-Kráka and the Spangereid-legend

It is doubtful how much of the adaptation process just described is to be attributed to the redactor of the older *Ragnars saga*, and how much of it is to be assumed to have taken place before the tradition came into his hands. The nature of *Skjǫldunga saga*'s relationship to the older *Ragnars saga* is uncertain, as Guðnason (1969, 32) points out; so also, as already indicated, is the extent of *Skjǫldunga saga*'s information on Ragnarr loðbrók and related matters. Nevertheless, it seems likely that *Skjǫldunga saga* knew of Ragnarr's marriages to Þóra and Áslaug, of the latter's parentage, of his sons (apart from Rǫgnvaldr, see Guðnason, 1982, 76, n. 11, and cf. ch. II, section (b) (*iii*) and p. 178, above) by both marriages, and of his death in England, and that this knowledge was acquired independently of the older *Ragnars saga*. The next step in the present argument is to consider the branch of the Ragnarr loðbrók tradition that conceived and developed the Kráka aspect of Áslaug. As will be shown below, this branch of the tradition is reflected in different ways in the 147 and 1824b texts of *Ragnars saga*; in the Faroese *Ragnars kvæði*, 'Gests ríma', and 'Brynhildar táttur'; in Müller's prose abstract of a lost Faroese poem about Osla and Kraaka; in Torfæus's and Ramus's prose accounts of oral traditions from the Lindesnæs area of southern Norway; and in the two Danish 'Kragelil' ballads. In calling the tradition represented by these texts a branch of the Ragnarr loðbrók tradition I am of course assuming, with K. Liestøl and others, that an awareness of Áslaug's involvement with Ragnarr loðbrók lay behind it from the beginning, even though this awareness is by no means always obvious from the surviving texts; and I further assume, while acknowledging that this is scarcely more obvious from the texts, that there also lay behind it from the start an awareness that Áslaug was the daughter of Sigurðr and Brynhildr.

The evidence suggests that this Áslaug-Kráka branch of the tradition, as it may be called, had no knowledge of Áslaug's additional name *Randalín*, or of her giving Ragnarr a protective garment; and no interest in her sons or stepsons, or in Ragnarr's death. All these items (including the name *Randalín*, even though the relevant parts of the 147 text are illegible, see Olsen, 1906–08, 181–94) clearly occurred in the X and Y versions of *Ragnars saga*, where, however, their presence seems to have been due not to the influence of the Áslaug-Kráka branch of the tradition, but to the more or less direct influence of the older *Ragnars saga*; otherwise the only references to them in the relevant texts are the brief ones involving Kráka's boneless child in the 'Gests ríma' (see part IIIC of the Analysis) and Ragnar's sons by Ásla in the C text of the *Ragnars kvæði* (see part VII of the Analysis). These, however, can be explained as results of the primary and secondary influence, respectively, of the Y version of *Ragnars saga* (cf. pp. 184–86, 194, below, and cf. the relative closeness of the C text of the *Ragnars kvæði* to the 1824b text of the saga, evident from parts IIIC, IVA, VII, and IX of the Analysis). Similarly, Ragnarr's death in the snake-pit, which occurs in the 147 and 1824b texts of *Ragnars saga* (presumably as part of their inheritance from the older *Ragnars saga*), is nowhere mentioned in the other reflexes of the Áslaug-Kráka branch of the tradition, though a memory of it seems to lie behind the heroine's reference, in the A and C texts of 'Karl og Kragelil', to her father's death in a snake-yard (see part IIIC of the

Analysis). The snake-yard motif may here be due, as de Vries (1915, 178) suggests, to the secondary influence of traditions about Ragnarr loðbrók or Gunnarr Gjúkason, or both, but on balance it seems to me more reasonable, as I shall explain below (pp. 186–88), to regard it as inherited from the older Ragnarr loðbrók tradition. The Áslaug-Kráka branch of the tradition, which of course presupposes an awareness of Áslaug, cannot however have sprung directly from this older tradition, if the latter was unaware of Áslaug, as suggested above (pp. 146–47); nor can it easily be thought to have derived from the older *Ragnars saga*, for if so, it would have to be explained how it came to drop the various items under discussion, apart from the motif of death in a snake-pit, i.e., Áslaug's additional name *Randalín*, her gift of a protective garment, and her sons and stepsons.

On the other hand the Áslaug-Kráka branch seems to depend for its very existence on an awareness of the stepmother and stepson relationship between Áslaug and Eirekr, if it can be accepted that, as argued earlier (see pp. 135–36, above), this idea drew into the Ragnarr loðbrok tradition the name of Craca, stepmother of Ericus Disertus. It seems safest to assume that the branch in question developed from a relatively early and most probably oral stage of the Ragnarr loðbrók tradition, underlying both *Skjǫldunga saga* and the older *Ragnars saga*, at which Áslaug had come to be regarded as the wife of Ragnarr loðbrók and stepmother of Eirekr, but which was in other respects identical to the tradition drawn on by the original 'Lindarorm' ballad, and described earlier (in section (b) of the present chapter). The application to Áslaug of the name *Randalín* may methodologically be attributed to the redactor of the older *Ragnars saga*, while the story of Þóra's clothes being given after her death to Áslaug seems, to judge from Müller's account (see parts III and IX of the Analysis), to have arisen within the Áslaug-Kráka branch of the tradition, where it must have had the function of establishing a link between Ragnarr's marriage to Áslaug and his previous marriage, rather than between the two serpent episodes of his career, since neither of the latter seems to have been at all prominent in this branch of the tradition (among the relevant texts they are mentioned only in the 147 and 1824b texts of *Ragnars saga*, which have surely derived the relevant information from the older *Ragnars saga*). That the Áslaug-Kráka branch preserved a memory of Ragnarr's death in the snake-pit, however, is suggested by the reference in the A and C texts of 'Karl og Kragelil' to the heroine's father's death in such circumstances, as I shall argue more fully below (see pp. 186–88). The story of the dead wife's clothes need not have been influenced by the motif of the protective costume given by Áslaug to Ragnarr, the presence of which in the older *Ragnars saga* may, therefore, be attributed to the redactor of that version of the saga, with the reservation that his use of it perhaps reflects the law of patterning characteristic of oral tradition (by this law, 'situations of the same sort' are made 'as similar as possible', Olrik, 1965, 137, and it was no doubt felt that Ragnarr ought to have a protective garment in the snake-pit, just as he had had one in fighting Þóra's serpent).

The Áslaug-Kráka branch of the Ragnarr loðbrók tradition accordingly developed independently of the older *Ragnars saga* on the basis of an idea also adopted by that version of the saga and transmitted thence to the X and Y versions: that Áslaug, the daughter of Sigurðr and Brynhildr, was the stepmother of Ragnarr's son Eirekr. It may be assumed that the presentation of Áslaug as Eirekr's stepmother, and perhaps also the title of *Krákumál*, led to the making of a connection between Áslaug and Craca, the stepmother of Ericus Disertus, thus bringing about the application to Áslaug of the additional name *Kráka*. As suggested earlier (see pp. 135–36, above), the connotations of this name were inappropriate to Áslaug in her heroic rôle, whether as valkyrie or avenging stepmother, interest in which, though maintained in the different versions of *Ragnars saga*, seems to have been rapidly abandoned by the Áslaug-Kráka branch of the tradition as it began its independent development. The introduction of the name *Kráka*, with its suggestions of evil stepmothers and ugly sisters, evidently led to an increased interest in Áslaug's childhood and youth, and to her being presented as suffering various misfortunes comparable to those of Cinderella, mainly at the hands of foster-parents, up to the time of her meeting and marrying Ragnarr loðbrók, who, however, is not always so named in the surviving texts. This stage in the branch's development seems to have taken place in southern Norway, particularly in the vicinity of Spangereid, an area clearly indicated in the 147 and 1824b texts of *Ragnars saga* (see Olsen 1906–08, 180, 6v, l. 3; 112, 122, 135), and in the accounts of Torfæus and Ramus. The term 'the Spangereid-legend' may be used as a blanket term for the relevant traditions as they developed orally in this part of Norway, though it should of course be recognized that they did not necessarily all develop in precisely the same place, or in direct contact with each other. The surviving reflexes of the Spangereid-legend—the 147 text of *Ragnars saga* (and 1824b where this fails), the Faroese and Danish ballad traditions, and the accounts of Müller, Torfæus, and Ramus—actually contradict each other surprisingly little, though their variety clearly reflects different aspects of the legend, and different stages of its development. The Spangereid-legend came to be influenced by material deriving by way of Denmark from the European continent on the one hand, and from England on the other, as I shall argue below; it was then drawn on by the redactor of the X version of *Ragnars saga*, whence it came to form part of the Y version also.

Thus the Aslaug-Kráka branch of the Ragnarr loðbrók tradition was introduced into the saga branch of the tradition (cf. p. 165, above) by way of the X version of *Ragnars saga*, while continuing to exist orally in Norway in the form of the Spangereid-legend. Because of the fragmentary state of the 147 text in which X is preserved, it is hard to determine the exact use made of the Spangereid-legend by the X redactor. The Y version of *Ragnars saga* preserved in 1824b is certainly of help here, but must be used with caution, since its first chapter in particular suggests that the Y redactor, without any obvious independent contact with the legend itself, has developed the X redactor's use of the relevant material. The Spangereid-legend clearly lived on in Norway, for the most part independently, though without altogether escaping secondary influence from the Ragnarr loðbrók tradition, into relatively modern times. This is shown by Torfæus's account, in particular, which bears witness to the influence of the Y version of *Ragnars saga* on the legend, as I shall argue below (see pp. 184–85); certain of the Faroese and Danish ballads deriving primarily from the Spangereid-legend also show the influence of the Y version of the saga, as I shall demonstrate.

It is obviously impossible to recover the Spangereid-legend in the forms in which it existed in oral tradition; some idea of these forms may, however, be obtained from a close study of the texts listed above (see p. 180), in which the Áslaug-Kráka branch of the tradition, and consequently the Spangereid-legend, have been preserved. The relevant parts of these texts will be summarized below in such a way as to give, it is hoped, as full and clear a picture as possible of the essential features of the legend. The summary will naturally cover some of the same ground as the Analysis of the heroic biographical pattern in the last chapter, and will make frequent reference to it; special attention will, however, be paid to those elements in the texts which for present purposes have not been adequately covered by the Analysis. It must at all times be remembered that the summary below is, of course, necessarily based on the surviving texts and may, therefore, include material extraneous to the legend itself; it may also include material which entered the legend as a result of secondary influence from the Ragnarr loðbrók tradition, but did not belong to it originally. Heimir and his harp, both mentioned in ch. 1 of the 1824b text of *Ragnars saga* (see part IIIC of the Analysis), seem to provide examples of these two types of material respectively.

It is true that Heimir, the foster-father of Brynhildr and subsequently of Áslaug in the *Vǫlsunga-Ragnars saga* sequence preserved in 1824b, is also presented as Brynhildr's foster-father in the eddaic *Grípisspá* (strs. 27–31; 39), a poem dating from the twelfth century (Sveinsson, 1962, 457, 528), and that *Grípisspá*, though it does not mention a daughter of Sigurðr and Brynhildr, may indirectly reflect a stage in the Áslaug-figure's development prior to its incorporation in the Ragnarr loðbrók tradition, as indicated above (pp. 174–75, 176–77). It has also been argued above, however (see pp. 177–78), that Áslaug entered this tradition with few credentials beyond the fact that she was the daughter of Sigurðr and Brynhildr, and it is indeed most unlikely that Heimir was thought of in connection with her at that stage, or that he himself entered the tradition prior to the writing of the X version of *Ragnars saga*, whose redactor, as I have hinted elsewhere (McTurk, 1977a, 571, 578–85), must have learnt of Heimir from *Vǫlsunga saga* and laid the basis for the development by the Y redactor of his foster-father relationship to Áslaug. No mention is made of Heimir in *Ragnarssona þáttr*, and, apart from the 'Gests ríma', where Gestur is clearly modelled on Heimir as presented in the Y version of *Ragnars saga*, none of the surviving reflexes of the Spangereid-legend shows any real awareness of Heimir (see however the discussion of 'Karl og Kragelil' at pp. 186–88, below). Torfæus and Ramus both know of him, it is true, but their knowledge is here based, as Helgason (1975, 79, n. 1) makes clear, on more or less direct acquaintance with *Vǫlsunga saga* and *Ragnars saga* as preserved in 1824b, and with *Grípisspá*; they do not include him in their accounts of the legend itself. No mention of him at all is made in the *Ragnars kvæði*, or in any part of 'Brynhildar táttur' (let alone the stanzas dealing with Áslaug), or in Müller's account, or in the

'Kragelil' ballads. It may thus be concluded that Heimir never at any stage formed part of the Spangereid-legend as this was defined (on p. 182, above), i.e. as a group of oral traditions on a certain subject developing in a particular part of Norway.

The case is not the same, however, with the harp in which, according to the 1824b text of *Ragnars saga*, Heimir concealed Áslaug and brought her to Spangarheiðr. The harp also occurs in the accounts of Torfæus and Ramus, where, though there is no Heimir-figure, Áslaug is washed ashore in a harp in the Spangereid area; and in the 'Gests ríma', where Gestur, who corresponds to Heimir, finds a harp by a river and takes it with him, apparently unaware of its contents, though it emerges after his death that Ásla is concealed inside it. According to Neckel (1920, 18), as indicated above (p. 161), the harp motif in the Ragnarr loðbrók tradition originates with the 'younger' version of *Ragnars saga*, by which it is reasonable to suppose that he means the Y version preserved in 1824b, since there is no evidence that this motif was present in the X version (McTurk, 1977a, 577–85). I shall argue below (in section (f)) in support of this view, tentatively suggesting that the Y redactor of *Ragnars saga* obtained from the Norwegian translation of Thomas's *Tristran*, with which brother Robert is credited (Tómasson, 1977, 76–78), the idea of a musical instrument being used as a portable hiding-place for a living being. Here, however, I shall simply follow Neckel (1920, 18) in suggesting that the idea of a harp as a container for Áslaug entered the Spangereid-legend as a result of secondary influence from the Ragnarr loðbrók tradition, stimulated by the Y version of *Ragnars saga*, and then combined with the Moses-motif, as Neckel calls it, which involved Áslaug being set afloat in a watertight vessel, and which, as Müller's account suggests, had developed as part of the Spangereid-legend before the latter was drawn on by the X version of *Ragnars saga*, in which the motif of the floating vessel (as opposed to the harp) may conceivably have occurred (cf. McTurk, 1977a, 585). This combination is reflected in the accounts of Torfæus and Ramus, who do not include Heimir in the Spangereid-legend as they report it. I have already argued that Heimir never came to form part of the Spangereid-legend, and the reason for this, I would now argue, may well be that the Moses-motif was sufficiently dominant in the legend to make Heimir's inclusion superfluous; the harp was, as it were, quite enough for the legend to take on. As for the 'Gests ríma', I suggest that the combination here of the Heimir figure

(Gestur) with the Moses-motif (of the harp found by a river) is due to the primary influence of the Y version of *Ragnars saga* in the former case and the secondary influence of the Spangereid-legend in the latter. I agree to a large extent with de Vries's view (1915, 182–88) that the 'Gests ríma' derives ultimately from what is here called the Y version of the saga; but differ from him in suggesting that its use of the Moses-motif betrays the secondary influence of the Spangereid-legend.

Not surprisingly, secondary influence from the Ragnarr loðbrók tradition has in some cases reached the surviving reflexes of the Spangereid-legend independently of the legend itself, and the summary below includes occasional instances of this kind of extraneous material also. Here it is relevant to mention *Regnfred* and *Sigurd*, the names of the hero and the heroine's father respectively in the A text of 'Regnfred og Kragelil'; these names, as Grundtvig (in DgF I, 1853, 330) and Storm (1878, 117) have indicated, may have been introduced into this text by the Danish grammarian and ballad-collector Peder Syv (1631–1702) on the basis of his knowledge of *Ragnars saga* and related works (including Saxo's *Gesta Danorum*, Book IX, from which he may have taken the name *Suanlogha* for the heroine, adapting it to the form *Svanelil*, not mentioned in the summary below, but see part IIIC of the Analysis).

I would accept, as de Vries (1928a, 286–89) apparently did in 1928, K. Liestøl's (1917, 105) and de Boor's (1923, 113–14) opinion that there is no reason to attribute the name *Brynnyll* for the heroine's mother in the A text of 'Karl og Kragelil' to secondary influence from the Ragnarr loðbrók tradition. As for the motif of the heroine's father's death in a snake-yard occurring in the A and C texts of this ballad, it will be remembered that, according to de Vries in 1915 (see de Vries, 1915, 178), this motif is to be regarded as a secondary borrowing from poetic traditions about heroes such as Gunnarr Gjúkason and Ragnarr loðbrók. This opinion is, however, clearly bound up with de Vries's view in 1915 that the Spangereid-legend originally had nothing to do with the Vǫlsungar and Gjúkungar, or with Ragnarr loðbrók (see pp. 149–56, above), a view he later came to modify in the light of Liestøl's (1917), Neckel's (1920), and de Boor's (1923) reviews; it is not certain that, after reading these, he continued to attribute the occurrence of the motif to secondary influence. It seems to me that, if it is really necessary to explain the snake-yard motif in 'Karl og Kragelil' in terms of secondary influence, there is no reason why it should not be derived from the Y version of *Ragnars saga*, where Ragnarr himself, of course, dies in a snake-pit; it could even be taken as reflecting a confused memory of the death in quite different circumstances of Heimir, Áslaug's foster-father, as recorded in that same version of the saga (see part IIIC of the Analysis).

Both these possibilities were considered by Grundtvig (DgF, 1853, I, 334), who also suggested that 'Karl og Kragelil' may have been influenced by a tradition according to which Sigurðr the serpent-slayer died in a snake-yard, and which apparently originated independently of the Ragnarr loðbrók tradition. If this view were accepted here, it would on balance have to be suggested that the influence took place after Áslaug was introduced into the Ragnarr loðbrók tradition, since it is by no means certain that the notion of Sigurðr's death in a snake-yard had developed by the time of her introduction or, if it had, that it formed part of the relatively little information that Áslaug brought with her, as it were, into the tradition (cf. p. 184, above). Grundtvig's suggestion as to Sigurðr's death in a snake-yard is in any case highly tentative, and his evidence scattered and fragmentary. Without disregarding these various possibilities, and without forgetting that it was probably Gunnarr's death in a snake-pit that first gave rise to the idea of Ragnarr's (cf. de Vries, 1923, 250–52), I would suggest that the simplest solution to the problem of the snake-yard motif in 'Karl og Kragelil' is to regard it as an echo of Ragnarr's death in the snake-pit as this was recorded in the older Ragnarr loðbrók tradition, i.e. before the introduction of Áslaug. It might indeed be explained in terms of the law of patterning (cf. p. 182, above): after Áslaug's introduction, the death of her father, Sigurðr the serpent-slayer, was assimilated to that of her husband, Ragnarr loðbrók, also a serpent-slayer. The assimilation may admittedly have been assisted by borrowed or inherited traditions of Gunnarr's death in a snake-pit, or even Sigurðr's, but it was, I suggest, stimulated primarily by an inherited memory of Ragnarr's death in these circumstances. This assimilation is reflected in the A and C texts of 'Karl og Kragelil', where, however, the Ragnarr-figure's death is not mentioned, presumably because it is not relevant to the ballad's narrative concerns.

If this view is accepted, the occurrence of the motif in these texts of the ballad may be used as evidence that, during its existence apart from the main branch of the Ragnarr loðbrók tradition, the Áslaug-Kráka branch did not entirely forget Ragnarr's death in

King Ella's snake-pit, even though it was far from centrally concerned with it. It may be repeated here that *Adellrun*, etc., the heroine's true name in all three texts of 'Karl og Kragelil', seems to derive independently of Áslaug's incorporation in the Ragnarr loðbrók tradition from a relatively early stage in the development of her presentation as the daughter of Sigurðr and Brynhildr, before the name *Áslaug* had become fully attached to her. Finally, it should be kept in mind in reading the summary that Ramus's account is largely based on Torfæus's, though he does make some additional points which in my view (a less sceptical view in this case than Helgason's, 1975, 86; see pp. 196–99, below) are not entirely without value for attempting to reconstruct the form and content of the Spangereid-legend.

The Spangereid-legend

Áslaug was the daughter of Sigurðr and Brynhildr (as emerges from 'Brynhildar táttur', see parts IA and IIA of the Analysis, and also from the 147 and 1824b texts of *Ragnars saga*, drawn on below. In the case of the saga, however, the information about Áslaug's parentage almost certainly derives independently of the Spangereid-legend from the older *Ragnars saga*, cf. p. 194, below. Ramus intimates that, in the local traditions available to him, she was known variously as 'Asløg' and as a king's daughter, see part III of the Analysis). She was set afloat by her mother (so 'Brynhildar táttur'; by her step-mother according to Ramus, see parts IIIA, III of the Analysis), and according to Ramus and Torfæus (the latter beginning his account at this point, without mentioning the girl's parentage) came to land in a harp in the Spangereid area, where she worked as a herdswoman, and where certain features of the landscape, including the brook Kraakebæk, appear to be named after her, the name *Kraake* having been applied to her, according to Ramus, because she wore black clothes (see part IIIC of the Analysis). Müller's account begins with Áslaug (here called Osla) being washed ashore in a chest; who her parents were, or where she landed, is not stated. She is brought up by a poor man named Kraaka who treats her badly because she is more beautiful than his own daughter (see part III of the Analysis); it is not told how they met.

In the 1824b text of *Ragnars saga* (as opposed to the 147 text, of which the relevant chapter does not seem to have formed part, see

p. 61, above), Áslaug, the daughter of Sigurðr and Brynhildr, is brought up with loving care by Heimir, to whom her mother had entrusted her in *Vǫlsunga saga*, ch. 29 (see Olsen, 1906–08, 69), until he is slain at Spangereid by a farming couple who then find her in the harp in which Heimir has concealed her (there is no story of her being set afloat). They name her Kráka after the farmer's wife's mother and seek to pass her off as their own daughter by rubbing her head with tar, giving her poor clothes, and making her do the worst jobs (cf. parts IIIC, IIID, and IX of the Analysis). The 'Gests ríma' differs little in outline from this account, from which it largely derives, see pp. 185–86, above; the main difference is that in the 'Gests ríma' there is no special relationship between Gestur (who here corresponds to Heimir) and Ásla (= Áslaug), since Gestur is apparently unaware that he is carrying Ásla in the harp, which he happens to find by a river (cf. part IIIC of the Analysis).

Spangereid is not mentioned in the 'Gests ríma', or in either of the two 'Kragelil' ballads. In neither of these latter does the heroine's name correspond to Áslaug, though her adopted name, *Kragelil*, closely resembles the name *Kráka*; nor can the hero's name in either ballad really be said to correspond to *Ragnarr* or *Loðbrók*, since the hero's name *Regnfred* in the A text of 'Regnfred og Kragelil' is apparently due to secondary influence from the Ragnarr loðbrók tradition, as indicated above (p. 186). In 'Regnfred og Kragelil' the heroine is presented as the abducted daughter of a king (whose name in the A text, *Sigurd*, evidently has no more independent weight than the hero's name *Regnfred*, see p. 186, above), and the hero seeks and finds her on the king's behalf. In 'Karl og Kragelil', on the other hand, she is found by messengers instructed by the hero to find him the fairest maiden the sun shines on. In both ballads she is found in a rural environment, tending herds. Much of her early history emerges in her replies to the question she is twice asked about her origins—by the hero in the case of 'Regnfred og Kragelil' and, in the case of 'Karl og Kragelil', by the hero's messenger(s) in the first instance, and by himself in the second. In reply to the first question she pretends, in both ballads, that her father is of peasant origin and that her name is *Kragelil*; in reply to the second, however, she gives, also in both ballads, her true name and origins. In 'Karl og Kragelil', which is evidently the more reliable of the two ballads in respect of names (see pp. 155–56 and 177, 186, above), she identifies her mother as the exiled Brynnyll (in the A text only, however; in the B and C texts she gives her mother's name as *Kremolt*); she gives her own name as *Adellrun* in all three texts of the ballad; while in the A and C texts she claims that her father (named Karl in all three texts) died in a snake-yard, and that she has lived ever since with the farmers who were responsible for his death (cf. part IIIC of the Analysis).

Neither Torfæus nor Ramus (in his account of the legend itself, cf. p. 184, above) mentions Ragnarr loðbrók; Torfæus says that Aadlow became Queen of Denmark after tending flocks at Spangereid, but Ramus says nothing of her meeting or marrying a hero-figure (cf. parts III, IIIC and IX of the Analysis). In the 1824b text of *Ragnars saga* (which it may be assumed mostly agrees from this point onwards with the text fragmentarily preserved in 147, as far as the Spangereid-legend is concerned), Ragnarr loðbrók sails to Norway after Þóra's death and lands near Spangereid; his men go to the farm to bake bread, see Kráka, and report to Ragnarr that their poor baking is due to the distraction of seeing a maiden no less beautiful than Þóra. He threatens them with severe punishment if her beauty should fall short of their estimate, and sends messengers to request that she should visit him under the three apparently impossible conditions described under heading IVA of the Analysis. In visiting him she fulfils the conditions in the manner there described; as she approaches Ragnarr's ship she speaks a verse (str. 2 of the 1824b text) in which, however, she refers to only two of the conditions in claiming to have fulfilled them; these are 'neither alone nor accompanied by man' and 'neither clad nor unclad'. She requests and is granted a safe-conduct in boarding the ship, where the dog she had brought with her in fulfilment of the condition 'neither alone nor accompanied by man' bites the hand Ragnarr stretches out to her in greeting, whereupon his men beat the dog and then strangle it (so 1824b; in 147 they hang it) with a bowstring (Olsen, 1906–08, 125, ll. 25–26; 178, Bl. 3r, l. 26). Speaking a half strophe each, Ragnarr and Kráka then recite str. 3 of the 1824b text, Ragnarr expressing his physical desire for her and Kráka reminding him of the safe-conduct. Prose then follows in which Ragnarr fails to persuade her to leave with him, or to spend the night on the ship; she says she prefers to wait until he has completed the voyage he had planned, in case he should change his mind about her. He recites a verse (str. 4 of the 1824b text), offering her a silver-embroidered shift (described as gold-embroidered in the prose) which had belonged to Þóra, and she replies with a verse (str. 5 in the 1824b text) in which she implies that it would not suit her, saying in fact that wretched garments do so, and that she is called Kráka because she has walked in coal-black clothes on stony ground and driven goats along the seashore (see further p. 197, below). Then in the prose she says she does not wish to dress in fine clothes while domiciled with a farmer, and suggests that Ragnarr might like her better if she were better dressed. Later, when Ragnarr returns from his voyage, she leaves with him, after first spending one more night at the farm and then wishing the farmer and his wife ill for the treatment they have given her, including (in the 1824b text, at least, cf. McTurk 1975, 58, n. 59 and 1977a, 585) the murder of her foster-father Heimir. Ragnarr wishes to sleep with her at once, but complies with her request that they should wait until they have been married in his kingdom (cf. part VII of the Analysis). The story then continues in the manner outlined above (in ch. II, section (b) (*i*)) in connection with the birth of Ívarr the boneless; Ragnarr eventually discovers Áslaug's true identity in the circumstances described in the summary of chs. 9–12 of the 1824b text of *Ragnars saga* given above (pp. 99–102; cf. also part IX of the Analysis); and no further mention is made of the shift until it is referred to in connection with the tunic Áslaug gives Ragnarr before he sails for England (cf. part V of the Analysis).

In the 'Gests ríma', Ragnar's men come to the farm to bake bread, as in *Ragnars saga* (though in the 'Gests ríma' the farm is not named); they see Ásla (here called Kráka by the farmer's wife) and Ragnar threatens them with the gallows in case they are mocking him when they explain that they have burnt the bread as a result of looking at a maiden fairer than Tóra. The ballad ends with Ásla calling her little dog to her when the men have returned to the farm to summon her to Ragnar (see part VII of the Analysis).

In the various relevant texts of the *Ragnars kvæði* (see also part VII of the Analysis), Ragnar's wife (Tóra) Borgarhjørt (see part V of the Analysis) prophesies on her death-bed that her clothes will be a perfect fit for his next wife, whom he will thus be able to identify (in two of the texts, see part VII of the Analysis, she specifies that this will be Ásla Sjúrðardóttir). Ragnar later arrives by ship at an unnamed place where his men attempt to bake bread at the home of an old man and his supposed daughter, on whose exceptional qualities the men report to Ragnar, implying that her presence has distracted them from baking, and comparing her with Tóra. In one text (see part VII of the Analysis), Ragnar threatens them with the gallows in case they are mocking him with this information. In all the relevant texts (see part IVA of the Analysis) he requests that she should visit him under two apparently impossible conditions, namely 'with a fellow who is not a fellow' and 'both clad and unclad'. She fulfils these by bringing a dog with her and by combing her hair in a special way. Some of the texts (see also under part IVA of the Analysis) betray an awareness of a third condition, 'neither fed nor unfed', corresponding to the second of the three conditions imposed in *Ragnars saga*. The maiden boards Ragnar's ship, and he questions her about her parentage. She replies that the old man is her father, that she (or in two texts he) keeps goats, and that her name is *Kráka*. He then makes her try on some clothes which, it is emphasized in most of the texts (see part VII of the Analysis), fit her perfectly; it is to be assumed that these are the clothes referred to earlier by Tóra. He then questions her again, more or less directly (see also under part VII of the Analysis), and she replies that she is Ásla, the daughter of Sjúrður and Brynhild. In Müller's account, finally, it is told how the widowed king of the country in which Osla has been brought up by a poor man named Kraaka (see part III of the Analysis, as well as p. 188, above) wishes to marry no-one but the woman whom his dead wife's clothes may happen to fit. They are found to fit Osla, who thus becomes queen; and when she is criticized for her humble origins she produces a letter, which her mother had placed in the chest in which she was washed ashore (see p. 188, above, and also parts III and IX of the Analysis). Her mother, who is still alive, is then contacted, and recognizes her.

*   *   *

It may be noted that Spangereid is mentioned by name only in the 1824b and 147 texts of *Ragnars saga* and in Torfæus's account, though Ramus, with his mention of Lindesnæs, is clearly aware that the Spangereid area is in question. As for the personal names involved in the legend, *Áslaug* and *Kráka* are easily the ones most frequently attested in its surviving reflexes. The name *Áslaug* occurs, in one form or another, in 1824b, 147, the 'Gests ríma', the *Ragnars kvæði*, 'Brynhildar táttur', and the accounts of Müller, Torfæus, and Ramus. The name *Kráka* occurs in all of these except 'Brynhildar táttur'; it also appears in the form *Kragelil* in what have here been called the two 'Kragelil' ballads. In Müller's account, it should be noted, the name *Kraaka* is applied not to the Áslaug-figure but to her evil foster-father; it should also be noted that, in all three texts of 'Karl og Kragelil', the Áslaug-figure's true name (as opposed to *Kragelil*, her nickname) is *Adellrun*. Áslaug's parents, Sigurðr and Brynhildr, are both mentioned by name in 1824b, 147, the *Ragnars kvæði*, and 'Brynhildar táttur', and Brynhildr's name appears in the form *Brynnyll* in the A text of 'Karl og Kragelil', the A and C texts of which perhaps show faint memories of Sigurðr (see p. 187, above), though without mentioning him by name, while the B and C texts give *Kremolt* as the name of the Áslaug-figure's (i.e. Adellrun's) mother.

Apart from the exceptional cases of *Adellrun* and *Kremolt*, the least frequently attested personal names are those of Ragnarr loðbrók and Þóra, which are mentioned only in 147, 1824b, the 'Gests ríma', and the *Ragnars kvæði*; the name *Regnfred*, obviously close in form to the name *Ragnarr*, is applied to the hero of 'Regnfred og Kragelil' only, it seems, as a result of secondary influence (see p. 186, above). Outside those texts in which he is mentioned by name, Ragnarr is represented by the hero-figure in the two 'Kragelil' ballads; by the king who seeks to marry Osla in Müller's account; and presumably by a king of Denmark in Torfæus's account, since Torfæus reports that Aadlow/Áslaug became Queen of Denmark. Neither the 'Brynhildar táttur' nor Ramus's account shows any awareness of him. Similarly Þóra is represented outside 147, 1824b, the 'Gests ríma', and the *Ragnars kvæði* only by the shadowy figure of the king's dead wife in Müller's account, whose clothes must be a perfect fit for the king's next wife if he is to marry again.

It must of course be remembered that the various texts reflecting the Spangereid-legend date from very much later than the time when the legend is likely to have informed the X version of *Ragnars saga*, i.e. towards the middle of the thirteenth century; nevertheless, it may be tentatively concluded from the distribution of personal names in these texts that, by the time it developed into the Spangereid-legend, the Áslaug-Kráka branch of the Ragnarr loðbrók tradition had become so preoccupied with its central figure—calling her mostly by the names *Áslaug* and *Kráka*, but also by the name *Adellrun*—as almost (though not entirely, cf. pp. 180–81, 186–88, above, and p. 225) to have forgotten the identity of Ragnarr loðbrók, whom Áslaug marries, and his earlier marriage to someone named Þóra. Both these items of information were, of course, known to the redactor of the older *Ragnars saga*, as *Ragnarssona þáttr* shows (see parts IVB, V, VI, and VII of the Analysis), and were transmitted from that version of the saga to the X and Y versions. The fact that Ragnarr and Þóra are correctly named in the 'Gests ríma' and the *Ragnars kvæði* is very likely due, in the case of the 'Gests ríma', to the primary influence of the Y version of *Ragnars saga*, for which I have argued above with reference to Heimir and Gestur (see pp. 184–86), largely following de Vries (1915, 182–88); and, in the case of the *Ragnars kvæði*, to the secondary influence of that same version of the saga, for which K. Liestøl (1917, 102–10; 1970, 44–51, 101–02) has argued, as also shown above (pp. 156–61). It may thus be suggested that the Áslaug-Kráka branch of the Ragnarr loðbrók tradition to some extent *needed* to unite with the saga branch by way of the Spangereid-legend and the X version of *Ragnars saga* for the identity of its heroine's husband and of his former wife to be confirmed.

I shall express below (pp. 198–99) a somewhat sceptical view of the authenticity of the lost Norwegian ballad referred to by Ramus, from which K. Liestøl (1917, 104–10) primarily derived the second part of the *Ragnars kvæði*, the part relevant here. I would recall here, however (from p. 159, above), the fact that K. Liestøl (1915, 215) further derived this so-called Ramus-ballad from the Spangereid-legend, and would accept his view in the following modified form: that the second part of the *Ragnars kvæði* descends primarily from the Spangereid-legend, and secondarily from the Y version of *Ragnars saga*.

The names of Áslaug's parents seem to have been rather better preserved in memory by the Spangereid-legend than those of Ragnarr loðbrók and Þóra, if not quite as well as Áslaug's own name and nickname. It is true that Sigurðr and Brynhildr are not mentioned in the 'Gests ríma', or in the legend as conveyed by Müller, Torfæus, or Ramus, and that 'Regnfred og Kragelil' shows no genuine memory of either of them. On the other hand, Brynhildr is remembered in one text of 'Karl og Kragelil' (see p. 186, above), and Sigurðr (perhaps) in two of them (cf. pp. 186–87, above), while 'Brynhildar táttur' is quite clear that it is Brynhild who abandons Ásla, her daughter by Sjúrður, to the waves (see part IIIA of the Analysis). Thus it is probably not solely due to the secondary influence of the Y version of *Ragnars saga* that Ásla's parents are correctly named in the *Ragnars kvæði*.

What is to be made of Ramus's statement that Asløg was set

afloat by her stepmother (see under main heading III of the Analysis)? As de Vries (1915, 156) indicates, this stepmother is mentioned nowhere else in the surviving reflexes of the Áslaug-Kráka branch of the Ragnarr loðbrók tradition. Now, if anybody qualifies for the title of Áslaug's stepmother in Norse heroic legend, it is presumably Guðrún, since it is she whom Sigurðr marries; he comes near to marrying Brynhildr, the mother of his daughter Áslaug, but does not in fact do so (see part IA of the Analysis). Sigurðr is killed by one of Guðrún's brothers at the instigation of Brynhildr who, having brought about the killing, commits suicide (*Vǫlsunga saga*, chs. 31–33). These events partly fulfil the curse laid by the dwarf Andvari on the ring Andvaranautr (*Vǫlsunga saga*, ch. 14), which Sigurðr gave to Brynhildr at Heimir's dwelling (*Vǫlsunga saga*, ch. 25), but later took from her while disguised as Gunnarr in her flame-encircled hall (*Vǫlsunga saga*, ch. 29), and then gave to Guðrún, as Guðrún herself reveals to Brynhildr (*Vǫlsunga saga*, ch. 30). There is little reason to expect that, after the deaths of Sigurðr and Brynhildr, their daughter, Áslaug, would be well treated by Guðrún or her brothers, and the opening sentences of the 1824b text of *Ragnars saga* indeed explain that Heimir, on hearing that Áslaug's parents are dead, conceals her in a harp and escapes with her because he fears that attempts will be made on her life (Olsen, 1906–08, 111), though it is not stated by whom. It must be emphasized that, with the possible exception of Ramus's information, this is the only surviving hint of hostile designs on Áslaug by Guðrún, whose stepmother-relationship to Áslaug is, as far as I know, nowhere made explicit. It may at the same time be pointed out that German traditions of the Nibelungs (who correspond to the Gjúkungar of Old Norse tradition), notably the *Nibelungenlied* dating from *c*.1200 and the *Lied vom hürnen Seyfrid* written probably in the fifteenth century (cf. Finch, 1965, xi, xvi, n. 1), assign the name *Kriemhilt* to the woman whose rôle in the German traditions corresponds to that of Guðrún in the Norse; that in the thirteenth-century Norwegian *Þiðriks saga af Bern*, based predominantly on German sources, the Guðrún-figure is named Grímhildr (see Bertelsen, 1905–11, II, 404–05); and that the name *Grímhildr* is otherwise applied in the Old Norse traditions of the Vǫlsungar and Gjúkungar not to Guðrún, but to the wife of Gjúki, the mother of Guðrún and her brothers. It is this Grímhildr, the mother of Guðrún, who gives Sigurðr a magic potion, thus causing him to forget Brynhildr and so marry Guðrún (*Vǫlsunga saga*, ch.

28), and who later, after Sigurðr's death, prepares for Guðrún another such potion which makes her forget her grief (*Vǫlsunga saga*, ch. 34). Thus as a sorceress, at least, she has a certain amount in common with the wicked stepmother-figure of folklore (see the discussion, pp. 119–22, above, of Craca in Saxo's story of Ericus Disertus), and it is noteworthy that the rôles of Grimhild and her daughter Guðrun occasionally merge with each other in the Scandinavian ballad-tradition, as K. Liestøl (1917, 94–95) has pointed out. In the Faroese 'Brynhildar tattur', for instance, it is Guðrun, rather than Grimhild her mother, who gives Sjúrður the potion of forgetfulness, though it is her mother who encourages her to do so (cf. part I A of the Analysis).

   If, on the basis of these considerations, it can be accepted that Ramus's reference to Asløg's stepmother points back to a tradition according to which Áslaug was set adrift by her cruel stepmother Guðrún-Grímhildr, this might give added significance to the fact that Adellrun's mother (though not her stepmother, be it noted) is called Kremolt in the B and C texts of 'Karl og Kragelil', and that Áslaug's ill-disposed foster-mother was called Gríma in the Y (and presumably also the X) version of *Ragnars saga*. If the evidence is not thought sufficient to support this view, then Ramus's information may be explained in terms of what de Vries (1928a, 279) has called the reduplication (*Verdoppelung*) of the stepmother-motif: once applied to Áslaug for the reasons suggested above (see pp. 119–22, 135–36), the name of Craca, stepmother of Ericus Disertus, led to the creation of the stepmother-figure for Áslaug in order partly to explain the attachment of such a name to her, and partly to help fill out the story of her life prior to her marriage (see pp. 136, 182, above). This view of Ramus's information is not necessarily inconsistent with the tentative one just offered in relation to Guðrún-Grímhildr; the reduplication envisaged by de Vries could well have been helped on its way by a tradition of Áslaug's ill-treatment by Guðrún-Grímhildr, or have stimulated such a tradition itself.

   It was noted above (pp. 190–91) that, in str. 5 of the 1824b text of *Ragnars saga*, Áslaug explains, among other things, that she is called Kráka because of her black clothes and the nature of her work as a goatherd. The relevant half-strophe may be compared with a stanza from the *Ragnars kvæði* on the one hand, and with one from 'Regnfred og Kragelil' on the other. The similarities between the two ballad-stanzas were pointed out by Olrik (1894a, 96), and all three passages were quoted by K. Liestøl in the course of his discussion of the ballad and saga traditions of Ragnarr loðbrók (K. Liestøl, 1917, 107–09); in this discussion, however, as already shown (pp. 156–60, above), Liestøl was more concerned with differences than with similarities between these two traditions:

Ragnars saga (1824b text, str. 5. Olsen, 1906–08, 127)

þvi em ek k*r*aca kavllvt	I am called Kráka because I
j kol svart*u*m vod*u*m.	have walked on stony ground
at ek hefi g*r*iot of g*e*ngit	in coal-black clothes and
ok geitr m*ed* sea Reknar.	driven goats along the sea-
	shore, OR: I am called 'Kráka
	in coal-black clothes' because
	I have walked on stony ground
	and driven goats etc.

Ragnars kvæði (G text, st. 84, Djurhuus & Matras, 1951–63, 243)

Hàki kall er fàðir àt màr,	The old man Haki is my father;
hvönn dàg goymi eg geit,	I tend goats every day; I
Kráka eri eg kallað sjálv,	myself am called Kráka; that
tàð er til navns at leita.	is indeed my name.

'Regnfred og Kragelil' (A text, st. 11, DgF, I, 1853, 331)

'En gammel mand er min fader,	My father is an old man; he
Hand genner de geder af mose:	chases the goats from the moors.
Selv da heder jeg Kragelild,	My own name is Kragelil; I will
Min byrd vil jeg ej rose.'	not boast of my descent.

K. Liestøl's purpose in quoting the first of these three passages was evidently to point out the similarity of its content to Ramus's information that, according to oral traditions in the Lindesnæs (i.e. Spangereid) area of southern Norway, Kráka was so called because she wore black clothes; his implication is that the half strophe in *Ragnars saga* and Ramus's statement derive independently of each other from the Spangereid-legend. Helgason (1975, 86), who is clearly sceptical of this view, nevertheless admits that Ramus, who knew Torfæus's account of relevant oral traditions from the same area, cannot have derived this particular item of information from Torfæus, who does not explain the name *Kráka*, though he does mention it (see part IIIC of the Analysis). According to Helgason, Torfæus 'cannot in this case have been an intermediary between the saga and Ramus'. What Helgason seems to be saying is that *Ragnars saga*, of which no edition or translation appeared until 1737 (when it was published in Stockholm in E. J. Björner's *Nordiska kämpadater* with translations into Swedish and Latin, see Hermannsson, 1912, 34, 1–2), was accessible in manuscript form to Torfæus (d. 1719), but not to Ramus (d. 1718). If this is so, it is surely more reasonable to suppose that Ramus obtained his explanation of the name *Kráka* as a result of making his own inquiries, independently of *Ragnars saga*, into traditions current in the relevant part of Norway, than that, as Helgason suggests, 'he conceived the idea himself, without the support of an older source.' Helgason seems to have been rather too heavily influenced here by Árni Magnússon's low opinion of Ramus as a researcher, to which he refers (Helgason, 1975, 85, n. 7), though at the same time he points out that the book in which Ramus gives his account (*Norriges Kongers Historie*, 1719, see p. 58, above), includes an 'Approbatio' written by Árni Magnússon himself. It may be assumed, then, that the explanation of the name *Kráka* in terms of black clothes originated with the Spangereid-legend, and that the verse referring to it and quoted above from the 1824b text of *Ragnars saga* also occurred in the X version of the saga preserved in 147, even though it cannot now be read in the relevant part of that manuscript (Olsen, 1906–08, 178–79).

Helgason is, however, probably right to be sceptical of Ramus's information about a Norwegian ballad according to which a king's daughter (presumably identical with Áslaug) was abandoned to the waves by her stepmother (see part III of the Analysis). No trace of this ballad has been found in later Norwegian tradition; if Ramus really knew such a ballad, it is surprising that he did not convey more of its content; and it is above all surprising that, if this ballad existed, neither Torfæus nor his chosen corroborator, Toldorph (cf. p. 58, above), should have made any mention of it. It is easier to believe that they might have omitted to mention the explanation of the name *Kráka* a relatively unimportant detail—than that they should have completely failed to mention the ballad. Yet Helgason (1975, 86–87) does not dismiss the 'Ramus-ballad' altogether; he admits that the stanzas in certain texts of the Faroese 'Brynhildar táttur' about Brynhild abandoning Ásla, her daughter by Sjúrður, to a fast-flowing river (cf. part IIIA of the Analysis) may seem to derive from a ballad such as Ramus describes. Helgason seems to have been the first to cast any doubt on the Ramus-ballad's authenticity; Grundtvig (in DgF I, 1853, 328), Storm (1878, 116–18), de Vries (1915, 154 79), and K. Liestøl (1915, 214; 1917,

85, 102–10; 1970, 49–50) all believed in it, and the three last-named scholars maintained that this Norwegian ballad formed the basis of the Danish ballads 'Regnfred og Kragelil' and 'Karl og Kragelil'. Doubt of the ballad's existence need not of course imply that the Spangereid-legend made no use at all of verse in the course of its oral development; if two at least of the three passages just quoted (see p. 197, above) derive independently of each other from the Spangereid-legend, it may indeed be concluded that the legend existed partly in verse form. Rather than commit myself to the idea of a lost Norwegian ballad, I would prefer to take the more cautious view that the Spangereid-legend developed partly in prose, partly in verse, in the course of oral tradition, and did not have so fixed a form as might be implied by an assumption of the Ramus-ballad's existence.

It would be idle to speculate in detail on the metrical form of the verse-elements in the Spangereid-legend, but it may be suggested that they developed gradually from scaldic to ballad metres, and that the scaldic stages in the metrical development are represented by strs. 2–5 of the 1824b text of *Ragnars saga* (all of which appear to have been transmitted to the Y version of the saga by way of the X version, even though none of them is now legible in the 147 text, cf. Olsen 1906–08, 178–79); while the ballad-stages are represented by the Faroese 'Gests ríma' and 'Brynhildar táttur', the two Danish 'Kragelil' ballads, and, less directly, the accounts of Müller and Ramus, both of whom seem to be referring to sources of ballad-type (see p. 161, above), but whose accounts are of course in prose. It is clear that the verse-element in the legend did not bulk large, however, in the traditions available to Torfæus and Toldorph.

It is relevant to mention here K. Liestøl's view (1970, 7–15; 97–98) that the ballad-metres in Scandinavia derived in part from 'forms of poetry of a more popular and less complex nature than true Scaldic verse'; Sveinsson's observation (1962, 125) that the verses of *Ragnars saga* tend to depart from the strict rules of the *dróttkvætt*, the metre most frequently employed by the scalds; and the fact that Snorri Sturluson in his prose *Edda* (*Háttatal*, str. 54, see F. Jónsson, 1931a, 238) attributes to Ragnarr loðbrók the metre he calls *Ragnars háttr*, illustrating it as the first in a series of irregular *dróttkvætt* forms. According to Snorri, the *Ragnars háttr* differs from strict *dróttkvætt* in having no internal rhyme in the first and third *vísuorð* of the half strophe, and one or two syllables before the alliterating syllable, or *hǫfuðstafr* ('head-stave'), in the second and fourth *vísuorð*. In strict *dróttkvætt*, there would be half-rhyme or *skothending* (i.e. agreement of post-vocalic consonants in certain positions, though not of the vowels preceding them) in the first and third *vísuorð*, and the *hǫfuðstafr* would be the first syllable in the second and fourth (Turville-Petre, 1976, xviii-xix). In other respects the *Ragnars háttr* resembles the *dróttkvætt*; in particular, as Snorri points out, it is characterized in the second and fourth *vísuorð* of the half strophe by full syllabic rhyme or *aðalhending* (i.e. agreement of pre-consonantal vowels in certain positions, and of the consonants following them). Snorri's information shows that, by the time of the composition of *Háttatal* (*c*.1225, see Faulkes, 1982, xiii, xv), the relevant part of his prose *Edda*, the name of Ragnarr loðbrók had come to be associated with a particular type of relatively loosely composed scaldic verse.

It is certainly true that the verses of *Ragnars saga* frequently depart from the strict rules of the *dróttkvætt*, if not in precisely the manner of the *Ragnars háttr* as described by Snorri. Of the thirty-seven scaldic strophes preserved in the 1824b text of *Ragnars saga* (seven of which are also preserved in *Hauksbók* as parts of *Ragnarssona þáttr*, while sixteen of them are preserved fragmentarily in the 147 text of the saga, see pp. 54–56, above), not a single one conforms exactly to the strict *dróttkvætt* pattern; on the other hand, not a single one of them conforms exactly to the *Ragnars háttr* as Snorri illustrates it. Internal rhyme occurs only sporadically, and in some strophes not at all; both *skothending* and *aðalhending* occur, but not necessarily in the appropriate *vísuorð*, and the *hǫfuðstafr* is often preceded by one or two syllables in the second and fourth *vísuorð* of the half-strophe, but this is by no means the general rule. It will be noticed that, in the above-quoted half strophe in which Kráka explains her nickname, there is no internal rhyme at all, and that the *hǫfuðstafr* is preceded by one syllable in the second and fourth *vísuorð*. In view of the theory, referred to by K. Liestøl (1970, 7–8, 97), that the eddaic *ljóðaháttr*-strophe played an especially important part in the development of the four-line ballad stanza in Scandinavia, it is particularly interesting to note that one of the scaldic strophes in the 1824b text of *Ragnars saga*, no. 21, seems to combine features of the *ljóðaháttr*-strophe with the irregular *dróttkvætt* measure generally characteristic of these strophes.

Once this point has been made, however, it must be emphasized that the strophe in question, which also occurs in a rather more strictly scaldic form in *Ragnarssona þáttr*, has no parallel in the ballad-traditions relating to Ragnarr loðbrók, and that its subject-matter—the heroic resolve of Ragnarr's son Hvítserkr, the speaker of the strophe, to set sail for Sweden with his brothers to avenge the slaying of their stepbrother Agnarr does not seem to have been a preoccupation of the ballad-traditions themselves, which in their surviving forms show no real awareness of Ragnarr's sons, even though, as argued above (pp. 165, 168–69, 179–82), an awareness of the sons does seem to have formed part of their background. It is the first half of str. 21 in the 1824b text that is relevant here; this may be quoted side by side with the corresponding half-strophe in *Hauksbók*.

Ragnars saga (1824b text, str. 21; Olsen, 1906–08, 145)	*Ragnarssona þáttr*, str. 6 (in Hb, 1892–96, 461, ll. 8–9)
hyggium at hinv aþr heiman farim. at hefnt megi verda. latum ymsa illa. agnarrs bana fagna.	HyGivm at aðr heitim að hefnt megi verða latvm ymsv illv Agnars bana fagna
(Let us consider this, before departing from home: that vengeance may be achieved. Let us allow various people to greet Agnarr's slayer unfavourably)	(Let us think about it, before we promise that vengeance may be achieved [OR: before we promise anything, let us think, so that vengeance may be achieved]. Let us allow Agnarr's slayer to encounter various misfortunes)

Most commentators emend the 1824b text here in *Hauksbók*'s favour, to a greater or lesser extent; the texts and translations given here may be compared with those of Finnur Jónsson in Hb (1892–96, 461), and in F. Jónsson (1915a, 237; 1915b, 256), and also with those of Olsen (1906–08, 209–10), and E. A. Kock (1927, 89–90). The *Hauksbók* half-strophe is obviously the closer of the two to the *dróttkvætt* form; it has the appropriate number of *vísuorð* and syllables per *vísuorð*, and uses alliteration according to the *dróttkvætt* pattern in the second pair of *vísuorð* (where vowel-alliteration is used) and in the manner of the *Ragnars háttr* in the first pair (where the second *vísuorð* has one syllable before the *hofuðstafr*). It also meets the requirements of the *dróttkvætt*, and indeed of the *Ragnars háttr*, in having full syllabic rhyme or *aðalhending* (on [-]*agn-*) in the fourth *vísuorð*, even though it has no other internal rhyme. The last two *vísuorð* of the 1824b passage differ in no way metrically from those of the *Hauksbók* passage, even though the reading *ymsa*, as opposed to *ymsv*, means that they differ grammatically, and hence semantically, from their *Hauksbók* counterparts. However, the first three *vísuorð* of the 1824b passage obviously differ in number and metre, as well as in meaning, from the two to which they correspond in *Hauksbók*; they seem in fact to constitute a *ljóðaháttr* half-strophe. It is true that the third *vísuorð* in such a half strophe would normally be expected to have independent double (sometimes triple) alliteration, but, as Sievers (1893, 83–84; cf. Bliss, 1971, 442–43) indicates, it may occasionally have only one alliterating word, which continues the alliteration of the preceding pair of *vísuorð*. This seems to be the case in the relevant part of the 1824b passage just quoted, where the word in question is of course *hefnt*. The strophe of which it forms part seems also to have occurred in the X version of *Ragnars saga*, but cannot now be read in the 147 text. It may be assumed that the half-strophe developed from an already rather loosely composed *dróttkvætt* form, such as *Hauksbók* represents, into an even looser combination of the *dróttkvætt* with the *ljóðaháttr* form, such as is represented by 1824b.

The *Ragnars kvæði* and Müller's account seem to preserve an older stage of the Spangereid-legend than is reflected in the 1824b text of *Ragnars saga*, at least, in that they make fuller and more logical use than the saga does of the motif of the hero's dead wife's clothes fitting the heroine perfectly. In the saga, Ragnarr simply offers Kráka-Áslaug the shift that had belonged to Þóra, because he thinks it would suit her (see str. 4 of the 1824b text, Olsen, 1906–08, 126–27; the 147 text is here illegible, Olsen, 1906–08, 179). Kráka-Áslaug, who at this stage of the narrative is still very much in the rôle of Kráka, appears not to agree (see str. 5, Olsen, 1906–08, 127), and although she hints that she may try it on later, it is not made clear whether she actually does so (see the summary of the Spangereid-legend, pp. 190–91, above). In the *Ragnars kvæði* and Müller's account, on the other hand, the perfect fit is clearly part of the process whereby Ásla/Osla is identified as the person the widowed hero must marry next. This difference, as de Vries (1928a, 289) shows convincingly, is due to the fact that the *Ragnars saga* texts reflect a later stage of the story's development, by which Kráka-Áslaug had come to be identified as the right wife for Ragnarr by the intelligence with which she fulfils the difficult conditions ('neither clad nor unclad') under which Ragnarr says she must visit him; once this idea had become established, the motif of the perfectly fitting clothes became almost superfluous, but could not be discarded altogether, since it provided a link between Ragnarr's marriage to Kráka-Áslaug and his earlier marriage to Þóra, as already indicated (see pp. 177–79, above). This view of de Vries's is consistent with K. Liestøl's view in the modified form I have given it above (p. 194), i.e. that the second part of the *Ragnars kvæði* derived primarily from the Spangereid-legend, and secondarily from the (Y) version of *Ragnars saga* reflected in 1824b. It seems clear that the *Ragnars kvæði* formed a two-part sequence from the earliest stages of their existence, as suggested earlier (see p. 166, above), and that the first part of the *Ragnars kvæði* derives mainly from the original 'Lindarorm' ballad, as K. Liestøl (1917, 102–04, 110; 1970, 44–47) has argued; but it is also indebted to the Spangereid-legend for its information that Ragnar's wife (Tóra) Borgarhjǫrt prophesies on her death-bed that his next wife will be the person for whom his present wife's clothes turn out to be a perfect fit (cf. part VII of the Analysis). It may incidentally be noted here that, just as the identities of Ragnarr loðbrók and Þóra may have become partly obscured as the Áslaug-Kráka branch of the tradition developed into the Spangereid-legend (see pp. 192–94, above), so may they also have become obscured as the Ragnarr loðbrók tradition in its 'pre-Áslaug' state developed into the original 'Lindarorm' ballad, in the manner suggested above (in section (b) of the present chapter); there is certainly no evidence in the surviving reflexes of this ballad that these figures were correctly named in the version of the ballad that formed a source for the *Ragnars kvæði*. It is possible that the secondary influence of the Y version of *Ragnars saga* on the *Ragnars kvæði* was of value to the latter in confirming these identities not only in relation to the Áslaug-Kráka branch of the tradition, as suggested earlier (p. 194, above), but also in relation to the branch represented by 'Lindarormen' and 'Ormekampen'.

Neither de Vries nor K. Liestøl seems to recognize the possibility that the *Ragnars kvæði* also preserve the motif of the apparently impossible conditions in a somewhat older form than is found in the 147 and 1824b texts of *Ragnars saga*. The saga has the following three conditions: 'Neither clad nor unclad, neither fed nor unfed, neither alone nor accompanied by man', whereas the *Ragnars kvæði* have only two, corresponding to the first and third of the three found in the saga (see part IV A of the Analysis). In some texts of the *Ragnars kvæði*, it is true, Ásla is presented as biting a leek while fulfilling these two conditions, which implies an awareness of the second condition in the saga ('neither fed nor unfed'), though this condition is not otherwise referred to in the *Ragnars kvæði*; the stanza supposedly describing it, which de Vries (1915, 151, n. 1) suggests the *Ragnars kvæði* have lost in the course of their transmission, is, as far as I can see, a complete invention on his part, however authentic it may appear. What he does not notice, any more than K. Liestøl, is that in str. 2 of the 1824b text of *Ragnars saga* (which also appears to have formed part of the 147 text, see Olsen, 1906 08, 178, n. to 3r 17), Kráka, who speaks this strophe, refers to only the first and third of the conditions found in the saga, the same two as are found in the *Ragnars kvæði*. These considerations might suggest a relatively early stage in the tradition's use of this motif at which two conditions were employed rather than three. The reference to the leek in the *Ragnars kvæði* would thus represent either an early stage in the transition from two to three conditions in the course of legendary development, or, more probably, the secondary influence of the Y version of *Ragnars saga*. A difficulty about this view, however, is that, according to de Vries (1928d, 228) at least, the motif probably involved three conditions when it was first adopted by the Ragnarr loðbrók tradition. If so, it would have to be explained how the number came to be reduced to two by the stage reflected in the *Ragnars kvæði*, and restored to three in the X and Y versions of *Ragnars saga*.

As de Vries (1928d, 14–29, 176–232; cf. McTurk, 1978, 278–82) has shown, the motif in question derives from the widespread international popular tale known as 'the clever peasant girl', AT no. 875, in which a clever peasant girl is required to visit a king or chieftain under a series of seemingly impossible conditions, and the king is so pleased by her successful fulfilment of them that he marries her. According to de Vries (1928d, 214 20), whose views on the history of the tale have, it should be noted, been to some extent called in question by Jackson (1961, 108–12), the form in which the series of conditions became available to the Ragnarr loðbrók tradition was most likely as follows: first, neither naked nor clothed; second, neither on foot nor on horseback; and third, neither fed nor unfed. Thus, if the *Ragnars kvæði* are left aside for the moment, it appears that, in the X and Y versions of *Ragnars saga*, the first and third conditions in the original series have been retained, while the second has been discarded; that the third condition in the original series has moved into second place in the saga; and that, in the latter, a new third condition, 'neither alone nor accompanied by man', has been added. This last condition, according to de Vries (1928d, 220–30), is intended to replace the second one in the original series, 'neither on foot nor on horseback', even though it occupies the third place in the saga. He argues most ingeniously and in the end convincingly that 'the clever peasant girl' tale has here combined with the tale-type now listed in AT (1961, 345) as no. 981: 'wisdom of hidden old man saves kingdom'. In the relevant variants of 'the clever peasant girl' tale, the fulfilment of the condition 'neither on foot nor on horseback' is often effected by the use of a goat as a means of transportation, but in de Vries's view (1928d, 219) it cannot have been thought appropriate for so great a lady as Áslaug, the daughter of Sigurðr and Brynhildr, to be presented in the ludicrous position of riding a goat, even in her rôle as Kráka. He does not seem to notice in this context the fact that, at this stage of her career, Kráka is working as a goatherd (see part IIIC of the Analysis), though whether it is strictly appropriate for a goatherd to ride one of her charges is admittedly a moot point.

Now the new condition, 'neither alone nor accompanied by man', to which Kráka responds by simply bringing a dog with her, arose, according to de Vries, as a result of the influence of the other tale just mentioned, 'wisdom of hidden old man saves kingdom', called by de Vries (1928d, 220) 'the legend of the slaying of the aged', which of course differs from version to version, but often takes the following form: the Romans act on a decision to kill all members of·their society whom old age and infirmity have made expendable in a time of famine, but then find themselves in difficulties without any old people left to give them sound advice. One of them has nevertheless secretly spared his father and maintained him in hiding, benefiting from his advice to such an obvious extent that his contemporaries suspect that his father is still alive. In an attempt to find out the truth they arrange for the king to invite him to a banquet in attending which he must fulfil certain difficult conditions, including those of bringing with him his best friend and his worst enemy. He fulfils these particular conditions by bringing his dog and his wife respectively; and it is clear that he has done what is required of him from the fact that, when he beats his dog, it remains faithful to him in spite of the beating, returning to him at once in friendly response to his call; whereas when he beats his wife, she betrays his secret by angrily revealing that his father is still alive.

If de Vries is right, it is easy to see how the new condition, 'neither alone nor accompanied by man', could arise once the combination of these two tales had taken place and the dog had been brought into prominence. In further support of his view that the Ragnarr loðbrók tradition was influenced by both tales and combined them in the manner just described, de Vries (1928d, 220–30) makes a number of points. Firstly, he shows that mediaeval literary versions of the story of the hidden old man's wisdom are recorded from France, Italy, England, and Germany; the oldest one listed by him is a Latin sermon by the Frankish-born Ratherius of Verona, who died in 974. Thus the story could easily have been brought to Scandinavia by way of the pilgrim-routes, which, as de Vries (1928a, 266–69; 1927c, 84–85) himself has shown, were an important channel for the transmission to Scandinavia of information deriving from further south on the continent (see also ch. II, pp. 109–10, above). The relevant information is likely to have included an originally Norman tradition according to which the Italian town of Luna was attacked by Vikings; this notion, which first finds expression in Book I of the *De moribus et actis primorum Normanniæ ducum* by the Norman chronicler Dudo of St. Quentin (*c*.1010) (see Lair, 1865, 132–38), may well derive, as de Vries argues (1928b, 122–25), from a misreading of the *Annales Bertiniani* for 849, where a sentence reporting the plundering of Luna by the Saracens immediately follows one recording an attack by the Norsemen on Périgueux in Aquitania. Now in *Ragnarssona páttr* (Hb, 1892–96, 464), the sons of Ragnarr loðbrók are said to have taken Lúna and to have contemplated for a time the taking of Rome; and in the 1824b text of *Ragnars saga* (ch. 14), as already shown (see pp. 109–10, above), they reach Lúna but are dissuaded from proceeding as far as Rome by an old man who convinces them that the journey would be too long. What little can be read of the relevant part of the 147 text (see Olsen 1906–08, 186) seems closer to the *páttr* than to 1824b, while Arngrímur, without actually mentioning Luna, gives essentially the same account as 1824b, but adds a scathing reference to a tradition according to which the old man was the apostle Peter, who was seeking to save Rome from attack; this information, according to Arngrímur, is on a par with the fabrications so often found in Saxo (Benediktsson, 1950,

465–66). In Dudo's account the Norsemen set out to conquer Rome after laying waste the whole of France; they arrive at Luna, where they employ the ruse of pretending their leader has died and asking permission to enter the town in order to bury him. He leaps from his bier at the last moment, takes the town with the help of his followers, and at first believes that it is indeed Rome he has won. What is particularly important in the present context is that, in Dudo's account, Alstignus, the leader of the Viking attack on Luna, is presented as one of a number of young men who were selected by lot for expulsion from their native country, Dacia, when it was threatened by overpopulation. This motif bears an obvious similarity to that of the slaying of the aged in a time of famine, an important element in the story of the hidden old man's wisdom; and the connection between the Norman tradition of a Viking attack on Luna and the Ragnarr loðbrók tradition, already obvious from the mention in both traditions of Rome and Luna in a Viking context, becomes even more so when it is noted that the later Norman chronicler William of Jumièges (c.1070) relates that the Viking leader Hastingus (i.e. Dudo's Alstignus) was assisted in his conquest of Luna by 'Lotbroci regis filio ... Bier Costae ... ferreae' (Marx, 1914, 5), who is clearly identifiable with Bjǫrn járnsíða, son of Ragnarr loðbrók (see part VII of the Analysis, and cf. pp. 1, 6–7, 41, 42–43, and 144, above). Williams's account also contains the motif of impending over-population; it was because of this that Bier's father, Lotbrocus, expelled him from his kingdom, sending Hastingus along with him as his 'pedagogus' (Marx, 1914, 8), as shown above (ch. II, section (b) (ii).

Secondly, de Vries points out (1928d, 228) that in the 1824b text of *Ragnars saga* (and also in 147, it may be added, see Olsen 1906–08, 178, cf. 125), the dog used in fulfilment of the third condition is slain because of its faithfulness to Kráka, whom it tries to protect from Ragnarr; in the 1824b text, at least, it seems that the dog is beaten (unless the word *drepa* here means 'kill', see Olsen, 1906–08, 125, ll. 24–26) before it actually dies (by strangling in the 1824b text; by hanging in 147). The beating and slaying of the dog have virtually no function in the plot of *Ragnars saga*, however; it is not necessary to establish the dog's faithfulness in the saga as it is in the story of the hidden old man's wisdom, where the beating is much more important. The slaying of the dog in the X and Y versions of *Ragnars saga* may thus be used in support of the view that the saga was influenced by the story of the hidden old man's wisdom and has preserved a memory of the suffering to which the dog is subjected in that story so that its faithfulness may be demonstrated. At the same time it should be noted that, although a dog is used in fulfilment of one of the two conditions in the *Ragnars kvæði*, no mention is made there of its being beaten or slain.

Thirdly, de Vries (1928d, 229) finds evidence in Scandinavian folk tradition for a combination of the story of the hidden old man's wisdom with the 'clever peasant girl' tale. The motif of the slaying of the aged occurs in the great majority of the Swedish variants of the 'clever peasant girl' tale known to him, and nine out of the ten relevant variants are popular rather than literary. Furthermore, the motif of conditions being fulfilled to appease the anger of a powerful person, which is found in a number of mediaeval versions of the story of the hidden old man's wisdom, is also found in two of the Norwegian popular variants of the 'king and the peasant's son' tale (AT 921) as documented by de Vries, both of which contain conditions of the type characteristic of the 'clever peasant girl' tale.

Fourthly and finally, de Vries (1928d, 229–30) draws attention to the fact that, in almost all the Danish variants of the 'clever peasant girl' tale known to him, the prince meets the maiden as a result of accidentally having to spend the night at a forest lodging, a situation obviously similar to the one in *Ragnars saga* where Ragnarr meets Kráka as a result of happening to land at Spangarheiðr. He might have added that the chance element in the encounter is even greater in the *Ragnars kvæði* than in the saga, since the *Ragnars kvæði* do not mention, as the saga does, that the hero was in the area for a specific purpose (i.e. visiting friends and relations, see p. 158, above).

From the third and fourth considerations just listed, de Vries concludes that the relevant episode of *Ragnars saga* derives partly from oral tradition; on the other hand, he credits a saga-redactor ('ein Sagaredakteur', de Vries, 1928d, 228) with responsibility for the process described above whereby the three conditions of the 'clever peasant girl' tale were adapted to those of the saga with the help of the story of the hidden old man's wisdom. In the same context (and on the same page) he refers to this redactor as 'Der Sagaverfasser, der im südlichen Norwegen lebte'; however, it is doubtful whether he is committing himself here to the view that a version of *Ragnars saga* was actually written in Norway, since he implies elsewhere (de Vries 1927c, 99–100), with reference to

Ragnars saga and the *fornaldarsǫgur* generally, that the art of saga-narration was so highly developed in Norwegian oral tradition as to merit description in such terms as 'Die Kunst des Sagaschreibens', even though the true home of saga-writing in the strict sense was, of course, Iceland rather than Norway. My own view, in any case, is that the adaptation process described by de Vries took place in Norwegian oral tradition as part of the Spangereid-legend; this seems to me to provide the most satisfactory explanation of why only two rather than three conditions are found in the *Ragnars kvæði* and in str. 2 of the 1824b text of *Ragnars saga*.

I would suggest a development on the following lines: while the Spangereid-legend was in process of formation, it was influenced by a version of the 'clever peasant girl' tale incorporating the following three conditions: neither naked nor clothed, neither on foot nor on horseback, neither fed nor unfed. Somewhat later, it was also influenced by the stipulation involving the faithful dog in the story of the hidden old man's wisdom, so that it came to substitute the new condition, 'neither alone nor accompanied by man', for the older 'neither on foot nor on horseback', very much as suggested by de Vries (1928d, 214–30). If it is objected here that de Vries's main reason for the substitution—i.e. the considerations of decorum which require a more respectable animal for Áslaug than a goat—is more what would be expected of a literary redactor than of legendary development, it may be replied, first, that the techniques of a skilled oral narrator are sometimes hard to distinguish from those of a literary artist, as de Vries (1927c, 99–100) himself seems to recognize, and secondly, that there may have been more pressure on the Spangereid-legend to accommodate the figure of a faithful dog than simply that exerted by the story of the hidden old man's wisdom, as I shall argue below (pp. 227–35).

If the argument so far is accepted, it is clear that the *Ragnars kvæði* and str. 2 of *Ragnars saga* in the 1824b text, which mention only two conditions, reflect a later stage in the legend's development than the substitution just described, since one of the two is the condition involving company. Since the other is the one involving clothing, these verse traditions seem to indicate that, after the substitution had taken place, the position of 'neither fed nor unfed', the third condition in the original series, was not entirely secure in the Spangereid-legend.

I would suggest three possible reasons for this. First, its position may not have been wholly secure even in its original context; according to de Vries (1928d, 219), it existed side by side with another possible third condition, 'neither by day nor by night', in the forms in which the 'clever peasant girl' tale is likely to have been available to the Ragnarr loðbrók tradition. Second, where a new condition has been substituted for one of three in the course of oral tradition, as in the case envisaged here, it would not be surprising if the tradition were at first preoccupied with the new condition to the exclusion of at least one of the other two. Third, it may be recalled that the heroine is twice questioned about her origins in the Spangereid-legend as reflected in the *Ragnars kvæði* (except in the C text, where she is questioned three times, see parts VII and IX of the Analysis) and the two 'Kragelil' ballads; in most cases the question is put both times by the hero, though in 'Karl og Kragelil' it is first asked by his messengers (see the summary of the legend, pp. 189–92, above). She gives a false answer the first time she is asked the question, but answers it correctly the second time (here again the C text of the *Ragnars kvæði* is an exception, see parts VII and IX of the Analysis, and cf. p. 180, above). The reason for only two conditions, the ones involving company and clothing, in the *Ragnars kvæði* and str. 2 of *Ragnars saga* in 1824b, may well be that the number of conditions has been assimilated to the number of times the question is asked, at the expense of 'neither fed nor unfed'. I would suggest that this assimilation in fact took place, and that it is reflected in the *Ragnars kvæði* and str. 2 of the 1824b text of *Ragnars saga*, while the prose texts of the saga preserved in 147 and 1824b reflect, albeit less clearly in the former case than in the latter, a still later stage which it may be assumed was represented in the X as well as the Y version of *Ragnars saga*, and by which the condition, 'neither fed nor unfed', never wholly forgotten, had been recovered and once again combined with the other two, in accordance with the demands of the law of three characteristic of oral narrative (see Olrik, 1921, 75). The motif of Ásla biting a leek found in some texts of the *Ragnars kvæði* is thus to be explained either as an example of the secondary influence of the Y version of *Ragnars saga*, as suggested earlier (see p. 204, above), or (this time rather more probably) as a relic of the condition 'neither fed nor unfed', from before the stage at which the assimilation just described had taken place. The fact that this condition occurs in a number of Italian variants of the 'clever peasant girl' tale, and the likelihood that it has its origin in fasting-practices, are, of course, wholly consistent with de Vries's view (1928a, 266–69; 1927c, 84–85) that some of the material for this and other parts of the Ragnarr loðbrók tradition reached Norway by way of the routes followed by West Scandinavian pilgrims returning homewards through Denmark. Finally, the absence of the dog's beating or slaying from the *Ragnars kvæði*, noted above (p. 208), is probably due to the Faroese ballad-poet's recognition of the superfluity of this motif in the Y version of *Ragnars saga*, if not in the Spangereid-legend in the form in which he knew it.

(e) The English contribution to the Spangereid-legend

So far, then, the evidence suggests that both the 'clever peasant girl' tale and the story of 'the hidden old man's wisdom' reached the Spangereid area from the European continent by way of Denmark, and were brought to Norway by Scandinavian pilgrims returning homewards. The Spangereid-legend must have provided a congenial setting for the 'clever peasant girl' tale, at least; the basic situation in the legend, where a girl of apparently humble origin comes to the attention of a king, who subsequently marries her, is similar to that in the tale. The heroine's name *Adellrun*, with its connotations of wisdom, noted above (pp. 174, 176–77), may indeed have helped to attract the influence of one or both of these tales, though it should of course be remembered that this name is unlikely to have been dominant in the legend and occurs in only one of its recorded versions (i.e. in 'Karl og Kragelil', see the summary of the legend above, pp. 189–90). The motif of the apparently impossible conditions is not as out of place in the Spangereid-legend as Schlauch (1930, xxxv), for instance, seems to think; when she writes that 'Ragnar is eager to have Kraka come to him, and it is hard to understand why he should wilfully put difficulties in her way', she fails to take account of the likelihood that his purpose in imposing the conditions is to find out if the maiden is as exceptional as she is said to be; and the *Ragnars kvæði* again seem to represent an earlier stage of development than the saga (as preserved in 147 and 1824b) in stressing her wisdom rather than her beauty in this context (cf. part VII of the Analysis). The motif of the conditions was clearly of value to the Ragnarr loðbrók tradition, as the *Ragnars kvæði* and the saga show, in helping to provide more of a build-up for the maiden's revelation of her true identity than was provided by the simple question-and-answer sequences reflected in the two 'Kragelil' ballads (see the summary of the Spangereid-legend, pp. 189–92, above).

These various considerations may be thought sufficient to explain the connection that developed between the Ragnarr loðbrók tradition on the one hand and the popular tales of 'the clever peasant girl' and the hidden old man's wisdom on the other. Further incentives to the making of this connection can however be found, I believe, among the traditions of English origin relating to Ragnarr loðbrók; and here it must be remembered that, as pointed out in connection with Rǫgnvaldr in the last chapter (ch. II, section (b) (*iii*)), there is evidence for the subject-matter of some of these traditions reaching Denmark from England and then being conveyed, very possibly by homeward-going pilgrims, to southern Norway. The traditions in question are preserved mainly in a number of Anglo-Latin writings of varying age and provenance; in the late tenth-century *Passio sancti Eadmundi*, written in England by a continental scholar, Abbo of Fleury, on the basis of apparently reliable information given him by Archbishop Dunstan of Canterbury (Whitelock, 1969, 218–19); and in *L'estoire des Engleis*, the mid twelfth-century Anglo-Norman verse chronicle by Geffrei Gaimar (ed. Bell, 1960; ed. and trans. Hardy & Martin, 1888, 1889). Insofar as they relate to Ragnarr loðbrók, these writings have been fairly thoroughly investigated by, among others, de Vries (1928b, 148–63), Loomis (1932, 1933), Whitelock (1969), and Lukman (1976, esp. 9–12); I shall discuss them here for the most part only insofar as they affect the development of the Spangereid-legend. In this context they are, I suggest, valuable in helping to fill in the background of three aspects of the legend in particular: first, the situation in which a woman summoned by a king arrives in humbler clothing than her true status requires; second, the three conditions; and third, the faithful dog.

There is no evidence that the combined name *Ragnarr loðbrók* was known to any of the writings just referred to or to their sources (cf. p. 7, above). Some of them are concerned with a figure whose name corresponds to *loðbrók*, though none of them mentions the name *Ragnarr*, or its equivalent, in a relevant context. Most of them refer to the ninth-century Viking leaders Inwære and Hubba, historical figures (on whom see ch. I, section (c), above) who came to be regarded as sons of Ragnarr loðbrók in Scandinavian tradition (under the names *Ívarr* and *Ubbo/Ubbi* respectively (see part VII of the Analysis, and pp. 40, 104–07, 154, above); and some of them refer to the English king Ælla, also a historical figure, who in Scandinavian tradition is represented as responsible for Ragnarr loðbrók's death in the snake-pit (under the names *Ella, Hella,* see parts V and X of the Analysis). According to de Vries (1927c, 81–83), the legend of Loðbrók and his sons first developed among Scandinavian settlers in England in the eleventh century, who found it necessary to supply, in the words of Schlauch (1930, xxxiv), 'so admirable a motive as revenge for a father's death' as an explanation of the Viking invasion of Northumbria in 866, and the slaying of King Edmund by Vikings in East Anglia three years later. The oldest source for these events, the *Anglo-Saxon chronicle,* compiled before 890, states (Earle & Plummer, 1892, 68–69) that there was civil strife among the people of Northumbria at the time of the invasion; that they had deposed their king Osbriht, and taken instead Ælla, a king not of royal birth; and that both kings were subsequently slain in the Northumbrian defeat at York (in 867). The leaders of the invasion are not named in the *Anglo-Saxon chronicle,* though the late tenth-century Latin chronicle of Æthelweard, based on a lost version of the *Anglo-Saxon chronicle* (Whitelock, 1969, 222), names Iguuar as one of the leaders of the army that arrived in East Anglia in 865 and invaded Northumbria the following year (Campbell, 1962, 35). Only manuscript F of the *Anglo-Saxon chronicle,* the least authoritative of the seven extant manuscripts and written *c.*1100, states that the Viking leaders who slew King Edmund in 869 were Ingware and Ubba (Stenton, 1971, 246, nn. 2 and 3); in the other manuscripts it is simply stated that the Danes defeated and killed him. To this information Æthelweard adds only a brief note of Edmund's burial at Bedricesworth (i.e. Bury St. Edmunds) and a statement that Iuuar (*sic*), the king of the victorious Vikings, died in the same year as King Edmund (for a refutation of the historical accuracy of this statement, see ch. I, p. 46, above). In the present discussion stories relating to Ælla will be found relevant to the motifs in the Spangereid-legend of the maiden coming to meet the king in humble clothing, and the three conditions; while stories relating to Edmund will be found relevant to the motif of the faithful dog.

The stories relating to Ælla tend to reflect both favourable and unfavourable attitudes towards him, as de Vries (1928b, 152–56) has shown, and this tendency presumably derives ultimately from the situation of civil strife in Northumbria in the context of which his name appears in the *Anglo-Saxon chronicle*. It seems clear, however, that the less favourable view of him was readily seized upon and developed by Danish settlers in Northumbria, who were anxious to justify as far as possible the Viking invasion of that kingdom in 866. This development, as de Vries implies, probably took place during the period of Danish ascendancy in England established by Sveinn Forkbeard (d. 1014) and Cnut the Great, and maintained until shortly after the latter's death in 1035 (cf. Kendrick, 1930, 257–73). It should however be noted that one of the writings considered by de Vries in this connection seems to date from before Sveinn's first appearance on the English scene in 994; this is the anonymous mid tenth-century *Historia de sancto Cuthberto*, wrongly believed by de Vries (1928b, 153) to be the work of Symeon of Durham (d. *c*.1130), who in fact used it as a source for his *Historia Dunelmensis ecclesiæ* (Craster, 1954, 177–78; Whitelock, 1979, 129).

As far as Ælla is concerned, the *Historia de sancto Cuthberto* (Arnold, 1882, 202) gives a curiously ambivalent and confusing account. It tells how Osberhtus, King of Northumbria, appropriated certain properties of the monks of St. Cuthbert, but was deprived a year later of his life and rule by God. He was succeeded by King Ælle (*sic*), who also took possession of monastery properties, thus breaking a promise to St. Cuthbert and incurring God's anger as well as the saint's. On hearing that Ubba, 'dux Fresciorum', was advancing on York with a large army of Danes, Ælle joined forces with his brother Osberhtus, but in the ensuing battle was defeated and slain after fleeing in terror before the divine wrath he had brought on himself. A sentence occurring a few lines later seems to suggest that Ælle's brother Osberhtus and the king succeeded by Ælle are one and the same person: 'Occiso igitur Ælle, et fratre ejus Osberto, nullus de cognatione eorum regnavit'. The account is thus ambivalent in presenting Ælle, in contrast to the *Anglo-Saxon chronicle*, as a brother of Osberhtus and so a legitimate heir to the throne, while at the same time suggesting that he thoroughly deserved his defeat by the Vikings for his treatment of St. Cuthbert's property; and it is confusing in that it reports the death of Osberhtus before going on to relate that the brothers joined forces against the Danes. It almost certainly represents a somewhat awkward conflation of two traditions, one more favourably inclined to Ælle than the other.

Symeon of Durham, in his *Historia Dunelmensis ecclesiæ* (Arnold,

1882, 54–55), lists Halfdene, Inguar and Hubba among the leaders of the Vikings who invaded England in the second half of the ninth century. He briefly records the expulsion of Osbertus by the Northumbrians and their adoption of Ælla as king in his place, but says nothing of Ælla's birth or background. He then goes on to describe the Viking invasion of Northumbria and the defeat of both kings at York, seeing their deaths as payment for the monastery properties they had appropriated, which are the same as those specified in the *Historia de sancto Cuthberto*. Two other writings appearing under Symeon's name, the *Historia regum* (Arnold, 1885, 75, 105, cf. xv–xvi) and a letter to a dean of York named Hugo (Arnold, 1882, 225), both seem to follow the tradition of the *Anglo-Saxon chronicle* in regarding Ælla as not of royal birth. The *Historia regum* adds the phrase 'tyrannum quendam' as a brief description of him, but makes no mention in this context of Viking leaders, while the letter says that the leaders of the Vikings were Ubba and Haldana.

Gaimar, in his *L'estoire des Engleis* (Bell, 1960, 83–91; Hardy & Martin, 1889, 84–92), tells how Osbrith, King of Northumbria, ravished the wife of a nobleman, Buern Bucecarle, while Buern was away at sea, on the watch for outlaws. The king, who had heard a report of this lady's beauty, called to eat at her home while hunting near York, his own place of residence, and forced himself upon her while his companions stood guard. On his return, Buern, here described as the bravest of seafarers, learned of the outrage from his wife, defied the king to his face, and went to bring the Danes to help him get his revenge; before they arrived, however, Osbrith was deposed by Buern's relatives, and a knight named Elle was installed in his place. When the Danes came, Osbrith was slain, and Elle, who was hunting in a wood at the time, hastened to oppose the Danes on hearing of their invasion from a blind man. He was defeated and slain after attempting unsuccessfully, in circumstances already described (see ch. II, pp. 99, 112, above), to save the life of his nephew Orin, who the blind man prophesied would be killed. The kings of the Vikings, Gaimar subsequently reveals (Bell, 1960, 91), were Ywar and Vbe.

In the anonymous *Narratio de uxore Aernulfi ab Ella rege Deirorum violata* (ed. Hardy & Martin, 1888, 328–38, cf. xlvii), no mention is made of Osbrith, and it is Ælla, as the title indicates, who is guilty of ravishing the wife of one of his subjects. The importance of this story, preserved in a manuscript of the early thirteenth century, does not seem to have been fully recognized by de Vries (1928b, 155–56) or Loomis (1933, 2, 6–8), and neither Whitelock (1969) nor Lukman (1976) makes any direct reference to it. It tells of a certain Aernulfus, who lived in Deira at the time of the hostile raids of Iwar and Ubba, and whose name, so the text says, would be *Aquilinus* in Latin. He was a rich and a just man, though not a Christian, and because his work as a merchant led him to travel by ship with exceptional frequency, he was called by the nickname *Seafar* ('seafarer'), glossed in Latin as *Pontivagus*. He also had a beautiful wife who, however, was as ignorant as he was of the true faith. Ælla, the king of Deira, who dwelt at York, the main city of the province, and was himself no Christian, knew of her beauty and greatly desired her. On one occasion, when Aernulfus was overseas on business, his wife moved from their home in York to stay in the country at Becwida, while Ælla was staying at Aelleswrdam, some six miles further along the same road. One day, two associates of the king, described as 'furfurarii regis' (Hardy & Martin, 1888, 331), who had set out from York with some dogs to visit the king's residence, broke their journey to take a meal in the company of Aernulfus's wife. When they met the king in the evening, he asked what they had heard on the way about the state of his kingdom, and they reported on its peace and harmony, the absence of plague and famine, the gentle climate and the fertile soil. Then, when he asked for further news, they told him of Aernulfus's absence and of his wife's beauty, declaring her worthy not of a countryman or pauper, but of a king and prince. Pleased with their report, Ælla made them masters of his huntsmen ('magistri ... venantium'), and then summoned some retainers ('clientes'), whom he ordered to bring the wife of Aernulfus to him, if necessary by force.

These retainers went next day to Aernulfus's wife, bidding her make haste to adorn herself and come with them to the king; and when she expressed reluctance to visit him in the absence of her husband, they said that if she refused to come they would take her by force. Resolving then to make herself as unattractive as possible, she accompanied them with her face unwashed, her hair uncombed, and wearing humble clothing ('nec lota facie, nec compto crine, in habitu minus precioso', Hardy & Martin, 1888, 333). When the king returned from hunting in the evening, he at once embraced her and said that he wished her to be his for the space of one night. She replied that in dishonouring the wife of one of his subjects he was dishonouring himself still more, and declared herself ill-suited to him since she was of humble birth, but he paid her no heed, thinking only of his carnal lust, which he proceeded to satisfy by force. When her husband returned, she exhorted him to avenge the outrage, but he dared not oppose the king; so, believing that her husband no longer loved her, she resolved to spend the rest of her life in mourning.

As de Vries (1928b, 154–56) demonstrates, these last two stories in particular show how the figure of Ælla has developed in significance since the ninth century; he is no longer the briefly mentioned, shadowy figure of the *Anglo-Saxon chronicle*, but is treated at some length as a force to have been reckoned with from several points of view. The Gaimar story, with its relatively favourable view of him and its suggestion that the failings of the king he replaced were what led to the Danish conquest of York, probably derives its colouring ultimately from the sentiments of Ælla's original Northumbrian supporters; while the story of Aernulfus's wife, in which Ælla is the only king mentioned and which emphasizes his violence and injustice as well as his power, no doubt reflects an elaboration by Danish settlers in Northumbria on the opinions of his Northumbrian opponents.

What does not seem to have been pointed out by previous commentators, however, is the resemblance this last story bears in some respects to the Spangereid-legend as reflected in the 147 and 1824b texts of *Ragnars saga*, and to a lesser extent in the *Ragnars kvæði*; the 'Gests ríma' does not have sufficient independent value to be relevant in this context (see pp. 185–86, 194, above). In referring to the saga here I shall rely on the 1824b text, on the assumption made earlier that, as far as the Spangereid-legend is concerned, there is little difference between it and the text preserved fragmentarily in 147; though it should of course be remembered that, in preserving the Y version of *Ragnars saga*, 1824b is at a further remove from the legend itself than 147, which reflects the X version. What is told of Ælla in relation to the wife of Aernulfus in the *de uxore Aernulfi* is comparable in several ways to what is told of Ragnarr in relation to Kráka-Áslaug in chs. 5–6 of the saga, and in the *Ragnars kvæði*. Ælla's encounter with the wife of Aernulfus takes place when he is away from his royal seat, just as Ragnarr is away from his own kingdom (in Norway according to the saga) when he meets Kráka (see part VII of the Analysis, and the summary of the Spangereid-legend given above).

It seems too that in the *de uxore Aernulfi*, as well as in the saga and the *Ragnars kvæði*, the king's associates who bring him news of the heroine are otherwise concerned with the provision of food. The word *furfurarius*, applied to these people in the plural in the *de uxore Aernulfi* (Hardy & Martin, 1888, 331), where it occurs as a substantive, is, as such, exceedingly rare; as an adjective it means 'of or belonging to bran' (Lewis & Short, 1879, 796), and as a substantive would seem to have the meaning of 'forager'. The context gives little help as to the meaning of the word, but it may be significant that the men are said to have dogs with them, and that du Cange (1774, 706) lists the word *furfuragium* as meaning 'bran for feeding dogs' ('furfur ad alendos canes'); it may also be significant that King Ælla, on hearing their report, promotes them to the rank of masters of his huntsmen; this might suggest that their earlier function had been the relatively humble one of feeding coarse bread to his hunting-animals. In the saga and the *Ragnars kvæði*, Ragnarr's followers (called 'matsveinar', 'kitchen-knaves', in the saga) go ashore to bake bread, but are distracted from their purpose by Kráka's presence; in the saga they are clearly stated to have burnt the bread. It may thus be argued that the food for which they are responsible, like that entrusted to the 'furfurarii', is of poor quality, though for different reasons.

Little can be made of the fact that the 'furfurarii' have dogs with them and that Kráka in both the saga and the *Ragnars kvæði* visits Ragnarr accompanied by a dog; there is insufficient similarity of context here to make this an important point. A difference between the Anglo-Latin and the Scandinavian accounts which, however, is not so great as to discourage the search for further similarities is the fact that, in the *de uxore Aernulfi*, the king's followers reporting to Ælla on Aernulfus's wife also report on mild weather, whereas in the saga the messengers who go next day (as in the *de uxore Aernulfi*) to fetch the heroine are prevented by a head-wind ('andvidri', Olsen, 1906–08, 124, l. 4) from going immediately.

Ælla's promotion of the 'furfurarii' to the rank of 'magistri ... venantium' (Hardy & Martin, 1888, 332) may be compared with the forgiveness which, according to the saga, Ragnarr promises the 'matsveinar' for their poor baking on condition that Kráka turns out to be as beautiful as they say, and a small point also worth noting is that the 'clientes' sent to bring the wife of Aernulfus to Ælla in the *de uxore Aernulfi* are not the same people as the 'furfurarii', just as the 'sendimenn' sent to fetch Kráka in the saga seem to be a different group of people from the 'matsveinar'.

No conditions under which the woman is to visit him are imposed by King Ælla in the *de uxore Aernulfi*, as they are by Ragnarr in the saga and the *Ragnars kvæði*; on the other hand, the wife of Aernulfus leaves her hair uncombed in order to make herself unattractive, and here it may be remembered that, in the saga, Kráka responds to the condition, 'neither clad nor unclad', not only by wearing a net, but also by allowing her hair, which is described as so long that it reaches to the ground, to fall about her over the net, so that no part of her body will be naked; and that in the *Ragnars kvæði* she combs her hair in such a way as to meet the condition, 'both clad and unclad'. The threefold state in which the wife of Aernulfus visits Ælla—face unwashed, hair uncombed, and humbly clad—is in fact reminiscent of the three conditions imposed by Ragnarr and fulfilled by Kráka in *Ragnars saga* and in the background, at least, of the *Ragnars kvæði* (see pp. 203–11, above); and the wording used to describe it, quoted above (p. 216) seems deliberately to suggest a three-part series. Furthermore, just as, in the *de uxore Aernulfi*, the wife of Aernulfus emphasizes her humble birth and assumed unattractiveness by dressing in common rags, so in the saga does Kráka, despite the fact that she is really Áslaug, the daughter of Sigurðr and Brynhildr, refuse Ragnarr's offer of Þóra's richly-embroidered shift on the grounds that such fine clothing would not suit her; wretched garments are what suit her, she says ('sama elig mer klędi'), in the first half of str. 5, in the second half of which she relates her name, *Kráka*, to her coal-black clothes and status as a goatherd (the similarity of this second half-strophe to a stanza in the *Ragnars kvæði*, where, however, Kráka's response to Ragnar's offer of Tóra's clothes is rather different, has been discussed above, pp. 196–202). The phrase 'vilibus ero pannis induta' of the *de uxore Aernulfi* (Hardy & Martin, 1888, 333) may indeed be compared with the phrases 'sama elig mer klędi' and 'j kol svartum vodum' (Olsen, 1906–08, 127) of this strophe; and the expressed intention of Aernulfus's wife to wear humble clothes so that she may not seem too glorious in the presence of the king—'ne coram rege nimis appaream gloriosa'—is reminiscent of Kráka's suggestion to Ragnarr in the saga that he might find her more attractive if she were better dressed: 'Kann vera, at ydr litiz betr a mik, ef ek bumzt betr', as she says just after refusing his offer of Þóra's shift (see Olsen, 1906–08, 127, and the summary of the Spangereid-legend in the preceding section). The fact that Aernulfus's wife is, by her own account at least, of humble birth, whereas Kráka, although brought up in humble circumstances, is really of noble origin, might seem to lessen the general validity of the comparison here being made, until it is remembered that in Gaimar's account, which is clearly a variant of the story told in the *de uxore Aernulfi*, the woman raped by King Osbrith does seem to be of noble birth; she is at any rate married to a nobleman rather than a merchant, and is referred to by the word *dame* (Bell, 1960, 83–84).

From now on the *Ragnars kvæði*, as opposed to *Ragnars saga*, cease to be relevant to the comparison, since they do not mention, as the saga emphatically does, Kráka's reluctance to have sexual relations with Ragnarr immediately. This motif seems to have been developed, as de Vries (1928a, 274–77) suggests, in such a way as to provide an explanation for Ívarr's nickname *beinlauss*, 'boneless', in terms of a curse placed on Kráka-Áslaug by her foster-parents to the effect that unless she postponed sexual intercourse for three nights after her marriage her child would be born without bones. This development must have taken place within the saga-branch of the Ragnarr loðbrók tradition, rather than as part of the Spanger-eid-legend in the early, independent stages of its growth, when it appears to have shown little or no interest in Ragnarr's sons, cf. p. 180, above; but there is no reason why the motif of feminine reluctance in the face of a man's sexual advances should not have played some part in the Spangereid-legend prior to the latter's incorporation in the saga-branch of the tradition, particularly if, as I shall suggest below (pp. 225–27), the legend was influenced by the story underlying both Gaimar's account and the *de uxore Aernulfi*. Ælla's words to the wife of Aernulfus, 'volo ut mea vel una sis nocte' (Hardy & Martin, 1888, 333), may be compared with Ragnarr's words, 'vil ek, at hun se min' ('I wish her to be mine', Olsen, 1906–08, 124, l. 8), which he says in ch. 5 of the saga just before imposing the conditions under which Kráka is to visit him, and with the request he makes after meeting her, reported in indirect speech in ch. 6, that she should spend the night on board his ship.

In neither Gaimar's account nor the *de uxore Aernulfi*, it is true, does the woman employ delaying tactics of the kind used by Kráka in *Ragnars saga*; this is partly because she has no choice, since the English king uses force in a way that Ragnarr does not, and partly because her attitude to the king is wholly different from Kráka's to Ragnarr; she would resist him altogether if she could, whereas Kráka wishes to marry Ragnarr, and only postpones intimate relations with him for what emerge as the following reasons: she wants to be sure that Ragnarr has honourable intentions towards her while still in ignorance of her true parentage—it is she rather than he who raises the subject of marriage, making it clear that she will not sleep with him before they are married; and she needs to be sure that she is free from the evil influence of her foster-parents (cf. the summary above, pp. 190–91; also ch. II, section (b) (*i*)). When Ragnarr expresses the wish, just referred to, that Kráka should stay on board his ship overnight, she says that that cannot happen until he has returned from the journey he has planned, by which time he may have changed his mind. Later, when he returns from the journey, she says that she will not join him to leave Spangarheiðr until the following morning; and on the way home with him to Ragnarr's kingdom she again refuses to sleep with him, pointing out that he owes it to her and their heirs to marry her first. Even on their bridal night, however, she excuses herself from intercourse, and, notwithstanding the scepticism expressed by Ragnarr as to the prophetic powers of her foster-parents, indicates to him that they must wait for three nights before consummating the marriage. At this point Ragnarr draws the line. There is nothing quite comparable to this in the *de uxore Aernulfi*, where the wife's violation by the king is delayed only by the short speech in which she impugns his honour and stresses her own humble origins (cf. pp. 216–17, above); still less delay is involved in Gaimar's account. Nevertheless, the words with which the *de uxore Aernulfi* continues immediately after the wife's speech of protest may be compared with those which, in *Ragnars saga*, immediately follow the strophe (str. 6) in which Kráka discourages consummation of the marriage until three nights have passed. The *de uxore Aernulfi* (Hardy & Martin, 1888, 334) has: 'Sic illa sermonicatur, sed ille non audit. Audit forsitan, sed non exaudit. Nihil putat melius fore quam desideria carnis implere. Implet ergo votum suum, vi reluctantem opprimens'. The saga (Olsen, 1906–08, 129) has: 'Ok þo hun kvẹdi þetta, gaf Ragnar at þvi enngan gaum ok bra a sitt rad' ('and although she recited this, Ragnarr paid no attention, and did what he wanted to do').

There are of course a number of differences between the English and Scandinavian stories here compared, and these have not been ignored or minimized in the foregoing survey; nevertheless the similarities between them are, I suggest, a good deal more convincing than those pointed out by Lukman (1976, 25–26) between this same part of *Ragnars saga* on the one hand and, on the other, the Frankish sources recording the sickness which, as some of these sources relate, caused the death of Reginheri/Ragenarius, the leader of the Viking attack on Paris in 845. The relevant sources are the *Annales Bertiniani* and the *Annales Xantenses* for 845, both written virtually contemporaneously with the events they describe (Skyum-Nielsen, 1967, 13, 15); the anonymous *Miracula sancti Germani in Normannorum adventu facta* (ch. 30), written between 849 and 858 (Skyum-Nielsen, 1967, 23); and Aimoin's *Miracula Sancti Germani* (Book I, ch. 12), based partly on the anonymous *Miracula* just mentioned, and written probably between 872 and 881 (Skyum-Nielsen, 1967, 41). The *Annales Bertiniani* do not mention the leader of the Viking attack on Paris by name or otherwise, but state (Rau, 1972, 66) that the Vikings involved were 'blinded by darkness and struck down by insanity' ('vel tenebris caecati vel insania sunt perculsi'); while the *Annales Xantenses* (Rau, 1972, 348) explicitly state that the Viking leader Reginheri died as a result of a disastrous plague, but do not specify the nature of the disease. The two versions of the *Miracula Sancti Germani* (Waitz, 1887, 16, and Carnandet, 1866, 789), on the other hand, expressly mention dysentery ('dissenteria') as the disease in question, before going on to give a considerably embroidered account of its fatal effect on the Viking leader Ragenarius; this account, which is substantially the same in both versions of the *Miracula*, has been outlined above (see ch. I, section (a); cf. part X of the Analysis). Now Saxo, though he does not use the actual word *dissenteria* in this connection, states (IX.iv, 22) that while preparing to attack the people of Biarmia, Regnerus Lothbrog and his followers were assailed by a disease which certainly looks very like dysentery from the way Saxo describes it: 'laxi ventris profluvium'. This consideration has been used as an argument in support of the view that Reginheri, the leader of the attack on Paris in 845, was a historical model for Ragnarr loðbrók (cf. McTurk, 1976, 95–96).

The *Annales Xantenses* do not specify the place of the Viking leader's death, but according to both versions of the *Miracula Sancti Germani* it took place in Denmark, shortly after his return from Paris. Ragnarr loðbrók's death in the snake-pit, on the other hand, took place in the British Isles according to those of the relevant accounts (see under part X of the Analysis) which actually specify where it occurred; *Krákumál* seems in fact to be the only one not to do so. *Ragnarssona þáttr* and the 1824b text of *Ragnars saga* place it unambiguously in England, and it may be assumed that the X version of *Ragnars saga* reflected in 147 did also (see Olsen, 1906–08, 186–89). Arngrímur, basing his account partly on the Y version of *Ragnars saga* (reflected in 1824b) and on Saxo's account (cf. pp. 57, 98, 206–07, above), also places it in England, while Saxo's location of it in Ireland is probably the result of confusion on the part of Saxo himself, as I have argued earlier (see pp. 87 and 108, above). Since these various accounts see the slaying of King Ella/Hella by the sons of Ragnarr loðbrók (or of Loðbrók in the case of *Krákumál*, where the name *Ragnarr* is not mentioned) as an act of vengeance for their father's death, and since Iguuar (= Ívarr), later regarded as a son of Ragnarr loðbrók, arrived in England in 865 (see Æthelweard, ed. Campbell, 1962, 35), while Ælla (= Ella) first appears in 866 (see the *Anglo-Saxon chronicle*, ed. Earle & Plummer, 1892, 68–69, and Stenton, 1971, 246, n. 3), they might seem to suggest that the historical prototype of Ragnarr loðbrók died at a time nearer to those dates than to 845, and in England rather than in France or Denmark. There is reason to believe, however, as de Vries (1928b, 156–62) has convincingly argued, that the notion of Loðbrók's death in England arose among Scandinavian settlers there as part of a gradual process of whitewashing the slaying of King Edmund—who was killed in 869 by Vikings in East Anglia, possibly under the leadership of Iguuar (Whitelock, 1969, 233)—by explaining it as an act of vengeance and by substituting the figure of Ella for that of Edmund.

However this may be, what Lukman (1976, 25–26) suggests in relation to the Frankish sources is that their descriptions of the affliction suffered by the Vikings in 845 show similarities to early medieval accounts of ergotism, the disease caused by the eating of grain that has been affected by the dark-violet fungus known as ergot; and he sees a connection between this type of fungus and the burnt or black bread of *Ragnars saga*, claiming that a memory of what happened to the Vikings in 845 lies behind the account of the 'matsveinar' burning the bread because of Kráka's beauty. I find it hard to agree with Lukman on either of these points. With regard to the first of them, it may be admitted that the insanity said to have struck the Vikings in the *Annales Bertiniani* for 845, and the loss of hearing said to have afflicted Ragenarius in both versions of the *Miracula Sancti Germani* (see further below), do perhaps correspond to certain of the symptoms recognized today as characteristic of ergotism (Critchley, 1978, 611). However, both versions of the *Miracula* state clearly that the disease in question was dysentery, and any symptoms they may mention that are inconsistent with dysentery are probably to be explained as a result of the exaggeration to which their authors clearly gave rein in developing the idea—already present in the *Annales Bertiniani* and the *Annales Xantenses* for 845—that the affliction was a divine punishment to the Vikings for their attack on Paris (see Rau, 1972, 66–67, 348–49). It may further be pointed out that the studies of ergotism to which Lukman (1976, 25, n. 36) himself refers hardly support his suggestion that the disease recorded in the accounts of the Viking attack on Paris in 845 shows similarities to ergotism as described in other mediaeval writings. Neither Ehlers (1896) nor Møller-Christensen (1944), both of whom are referred to by Lukman, seems to have found these accounts sufficiently illustrative of ergotism to be worth including in their studies of the subject; both of them, indeed, give an example from the *Annales Xantenses* for 857 (rather than for 845) as the earliest known clear-cut instance of ergotism (Ehlers, 1896, 26; Møller-Christensen, 1944, 163). Furthermore, the main symptoms of the disease, according to the accounts summarized by these two writers (Ehlers, 1896, 26–61, cf. 153; Møller-Christensen, 1944, 163–73), seem to have been the wasting away of the arms and legs and the loss of the hands and feet, while according to both versions of the *Miracula Sancti Germani*—the only accounts of the 845 disease which record its symptoms in any detail—Ragenarius's body burst in the middle after the senses of hearing, sight, smell, and taste had departed from it, and all his entrails spilled onto the earth (Waitz, 1887, 16; Carnandet, 1866, 789). It is not difficult to see this description as a deliberately exaggerated account of the symptoms of dysentery.

Even if it were admitted that ergotism was, or was thought to be, the disease to which these sources refer, there would still be the problem of Lukman's second point, his suggestion of a link between this disease and the burning of the bread in *Ragnars saga*. Not that there is no link at all between the Frankish accounts and *Ragnars saga*; the formal hero of the saga, Ragnarr loðbrók, clearly has origins in common with Regnerus Lothbrog, the main figure of Book IX of Saxo's *Gesta Danorum*, and this Regnerus seems to have suffered from a dysenteric disease, as the Ragenarius of the Frankish accounts is said to have done; furthermore, the death of Reginheri/Ragenarius as recorded in the Frankish sources is comparable, at least in respect of its exceptional, 'miraculous' nature, to Ragnarr's death in the snake-pit as recorded in the various Scandinavian accounts, including *Ragnars saga*, that are summarized under part X of the Analysis (cf. the remarks of de Vries, 1923, 252, quoted there). These considerations, and the fact that *Reginheri/Ragenarius* and *Ragnarr/Regnerus* are basically the same name (cf. Noreen, 1923, 65; Janzén, 1947, 87, 100; Hornby, 1947, 197), make it quite possible that the Reginheri/Ragenarius of the Frankish sources was indeed a historical model for the Ragnarr loðbrók of Scandinavian tradition (cf. McTurk, 1976, 95–96). Apart from the points noted here, however, there is very little that the Frankish and Scandinavian narratives can be said to have in common, and Lukman's reference to dark-coloured fungus and black bread as a point of similarity or connection between them seems to me far-fetched in the extreme.

Since the meaning of the word *furfurarius* is uncertain, my suggestion of a link between the 'furfurarii' of the *de uxore Aernulfi* and the 'matsveinar' of *Ragnars saga* may at first sight seem tenuous, but it should be emphasized that (as I hope to have shown) this is by no means the only similarity between the two stories compared above, viz., the story reflected mainly in the *de uxore Aernulfi*, though also in Gaimar, of the rape perpetrated by a king of Northumbria, and the Spangereid-legend as reflected mainly in *Ragnars saga*, though also in the *Ragnars kvæði*. In both stories menials of a king report to him, while he is away from his royal seat, on the beauty of a woman they have seen; and in both stories messengers are then sent to bring her to him, and she arrives having prepared herself in three ways, one of which, in both stories, involves her hair falling loosely about her. In both stories (though in different ways) the woman is, as it were, of both humble and noble status; and in both stories she emphasizes her lowly station by means of humble clothing, and attempts to resist the king's advances to no avail. The similarities thus extend throughout a whole narrative sequence corresponding to chs. 5–6 of the 1824b text of *Ragnars saga*; it is not simply a question of one or two isolated points of rather dubious similarity such as those to which Lukman draws attention in discussing this part of the saga in relation to certain events of 845 as reported in Frankish sources.

It is of course also significant that the names *Ywar/Iwar*, *Ube/Ubba* and *Elle/Ælla* occur in both Gaimar's account and the *de uxore Aernulfi*; the first two of these names, which refer in these accounts to Viking invaders of Northumbria, correspond to those of Ívarr and Ubbo, sons of Ragnarr loðbrók in Scandinavian tradition (though Ubbo occurs only in east Scandinavian tradition, see pp. 105–07, above and part VII of the Analysis); and Ella/Hella is the name of the king in whose snake-pit Ragnarr loðbrók dies according to the major Scandinavian accounts summarized under part X of the Analysis. It is true that the Spangereid-legend, with which we are here mainly concerned, shows little or no interest in the sons of Ragnarr loðbrók or in the manner of his death; on the other hand, it has been argued above that an awareness of his sons and of his death lay from the beginning behind the Áslaug-Kráka branch of the Ragnarr loðbrók tradition, from which the Spangereid-legend developed (see pp. 179–82, above); that the Spangereid-legend did not entirely forget the story of Ragnarr's death in King Ella's snake-pit (see pp. 186–88, above); and that an awareness of this story also implies an awareness of Ragnarr's avenging sons (pp. 168–70, above). If, as I shall argue, the story reflected in Gaimar's account and the *de uxore Aernulfi* travelled from England to Denmark and there combined with other traditions relating to Ragnarr loðbrók before travelling on to Norway and there influencing the Spangereid-legend, there can be little doubt that this combination was stimulated by, among other things, the story's inclusion of one or more of these three names in the form in which it reached Denmark.

Lukman (1976, 11–12) implies that at least one element in the Spangereid-legend—the motif of hair worn long as a partial cover for nakedness (cf. part IVA of the Analysis)—derives from an English source; he compares Kráka's response to Ragnarr's condition, 'neither clad nor unclad', in ch. 5 of *Ragnars saga*, with Roger of Wendover's account (Coxe, 1841, 497), dating from the early thirteenth century (Galbraith, 1944, 15–17), of how Lady Godiva finally managed to dissuade her husband from imposing a heavy tax on the people of Coventry by riding naked through the town on horseback, covered only by her long hair. It is indeed rather surprising that in looking for parallels to the bread-burning motif in *Ragnars saga* Lukman does not find one in the well-known story of King Alfred burning the cakes; at least one version of this, found in the mid thirteenth-century chronicle attributed to John of Wallingford (Vaughan, 1958, 32–33; cf. Keynes & Lapidge, 1983, 197–202), relates the story explicitly, if indirectly, to the Viking invasion of England by Igguar and Hubba. Whatever the origins of these details, my own view, as already hinted, is that the Northumbrian story of the rape by the king influenced the Spangereid-legend, and travelled from England to Norway by the route described in the last chapter (see pp. 104 13, above) in connection with what was there called the eastern branch of the Rægnald-tradition, i.e. by way of Denmark. Just as Saxo, as indicated in the last chapter (see p. 112, above), shows a faint recollection of the story of Rǫgnvaldr in the form in which it was told in Denmark, so, it may be argued, does he show an awareness of the story of the rape in his account (IX.iv, 18–19) of Regnerus's affair with the lowly-born daughter of Hesbernus, who becomes the mother of his son Ubbo (cf. p. 154, above). If this argument is accepted, then it is clear that in the version of the story known to Saxo, the rôle of the Northumbrian king had become transferred to the figure represented in his account by Regnerus Lothbrog, and although it is not necessary to assume that this development had taken place in England before the story reached Denmark, it is quite possible that this was the case, since the story, which is by no means entirely to the English king's credit, could easily have been transferred in an English environment from an English to a Scandinavian leader—perhaps even to the father of the Viking invaders Inwære and Hubba.

In Denmark, I suggest, this story combined with the stories told by Scandinavian pilgrims returning from southern Europe, which, as shown in the last chapter (pp. 108–10, above), seem to have included in their subject-matter the destruction of Vífilsborg by the sons of Loðbrók, and Gunnarr's death in the snake-pit, which was believed to have taken place near Luna. If these stories already included the motif of the three conditions characteristic of the 'clever peasant girl' tale, as is possible (since the motif also appears in a striking number of southern European variants, as de Vries, 1928d, 218–19, has shown), then the Northumbrian story, with its emphasis on the threefold manner in which the woman prepares herself to meet the king, is likely to have reinforced their inclusion of it. On the other hand, it is also possible that the Northumbrian story itself included this motif before it reached Denmark from England, since, as Jackson (1961, 106–12) has shown, the motif was known in the British Isles as early as the eleventh century; in this case the Northumbrian story could have introduced the motif in Denmark to the narrative material relating to Ragnarr loðbrók that the Scandinavian pilgrims appear to have brought with them from the continent. It is impossible to say which of these two explanations is the more likely, just as it cannot be known for certain whether the name Loðbrók had already become attached to the Northumbrian story before the story travelled to Denmark. It may in any case be assumed that the story was conveyed by homeward-going West Scandinavian pilgrims from Denmark to Norway, and there influenced the Spangereid-legend, to which it was clearly of value, as already indicated (see pp. 183, 219–20, above), in either introducing or helping to establish the motif of the three conditions, thus adding to the suspense leading up to the maiden's revelation of her true identity; in helping with its emphasis on the woman's humble clothing to dramatize the situation in which a maiden of apparently humble origin meets a king; and in introducing the motif of the king's sexual importunity, which in Saxo's account seems to be reflected in the lengths to which Regnerus goes to disguise himself in order to gain access to the daughter of Hesbernus, and which must have added to the interest of the story. It must indeed have been of value to the X redactor of *Ragnars saga*, who used it as part of his explanation of Ívarr's nickname 'beinlauss', and was followed in this respect by the Y redactor, as the 147 and 1824b texts show (Olsen, 1906–08, 178–79, cf. 123–29).

As shown above (pp. 203–11), de Vries (1928a, 275–76; 1928d, 227–28; cf. 1928b, 117–35) provides reasonably convincing evidence that the motif of the faithful dog reached what has here been called the Spangereid-legend from the European continent, and was also brought to Norway by pilgrims returning homewards through Denmark. This motif is often found in association with the tale of the hidden old man's wisdom, and de Vries notes that the Norman chroniclers Dudo of St. Quentin (Lair, 1865, 129–38) and William of Jumièges (Marx, 1914, 7–17) use a variant of the motif of the slaying of the aged, an essential element in the tale (see AT, 1961, 345), in reporting the conquest of Luna by Vikings who, in William's account, include the one who is described as a son of Lotbroc and named *Bier Costae ferreae* (cf. *Bjǫrn járnsíða*, and pp. 40–43, above). To judge from Nicholas of Þverá's account (see pp. 108–10, above), Scandinavian pilgrims associated the Italian town of Luna with Gunnarr's death in the snake-pit, just as they also associated the central European town of Vífilsborg, another point on their route, with the sons of Loðbrók; and Luna is, of course, one of the places conquered by the sons of Ragnarr loðbrók in *Ragnarssona þáttr* (Hb, 1892–96, 464) and *Ragnars saga* (1906–08, 152–53, cf. 186), as Vífilsborg also is in the saga (Olsen, 1906–08, 150–52, 185–86). Furthermore, the fact that the dog is beaten in

Ragnars saga as a result of its loyalty to its mistress suggests the influence of the tale of the hidden old man's wisdom (cf. pp. 207–08, above).

On the other hand, it should be pointed out that the motif of the faithful dog is not an obligatory element in the story in AT 981, the story of the hidden old man's wisdom, as appears from the way the tale-type is formulated in AT (1961, 345, 319), where 'best friend, worst enemy' (i.e. dog and wife respectively) is listed as sub-type B of AT 921, the 'king and the peasant's son' tale; and there seems to be no hint of the dog-motif in Dudo's or William's accounts; it does not appear to have had an especially secure position in the relevant narrative material brought northwards by the pilgrims. Reservations have moreover been expressed above (pp. 205, 209) about de Vries's main reason (i.e. that Áslaug deserves a nobler animal than a goat) for the replacement of the condition, 'neither on foot nor on horseback' (usually fulfilled by means of a goat), by one involving a dog, and deriving from the 'hidden old man's wisdom' tale; this new condition was presumably, at first, something like 'with best friend and worst enemy', and later developed into 'neither alone nor accompanied by man.' While de Vries's argument here is not without its point, as already acknowledged (see p. 209, above), it would be helpful to the present investigation if a still more compelling reason could be found for the use in the Spangereid-legend of the motif of the faithful dog.

Such a reason can, I suggest, be found if Roger of Wendover's story (Coxe, 1841, 303–10) of how the dead body of Lothbrocus, the father of Hinguar and Hubba, was guarded by a faithful greyhound, is considered in relation to the Spangereid-legend. This story appears to have developed in the Danelaw independently of the mainland Scandinavian traditions of Ragnarr or Loðbrók (de Vries, 1928b, 158–61), and since it was evidently partly intended to ease relations between Danish settlers and the local inhabitants during the reign of Cnut the Great (d. 1035), it is likely that it spread to Denmark during that period or later (de Vries, 1928b, 160–61, 163). I would suggest that the story did indeed travel to Denmark, and that, in combining there with the continental traditions of Loðbrók brought by pilgrims to Scandinavia in the twelfth century, it helped to reinforce the position of the motif of the faithful dog among these traditions, which had already been influenced by the tale of the hidden old man's wisdom, as William of Jumièges in particular seems to indicate (see pp. 204–07, above).

So prominent did the motif become as a result of this combination, I would further suggest, that it could not be omitted altogether from the Spangereid-legend (as witness the accounts of the beating or slaying in the 147 and 1824b texts of the saga, see pp. 207–08, above), even though the dog had by then come to be regarded as the faithful follower of the Áslaug-figure rather than of the Ragnarr-figure, and even though its function was by then not so much to be faithful as simply to fulfil the condition 'neither alone nor accompanied by man.' The beginnings of the dog's attachment to a female rather than a male figure can perhaps be glimpsed in the story of the dog that protects Lathgertha and is killed by Regnerus in Saxo's account (IX.iv, 2–3; see parts IIIB, IVA, and VII of the Analysis), which may thus represent a Danish stage on the route from England to Norway in the case of the faithful dog motif, as it does in the case of the eastern branch of the Rægnald-tradition and in that of the Northumbrian story of the rape, as shown above (p. 112; cf. pp. 226–27).

For its significance in the present context to be fully appreciated, Wendover's account should be seen in relation to Abbo of Fleury's late tenth-century *Passio sancti Eadmundi*, which clearly influenced it. In Abbo's account (Arnold, 1890, 9–19) the Danes Inguar and Hubba (who are here described not as brothers, but as fellow-pirates) first came to Northumbria, which they overran. Leaving Hubba there, Inguar proceeded to East Anglia, where he ravaged and burned a city, and on discovering that Edmund, King of East Anglia, was at Hægelisdun (probably Hellesdon, see Whitelock, 1969, 220), sent a messenger to him requiring him to halve his treasures with him and rule as his vassal. After consulting with a bishop who advised flight or surrender, Edmund sent back word that he would submit only if Inguar became a Christian. At Inguar's command, consequently, Edmund was seized, tied to a tree, mocked, and cruelly scourged; he was shot full of arrows so that he bristled with them like a hedgehog or a thistle and resembled the martyr St. Sebastian. Finally, on Inguar's orders, he was beheaded; but first he was pulled from the tree half-dead, 'with the hollows between his ribs opened up by frequent piercings, and as if he had been stretched on a rack or disfigured by savage claws' (Arnold, 1890, 15: 'retectis costarum latebris præ punctionibus crebris, ac si raptum eculeo aut sævis tortum ungulis').

According to de Vries (1928b, 161–62) and Lukman (1976, 12), it is from a partial misunderstanding of this passage, involving the information about the ribs and confusion of the Latin word *eculeus* ('rack') and *aquila* ('eagle'), that the notion of the blood-eagle being cut on Ella's back derives. This form of torture, which appears to have involved cutting the ribs from the backbone and pulling out the lungs in a manner suggestive of an eagle's wings, seems to be applied to King Hella/Ella in Saxo's account (IX.v, 5), *Ragnarssona þáttr.* (Hb 1892–96, 464), and *Ragnars saga* (Olsen, 1906–08, 167–68, 193); the *þáttr* and the 147 text of *Ragnars saga* differ however from Saxo and the 1824b text in specifying the cutting of the ribs from the spine and the pulling out of the lungs, and in quoting Sigvatr Þórðarson's *Knútsdrápa* (c. 1038, de Vries, 1964, 252), which, in the half strophe quoted (cf. pp. 55, 56, above), appears to state that in York Ívarr had an eagle cut on Ella's back ('Ok Ellu bak, / at, lét, hinn's sat, / Ívarr, ara, / Jórvík, skorit,' see F. Jónsson 1912b, 232; and cf. E. A. Kock, 1940, 17–18). Other instances of the torture are listed by de Vries (1956, 411–12), who sees it as a sacrifice to Óðinn, and argues that scepticism as to the supposedly historical instances of the sacrifice (including the case of Ella) need not imply that the sacrifice itself was unhistorical. Frank (1984), on the other hand, has recently argued that the whole idea of the blood-eagle has arisen from a misunderstanding of Sigvatr's half strophe. According to Frank (1984, 336–40), *ara* is here to be taken as an instrumental dative form of *ari*, 'eagle', and as referring to the eagle as a conventional 'carrion beast', seeking out and mutilating the bodies of warriors slain in battle; she translates the passage as follows: 'Ívarr had Ella's back scored by an eagle'. I do not find this argument convincing. If *ara* did refer here to a 'carrion bird', as Frank suggests, the dative would be more likely to express an indirect object than to be instrumental; indeed the reading of *ara* here as an instrumental dative (which is not as original as Frank, 1984, 337, implies) is by no means inconsistent with the idea of the blood-eagle, as F. Jónsson, 1931b, 15, 505 (under 'ari' and 'skera' respectively) seems to recognize, though E.A. Kock (1940, 17)—without rejecting the idea of the blood-eagle—thinks differently. Frank's reading of *ara* as used here by Sigvatr is in my view more consistent with the idea of the blood-eagle than with that of the 'carrion beast' she herself proposes. Furthermore, the Old Norse, Latin and Old English passages adduced by Frank as parallels to Sigvatr's half strophe, though close sometimes in meaning, and sometimes in grammar, to the half-strophe as she interprets it, do not seem to me to coincide enough in meaning and grammar to provide convincing parallels.

Abbo goes on to relate that after Edmund's death, which was witnessed by a Christian hiding nearby, the Danes left the body at the place of the martyrdom, but concealed the head in a neighbouring wood (called Haglesdun, cf. Hægelisdun, p. 229, above), so that the body would not be buried intact by the Christians. These later found the body, and, guided by the eyewitness, searched in the wood for the head, keeping in touch with each other by means of horns, pipes and their own voices, so as not to cover the same ground twice. Miraculously, the head replied in English to the calls of the search-party, crying out 'Here!

Here! Here!' in answer to the question, 'Where are you?' Eventually the head was found between the paws of a monstrous wolf, which was protecting it from other animals. The head was then brought to the body, and the wolf followed the mourners to the place of burial. 'After following them, and as if mourning for the pledge it had lost—since although provoked it hurt no one and was troublesome to none—it returned unharmed to the retreats of blissful solitude that it knew so well, and a wolf of such terrible appearance was not seen again in those places' (Arnold, 1890, 19: 'Qui eis a tergo imminens, et quasi pro perdito pignore lugens, cum neminem etiam irritatus læderet, nemini importunus existeret, nota dilectæ solitudinis secreta illæsus repetiit, nec ulterius in illis locis lupus specie tam terribilis apparuit'). The head was then fitted to the body and a simple chapel was built over the grave; and many years later, after miracles had taken place there, it was decided to build a wooden church at Bedricesworth and to move the body there. This was done, and the church became the scene of many more miracles.

Abbo makes no mention of Loðbrók, or of any blood-relationship between Inguar and Hubba. In Roger of Wendover's account, on the other hand, Hinguar and Hubba appear as sons of Lothbrocus, a combination which first finds clear expression in the twelfth-century *Annals of St. Neots*, as noted in the last chapter (see pp. 105–106). Roger of Wendover, a monk of St. Albans, wrote his *Flores historiarum* most probably in the period 1219–35 (Galbraith, 1944, 15–21), and it is the part of this work dealing with the events leading up to St. Edmund's martyrdom (Coxe, 1841, 303–10) that is relevant here. It may be mentioned that among the mediaeval copies of Wendover's account (Smyth, 1977, 55) are two apparently by Matthew Paris; one in Matthew's *Chronica majora* (Luard, 1872, 393–98), and one in a work also entitled *Flores historiarum* (Luard, 1890, 433–38; not to be confused with Wendover's work of that name) and now attributed, in part at least, to Matthew Paris (Galbraith, 1944, 25, 31–34, 45 46). This Matthew, another monk of St. Albans, reproduced and continued Wendover's work, but makes no significant additions or alterations to the account here in question. This is all the more regrettable in that in 1248 (by which date the X version of *Ragnars saga* had possibly been written, cf. p. 54, above) Matthew Paris visited by way of Bergen the Benedictine monastery of Holm on the island of Nidarholm in western Norway (Madden, 1869, xv–xix). If there were significant differences between Matthew's account and Roger's, the interesting question would arise as to whether they were to be explained by reference to information acquired by Matthew on his visit to Norway; but this, unfortunately, is not the case.

Wendover's account may now be summarized: Lothbrocus, a member of the Danish royal family and the father of Hinguar and Hubba, set out alone with a hawk in a small boat to hunt waterfowl. A sudden storm drove him out to sea, and after several days of peril he was cast ashore in Norfolk, and taken by the local inhabitants to the court of King Edmund of the East Angles, where he was honourably received. Because of the closeness of Danish to English, he was able to tell Edmund of the circumstances of his arrival; and he was so impressed by Edmund's court that he asked permission to stay there to study its customs. Permission was granted, and Lothbrocus attached himself to Bernus, the king's huntsman, in order to practise the art of hunting, in which he was already highly skilled. His skill indeed turned out to be superior to that of Bernus, whose jealousy was thus aroused; and one day, when they were hunting together, Bernus murdered Lothbrocus, hiding his body in the depths of a wood. When he recalled the hounds, one of them, a greyhound ('leporarius') of which Lothbrocus had taken charge and which was deeply attached to him, remained by the body. When Lothbrocus's absence from the king's table was noticed the next day, Bernus said that Lothbrocus had stayed behind in the wood and that he had not seen him since. No sooner had he said this than the greyhound appeared in the palace, making friendly advances to the king in particular, who gave it food, hoping that the hound's arrival heralded that of its master. Once it had had enough to eat, however, it returned to the body. When the greyhound came back for more food three days later, the king had it followed when it left the court, and the body of Lothbrocus was thus discovered. The king arranged for it to be honourably buried, and realized Bernus's guilt. It was then decided by the court that, as a punishment, Bernus should be set adrift in Lothbrocus's boat without any means of navigation, to see if God wished to preserve him from danger. This was done, and after a few days Bernus was cast ashore in Denmark, where the harbour-guards, recognizing the boat as Lothbrocus's, conducted him to Hinguar and Hubba. These questioned him with the help of torturers about what had happened to their father, and Bernus lied that Lothbrocus had been put to death on the orders of King

Edmund. The brothers then swore vengeance on the innocent Edmund, and, taking Bernus with them as a guide, set sail for East Anglia, where they eventually arrived after being driven off course by adverse winds and forced to land near Berwick-on-Tweed. They killed everyone they found in East Anglia, and Hinguar sent a message to King Edmund, who was then at Haeilisdune (cf. Hægilisdun, Haglesdun, pp. 229–30, above), challenging him to battle. After consulting with a bishop who advised flight, Edmund met the Danes in battle, but the English suffered such severe losses that the pious king decided to surrender his own person to avoid further bloodshed. The story of his martyrdom then follows, as told by Abbo of Fleury (see pp. 229–31, above).

As de Vries (1928b, 160–61) confirms, this account betrays an origin among Scandinavian settlers in England in the eleventh century, with its attempts to excuse the actions of the Danes as well as the English in connection with the Viking invasion of East Anglia in 869. The slaying of Edmund by Hinguar and Hubba is here seen as an understandable act of vengeance for the slaying of their father Lothbrocus. Bernus the huntsman, who in bringing the Danes to the scene of conflict plays a part comparable to that of Buern Bucecarle in Gaimar's story, summarized earlier (p. 215, above), contributes to this whitewashing tendency; according to Wendover it is Bernus's treachery and lies that bring the Danes to East Anglia in search of vengeance, rather than aggression on their part or provocation on the part of the English. Wendover's account also shows the influence of Abbo's *Passio* in the story of Lothbrocus's death: the hiding of his body in a wood, and the fact that it is guarded by a greyhound, parallel what is told of Edmund's head and its protection by a wolf in the *Passio*. J. de Vries (1928b, 161–62) also argues convincingly that the gradual replacement in Scandinavian tradition of the figure of Edmund by that of Ella, of which Sigvatr Þórðarson's *Knútsdrápa* (mentioning Ella but not Edmund) gives the oldest surviving indication (dating from *c.*1038, see p. 230, above), and which seems to be complete in Saxo and the 1824b text of *Ragnars saga* (as opposed to the *þáttr* and the 147 text, which both mention Edmund, i.e. Játmundr, as well as Ella, see McTurk 1975, 74 75), had its origins in the Danelaw during the reign of Cnut (d. 1035). Since its purpose was to present the ninth-century Viking harassment of England in a relatively favourable light by providing it with the motive of vengeance, the substitution was assisted by the fact that Ælla, in contrast to the famous martyr Edmund, was a relatively unimportant upstart, and by the fact that the passage quoted earlier from Abbo's *Passio* could be misunderstood as referring to the cutting of the blood-eagle on the victim's back—a form of killing which, according to de Vries (1928b, 161–62; cf. 1956, 411–12), was especially associated with vengeance for a slain father.

It is less easy to see how the motif of the slaying of the aged, or even the 'best friend, worst enemy' type of condition sometimes associated with it, could have combined with the story preserved by Wendover, and just outlined, than it is to imagine the conditions of the type characteristic of the 'clever peasant girl' tale combining with the Northumbrian story of the rape, outlined earlier (pp. 215–17, above), especially as it is preserved in the *de uxore Aernulfi*, where the king does not seek out the woman he desires (as in Gaimar), but requires her to come to him. For this reason I prefer to assume that the story of Lothbrocus's faithful greyhound had no contact with the 'hidden old man's wisdom' tale or its associated motifs before it reached Denmark from England, but would leave open the possibility, suggested earlier (pp. 226–27, above), that the Northumbrian story of the rape did combine with motifs character-istic of the 'clever peasant girl' tale before it travelled to Denmark. On the other hand there is little doubt that the name *Loðbrók* formed part of the greyhound story before it left its English environment; whether it also formed part of the story of the rape before that story travelled from England to Denmark is an open question.

As suggested above (p. 229), the route by which these two stories reached Norway from England is essentially the same as that suggested for the eastern branch of the Rægnald-tradition in the last chapter (see pp. 104 13). It is not impossible that this branch of the Rægnald-tradition travelled from England to Denmark in combina-tion with the Northumbrian story of the rape, since in Gaimar's account this story is closely followed by an account of Orin's death, which, as argued earlier (p. 112, above), is comparable to Rǫgnvaldr's death as reported in the 1824b (and also, it may be assumed, the 147) text of *Ragnars saga*. It cannot easily be suggested, however, that the relevant information about Rægnald-Rǫgnvaldr reached Norway from Denmark in combination with the English material that informed the Spangereid-legend, since the legend shows no awareness of Rǫgnvaldr (and no interest, indeed, in any of Ragnarr loðbrók's sons, see pp. 180, 201, above). It may be assumed, therefore, that the eastern branch of the Rægnald-tradition reached the X redactor of *Ragnars saga* by way of Denmark and Norway, as suggested earlier (pp. 104–13), but independently of the Spangereid-legend.

(f) The contribution of *Tristrams saga ok Ísöndar*

Now that the major sources of the Spangereid-legend have (it is hoped) been accounted for, I should like to substantiate a point made earlier only in passing (see p. 185, above), i.e. that the Y version of *Ragnars saga* derived the idea of Áslaug being concealed in a harp from *Tristrams saga ok Ísöndar* (ed. Brynjúlfsson, 1878; here called simply *Tristrams saga*), the Norwegian prose translation of Thomas's *Tristran* attributed to brother Robert, dating in all likelihood from 1226 (though see Tómasson, 1977, 70–78), and preserved in Icelandic manuscripts of the fifteenth, seventeenth, and eighteenth centuries (Schach, 1957–61, 104–05; 1969a, 298–99, 306). The motif of the harp is found in one form or another in the 1824b text of *Ragnars saga* (ch. 1), the 'Gests ríma', and the accounts of Torfæus and Ramus (see part IIIC of the Analysis); and it was suggested earlier (see p. 185, above) that the motif first appeared in the Ragnarr loðbrók tradition in the Y version of *Ragnars saga* (as opposed to the X version, which almost certainly did not contain it, see pp. 61, 66, 185, above), and that it made its way from there primarily to the 'Gests ríma' and secondarily to the Spangereid-legend, whence Torfæus and Ramus derived it. It should be made clear at the outset that in its surviving form *Tristrams saga* makes no reference to the use of a harp or of any other musical instrument for containing or concealing a living being; in its original form, however, it may have done so.

Only the last sixth of Thomas's *Tristran* survives, but the content of the first five sixths of the poem may be to a large extent deduced from *Tristrams saga* itself, and from the poem's two other main derivatives (see Schach, 1969b, 86): Gottfried von Strass-burg's Middle High German poem *Tristan* (ed. Ganz, 1978), dating from 1205–20 (see Ganz, 1978, I, xi), and the anonymous late Middle English poem *Sir Tristrem*, dating from *c.*1300 (ed. McNeill, 1886, see pp. xxxii–xlv). *Tristrams saga* survives only in very young manuscripts, as already indicated, and Mundt (1971, 132–33) has argued that the motif of the spear coming apart in

Ragnars saga in the course of Ragnarr's serpent-fight (see part V of the Analysis) derives from the account of Tristram's fight with the dragon in *Tristrams saga*, even though this motif does not occur in the relevant chapters of that work (chs. 35–45, see esp. ch. 36, Brynjúlfsson, 1878, 74–75, where Tristram uses a spear to kill the dragon, it is true, but the spear remains intact). Since it does occur, however, in the corresponding part of Gottfried's *Tristan* (ll. 9210–24, see Ganz 1978, I, 318, where the steward who falsely claims to have killed the dragon breaks his spear and thrusts part of it down the dragon's throat to provide evidence that he has fought it), and of *Sir Tristrem* (ll. 1435–56, McNeill, 1886, 41, where Tristrem's own spear breaks in the course of the dragon fight), Mundt concludes that it occurred in the relevant context in Thomas's *Tristran* and must also have done so in the original text of *Tristrams saga*, whence *Ragnars saga* derived it. (It should be emphasized that, in the Ragnarr loðbrók tradition, it is only in the Y version of *Ragnars saga* as reflected in 1824b, and in the *Ragnars kvæði*, which derive partly from Y, that this motif occurs, see parts V and VII of the Analysis and cf. pp. 180, 194, above; it is not necessary to assume, therefore, that *Tristrams saga* influenced any other version of *Ragnars saga* than Y, at least as far as this motif is concerned.) More recently, M. F. Thomas (1983, 64; not to be confused with the twelfth-century Anglo-Norman poet of *Tristran*) has argued that 'The German version [i.e. Gottfried's poem] may represent a more detailed reproduction of Thomas's story than the extant ... Icelandic manuscripts of the latter preserve; it is conceivable that an early version of the *Translated Tristram* [i.e. *Tristrams saga*] may have contained similar information to the German poem.'

Against the background of these considerations, I would note that in *Tristrams saga* (ch. 63, Brynjúlfsson, 1878, 136–37), Gottfried's *Tristan* (ll. 16275–87, Ganz, 1978, II, 202), and *Sir Tristrem* (ll. 2399–2420, McNeill, 1886, 67–68), the hero sends his beloved (called Ísönd, Isolt, and Ysonde in each of these works respectively) a dog as a present; in *Tristrams saga* this dog is referred to by the word *rakki*, which means simply 'dog' (though according to Blöndal's dictionary of Modern Icelandic, Blöndal, 1920–24, 634, it has the archaic meaning 'little dog' or 'puppy'); in Gottfried's poem and *Sir Tristrem* it is referred to by the words *hundelin* ('little dog') and *welp* ('puppy') respectively. In *Tristrams saga* and in Gottfried's poem the messenger by whom the dog is sent is a musician, and in Gottfried's poem only, l. 16284 (see Ganz, 1978, II, 202), the messenger conveys the dog to Isolt 'in síner rotten', i.e. in his rote or fiddle. I would suggest that this last motif occurred in Thomas's *Tristran* (even though Bédier, 1902, 225, does not include it in his reconstruction of the poem's content); that it also occurred in the original text of *Tristrams saga*; and that the Y redactor of *Ragnars saga* derived it from there, and developed from it the idea of Áslaug being concealed in a harp. If this seems a ludicrous development of the already scarcely credible idea of a dog (however small) being put inside a fiddle, it may be pointed out that the idea is carried still further in Old Icelandic literature in chs. 11–13 of the older *Bósa saga*, whose late fourteenth-century redactor probably knew both the Y version of *Ragnars saga* and *Ragnarssona þáttr* (see Jiriczek, 1893, lv–lvi, ivl–iiil; cf. however Edzardi, 1880, xli–xliv). Here Bósi rescues Hleiðr, the sister of King Goðmundr of Glæsisvellir, from her wedding to Siggeirr, her unloved suitor, by hiding her in a harp, which is described as 'so big that a man could stand upright inside it' ('svó stór, at maðr mátti standa réttr í ... henni', Jiriczek, 1893, 46). The final chapter (16) of the older *Bósa saga* also contains a brief account of Ragnarr's winning of Þóra by slaying the serpent, which is here described as having been found in a vulture's egg which, earlier in the saga (ch. 8), the foster-brothers Bósi and Herrauðr had found in a pagan temple in Bjarmaland. Because I accept Jiriczek's view that, as far as Ragnarr loðbrók is concerned, *Bósa saga* has no independent value (cf. p. 157, above), this account is not included in the list of analogues and versions of *Ragnars saga* given in section (a) of the preceding chapter.

As Mundt (1971, 131–33, 139–40) shows, the account of Ragnarr's serpent-fight in the 1824b text of *Ragnars saga* fails to make the fullest possible use of the broken spear motif; Ragnarr leaves his spearhead in the serpent's body after killing it, and is later identified as its slayer when he matches his spearshaft with the spearhead, but in the meantime no rival has presented himself as the slayer by claiming the spearhead as his own; the motif of 'identification by broken weapon' (Boberg, 1966, 149) here lacks the suspense and excitement that the introduction of a rival claimant would provide. In the *Ragnars kvæði*, on the other hand, which as far as the serpent-fight is concerned derive primarily from the original 'Lindarorm' ballad and secondarily from the Y version of *Ragnars saga*, as indicated above (pp. 156–58, 159–60), this motif is handled with a greater sense of its narrative potential, even though the means by which the identification is finally made are left rather unclear (cf. part VII of the Analysis). Here a slave finds the weapon (or part of a weapon, see part V of the Analysis) left behind at the scene of the killing, and claims to be the slayer; thus a greater effect of suspense is achieved in the *Ragnars kvæði* than in the saga.

In *Tristrams saga* (chs. 35–45) as it survives (see Brynjúlfsson, 1878, 72–95), a steward cuts off the dragon's head, from which Tristram, its true slayer, has previously extracted the tongue, and claims to have done the killing (ch. 37); his claim is shown to be false, however, when Tristram produces the tongue (ch. 45). Although a spear figures in this account, as shown above (pp. 235–36), no mention is made of its breaking, or of its parts being used as evidence in identifying the slayer. Mundt (1971, 131–33), however, has argued, as also shown above, that the motif of the broken spear did form part of *Tristrams saga*'s account of the slaying in its original form, and I am inclined to accept her view. The broken spear motif occurs in both Gottfried's *Tristan* and the Middle English *Sir Tristrem*, as already indicated (pp. 235–36, above). In both these poems, it is true, the hero uses the dragon's tongue as evidence that he has killed it, and in both poems also (logically enough) the rival claimant uses the dragon's head in claiming to have done so. In Gottfried's poem, however, the rival uses the broken spear as well as the dragon's head in this context.

Since the identification motif is not found in either 'Lindarormen' or 'Ormekampen', which represent the *Ragnars kvæði*'s main source for their account of Ragnarr's serpent-fight (cf. pp. 156–60, above), the foregoing considerations raise the question of whether the composer of the *Ragnars kvæði*, with his reasonably full and logical use of the motif, knew *Tristrams saga* in some form, or whether he knew the Y version of *Ragnars saga* in a form different from that in which it survives in 1824b, and including the rival claimant figure. In my view it is not necessary to make either of these assumptions. It is certainly possible that the poet of the *Ragnars kvæði* knew *Tristrams saga*; the Faroese ballad known as 'Tístrans táttur' (which deals almost exclusively with the deaths of the hero and heroine, and not at all with the dragon-fight) probably derives largely from *Tristrams saga* (see Schach, 1964, 286, 297); it is also possible that the Y version of *Ragnars saga*, in the form in which it was known to the poet of the *Ragnars kvæði*, gave a fuller and better account of the serpent fight than 1824b—though it has not as yet been found necessary in this monograph to assume any difference between the form in which the Y version of *Ragnars saga* survives in 1824b, and any other form of that same version. I would suggest that the poet of the *Ragnars kvæði* knew the Y version of *Ragnars saga* in a form close or identical to that which survives in 1824b; that he recognized the deficiencies in its account of the serpent-fight; and that, without necessarily being aware of any other version of the story, he used his own intelligence in touching up this account by supplying the rival claimant figure.

(g) Concluding remarks

The argument of this chapter is summarized in the stemma on p. 241, which may be compared and contrasted with de Vries's stemmata of 1915, reproduced on p. 240. It should be emphasized that de Vries's stemmata represent his views in a relatively early and extreme form, even though the modifications he made in 1928 were hardly extensive (see pp. 149–61, 168–73, above); and that my own stemma is intended not only as a summary of the argument of this chapter, but also to show the relationship, as I see it, of *Ragnars saga* to its major Scandinavian analogues, as listed in ch. II, section (a), above; it thus includes certain items which, since they were not central to de Vries's concerns in 1915, do not appear in his stemmata. The square brackets in fig. 3 on p. 240 have been introduced to mark off information which, though clearly available to Ramus (from Torfæus, if from no other source), does not in fact form part of Ramus's account, a point disregarded by de Vries; and in my own stemma, certain abbreviations not used elsewhere in this monograph are used, as follows: Krm (*Krákumál*); Skj (*Skjǫldunga saga*); oRs (older *Ragnars saga*); Rsþ (*Ragnarssona páttr*); Vs (*Vǫlsunga saga*); incl. (including); and Bk (Book). X and Y refer, of course, to the X and Y versions of *Ragnars saga* (represented by 147 and 1824b respectively), and the figures preceded by the abbreviation AT indicate folk-tale types as numbered in Aarne-Thompson (1961; see under AT in the Bibliography). With regard to my own stemma in particular, it should be noted that the direction implied by all non-horizontal lines is downward, unless arrows indicate otherwise, and that this direction in turn implies a movement forward in time (as also do the arrows, wherever they are used), though the lines in question are not necessarily proportionate in length to periods of historical time. Words in round brackets placed alongside

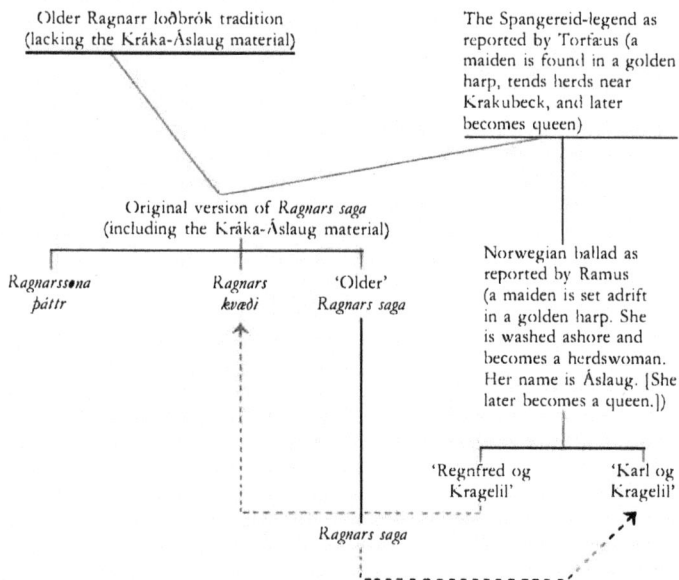

Fig. 3: adapted from de Vries (1915, 179)

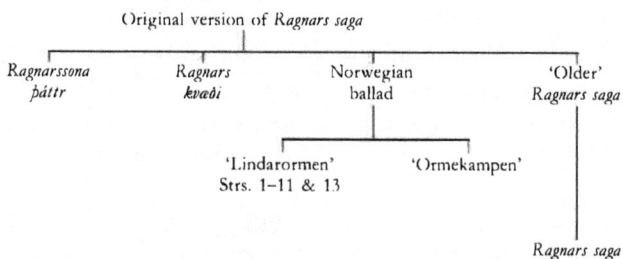

Fig. 4: adapted from de Vries (1915, 148)

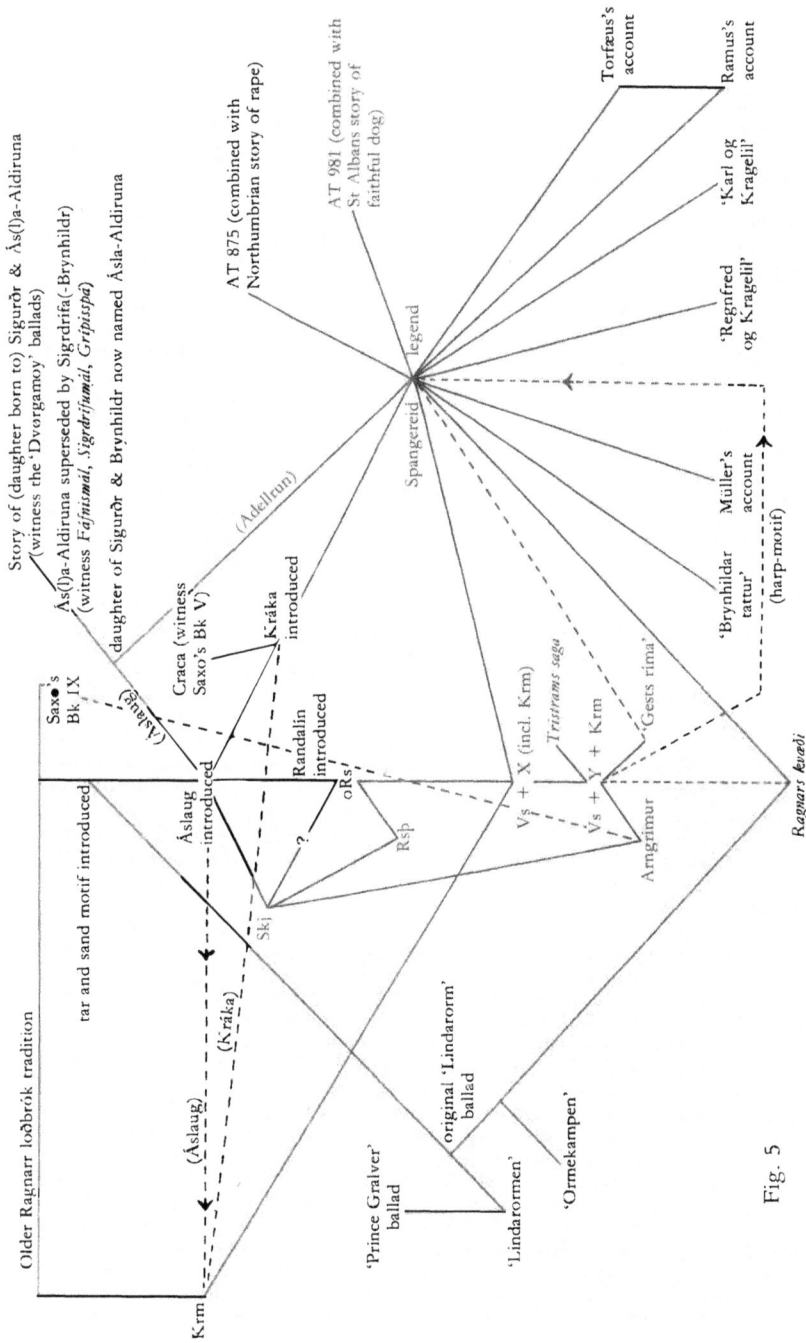

Fig. 5

certain lines indicate the material of which these lines represent the transmission; and I follow de Vries in using dotted lines to indicate the more important cases of secondary influence.

It will be remembered from ch. II (see p. 118, above) that *Ragnarssona þáttr* and the 147 text of *Ragnars saga* differ from the 1824b text of the latter in presenting two of Ragnarr's sons (Bjǫrn and Hvítserkr in the *þáttr*, and very possibly also in 147, see Hb, 1892–96, 460, l. 17, and Olsen, 1906–08, xcii; 183, Bl. 8v, ll. 21–25) as playing a board-game ('tafl'), when they hear from their mother, Áslaug, of the deaths of their stepbrothers Eiríkr and Agnarr, Ragnarr's sons by Þóra. The 1824b text of the saga does not mention a board-game in this context; nor does Saxo, who in any case reports the deaths of Ericus and Agnerus rather differently from the *þáttr* and the saga (see p. 135, above). On the other hand, 1824b has in common with Saxo and 147, though not the *þáttr*, the fact that it presents certain of Ragnarr's sons as playing a board-game ('hneftafl', see Olsen, 1906–08, 161, l. 7) when they hear from messengers in Denmark the news of their father's death in the British Isles; the sons in question are Sigurðr and Hvítserkr in 1824b and apparently also in 147 (see Olsen, 1906–08, 161–62, 190), and just Biornus in Saxo (IX.v, 3). In the saga (to judge from 1824b), Hvítserkr, who is holding one of the pieces used in the game, squeezes it so hard on hearing the news that each of his fingers bleeds from under the nail; and in Saxo's account, Biornus, who is playing a dice-game ('tesserarum iactus'), reacts to the news by squeezing a die so violently that the blood drips from his fingers onto the board.

Bugge (1908, 206–07) drew attention to similarities between these accounts on the one hand and, on the other, an account in the early ninth-century Irish saga *Cath Maige Mucrama* (Carney, 1968, 148; cf. O Daly, 1975, 18) of how Lugaid Mac Con, having fled from Ireland and taken refuge with the king of Scotland, from whom he conceals his identity, is playing a board-game ('fidchell', see O Daly, 1975, 45) with the king when a stranger arrives with the news that Lugaid's relatives in Ireland are in a state of subjection to Éogan, son of Ailill. On hearing this news Lugaid places his finger on two or three of the pieces used in the game, thus knocking down the row of pieces in front of him; and the king then realizes who he is.

Herrmann (1922, 655–56) and de Vries (1928a, 264) both use this Irish account as 'ein Beweis mehr dafür, daß die Wikingersaga von Ragnar entweder von England ausgegangen ist oder über England den Isländern vermittelt ist' (Herrmann, 1922, 655). If this means that the Icelandic saga-tradition of Ragnarr loðbrók derived the board-game motif more or less directly from England, a difficulty arises in that the older as opposed to the X or the Y version of *Ragnars saga* appears (to judge from *Ragnarssona þáttr*) to have used this motif in connection with the deaths of Ragnarr's sons Eiríkr and Agnarr rather than with Ragnarr's own death, whereas it is altogether likely that the Ragnarr loðbrók tradition, if it did obtain this motif from England, used it originally in connection with the father's death, as opposed to that of any of his sons (cf. pp. 89–90, 213, above). The X version of the saga (to judge from 147) uses the motif in connection with Ragnarr's death as well as Eiríkr's and Agnarr's; while the Y version (to judge from 1824b) uses it exclusively in connection with Ragnarr's. Thus the X version seems to represent a transitional stage in a process whereby the saga-tradition completely transferred to Ragnarr a motif it had earlier used only in connection with his sons Eiríkr and Agnarr. Saxo, as already indicated, resembles the Y version in using the motif exclusively in connection with the death of Regnerus, the father figure; and I would venture to explain this, not as a result of the influence of West Norse tradition, which is presumably how Herrmann and de Vries would explain it, but as another example of Saxo's account reflecting material that reached Scandinavia directly from England by way of Denmark. I would suggest, in fact, that the motif reached Iceland from England primarily by way of Denmark and Norway, i.e. by the route described earlier in connection with Rægnald/Rǫgnvaldr (see pp. 104 12, above) and the English stories of the rape and the faithful dog (see pp. 225–29, 233–35, above). I would further suggest that in Denmark, where the motif first reached Scandinavia, it was used exclusively in connection with the Ragnarr-figure's death (as in Saxo's account), but that, as the motif travelled to Western Scandinavia, this use of it took time to impinge on West Norse tradition, which at first connected it with the deaths of Eiríkr and Agnarr, but later came to apply it to Ragnarr's death as a result of additional information emanating from Denmark, or the British Isles, or both.

It is possible that the motif of 'deceptive land purchase' (see Boberg, 1966, 168) by the use of an animal's skin, as it occurs in the Ragnarr loðbrók tradition, also reached Iceland from England by way of mainland Scandinavia, and primarily by way of Denmark.

Storm (1878, 99–100) at any rate seemed to think that it travelled from England to Denmark in the mid-twelfth century, and Guðnason's (1963, 185–87) more recent remarks appear to build largely on Storm's. It occurs in Saxo's account (IX.v, 4), in *Ragnarssona þáttr* (Hb, 1892–96, 463), in the 147 and 1824b texts of *Ragnars saga* (Olsen, 1906–08, 192, 164–65), and in Arngrímur's account (Benediktsson, 1950, 466). The precise form of the motif in 147 is difficult to determine because of the fragmentary and largely illegible state of that manuscript; and in Arngrímur's account it occurs in such a condensed form as to be scarcely recognizable. Arngrímur's account has in any case no independent value on this point, since he appears to have derived the motif from the Y version of *Ragnars saga* reflected in 1824b, if not from 1824b itself (Benediktsson, 1957, 262); he thus cannot be said to provide evidence that the motif occurred in the lost *Skjǫldunga saga*, though its occurrence in *Ragnarssona þáttr* perhaps does provide such evidence (cf. pp. 56, 57, above). In the *þáttr*, Ívarr, after his father's death in King Ella's snake-pit, makes terms with Ella, who agrees to grant him in compensation as much land as Ívarr can cover with the hide of an old bull. Taking the largest hide he can find, Ívarr has it stretched and cut in such a way as to form a strip with which he marks out an area of flat ground on which he founds York ('Jórvík'). He wins the support of the local chieftains and sends for his brothers, encouraging them to avenge their father while at the same time deceiving Ella into believing that he is trying to dissuade them from doing so. In the battle which follows, a number of chieftains transfer their loyalty from Ella to Ívarr, and Ella is defeated, captured, and put to death (cf. pp. 106, 230, above). The motif is found in essentially the same form in Saxo's account and 1824b; in Saxo's account, however, a horse's hide rather than a bull's is used and the city founded is not named, while in 1824b (as in Arngrímur's account) the city is named London ('Lundúnaborg', 'Londinium') rather than York. Neither the type of hide used nor the name of the city emerges from what can be read of 147, but there is nothing to suggest that the X version of *Ragnars saga* reflected in 147 does not represent, in this as in other respects, an intermediate stage between the older *Ragnars saga* (reflected in *Ragnarssona þáttr*) and the Y version of *Ragnars saga* (reflected in 1824b).

This motif, sometimes called the Dido motif, since according to Virgil's *Aeneid*, Book I, ll. 365–68 (Fairclough, 1956, 266–67), Dido and others founded the city of Carthage by marking out its site with a bull's hide, is also found in Geoffrey of Monmouth's *Historia regum Britanniæ* (part VI, chs. 10–11), dating from the first half of the twelfth century (see Griscom, 1929, 42, 366–70). Here Hengist, the leader (with his brother Horsa) of the Saxons, who have recently arrived in Britain, asks the king of Britain, Vortigern, who has welcomed them as allies against the Picts, to grant him as much land as can be encircled by a single thong. The king does so, and Hengist, with a thong cut from a bull's hide, marks out an area on which he founds the fortress known in Saxon as Thanceastre. Geoffrey's *Historia* was translated into Icelandic around 1220 (see Guðnason, 1963, 185), but it cannot be assumed that the translation was the means by which the motif under discussion became known in Scandinavia, not least because it is by no means certain that the episode just outlined was included in the translation (Guðnason, 1963, 186). Although the motif is a widespread one, I would agree with Guðnason (1963, 187) that there is enough similarity of context between the uses of it by Geoffrey on the one hand and the Ragnarr loðbrók tradition on the other to suggest that the latter derived it from the British Isles. I would follow Guðnason in suggesting that it was conveyed orally to Scandinavia, and Storm (1878, 99) in maintaining that it travelled in the first instance from England to Denmark. Saxo, who, as already noted, mentions a horse's hide rather than a bull's, and does not name the city founded, is not so much of an exception in these respects as he seems at first to be, since it is likely that his idea of a horse's hide in this context derives from a misunderstanding of the Old Norse name for York, *Jórvík*, the first syllable of which, though it in fact derives from Old English *eofor*, 'boar' (Noreen, 1923, 172), is identical in form with an Old Norse poetic word for 'stallion' or 'steed' (see Guðnason, 1963, 186, and cf. F. Jónsson, 1931b, 330). I would conclude that Geoffrey of Monmouth's account and the ones corresponding to it in the Ragnarr loðbrók tradition derive from a common source, a story orally current in the British Isles; that the story came to be told in connection with Inwære and York in the Danelaw, whence it travelled to Iceland by the same route as the board-game motif discussed above; that its association with York, somewhat obscurely reflected in Saxo's account, was retained in the older *Ragnars saga*, as *Ragnarssona þáttr* confirms (and also in *Skjǫldunga saga*, if the latter included the story); but that, by the Y stage of the saga-tradition, London had come to be substituted for York, as the 1824b text shows.

Geoffrey's *Historia regum Britanniæ* (part VI, ch. 14, see Griscom, 1929, 374–75) also includes an account, apparently deriving from the ninth-century *Historia Brittonum* attributed to Nennius (Thorpe, 1966, 163, n. 1; Whitelock, 1979, 125–26), of how Vortigern's eldest son Vortimer, who frequently defeated the Saxons, asked to be buried after his death at the point on the British coast where the Saxons most often landed, in the hope that they would abandon their invasions at the sight of his tomb. In the event, however, he was buried elsewhere, and the invasions continued. It is no more certain than in the case of the story of Hengist, just discussed, that this account was included in the Icelandic translation of Geoffrey's *Historia* (see *Annaler*, 1849, pp. 8–9 and cf. Guðnason, 1963, 186). As Lukman (1976, 39 40) points out, the Vortimer story is paralleled in what is told of Ívarr, son of Ragnarr loðbrók, in ch. 18 of the 1824b text of *Ragnars saga* (see Olsen 1906–08, 169): after his death in England, Ívarr is buried in a mound at a place where the country is exposed to invasion. He had requested this himself, prophesying that invaders who landed there would not gain victory. The saga goes on to report that, according to what many people say, King Haraldr Sigurðarson (elsewhere called 'harðráði', 'the tyrannical') later met his defeat near Ívarr's burial-mound, and that Vilhjálmr bastarðr ('the bastard', i.e. William the Conqueror) was able to conquer England only after he had had Ívarr's body exhumed and burnt.

Since it occurs in 1824b, this story may be assumed to have formed part of the Y version of *Ragnars saga*, but its occurrence in ch. 18 of the 1824b text means that it can hardly have formed part of the X version (cf. p. 61, above). It seems indeed to have no very convincing parallel elsewhere in the Ragnarr loðbrók tradition; *Ragnarssona þáttr* (Hb, 1892–96, 465, l. 13) and Arngrímur (see Benediktsson, 1950, 466, l. 29) both mention Ívarr's burial in England, the former specifying that he was buried in a mound ('heygðr'), and the latter emphasizing the ancient (i.e. pre-Christian) manner of the burial ('veteris sæculi more inhumatus est'), but neither gives any further details. Saxo (IX.v, 6), who does not record the death of Ivarus, does, it is true, mention burial-mounds ('colles') just before mentioning him for the last time, but only to the extent of pointing out that such mounds mark the scene of a victory won off Schleswig by certain of Regnerus's sons (while Ivarus was in England) over two rebels named (coincidentally enough) Siwardus and Ericus. It may however be noted that

Gaimar in his *L'estoire des Engleis* (Bell, 1960, 100; 244–45) records in a passage partly deriving from a lost version of the *Anglo-Saxon chronicle* that Ube, 'the brother of Ywar and of Haldene', was defeated and slain in a wood called Pene (probably Penselwood on the Somerset-Wiltshire border) and that the Danes (his compatriots) raised a mound over his body in Devonshire. In ch. I, pp. 30–50, above, it was maintained that the Ívarr of *Ragnars saga* and Gaimar's Ywar were historically the same person, the Inwære of the *Anglo-Saxon chronicle*; and that this Inwære and the persons called Ube and Haldene by Gaimar were among the five sons of Loðbróka, a woman whose name appears to be misremembered as *Loðbrók* in the Maeshowe runic inscription numbered XIX-XX. Taking together the relevant accounts of Geoffrey of Monmouth, Gaimar, and the 1824b text of *Ragnars saga*, de Vries (1928a, 260–63) argues convincingly that the motif of the burial-mound giving protection against invasion first became attached to Ívarr/Inwære in England among Scandinavian settlers, surely the most likely environment for the development of a story in which a Viking leader seems to be presented as a guardian spirit of the English people. He further suggests that the Maeshowe inscription represents a link between the English and the Icelandic stages of the story's development. Maeshowe itself appears to have been a grave-mound (see Farrer, 1862, 14; cf. Elliott, 1963, 27), and in referring to Loðbrók's mound and to her sons the inscription shows that in twelfth-century Orkney the sons of Loðbrók(a) were thought of in connection with a mound. It would be rash to make assumptions about the precise route or routes whereby the story reached Iceland from England, but there seems little doubt that the Orkneys played an important part in its transmission from England to Scandinavia.

Throughout this monograph I have tried as far as possible to make sense of existing records without assuming more (or less) about their background than is indicated in the records themselves—an approach which has involved placing more trust in the records than de Vries often seemed to do in his various relevant writings. In my first chapter, for instance, I have chosen to assume that William of Jumièges came near to being historically accurate in describing Bier Costae ferreae as a son of Lotbroc(us), and not to accept de Vries's more complicated view that William was here adapting a source now lost in which Inwære/Inguar was so described (see pp. 42–43). In my second chapter I have differed from de Vries in taking the absence from *Ragnarssona þáttr* of Rǫgnvaldr and the cow-slaying episodes, as well as of Kráka and *Krákumál*, as an indication that these items were also absent from the *þáttr*'s sources (see pp. 102–14, 132–33, 135–36); and Saxo's failure to mention Áslaug, Kráka, or Randalín in Book IX of his *Gesta Danorum* as a similar indication that these figures formed virtually no part of that book's background (see pp. 123–25). In the same chapter I have also argued, against de Vries, that *Krákumál* differs little in its surviving form from that in which it was composed (see pp. 125–32). In the present chapter I have, it is true, found it necessary to assume rather more about the background of 'Lindarormen' and 'Ormekampen' than is perhaps apparent from these poems in their surviving forms; but I have at any rate argued for a reduction in the amount of their source-material as envisaged by de Vries (see ch. III, section (b), above), whereas I have placed greater faith than he initially did in hints provided in certain records of the Spangereid-legend to the effect that Áslaug's marriage to Ragnarr loðbrók, and her filial relationship to Sigurðr and Brynhildr, were known to the legend from its beginnings (see pp. 149–56, 160–61, 176–83). Thus I have often (though by no means always) disagreed with de Vries, and found myself modifying or adjusting his views. This does not mean, of course, that I believe now, any more than de Vries (1923, 272) believed in 1923, 'dass meine obigen Ausführungen in allen Punkten das Richtige getroffen haben', or that I do not regard my debt to him as immeasurable. This debt is apparent, I suspect, on almost every page of this monograph, and especially, perhaps, in my discussion and use of the heroic biographical pattern in the first and second chapters. In conclusion I would say of de Vries, as Dryden in a different context said of Chaucer, that while I have often disagreed with him, 'I must at the same time acknowledge, that I could have done nothing without him'.

BIBLIOGRAPHY

Apart from the fact that V and W have been treated as separate letters, the alphabetical order of *Kulturhistorisk leksikon for nordisk middelalder* ... (22 vols., Copenhagen and elsewhere, 1956–78) has been adopted here as the one most appropriate for the large number of Scandinavian names listed. All sources, whether primary or secondary, are placed in the alphabetical sequence under the designations used in the text to indicate specific references to them, i.e. references by page or column number (except in the case of Saxo, where a different system has been used, see under his name, below). Thus where a primary source is not listed under its own title or its author's name, it will be found under its editor's name, or the title of the edition or collection in which it appears, as indicated in the text. In cases where a primary source is referred to with exceptional frequency in the text, or where additional clarity has seemed necessary, both the source itself (or its author where known) *and* the relevant editor or edition are listed. All the items listed on pp. 53–61, above, for instance, have been treated in this way.

ADALBJARNARSON, Bjarni, 1941 (ed). *Heimskringla*, vol. I, Íslenzk fornrit, XXVI, Reykjavík.

AFANAS'EV, Aleksandr, 1946 (collector). *Russian fairy tales*, London (translated by Norbert Guterman; rpt. 1976).

ANNALER, 1849. *Annaler for nordisk Oldkyndighed og Historie*, Copenhagen (contains on pp. 3–145 an edition with a facing Danish translation, continued from *Annaler*, 1848, of *Breta sögur*, the Icelandic translation of Geoffrey of Monmouth's *Historia regum Britanniæ*).

ARENT, A. Margaret, 1969. The heroic pattern: old Germanic helmets, *Beowulf*, and *Grettis saga*, in *Old Norse literature and mythology: a symposium*, ed. Edgar C. Polomé, Austin, Texas, pp. 130–99.

ARNGRÍMUR (Jónsson). See under Jónsson, Arngrímur.

ARNOLD, Thomas, 1882 (ed). *Symeonis monachi opera omnia*, vol. I, Rerum Britannicarum medii ævi scriptores, London.

— 1885 (ed). *Symeonis monachi opera omnia*, vol. III, Rerum Britannicarum medii ævi scriptores, London.

— 1890 (ed). *Memorials of St. Edmund's abbey*, vol. I, Rerum Britannicarum medii ævi scriptores, London.

'ÁSLU RÍMA'. See 'Gests ríma'.

AT (1961). *The types of the folktale* ... Antti Aarne's *Verzeichnis der Märchentypen* (FF communications, 3), trans. and enlarged by Stith Thompson ..., second revision, FF communications, 184, Helsinki (first published 1910, revised 1928).

BÉDIER, Joseph, 1902 (ed). *Le roman de Tristan par Thomas. Poème du XIIe siècle*, vol. I (text), Société des anciens textes français, LXXV, Paris.

BELL, Alexander, 1960 (ed). Geffrei Gaimar, *L'estoire des Engleis*, Anglo-Norman Text Society, XIV–XVI (for 1956–58), Oxford.

BENEDIKTSSON, Jakob, 1950 (ed). *Arngrimi Jonae opera Latine conscripta*, vol. I, Bibliotheca Arnamagnæana (ed. Jón Helgason), IX, Copenhagen.

— 1957 (ed). *Arngrimi Jonae opera Latine conscripta*, vol. IV, *Introduction and notes*, Bibliotheca Arnamagnæana (ed. Jón Helgason), XII, Copenhagen.

— 1968 (ed). *Íslendingabók, Landnámabók*, Íslenzk fornrit, I (in two parts, continuously paginated), Reykjavík.

BERTELSEN, Henrik, 1905–11 (ed). *Þiðriks saga af Bern*, vols. I–II (each volume separately paginated), Samfund til udgivelse af gammel nordisk litteratur, XXXIV, Copenhagen.

BIBLE, THE NEW ENGLISH, WITH THE APOCRYPHA, 1970. Oxford (second edition of New Testament; first edition of Old Testament and Apocrypha).

BLISS, A. J., 1971. Single halflines in Old English poetry, *Notes and queries*, new series, 18 (continuous series, 216), pp. 442–49.

BLÖNDAL, Sigfús, 1920–24. *Íslensk-dönsk orðabók*, Reykjavík.

BOBERG, Inger M., 1966. *Motif-index of early Icelandic literature*, Bibliotheca Arnamagnæana (ed. Jón Helgason), XXVII, Copenhagen.

BOER, R. C., 1892 (ed). *Qrvar-Odds saga*, Altnordische Saga-bibliothek (ed. Gustaf Cederschiöld *et al.*), 2, Halle.

BOOR, H(elmut) de, 1920. Die færöischen Dvörgamoylieder, *Arkiv för nordisk filologi*, 36, pp. 207–99.

— 1923. Review of de Vries, 1915 (*q.v.*), in *Zeitschrift für deutsche Philologie*, 49, pp. 104–14.

— 1956 (ed). *Das Nibelungenlied*, ed. by de Boor on the basis of Karl Bartsch's edition. Deutsche Klassiker des Mittelalters (inst. Franz Pfeiffer), Wiesbaden (thirteenth edition, revised; Bartsch's edition first published in three vols., Leipzig, 1870–80).

BOSWORTH, Joseph, and T. Northcote TOLLER, 1929 (eds). *An Anglo-Saxon dictionary*, Oxford (rpt. of the first edition, 1898).

'BRYNHILDAR TÁTTUR'. As edited in Djurhuus & Matras, 1951–63 (*q.v.*), pp. 1–214.

[BRYNJÚLFSSON, Gísli,] 1878 (ed). *Saga af Tristram ok Isönd samt Möttuls saga*, Copenhagen.

BUGGE, S(ophus, 1862). References to the variants of 'Lindarormen' discussed by Bugge are to DgF III, 1862 (*q.v.*), pp. 798–99.

— 1867 (ed). *Norræn fornkvæði: islandsk Samling af folkelige Oldtidsdigte om Nordens Guder og Heroer almindelig kaldet Sæmundar Edda hins fróða*, Christiania (rpt. Oslo 1965).

— 1908. *Norsk Sagaskrivning og Sagafortælling i Irland*, Christiania.

BYRNE, Francis John, 1963. Review of *Proceedings of the international congress of Celtic studies held in Dublin, 6 10 July, 1959* (Dublin 1962), in *Irish historical studies*, 13, pp. 269–71.

CAMPBELL, A., 1962 (ed). *The chronicle of Æthelweard*, Medieval texts (ed. V. H. Galbraith *et al.*), London.

CANGE, Charles du Fresne, Seigneur du, 1774. *Glossarium manuale ad scriptores mediae et infimae Latinitatis* . . ., vol. III, Halle.

CARNANDET, Joanne, 1866 (ed.). Historia miraculorum et translationum ob irruptiones Normannicas. Auctore Aimoino Monacho Pratensi seculo IX, in *Acta Sanctorum* . . . collecta . . . a Godefrido Henschenio et Daniele Papebrochio (new edition). *Maii* tomus sextus . . . operam et studium conferentibus Francisco Baertio et Conrado Ianningo, Paris, pp. 786–96 (first edition, Antwerp, 1688).

CARNEY, James, 1968. Cath Maige Muccrime, in *Irish sagas*, ed. Myles Dillon, Mercier paperback, Cork, pp. 148–61.

CARNEY, Maura, and Máirín O Daly, 1975 (arranged by). *Contributions to a dictionary of the Irish language* (general editor E. G. Quin) *B*, Dublin (references are to columns, not pages).

CHADWICK, Nora K., 1959. The monsters and Beowulf, in *The Anglo-Saxons. Studies in some aspects of their history and culture presented to Bruce Dickins*, ed. by Peter Clemoes, London, pp. 171–203.

CLARKE, D. E. Martin, 1923 (ed. and trans.). *The Hávamál* . . ., Cambridge.

CLEASBY, Richard, Gudbrand VIGFUSSON, and Sir William A. CRAIGIE, 1957 (eds). *An Icelandic-English Dictionary*, second edition, Oxford (rpt. 1962; first edition 1874).

COXE, Henricus O., 1841 (ed). *Rogeri de Wendover chronica sive flores historiarum*, vol. I, London.

CRASTER, Edmund, 1954. The patrimony of St. Cuthbert, *English historical review*, 69, pp. 177–99.

CRITCHLEY, Macdonald, 1978 (ed.). *Butterworths medical dictionary*, second edition, London (first published 1961, ed. by Sir Arthur Salusbury MacNalty; revised 1963; first published under this title, 1965).

DAVIDSON, Hilda Ellis, and Peter FISHER, 1980. Saxo Grammaticus, *The history of the Danes, Books I–IX*, vol. II: *Commentary*, Cambridge.

DE BOOR, Helmut. See under Boor, Helmut de.

DE VRIES, Jan. See under Vries, Jan de.

DgF I, 1853. *Danmarks gamle Folkeviser*, pt. 1, ed. Svend Grundtvig, Copenhagen.

DgF III, 1862. *Danmarks gamle Folkeviser*, pt. 3, ed. Svend Grundtvig, Copenhagen.

DgF XII, 1976. *Danmarks gamle Folkeviser* . . ., *Old popular ballads of Denmark: index volume* . . ., ed. Ellen Grüner-Nielsen *et al.*, Copenhagen.

DICKINS, Bruce, 1930. *The runic inscriptions of Maeshowe*, Kirkwall (reprinted from vol. VIII of the *Proceedings of the Orkney Antiquarian Society*).

DIETRICHSON, L., 1906. *Monumenta Orcadica, Nordmændene paa Orknøerne og deres efterladte mindesmærker* . . ., Christiania.

DILLON, Myles, 1948. *Early Irish literature*, Chicago (fourth impression, 1969).

DJURHUUS, N., and Chr. MATRAS, 1951–63 (eds). *Føroya kvæði, corpus carminum Færoensium a Sv. Grundtvig et J. Bloch comparatum*, I, Copenhagen.

DOWSON, John, 1968. *A Classical Dictionary of Hindu mythology and religion, geography, history and literature*, Trubner's Oriental series, London (eleventh edition; first edition, 1879).

DRONKE, Ursula, 1969a (ed. and trans.). *The poetic Edda*, vol. I. *Heroic poems*, Oxford.

—— 1969b. Beowulf and Ragnarǫk, *Saga-Book*, 17, pp. 302–25.

DU CANGE, See under Cange, Charles du Fresne, Seigneur du.

DUNDES, Alan, 1965. *The study of folklore*, Englewood Cliffs, New Jersey.

EARLE, John, and Charles PLUMMER, 1892 (eds.). *Two of the Saxon chronicles parallel, with supplementary extracts from the others: a revised text*, vol. I, *Text, appendices and glossary*, Oxford (rpt. 1952 with additional notes by D. Whitelock).

EDDA, the poetic. References to eddaic poems are to the texts as edited in Neckel, 1962, unless otherwise stated.

EDDA, the prose, Snorri's prose. See *Snorra Edda*.

EDZARDI, A., 1880 (ed.). *Volsunga- und Ragnars-saga nebst der Geschichte von Nornagest* (second edition, fully revised, of F. H. von der Hagen's German translation of 1814), Altdeutsche und altnordische Heldensagen, 3, Stuttgart.

EHLERS, E., 1896. *L'ergotisme. Ignis sacer*, Encyclopédie scientifique des aide-mémoire, 158B, Paris.

EKWALL, Eilert, 1960. *The concise Oxford dictionary of English place-names*, fourth edition, Oxford (rpt. 1964; first edition 1936).

ELLIOTT, R. W. V., 1963. *Runes, an introduction*, Manchester (rpt. with minor corrections of first edition, 1959; rpt. 1971).

ELTON, Oliver, 1894 (trans.). *The first nine books of the Danish history of Saxo Grammaticus*, with some considerations on Saxo's sources ..., by Frederick York Powell ..., Publications of the Folk-lore Society (1893), London.

FAIRCLOUGH, H. Rushton, 1956 (ed. and trans.) *Virgil ... in two volumes*, vol. 1 (*Eclogues, Georgics, Aeneid I VI*), The Loeb classical library (founded by James Loeb), London (rpt. of revised edition 1935; first edition 1916).

FALK, Hjalmar, 1919. *Altwestnordische Kleiderkunde mit besonderer Berücksichtigung der Terminologie*, Videnskapsselskapets Skrifter, II, Hist-filos. klasse, 1918, No. 3, Christiania.

FARRER, James, 1862. *Notice of runic inscriptions discovered during recent excavations in the Orkneys*, Edinburgh.

FAULKES, Anthony, 1982 (ed). Snorri Sturluson, *Edda: prologue and Gylfaginning*, Oxford.

FINCH, R. G., 1965 (ed. and trans.). *The saga of the Volsungs*, Icelandic texts, London.

—1983. Personal letter to R. W. McTurk dated July 28 (unpublished).

FISHER, Peter, 1979 (trans.; Hilda Ellis DAVIDSON, ed.). Saxo Grammaticus, *The history of the Danes*, vol. I: *English text*, Cambridge.

FOOTE, Peter, and David M. WILSON, 1973. *The Viking achievement. The society and culture of early medieval Scandinavia*, London (second impression, with additional bibliography; first published 1970).

FRANK, Roberta, 1970. Onomastic play in Kormakr's verse: the name Steingerðr, *Mediaeval Scandinavia*, 3, pp. 7–34.

— 1984. Viking atrocity and scaldic verse: the rite of the blood-eagle, *English historical review*, 99, pp. 332–43.

FRIESEN, Otto von, 1932–34. Har det nordiska kungadömet sakralt ursprung? *Saga och sed*, Uppsala, 1934, pp. 15–34.

FRITZNER, Johan, 1891. *Ordbog over det gamle norske Sprog* (revised and enlarged edition), vol. II, *Hl P*, Christiania (vol. II of second edition, in three vols., 1883–96; first edition in one vol., 1867).

— 1973. *Ordbog over det gamle norske Sprog*, vols. I–IV (fourth edition, revised, enlarged, and improved), Oslo (third edition in three vols., 1954; for earlier editions, see under Fritzner, 1891).

FS, 1835. *Fornmanna sögur eptir gömlum handritum útgefnar að tilhlutun hins konúngliga norræna fornfræða félags*, X, Copenhagen (editor not named).

GALBRAITH, V. H., 1944. *Roger Wendover and Matthew Paris*, ... the eleventh lecture on the David Murray Foundation in the University of Glasgow ..., Glasgow University Publications LXI, Glasgow.

GANZ, Peter F., 1978 (ed.). Gottfried von Strassburg, *Tristan*, on the basis of Reinhold Bechstein's edition (first published 1869–70), Deutsche Klassiker des Mittelalters (inst. Franz Pfeiffer), new series, 4 (in two parts, separately paginated, and here numbered I–II), Wiesbaden.

GERTZ, M. Cl., 1917–18 (ed). *Scriptores minores historiæ Danicæ medii ævi*, I (fascicles I–II), Selskabet for Udgivelse af Kilder til dansk Historie, Copenhagen (rpt. 1970).

'GESTS RÍMA' ('Áslu ríma'). As edited in Djurhuus & Matras, 1951–63 (*q.v.*), pp. 244–47.

GODEFROY MENILGLAISE, D. C., 1855 (ed). Lambertus Ardensis, *Chronicon Ghisnense et Ardense* (918–1203) ..., Paris (contains a fifteenth-century French translation facing the Latin text).

GODLEY, A. D., 1957 (ed. and trans.). *Herodotus ... in four volumes*, vol. II (*Books III and IV*), The Loeb classical library (founded by James Loeb), London (rpt. of revised edition, 1938; first edition, 1921).

GORDON, E. V., 1957. *An introduction to Old Norse*, second edition revised by A. R. Taylor, Oxford (rpt. 1962 and later; first edition, 1927).

GRAVES, Robert, 1958. *Greek Myths*, London (rpt. 1980; first published in two vols. by Penguin Books, 1955).

GRIFFITH, Ralph T. H., 1870 (trans.). *The Rámáyan of Válmíki translated into English verse*, vol. I, London.

GRISCOM, Acton, 1929 (ed.). *The historia regum Britanniæ of Geoffrey of Monmouth ...* together with a literal translation of the Welsh manuscript no. LXI of Jesus College, Oxford, by Robert Ellis Jones ..., London.

GRØNBECH, Vilhelm, 1955. *Vor folkeæt i oldtiden*, pt. 1, Copenhagen (first published 1909–12; revised and enlarged edition).

GUÐMUNDSSON, Finnbogi, 1965 (ed.). *Orkneyinga saga ...*, Íslenzk fornrit, XXXIV, Reykjavík.

GUÐNASON, Bjarni, 1963. *Um Skjöldunga sögu*, Reykjavík.

— 1969. Gerðir og ritþróun Ragnars sögu loðbrókar, in *Einarsbók. Afmæliskveðja til Einars Ól. Sveinssonar...*, ed. Bjarni Guðnason *et al.*, Reykjavík, pp. 28–37.

— 1982 (ed.). *Danakonunga sǫgur ...*, Íslenzk fornrit, XXXV, Reykjavík.

GUTENBRUNNER, Siegfried, 1937. Zu den Strophen des 'Holzmannes' in der Ragnarssaga, *Zeitschrift für deutsches Altertum und deutsche Literatur*, 74, pp. 139–43.

GÖDEL, Vilhelm, 1892. *Katalog öfver Upsala Universitets biblioteks fornisländska och fornnorska handskrifter*, Skrifter utgifna af Humanistiska Vetenskapssamfundet i Upsala, II.1, Uppsala.

HAMMERSHAIMB, V. U., 1851 (ed.). *Færöiske kvæder*, I, Copenhagen.

HANDFORD, S. A., 1970 (trans.). Tacitus, *The Agricola and the Germania*, trans. ... by H. Mattingly, translation revised by S. A. Handford, The Penguin Classics (founder editor E. V. Rieu), Harmondsworth (Mattingly's translation first published 1948).

HARDY, Sir Thomas Duffus, and Charles Trice MARTIN, 1888 (eds.). *Lestorie des*

Engles solum la translacion Maistre Geffrei Gaimar, vol. I: *Text*, Rerum Britannicarum medii ævi scriptores, London.

— 1889 (transs). *Lestorie des Engles solum la translacion Maistre Geffrei Gaimar*, vol. II: *Translation*, Rerum Britannicarum medii ævi scriptores, London.

HB, 1892–96. *Hauksbók, udgiven efter de arnamagnæanske håndskrifter no. 371, 544 og 675 4to samt forskellige papirshåndskrifter* [ed. by Finnur Jónsson and Eiríkur Jónsson], Det kongelige nordiske Oldskrift-selskab, Copenhagen.

HEGGSTAD, Leiv, 1930. *Gamalnorsk ordbok med nynorsk tyding* (a revised and augmented edition of Hægstad & Torp, 1909, *q.v.*), Oslo (rpt. 1958, 1963; third edition by Heggstad, Hødnebø & Simensen, 1975, *q.v.*).

HEGGSTAD, Leiv, Finn HØDNEBØ, and Erik SIMENSEN, 1975 (eds.). *Norrøn ordbok* (third edition), Oslo (cf. Heggstad, 1930).

HELGASON, Jón, 1953. Norges og Islands digtning, in *Litteraturhistorie B. Norge og Island*, ed. by Sigurður Nordal, Nordisk kultur (ed. Johs. Brøndum-Nielsen *et al.*), VIII:B, Stockholm, pp. 3–179.

— 1975. Åtlaug på Spangereid. Oversigt over optegnelser af et norsk lokalsagn, in *Nordiske studier, festskrift til Chr. Westergaard-Nielsen ...*, ed. by Johs. Brøndum-Nielsen *et al.*, Copenhagen, pp. 79–89.

HENDERSON, George, 1899 (ed. and trans.). *Fled Bricrend. The feast of Bricriu ...*, Irish Texts Society, II, London.

HENNESSY, William M., 1887 (ed. and trans.). *Annals of Ulster ...*, vol. I, *A.D., 431–1056*, Dublin.

HERMANNSSON, Halldór, 1912. *Bibliography of the mythical heroic sagas (Fornald arsögur)*, Islandica ... (ed. by George William Harris), V, Ithaca, N.Y.

HERRMANN, Paul, 1922. *Erläuterungen zu den ersten neun Büchern der dänischen Geschichte des Saxo Grammaticus*, pt. 2: *Kommentar (Die Heldensagen des Saxo Grammaticus)*, Leipzig.

HEUSLER, Andreas, and Wilhelm RANISCH, 1903 (eds.). *Eddica minora. Dichtungen eddischer Art aus den Fornaldarsögur und anderen Prosawerken*, Dortmund (rpt. 1974, Wissenschaftliche Buchgesellschaft, Darmstadt).

HOLTSMARK, Anne, 1966. Heroic poetry and legendary sagas, in *Bibliography of Old Norse-Icelandic studies 1965*, Copenhagen, pp. 9–21.

HORNBY, Rikard, 1947. Fornavne i Danmark i middelalderen, in *Personnavne*, ed. Assar Janzén, Nordisk kultur (ed. Johs. Brøndum-Nielsen *et al.*), VII, Stockholm, pp. 187–234.

HUGHES, Kathleen, 1972. *Early Christian Ireland: introduction to the sources*, The sources of history: studies in the uses of historical evidence (ed. by G. R. Elton), London.

HÜSING, Georg, 1906. *Beiträge zur Kyros-Sage ... Verbesserte und vermehrte Sonderabzüge aus der Orientalischen Litteratur-Zeitung*, 1903–06, Berlin.

HÆGSTAD, Marius, and Alf TORP, 1909. *Gamalnorsk ordbok med nynorsk tyding*, Christiania (see under HEGGSTAD for later editions).

JACKSON, Kenneth Hurlstone, 1961. *The international popular tale and early Welsh tradition*, The Gregynog lectures, 1961, Cardiff.

JANZÉN, Assar, 1947. De fornvästnordiska personnamnen, in *Personnavne*, ed. Assar Janzén, Nordisk kultur (ed. by Johs. Brøndum-Nielsen *et al.*), VII, Stockholm, pp. 22–186.

JESSEN, C. A. E., 1862. *Undersögelser til nordisk oldhistorie*, Copenhagen.

JIRICZEK, Otto Luitpold, 1893 (ed.). *Die Bósa-saga in zwei Fassungen nebst Proben aus den Bósa-rímur*, Strassburg.

JÓNSSON, Arngrímur. References to Arngrímur's account of Ragnarr loðbrók are to the edition of Benediktsson, 1950 (*q.v.*), pp. 358–59, 464 66.

JÓNSSON, Finnur, 1912a (ed.). *Den norsk-islandske skjaldedigtning* ..., *A, tekst efter hånd skrifterne*, vol. I, Copenhagen (rpt. 1967).

— 1912b (ed.). *Den norsk-islandske skjaldedigtning* ..., *B, rettet tekst*, vol. I, Copenhagen (rpt. 1973).

— 1915a (ed.). *Den norsk-islandske skjaldedigtning* ..., *A, tekst efter håndskrifterne*, vol. II, Copenhagen (rpt. 1967.)

— 1915b (ed.). *Den norsk-islandske skjaldedigtning* ..., *B, rettet tekst*, vol. II, Copenhagen (rpt. 1973).

— 1923. *Den oldnorske og oldislandske litteraturs historie* (second edition), vol. II, Copenhagen (first edition, 1898–1901).

— 1931a (ed.). *Edda Snorra Sturlusonar udgivet efter håndskrifterne...*, Copenhagen.

— 1931b. *Lexicon poeticum antiquæ linguæ septentrionalis* ... (originally by Sveinbjörn Egilsson; second edition, Copenhagen (rpt. 1966. Egilsson's edition, 1860; Jonsson's first edition 1913–16).

JÓNSSON, Jón, 1910. Merki 'Loðbrókarsona', *Arkiv för nordisk filologi*, 26, pp. 371–76.

JØRGENSEN, Ellen, 1920 (ed.). *Annales Danici medii ævi*, Selskabet for Udgivelse af Kilder til dansk Historie (in two parts, continuously paginated), Copenhagen.

KAHLE, B., 1905 (ed.). *Kristnisaga, þáttr Þorvalds ens víðfǫrla* ..., Altnordische Saga-bibliothek (ed. by Gustaf Cederschiöld, *et al.*), 11, Halle.

'KARL OG KRAGELIL'. As edited in DgF I, 1853 (*q.v.*), 334 42.

KENDRICK, T. D., 1930. *A history of the Vikings*, London (rpt. 1968).

KEYNES, Simon, and Michael LAPIDGE, 1983 (trans. and introd.). *Alfred the Great. Asser's Life of King Alfred and other contemporary sources*, The Penguin Classics (founder editor: E. V. Rieu), Harmondsworth.

KING, K. C., 1958 (ed.). *Das Lied vom hürnen Seyfrid*, Manchester.

KIRK, G. S., 1971. *Myth, its meaning and functions in ancient and other cultures*, Sather Classical lectures, 40, Cambridge (first published 1970).

KNUDSEN, Gunnar, Marius KRISTENSEN, and Rikard HORNBY, 1954–64 (eds.) *Danmarks gamle Personnavne* ..., vol. II, *Tilnavne*, pt. 2, L-Ø ..., Copenhagen (references are to columns, not pages).

KOCK, Axel, 1898. Studier i de nordiska språkens historia, *Arkiv för nordisk filologi*, 14, pp. 213–70.

KOCK, Ernst Albin, 1923. *Notationes Norrænæ. Anteckningar till Edda och skaldediktning* [pt. 1], *Lunds Universitets årsskrift*, new series, pt. 1, vol. 19, no. 2.

— 1927. *Notationes Norrænæ. Anteckningar till Edda och skaldediktning*, pt. 9, *Lunds Universitets årsskrift*, new series, pt. 1, vol. 23, no. 7.

— 1940. *Notationes Norrænæ. Anteckningar till Edda och skaldediktning*, pt. 26, *Lunds Universitets årsskrift*, new series, pt. 1, vol. 37, no. 2.

KOHT, Halvdan, 1921. *Innhogg og utsyn i norsk historie*, Christiania.

— 1931. *The Old Norse sagas*, London.

KRÁKUMÁL. As edited in F. Jónsson, 1912a (*q.v.*), pp. 641–49, and 1912b (*q.v.*), pp. 649–56.

KRAPPE, Alexander Haggerty, 1928–29. La légende de Gunnar Half (Olafs saga Tryggvasonar, Chap. 173), *Acta philologica Scandinavica*, 3, pp. 226–33.

— 1941–42. Sur un épisode de la saga de Ragnar Lodbrok, *Acta philologica Scandinavica*, 15, pp. 326–38.

KRISTENSEN, Anne K. G., 1969. *Danmarks ældste annalistik. Studier over lundensisk annalskrivning i 12. og 13. århundrede*, Skrifter udgivet af det historiske Institut ved Københavns Universitet, III, Copenhagen.

KRISTJÁNSSON, Jónas, 1956 (ed.). *Eyfirðinga sǫgur* ..., Íslenzk fornrit, IX, Reykjavík.

KRUSCH, Bruno, 1888 (ed.). *Fredegarii et aliorum chronica*, in *Monvmenta Germaniæ historica* (ed. Societas aperiendis fontibus rervm Germanicarum medii aevi), *Sciptores rervm Merovingicarvm*, II, Hanover, pp. 1–194.

KUHN, Hans, 1968. *Edda, die lieder des Codex regius nebst verwandten denkmälern*, ed. by Gustav Neckel, vol. II, *Kurzes wörterbuch*, Germanische Bibliothek (fourth series), Heidelberg (second vol. of Neckel, 1962, *q.v.*; third edition, revised, of Neckel's glossary, first published 1927).

KUNTZE, Franz, 1917. Die Ragnar-Lodbrok-Sage, *Neue Jahrbücher fur das klassische Altertum*, 39, pp. 447–72.

[KÅLUND, Kr.,] 1900. *Katalog over de oldnorsk-islandske håndskrifter i det store kongelige bibliotek og i universitetsbiblioteket* ..., Copenhagen.

KÅLUND, Kr., 1908 (ed.). *Alfræði íslenzk. Islandsk encyklopædisk litteratur, I. Cod. Mbr. AM 194, 8vo*, Samfund til udgivelse af gammel nordisk litteratur, XXXVII, Copenhagen.

LAIR, Jules, 1865 (ed.). *De moribus et actis primorum Normanniæ ducum auctore Dudone Sancti Quintini decano*, Memoires de la Société des Antiquaires de Normandie, XXIII, Caen.

LANDSTAD, M. B., 1853 (ed.). *Norske Folkeviser*, Christiania.

LANGEBEK, Jacobus, 1772 (ed.). *Scriptores rerum Danicarum medii ævi* ..., I, Copenhagen.

LEACH, Edmund, 1983. Anthropological approaches to the study of the Bible during the twentieth century, in *Structuralist interpretations of biblical myth*, ed. by Edmund Leach and D. Alan Aycock, Cambridge, pp. 7–32.

LEWIS, Charlton T., and Charles SHORT, 1879. *A Latin Dictionary* ..., Oxford (rpt. 1975).

LID, Nils, 1942. Gudar og gudedyrking, in *Religionshistorie*, ed. by Nils Lid, Nordisk kultur (ed. by Johs. Brøndum-Nielsen *et al.*), XXVI, Stockholm, pp. 80–153.

LIDÉN, Evald, 1928. Gullvarta-Síbilia, in *Festskrift til Finnur Jónsson 29. maj 1928*, ed. by Johs. Brøndum-Nielsen *et al.*, Copenhagen, pp. 358–64.

LIE, Hallvard, 1950. Tanker omkring en 'uekte' replikk i Eyrbyggjasaga, *Arkiv för nordisk filologi*, 65, pp. 160 77 (rpt. in Hallvard Lie, *Om sagakunst og skaldskap. Utvalgte avhandlinger*, Øvre Ervik, 1982, pp. 342–59).

— 1957. '*Natur*' og '*unatur*' i skaldekunsten, Avhandlinger utgitt av Det Norske Videnskaps-Akademi i Oslo, II. Hist.-filos. klasse. No. 1 (rpt. in Hallvard Lie, *Om sagakunst og skaldskap. Utvalgte avhandlinger*, Øvre Ervik, 1982, pp. 201–315).

LIEBRECHT, Felix, 1861. Die Ragnar Lodbrokssage in Persien, in (Benfey's) *Orient und Occident*, I, pp. 561–67.

LIESTØL, Aslak, 1968. The Maeshowe runes: some new interpretations, in *The fifth Viking Congress, Tórshavn, July 1965*, ed. by Bjarni Niclasen, Tórshavn, pp. 55–61.

LIESTØL, Knut, 1915. *Norske trollvisor og norrøne sogor*, Christiania.

— 1917. Færøyske og norske folkevisor, *Maal og minne*, Christiania, pp. 81–110 (extended review of de Vries, 1915, *q.v.*).

— 1970. *Den norrøne arven*, Scandinavian University Books, Oslo.

LIND, E. H., 1920–21 (ed.). *Norsk-isländska personbinamn från medeltiden, samlade ock utgivna med förklaringar*, Uppsala (references in arabic (as opposed to roman) numerals are to columns, not pages).

'LINDARORMEN'. As edited in Landstad, 1853 (*q.v.*), pp. 139–45; cf. also DgF III, 1862 (*q.v.*), pp. 798–99.

LOOMIS, Grant, 1932. The growth of the Saint Edmund legend, *Harvard studies and notes in philology and literature*, 14, pp. 83–113.

— 1933. Saint Edmund and the Lodbrok (Lothbroc) legend, *Harvard studies and notes in philology and literature*, 15, pp. 1–23.

LUARD, Henry Richards, 1872 (ed.). *Matthæi Parisiensis, monachi sancti Albani, chronica majora*, vol. I, Rerum Britannicarum medii ævi scriptores, London.

— 1890 (ed.). *Flores historiarum*, vol. I, Rerum Britannicarum medii ævi scriptores, London.

LUKMAN, Niels, 1976. Ragnarr loðbrók, Sigifrid, and the saints of Flanders, *Mediaeval Scandinavia*, 9, pp. 7–50.

LÖNNROTH, Lars, 1976. *Njáls saga: a critical introduction*, Berkeley, California.

MCNEILL, George P., 1886 (ed.). *Sir Tristrem*, The Scottish Text Society, 8, Edinburgh.

MCTURK, R(ory). (W)., 1975. The extant Icelandic manifestations of *Ragnars saga loðbrókar*, *Gripla*, 1, Stofnun Árna Magnússonar á Íslandi, rit 7, pp. 43–75.

— 1976. Ragnarr loðbrók in the Irish annals? in *Proceedings of the seventh Viking Congress, Dublin, 15 21 August, 1973*, ed. by Bo Almqvist and David Greene, Dublin, pp. 83–123.

— 1977a. The relationship of *Ragnars saga loðbrókar* to *Þiðriks saga af Bern*, in *Sjötíu ritgerðir helgaðar Jakobi Benediktssyni 20. júlí 1977*, pt. 2, ed. by Einar G. Pétursson and Jónas Kristjánsson, Stofnun Árna Magnússonar á Íslandi, rit 12, Reykjavik, pp. 568–85 (in two parts, continuously paginated).

— 1977b. Review of Alfred P. Smyth, *Scandinavian York and Dublin. The history and archaeology of two related Viking kingdoms*, vol. I (Dublin, 1975), in *Saga-Book*, 19, pp. 471 74.

— 1977c. Review of J. M. Wallace-Hadrill, *The Vikings in Francia, The Stenton lecture, 1974, University of Reading* (Reading, 1975) in *Saga-Book*, 19, pp. 474–76.

— 1978. An Irish analogue to the Kráka-episode of Ragnars saga loðbrókar, *Éigse. A Journal of Irish Studies*, 17, pp. 277–96.

— 1980. Review of Smyth, 1977 (*q.v.*), *Saga-Book*, 20, pp. 231–34.

— 1981a. Variation in *Beowulf* and the poetic *Edda*: a chronological experiment, in *The dating of Beowulf*, ed. by Colin Chase, Toronto Old English series, 6, Toronto, pp. 141–60.

— 1981b. 'Cynewulf and Cyneheard' and the Icelandic sagas, *Leeds Studies in English*, new series, 12 (for 1980 and 1981), *Essays in honour of A. C. Cawley*, ed. by Peter Meredith, pp. 81–127.

MADDEN, Sir Frederic, 1869 (ed). *Matthæi Parisiensis, monachi sancti Albani, historia Anglorum . . .*, vol. III, Rerum Britannicarum medii ævi scriptores, London.

MAGOUN, Francis P., jr., 1944. The pilgrim-diary of Nikulás of Munkathverá: the road to Rome, *Mediaeval studies*, 6, pp. 314 54.

MARTIN, John Stanley, 1981. *Ár vas alda*. Ancient Scandinavian creation myths reconsidered, in *Specvlvm norroenvm. Norse studies in memory of Gabriel Turville-Petre*, ed. by Ursula Dronke *et al.*, Odense, pp. 357–69.

MARWICK, Hugh, 1929. *The Orkney Norn*, Oxford.

MARX, Jean, 1914 (ed.). Guillaume de Jumièges, *Gesta Normannorum ducum*, Rouen.

MAWER, Allen, 1909. Ragnar Lothbrók and his sons, *Saga-Book of the Viking Club*, 6, pp. 68–89.

MEISSNER, Rudolf, 1921. *Die Kenningar der Skalden. Ein Beitrag zur skaldischen Poetik*, Rheinische Beiträge und Hülfsbücher zur germanischen Philologie und Volkskunde (ed. by Theodor Frings *et al.*), I, Bonn.

MENILGLAISE, GODEFROY D. C. See under GODEFROY MENILGLAISE.

MITCHELL, P. M., 1957. *A history of Danish literature*, with an introductory chapter (pp. 11–29) by Mogens Haugsted, Copenhagen.

MUCH, Rudolf, 1967 (ed. and trans.). *Die Germania des Tacitus* (third edition, enlarged, by Herbert Jankuhn and Wolfgang Lange), Germanische Bibliothek (fifth series), Heidelberg (first edition, 1937).

MUDRAK, Edmund, 1943. *Die nordische Heldensage*, Jahrbuch für historische Volkskunde (inst. Wilhelm Fraenger), X, Berlin.

MUNCH, P. A., 1967. *Norrøne gude- og heltesagn*, revised edition, ed. Anne Holtsmark, U bøkene, 52, Oslo (fourth edition, reprinted 1970; first edition 1840).

MUNDT, Marina, 1971. Omkring dragekampen i Ragnars saga loðbrókar, *Arv*, 27, pp. 121–40.

MURPHY, Gerard, 1971. *Saga and myth in ancient Ireland*, foreword by Nessa Ní Shé. Irish life and culture, X, Cork (updated edition; formerly published 1955, 1961).

MÜLLER, P. E., (1818). References to Müller's account of the lost Faroese ballad about Osla and Kraaka are to his *Sagabibliothek*, vol. II, Copenhagen (1818), p. 481.

MØLLER-CHRISTENSEN, Vilhelm, 1944. *Middelalderens lægekunst i Danmark*, Acta historica scientiarum naturalium et medicinalium, 3, Copenhagen.

NECKEL, G(ustav), 1920. Review of de Vries, 1915 (*q.v.*), in *Anzeiger für deutsches Altertum*, 39, pp. 17–19.

— 1962 (ed). *Edda, die lieder des codex regius nebst verwandten denkmälern*, vol. I., *Text* (fourth edition, revised by Hans Kuhn), Germanische Bibliothek (fourth series), Heidelberg (first edition, 1914).

NOLSØE, Mortan, 1976. Noen betraktninger om forholdet mellom ballade och sagaforelegg, *Sumlen*, Stockholm, pp. 11–19.

NORDAL, Sigurður, 1933 (ed.). *Egils saga Skalla-Grímssonar*, Íslenzk fornrit, II, Reykjavík.

— 1978 (ed). *Vǫluspá*, trans. by B. S. Benedikz and John McKinnell, Durham and St. Andrews medieval texts (ed. by Paul Bibire and John McKinnell), 1, Durham (first published in Icelandic, Reykjavík, 1923).

NORDAL, Sigurður, 1978–79. The author of *Vǫluspá*, trans. by B. S. Benedikz, *Saga-Book*, 20, pp. 114–30 (first published in Icelandic in 1923–24).

NOREEN, Adolf, 1923. *Altnordische grammatik I. Altisländische und altnorwegische grammatik (laut- und flexionslehre) unter berücksichtigung des urnordischen*, Halle (rpt. in 1970 as no. 19 in the Alabama linguistic and philological series, The University, Alabama).

NORNAGESTS ÞÁTTR. As edited by Ernst Wilken in his *Die prosaische Edda im Auszuge, nebst Vǫlsunga-saga und Nornagests þáttr*, pt. I, *Text*, Bibliothek der ältesten deutschen Literatur-Denkmäler, XI, pt. I, Paderborn, 1912 (second edition, revised), pp. 235–61 (first edition, 1877).

NYGAARD, M., 1905. *Norrøn syntax*, Christiania.

Ó CATHASAIGH, Tomás, 1977. *The heroic biography of Cormac mac Airt*, Dublin.

Ó CORRÁIN, Donnchadh, 1979. High-kings, Vikings and other kings, *Irish historical studies*, 21 (no. 83, March), pp. 283–323 (title page misprints vol. no. as 22).

O DALY, Máirín, 1975 (ed. and trans.). *Cath Maige Mucrama. The battle of Mag Mucrama*, Irish Texts Society, L, Dublin.

OLAF OLSEN, See under OLSEN, Olaf.

OLRIK, Axel, 1894a. *Kilderne til Sakses oldhistorie. En literaturhistorisk undersøgelse*, vol. II: *Norröne sagaer og danske sagn*, Copenhagen.

— 1894b. Skjoldungasaga i Arngrim Jonssons udtog, *Aarbøger for nordisk oldkyndighed og historie*, second series, 9, pp. 83–164.

— 1905. Nordisk og lappisk gudsdyrkelse. Bemærkninger i anledning af solvognen fra Trundholm, *Danske studier*, Copenhagen, pp. 39–57.

— 1921. *Nogle grundsætninger for sagnforskning* (ed. by Hans Ellekilde after the author's death), Danmarks folkeminder, 23, Copenhagen.

— 1965. Epic laws of folk narrative, Dundes, 1965 (*q.v.*) pp. 129–41.

OLRIK, J., and H. RÆDER, 1931 (eds.). *Saxonis gesta Danorum . . .*, vol. I, Copenhagen.

OLSEN, Magnus, 1906–08 (ed.). *Vǫlsunga saga ok Ragnars saga loðbrókar*, Samfund til udgivelse af gammel nordisk litteratur, XXXVI, Copenhagen.

— 1912. *Stedsnavnestudier*, Christiania.

— 1935. Krákumál, *Maal og minne*, Oslo, pp. 78–80.

— 1962. *Edda- og skaldekvad. Forarbeider til kommentar. V. Hávamál*, Avhandlinger utgitt av Det Norske Videnskaps-Akademi i Oslo, II. Hist.-filos. klasse. New series, No. 3, Oslo.

OLSEN, Olaf, 1966. *Hørg, hov og kirke. Historiske og arkæologiske vikingetidsstudier, Aarbøger for nordisk oldkyndighed og historie*, 1965, Copenhagen.

ORKNEYINGA SAGA. As edited in Guðmundsson, 1965 (*q.v.*), pp. 1–300.

'ORMEKAMPEN'. As edited in DgF I, 1853 (*q.v.*), pp. 342–48.

PERTZ, G. H., 1829 (ed.). Fragmentum chronici Fontanellensis a. 841–859, in *Monvmenta Germaniae historica* (ed. by G. H. Pertz), *Scriptores*, II, Hanover, pp. 301 04.

POLOMÉ, Edgar Charles, 1969. Some comments on *Vǫluspá*, stanzas 17–18, in *Old Norse literature and mythology: a symposium*, ed. by Edgar C. Polomé, Austin, Texas, pp. 265–90.

RADNER, Joan Newlon, 1978 (ed. and trans.). *Fragmentary annals of Ireland*, Dublin.

RAGNARS KVÆÐI. As edited in Djurhuus & Matras, 1951–63 (*q.v.*), pp. 215–43.

RAGNARS SAGA. References to the X and Y versions of the saga, as reflected in 147 and 1824b respectively, are to the edition of Olsen, 1906–08 (*q.v.*), pp. 176–94; 111–75.

RAGNARSSONA ÞÁTTR. As edited in Hb, 1892–96 (*q.v.*), pp. 458–67.

RAMUS, Jonas. References are to Ramus's *Norriges Kongers Historie* (published 1719) as excerpted in Helgason, 1975 (*q.v.*), pp. 85–86.

RAU, Reinhold, 1969 (ed.). *Jahrbücher von Fulda . . .*, in *Quellen zur karolingischen Reichsgeschichte*, pt. III, Ausgewählte Quellen zur deutschen Geschichte des Mittelalters, Freiherr vom Stein-Gedächtnisausgabe (ed. by Rudolf Buchner), VII, Darmstadt (second edition, revised; first edition, 1960).

— 1972 (ed.). *Jahrbücher von St. Bertin . . . Xantener Jahrbücher* in *Quellen zur karolingischen Reichsgeschichte*, pt. II, Ausgewählte Quellen zur deutschen Geschichte des Mittelalters, Freiherr vom Stein-Gedächtnisausgabe (ed. Rudolf Buchner), VI, Darmstadt (rpt. of the 1969 edition).

— 1974 (ed.). *Die Reichsannalen* ... in *Quellen zur karolingischen Reichsgeschichte*, pt. I, Ausgewählte Quellen zur deutschen Geschichte des Mittelalters, Freiherr vom Stein-Gedächtnisausgabe (ed. Rudolf Buchner), V, Darmstadt (rpt., with revisions, of the 1955 edition).

'REGNFRED OG KRAGELIL'. As edited in DgF I, 1853 (*q.v.*), pp. 327–33.

REINHOLD, Meyer, 1972. *Past and present. The continuity of classical myths*, Toronto.

ROSSENBECK, Klaus, 1974. Siegfried, Arminius und die Knetterheide, *Zeitschrift für deutsches Altertum und deutsche Litteratur*, 103, pp. 243–48.

RUDBERG, Gunnar, 1965 (trans.). Rimbert, *Ansgars levnad* ... Med historisk inledning av Nils Ahnlund, Stockholm.

SAHLGREN, Jöran, 1918. Förbjudna namn, *Namn och bygd*, 6, pp. 1–40.

SAXO (Grammaticus). References are by number to the relevant book, section, and paragraph of Saxo's *Gesta Danorum* as edited by Olrik & Ræder, 1931, *q.v.*

SCHACH, Paul, 1957–61. Some observations on *Tristrams saga*, *Saga-Book*, 15, pp. 102–29.

— 1964. Tristan and Isolde in Scandinavian ballad and folktale, *Scandinavian studies*, 36, pp. 281–97.

— 1969a. The Reeves fragment of Tristrams saga ok Ísöndar, *Einarsbók. Afmæliskveðja til Einars Ól. Sveinssonar...*, ed. Bjarni Guðnason et al., Reykjavík, pp. 296–308.

— 1969b. Some observations on the influence of *Tristrams saga ok Ísöndar* on Old Icelandic literature, in *Old Norse literature and mythology: a symposium*, ed. by Edgar C. Polomé, Austin, Texas, pp. 81–129.

— 1983. Some thoughts on *Völuspá*, in *Edda: a collection of essays*, ed. by Robert J. Glendinning and Haraldur Bessason, The University of Manitoba Icelandic Studies (ed. by Haraldur Bessason and Robert J. Glendinning), 4, Winnipeg, pp. 86–116.

SCHIER, Kurt, 1970. *Sagaliteratur*, Sammlung Metzler, Realienbücher für Germanisten, Abt. D: Literaturgeschichte, 78, Stuttgart.

SCHIERN, Frederik, 1858. Om Navnet Lodbrog hos Angelsaxerne, *Annaler for nordisk Oldkyndighed og Historie*, Copenhagen, pp. 8–11.

SCHLAUCH, Margaret, 1930 (trans.). *The saga of the Volsungs, the saga of Ragnar Lodbrok together with the lay of Kraka*, Scandinavian classics, XXXV, New York.

SCHÜCK, Henrik, 1900. Till Lodbroks-sagan, *Svenska Fornminnesföreningens tidsskrift*, 11, pp. 131–40 (published in 1900 in no. 1 of vol. 11; 1902 appears on the title-page of the volume).

SEELOW, Hubert, 1981 (ed.). *Hálfs saga ok Hálfsrekka*, Stofnun Árna Magnússonar á Íslandi, rit 20, Reykjavík.

SEIP, Didrik Arup, 1954. *Palæografi B. Norge og Island*, Nordisk kultur (ed. Johs. Brøndum-Nielsen et al.), XXVIII:B, Stockholm.

SIEVERS, Eduard, 1893. *Altgermanische metrik*, Sammlung kurzer grammatiken germanischer dialekte (ed. by Wilhelm Braune), supplementary series II, Halle.

SKYUM-NIELSEN, Niels, 1967. *Vikingerne i Paris* (second edition, revised), Selskabet til historiske kildeskrifters oversættelse, Copenhagen.

SMITH, A. H., 1935. The sons of Ragnar Lothbrok, *Saga-Book*, 11, pp. 173–91.

SMYTH, Alfred P., 1977. *Scandinavian kings in the British Isles 850–880*, Oxford historical monographs (ed. by Barbara Harvey et al.), Oxford.

SNORRA EDDA. As edited in F. Jónsson, 1931a, *q.v.*

SOLHEIM, Svale, 1940. *Nemningsfordomar ved fiske*, Oslo.

SPEIRS, John, 1957. *Medieval English poetry: the non-Chaucerian tradition*, London (later edition 1971).

SPRINGER, Otto, 1950. Mediaeval pilgrim routes from Scandinavia to Rome, *Mediaeval studies*, 12, pp. 92 122.

STEENSTRUP, Johannes C. H. R., 1876. *Normannerne*, vol. I: *Indledning i Normannertiden*, Copenhagen (rpt. 1972, Selskabet for udgivelse af kilder til dansk historie).

— 1878. *Normannerne*, vol. II: *Vikingetogene mod Vest i det 9de Aarhundrede*, Copenhagen (rpt. 1972, Selskabet for udgivelse af kilder til dansk historie).

STENTON, F. M., 1971. *Anglo-Saxon England*, third edition, The Oxford History of England (ed. by Sir George Clark), II, Oxford (first edition, 1943).

STEVENSON, William Henry, 1959 (ed.). *Asser's life of King Alfred, together with the annals of St. Neots erroneously ascribed to Asser*, new impression with article . . . by Dorothy Whitelock, Oxford (first edition 1904).

STORM, Gustav, 1878. *Kritiske Bidrag til Vikingetidens Historie (I. Ragnar Lodbrok og Gange-Rolv)*, Christiania (the relevant parts of this book, pp. 34–129, 193-200, were in fact first published in 1877, under the title 'Ragnar Lodbrok og Lodbrokssönerne. Studie i dansk Oldhistorie og nordisk Sagnhistorie' in the Norwegian *Historisk Tidsskrift*, series 2, vol.1, pp. 371–491).

STRAND, Birgit, 1980. *Kvinnor och män i Gesta Danorum*, Kvinnohistoriskt arkiv, 18, Gothenburg.

STRÖMBÄCK, Dag, 1935. Kungshatt. Sägen och dikt omkring ett ortnamn, *Namn och bygd*, 23, pp. 135–44.

SVEINSSON, Einar Ól., 1934 (ed). *Laxdæla saga . . .*, Íslenzk fornrit, V, Reykjavík.

— 1936. Nafngiftir Oddaverja, in *Bidrag till nordisk filologi tillägnade Emil Olson den 9. juni 1936*, Lund, pp. 190–96.

— 1954 (ed). *Brennu-Njáls saga*, Íslenzk fornrit, XII, Reykjavík.

— 1962. *Íslenzkar bókmenntir í fornöld*, vol. I, Reykjavík.

SWEET [Henry,] 1967. *Sweet's Anglo-Saxon reader in prose and verse*, revised throughout by Dorothy Whitelock, Oxford (first edition 1876).

SYDOW, C.W. von, 1919. Review of de Vries, 1915 (*q.v.*) in *Arkiv för nordisk filologi*, 35, pp. 107 11.

THOMAS, M. F., [1983]. The briar and the vine: Tristan goes north, *Arthurian literature*, 3, pp. 53–90.

THORPE, Lewis, 1966 (trans. and introd.). *Geoffrey of Monmouth: the history of the kings of Britain*, The Penguin Classics (founder editor: E. V. Rieu), L 170, Harmondsworth.

TÓMASSON, Sverrir, 1977. Hvenær var Tristrams sögu snúið? *Gripla*, 2, Stofnun Árna Magnússonar á Íslandi, rit 16, pp. 47–78.

TORFÆUS (Þormóður Torfason). References are to Torfæus's *Historia rerum Norvegicarum* (published 1711) as excerpted in Helgason, 1975 (*q.v.*), p. 83.

TRILLMICH, Werner, 1961 (ed. and trans.). *Rimbert Leben Ansgars, Adam von Bremen Bischofsgeschichte der Hamburger Kirche . . . in Quellen des 9. und 11. Jahrhunderts zur Geschichte der hamburgischen Kirche und des Reiches*, Ausgewählte Quellen zur deutschen Geschichte des Mittelalters, Freiherr vom Stein-Gedächtnisausgabe (ed. by Rudolf Buchner), XI, Berlin.

TURVILLE-PETRE, E. O. G., 1964. *Myth and religion of the north: the religion of ancient Scandinavia*, History of religion, London.

— 1969. Fertility of beast and soil in Old Norse literature, in *Old Norse literature and mythology: a symposium*, ed. by Edgar C. Polomé, Austin, Texas, pp. 244–64.

— 1976. *Scaldic poetry*, Oxford.

VAFÞRÚDNISMÁL. As edited in Neckel, 1962 (*q.v.*), pp. 45–55.

VAUGHAN, Richard, 1958 (ed). *The chronicle attributed to John of Wallingford*, Camden miscellany, XXI (Camden third series XC), London.

VOGEL, Walther, 1906. *Die Normannen und das fränkische Reich bis zur Gründung der Normandie (799–911)*, Heidelberger Abhandlungen zur mittleren und neueren Geschichte (ed. by Karl Hampe *et al.*), 14, Heidelberg.

VON FRIESEN, Otto. See Friesen, Otto von.

VON SYDOW, See Sydow, C. W. von.

VRIES, Jan de, 1915. *Studiën over Færösche balladen*, Haarlem.

— 1923. Die historischen Grundlagen der Ragnarssaga Loðbrókar, *Arkiv för nordisk filologi*, 39, pp. 244–74.

— 1927a. Die ostnordische Überlieferung der Sage von Ragnar Lodbrók, *Acta philologica Scandinavica*, 2, pp. 115–49.

— 1927b. Die Krákumál I, *Neophilologus*, 13, pp. 51–60.

— 1927c. Die Wikingersaga, *Germanisch-romanische Monatsschrift*, 15, pp. 81–100.

— 1928a. Die westnordische Tradition der Sage von Ragnar Lodbrok, *Zeitschrift für deutsche Philologie*, 53, pp. 257–302.

— 1928b. Die Entwicklung der Sage von den Lodbrokssöhnen in den historischen Quellen, *Arkiv för nordisk filologi*, 44, pp. 117–63.

— 1928c. Die Krákumál II, *Neophilologus*, 13, pp. 123–30.

— 1928d. *Die Märchen von klugen Rätsellösern. Eine vergleichende Untersuchung*, FF communications, 73, Helsinki.

— 1931. Bemerkungen über die Quellenverhältnisse der färöischen Balladen, *Zeitschrift für deutsche Philologie*, 56, pp. 129–45.

— 1956. *Altgermanische Religionsgeschichte*, vol. I (second edition, fully revised), Grundriss der germanischen Philologie (inst. Hermann Paul), 12/I, Berlin (first edition, 1935).

— 1957. *Altgermanische Religionsgeschichte*, vol. II (second edition, fully revised), Grundriss der germanischen Philologie (inst. Hermann Paul) 12/II, Berlin (first edition, 1937).

— 1963. *Heroic song and heroic legend*, trans. by B. J. Timmer, London (originally published in Holland, 1959).

— 1964. *Altnordische Literaturgeschichte*, vol. I (second edition, fully revised), Grundriss der germanischen Philologie (inst. Hermann Paul), 15, Berlin (first edition, 1941).

— 1967. *Altnordische Literaturgeschichte*, vol. II (second edition, fully revised), Grundriss der germanischen Philologie (inst. Hermann Paul), 16, Berlin (first edition, 1942).

— 1977. *Altnordisches etymologisches wörterbuch* (second edition, revised) Leiden (first edition, 1957–60; revised 1962).

VǪLSUNGA SAGA. As edited in Olsen, 1906–08 (*q.v.*), pp. 1–110.

WAITZ, G., 1887 (ed). Ex miraculis sancti Germani in Normannorum adventu factis, in *Monvmenta Germaniae historica* (ed. Societas aperiendis fontibus rerum Germanicarum medii aevi), *Scriptores*, XV, pt. I, Hanover, pp. 10–16.

WECHSLER, Adolf, 1875. Die Sage von Aslög, der Tochter Sigurds, und ein Versuch ihrer Deutung, *Verhandlungen des Vereins für Kunst und Altherthum von Ulm*, new series, 7, pp. 10–14.

WHITELOCK, Dorothy, *et al.* (eds.), 1965. *The Anglo-Saxon chronicle, a revised translation*, London (second, corrected impression of first edition, 1961).

WHITELOCK, Dorothy, 1969. Fact and fiction in the legend of St. Edmund, *The Proceedings of the Suffolk Institute of Archaeology*, 31, pp. 217–33 (rpt. as no. XI in Dorothy Whitelock, *From Bede to Alfred*, Variorum reprints. Collected studies series, 121, London 1980, with same pagination).

— 1979 (ed.). *English historical documents c.*500–1042 (second edition), English historical documents (ed. David C. Douglas), I, London (first edition, 1955).

WILSON, H. H., 1972 (TRANS.). *The Vishńu Puráńa. A system of Hindu mythology and tradition* ..., with an introduction by Dr. R. C. Hazra, Calcutta (rpt. of third edition, Calcutta 1961; first edition, London, 1840; second edition, ed. by Dr. F. Hall, London 1888).

WLISLOCKI, Heinrich v., 1887. Die Ragnar Lodbrokssage in Siebenbürgen, *Germania*, 32, pp. 362–66.

WORMALD, C. Patrick, 1982. Viking studies: whence and whither? in *The Vikings*, ed. by R. T. Farrell, London, pp. 128–53.

YOUNG, Jean, 1933. Does Rígsþula betray Irish influence? *Arkiv för nordisk filologi*, 49, pp. 97–107.

ÞIDRIKS SAGA AF BERN. As edited in Bertelsen, 1905–11, *q.v.*

INDEX

The Index is selective, and does not, for example, include items listed in the Bibliography, or the items numbered 1-18 in the List of items analysed in ch. II, section (a), cf. pp. 53-61 and 249, above. As in the Bibliography, the alphabetical order treats V and W as separate letters, but otherwise follows that of *Kulturhistorisk leksikon for nordisk middelalder* (22 vols., Copenhagen and elsewhere, 1956-78). It should be noted that the Index differs from the Bibliography in listing Icelanders by their forenames rather than by their patronymics; that medieval authors (such as William of Jumièges) are listed in the Index by their names rather than by the places with which they may be associated; that works by known authors are listed by the latter's names rather than by their titles; and that nicknames not indexed separately will be found under the proper names to which they are most commonly attached.